THAI
REFERENCE GRAMMAR

THAI
REFERENCE GRAMMAR

THAI
REFERENCE GRAMMAR

The Structure of Spoken Thai

James Higbie & Snea Thinsan

Orchid Press
Bangkok 2003

James Higbie & Snea Thinsan
THAI REFERENCE GRAMMAR:
The Structure of Spoken Thai

First Published 2002
Reprint 2003

ORCHID PRESS
P.O. Box 19,
Yuttitham Post Office,
Bangkok 10907
Thailand

ISBN: 974-8304-96-5

CONTENTS

4: QUESTIONS

5: EXPANDED SENTENCES

6: TENSES

10: USING *GAW*

11: QUANTIFIERS

12: COMPARISONS

13: PREPOSITIONS

14: PARTICLES & INTERJECTIONS

15: TIME PHRASES

APPENDIX: CLASSIFIERS

INTRODUCTION

This book was written to give students of the Thai language information on the advanced sentence structure of the language, especially the spoken form used throughout Thailand. "Grammar" refers to the rules governing the formation of sentences in a language. In Thai this refers mostly to word order and the use of words like *dai* and *laeo* (here called "function words") that have basic meanings related to time and action.

Some Western grammar terms such as "tense", "conjunction", and "preposition" are used in this book to categorize Thai patterns and vocabulary. This was done for convenience only, not to provide an analysis of Thai grammar in Western terms. A word like "far", for example, is included with prepositions because it describes a location, not because it should be categorized as a preposition in a grammatical scheme.

In researching this book we collected samples of language from conversations, TV, radio, magazine interviews, and even comic books, trying to find examples of all the common patterns and function words of spoken Thai. We also translated English sentences into Thai to find equivalents between the languages, such as how a word like "for" in English compares to *sam-rap* or *pheua* in Thai. We then analyzed each word and pattern by the following points:

- Is it acceptable as correct by native Thai speakers?
- What are the variations in the way it's used?
- How does it compare to equivalent words or patterns in English?
- What kind of situations is it used in? Is it only formal or informal?

Finally we wrote sample sentences that showed the different ways the word or pattern is used.

Our informants were all native speakers of Thai who worked as language teachers and who showed a strong interest in analyzing the correct use of their language. The results, we hope, will provide a greater understanding of the rules of Thai, leading to clearer expression and communication in the language.

CHARACTERISTICS OF THAI

Thai is a very concise language, and people used to Western languages are often surprised at its logical word order and the way complex meanings are expressed by combining all the words in a phrase into a single meaning. In Thai, function words like *ja*, *hai*, *dai*, and *theung* alter tenses or give phrases and sentences different shades of meaning. These words are used over and over in different patterns, always keeping their basic meanings.

In Thai, words are often interchangable as parts of speech and Thai speakers enjoy making clever use of this in conversation. Thai, however, is also very idiomatic and one of the requirements of advanced speaking is knowing exactly how a native speaker would say something, as there is often only one common way to express a meaning.

In Thai, some of the words in a sentence may be optional. All Thai sentences have a complete form, from which words may be omitted depending on the context and the formality of the situation. (In general the more words a sentence has the more formal it sounds.) In this book optional words are put in parentheses as in this example:

Have you been in Thailand long?

Koon yoo meuang Thai (ma) nan (laeo) reu yang?

คุณอยู่เมืองไทย(มา)นาน(แล้ว)รึยัง

The two words in parentheses yield four ways to state the question:

Koon yoo meuang Thai nan reu yang?

Koon yoo meuang Thai ma nan reu yang?

Koon yoo meuang Thai nan laeo reu yang?

Koon yoo meuang Thai ma nan laeo reu yang?

Other options are to include *ka* or *krup* at the end for politeness and to omit "you" (more informal) or to use a substitute for "you" such as the person's name or a relationship term. It's best to use a polite version of the sentence (longer and with *koon* and *ka* or *krup*) if you're in a formal situation or talking to someone you don't know or who is older than you.

Words may also be omitted to produce a typical Thai sentence rhythm which comes from the number of syllables in the sentence and their tones and vowel lengths. Developing a good speaking rhythm that can fit naturally into a conversation is part of becoming fluent, as is being able to change your style to conform to various social situations.

ACKNOWLEDGMENTS

We would like to thank the following people for kindly giving their time to help with the writing of this book:

Ekaraj Ragwanas, Pinanong Khoonukoon, Athikom Jeerapairotekun, Pawadee Kucita, Puangtong Wilkins, Sitthichai Thepsura, Duangrath Kaewkomorn, Borworn Pitaksanonkun, Srinuan Bunharn, Supaporn Wetchupakorn, Atsama Anongkanatrakool, Porntip Bokham, Benjawan Kajonrit, Supa Harirakaapitok, Sutthida Malikaew, Saisamorn Wattanasomboon, Suwat Supapondee, Waree Sudhidee, Kitchakan Ratanakaew, David Murray, Benjawan Pornpattananikhom, Tom Riddle, Greg Wilkins, Somboun Thavisay

Drawings: Puangtong WIlkins

Cover design: Kongphat Luangrath

PRONUNCIATION

There are five different tones in Thai and two distinct vowel lengths—long, with the pronunciation drawn out, and short with a quicker, cut off pronunciation. There are therefore ten possible pronunciations for any syllable or one-syllable word in Thai, although no "word" has meanings for all ten (*mai* and *kao* have the most with six each).

Following are the five tones, each with two vowel lengths, written with the visual tone symbols used in this book. Short vowel-length words are marked with an asterisk.

mid tone - Your normal speaking voice. (asterisk = short vowel length)

mid-short	yang	still/yet	ยัง
mid-long	yang	rubber	ยาง

low tone - Lower than your normal voice. (underlined)

low-short	gae	to undo	แกะ
low-long	gae	old	แก่

falling tone - Start high and go down to a mid sound. (high line curving down)

falling-short	kao	to enter	เข้า
falling-long	kao	rice	ข้าว

high tone - Higher than your normal voice. With a long vowel length the tone rises a little at the end. (straight line above)

high-short	mai	interrogative	มั้ย
high-long	mai	wood	ไม้

rising tone - Start low and go up to a mid tone. (low line curving up)

rising-short	lai	to flow	ไหล
rising-long	lai	many/a lot	หลาย

Consonants - The following letters have the same consonant sounds as in English:

| b | d | f | h | k | l | m | n | s | w |

The following letters have different sounds from English. Two of them may be difficult for English speakers. These are the hard *p* sound and the hard *t* sound. The sound of the first is a cross between "p" and "b", and the second is a cross between "t" and "d" (like the "t" in "sixty").

p	a hard p/b sound
ph	pronounced as "p" in English, not "f"
t	a hard t/d sound
th	pronounced as "t" in English, not "th"
g	has a harder sound than in English, between "g" and "k"
j	has a harder sound than in English
r	slightly rolled, pronounced "l" in colloquial Thai
ng	used at the beginning of words as well as at the end

Vowels - Thai has many vowel sounds and some of them may be difficult for English speakers. Two sounds as written here may be mispronounced if read as in English. The first, the letter *a*, is pronounced *ah* as in "father", so the word for house, *ban*, is pronounced "bahn", not as "ban" in English. Second is the single letter *o* which has the *oh* sound in "boat". The word *rot* ("vehicle") is pronounced "rote". Similarly *mot* ("used up") is "mote" and *jop* ("to finish") is "jope".

a	as in "father"
ay	between "ay" as in "say" and "eh" as in "met" (varies)
ae	as in "cat"
e	as in "met"
ee	as in "see"
i	as in "bit"
ai	as in "Thai"
aw	as in "saw"
o	as in "coat"
u	as in "but"
oo	as in "boot"
eu	the sound when you say "good" while smiling
euh	as in "love" or "above"

Vowel combinations - Here two or more vowel sounds are combined into one smooth sound.

ao	ah + oh, as in "how"
oi	aw + ee
oy	oh + ee, as in "Chloe"
eo	ay + oh, as in "mayo"
aeo	ae + oh
ia	ee + uh, as in "Pia"
io	ee + oh as in "Leo"
iu	ee + oo, as in "mew"
ua	oo + uh, as in "Kahlua"
ui	oo + ee, as in "Louie"
uay	oo + ay + ee (ends with a very short "ee" sound)
eua	eu + uh
euy	euh + ee
euay	eua + ay + ee (also ends with a very short "ee" sound)

NOTES ON PRONUNCIATION

Colloquial pronunciation - There are differences in all languages between the ideal form and the way it's commonly spoken. Following are some characteristics of informal, colloquial Thai:

- *R* is often pronounced *l* in informal speech, for example, *rong-raem* ("hotel") may be pronounced *long-laem*.

- *R* or *l* is often omitted when it's the second consonant sound of a word. *Krup*, the polite word for men, may be pronounced *kup*, and *pla* ("fish") pronounced *pa*.

- In some areas of Central Thailand a *kw* or *gw* sound may change to an *f*, for example, *kwa*, meaning "right" (opposite of "left") is pronounced *fa*, and *mai gwat*, meaning "broom", is *mai fat* ("faht").

Some common words have informal pronunciations with their own spellings in Thai which are used when informal quotes, dialogue, etc, are written out. In this book the informal spellings are used. (One exception is *chan*, "I" for women, pronounced high/short informally but spelled in the usual way.) Following are some examples of these informal changes:

	formal/written form		informal form	
he/she	kaoj	เขา	kao	เค้า
how	yang-rai	อย่างไร	yang-ngai	ยังไง
interrogative	maij	ไหม	mai	มั้ย

Tone changes on unstressed syllables - In spoken Thai, unstressed syllables in multisyllable words may be given mid tones instead of the high, low, or rising tone they should have according to their Thai spelling. In this book the common spoken form is used, and these syllables are given mid tones. Following are some examples of words where this happens:

	as spelled in Thai	as commonly pronounced
comfortable	sa-bai	sa-bai
westerner	fa-rang	fa-rang
lime	ma-nao	ma-nao
clock/watch	na-lee-ga	na-lee-ga
book	nang-seu	nang-seu

Final sound omitted - In some multisyllable words the final consonant sound of the first syllable may be left out. In formal/correct pronunciation the word follows its Thai spelling and includes the sound. Some examples:

advertise/advertisement	kot-sa-na	"t" not pronounced
art	sing-la-pa	"n" not pronounced
free/freedom	eet-sa-ra	"t" not pronounced
fruit	phong-la-mai	"n" not pronounced
religion	sat-sa-na	"t" not pronounced
wife (polite word)	phan-ra-ya	"n" not pronounced, "r" is "l"

Variations in vowel sounds - Most descriptions of Thai try to make an exact correspondence between Thai letters and English letters, with each Thai letter given an English equivalent. However, we found variations in the pronunciation of the following Thai vowel letters:

- The short vowel-length letter ˘ is pronounced both *ah* and *uh*. For example, in *wat* ("temple") the pronunciation is *ah* while in *fun* ("tooth" or "teeth") it's closer to *uh*. Some words may be pronounced either way depending on the speaker, for example, *chan* ("I" for woman) is also pronounced *chun*.

- The letter เ can be pronounced either *ay* or *eh*, or somewhere in between. For example, the *ay* sound in *phlayng* ("song") and the *e* sound in *geng* ("well/expertly") are both spelled with this letter.

- The short vowel-length letter ˆ is either *i* or *ee*. This letter is used in both *kit* ("to think") and *hee-ma* ("snow").

1. FUNDAMENTALS

PRONOUNS

Pronouns vary in Thai according to age, status, and the relationship the people speaking have to each other. The best pronouns for "I" for non-Thais are *phom* for men and *chan* for women. These are neither too respectful nor too intimate. When talking with a friend the person's name may be used for "you", especially the one-syllable nicknames that most Thais have. Some people also use their own names for "I".

In Thai, pronouns are often omitted in informal conversation, especially "I" and "you", but also "she/he/they" if it's understood in context whom you're referring to. Pronouns don't change with part of speech. The same words are both "I" and "me", "he" and "him", etc. Some Thai pronouns may be used in more than one way, for example, *theuh* is both "she" and "you", and *rao* can mean "we", "I", or "you".

I (said by women) -

chan (ฉัน) - This is the most common, informal word for "I" for women. The pronunciation is high/short informally, but rising/short in its written or formal form.

dee-chan (ดิฉัน) - More formal, could be used, for example, in a meeting where you don't know the people well. Too formal for everyday conversation.

rao (เรา) - An informal way to say "I" for women.

kao (เค้า) - Informal for "I" among close female friends.

noo (หนู) - "I" for young women, teenagers and under. Means "mouse" or "rat", sounds cute.

I (said by men) -

phom (ผม) - The most common word for "I" for men, neither too formal nor informal.

chan (ฉัน) - Same as "I" for women but more informal and intimate when used by men. Used with children and intimate friends only.

rao (เรา) - Informal and intimate.

gan (กัน) - For "I" when talking with close male friends.

I (said by children) -

noo (หนู) - This is both "I" and "you", said by and to talk to children.

I (very formal) -

ka-pha-jao - (ข้าพเจ้า) - Used mostly in speeches.

you -

koon (คุณ) - The general way to say "you", sounds polite.

than (ท่าน) - Respectful.

thook than (ทุกท่าน) - Literally "all of you", used in speeches and announcements.

theuh/rao/nooj (เธอ/เรา/หนู) - For addressing children.

gae (แก) - For addressing close friends, either male or female. May sound rude with people other than friends.

theuh/tua (เธอ/ตัว) - "You" by close female friends.

nai (นาย) - "You" by close male friends.

theuh (เธอ) - "You" by couples when addressing each other.

he/she/it -

kao (เค้า) - The general word for both "he" and "she".

theuh (เธอ) - For "she", sounds more polite than *kao*.

gae (แก) - Familiar, used to refer to friends, both male and female.

lawn (หล่อน) - "She" in writing, mostly in novels.

mun (มัน) - Means "it", sometimes used to refer to people in a derogatory way.

they -

kao (เค้า) - Informal for "they", the same as "he/she".

phuak kao (พวกเค้า) - More formal and precise, used formally or when there may be uncertainty whether you're referring to one or more people.

we -

rao (เรา) - The general word for "we".

rao sawngj kon (เราสองคน) - Means "we two" or "the two of us".

phuak rao (พวกเรา) - Means "all of us".

kon rao (คนเรา) - Means "we the people" or "we of the world".

RELATIONSHIP TERMS USED AS PRONOUNS

When people of different ages speak to each other they often use relationship terms for "I" and "you". This makes the conversation sound more intimate and also indicates respect for the older person by the younger. The following terms are both pronouns and titles put before people's first names:

phee (พี่) - Used to address a person who is older than you are but from the same generation, and also to refer to yourself when talking to someone younger.

nawng (น้อง) - Used to address a person who is younger than you are but from the same generation, or "I" for a younger person when talking to someone older.

na/ah (น้า/อา) - For people from your parents' generation who are younger than they are. These words actually refer to younger aunts and uncles (maternal/paternal).

pa (ป้า) - For women from your parents' generation who are older than they are. It actually refers to the older sister of your mother or father.

loong (ลุง) - For men from your parents' generation who are older than they are. It actually refers to the older brother of your mother or father.

yai/ya (ยาย/ย่า) - For grandmother-aged women, actually for your maternal and paternal grandmothers.

ta/poo (ตา/ปู่) - For grandfather-aged men, actually for your maternal and paternal grandfathers.

In this dialogue *phee* and *nawng* are used for "you" (A is younger than B).

A: Have you eaten yet?

Phee gin kao reu yang?

พี่กินข้าวรึยัง

B: No. What about you?

Yang. Laeo nawng, la?

ยัง แล้วน้องละ

A: I've eaten already.

Gin laeo, ka/krup.

กินแล้วค่ะ/ครับ

OTHER WORDS USED TO ADDRESS PEOPLE

phaw/mae/look (พ่อ/แม่/ลูก) - These are "father", "mother", and "child/children", for parents and children when talking to or referring to each other.

kroo/a-jan (ครู/อาจารย์) - "Teacher" and "professor". *Ajan* is for higher-level teachers.

mawj/koon mawj (หมอ/คุณหมอ) - For doctors.

jay (เจ๊) - For female shop or restaurant owners, usually Chinese.

thao-gae (เถ้าแก่) - For owners of businesses and factories, originally for Chinese but now also used with Thais.

maem (แหมม) - For Western women.

Other words are *pheuan* for a friend or friends and *faen* for a spouse or partner. These words aren't used for "I" or "you" but only for "he", "she", or "they".

A: Where did your friend(s) go?

Pheuan pai nai?

เพื่อนไปไหน

B: He/she/they went to work.

Pheuan pai tham-ngan laeo.

เพื่อนไปทำงานแล้ว

A: Where's your girlfriend from? (boyfriend/husband/wife)

    Faen pen kon thee-nai?

       แฟนเป็นคนที่ไหน

B: She's from Chiang Mai. ("She's a Chiang Mai person.")

    Faen pen kon Chiang Mai.

       แฟนเป็นคนเชียงใหม่

Impolite pronouns/cursing - Thais generally don't speak abusively, but there are a few cursing terms including the following crude-sounding pronouns. These words are impolite and shouldn't be used in public.

goo (กู) - A tough and crude way to say "I".

meung (มึง) - A crude term for "you", used together with *goo*.

ai (ไอ้) - "You", derogatory when talking to a man.

ee (อี) - "You", derogatory for women.

Ai and *ee* sound very derogatory for "you", but may be used before names among close friends or by older people to younger people without sounding rude (although they're still not polite). *Ai* and *ee* are also used before names of pets such as dogs and water buffalo, and *ai* can be put before names of objects to make them sound detestable, as in this example.

This **** watch breaks a lot.

    Ai na-lee-ga nee chawp sia boi-boi.

       ไอ้นาฬิกานี่ชอบเสียบ่อยๆ

TITLES

Titles are put before first names in Thai.

koon (คุณ) - This is the equivalent of Mr or Ms although it's put before first names. It's common in offices and on the telephone.

nai (นาย) - Very formal for "Mr" or "master" (may be said by low-level workers).

nang (นาง) - A formal title put before the first names of married women, the equivalent of "Mrs".

nang-sao (นางสาว) - A formal title put before the first names of unmarried women, the equivalent of "Miss".

koon ying (คุณหญิง) - The Thai equivalent of "Lady", used by women who have been conferred the title.

sia (เสี่ย) - For tycoons and godfathers (from Chinese).

BASIC WORD ORDER

The word order of Thai sentences isn't very complicated but follows definite rules. Basic sentences have the same subject-verb-object order of English, however the object may be stated first when it's the topic of the sentence as in the first point here.

Stating the topic first - When the topic is stated first the subject pronoun is often omitted. Here "I" is in parentheses.

I don't want this one. ("This one I don't want.")

    Un nee (chan) mai ao. (or *phom* for men; pronouns alternate in examples)

    อันนี้(ฉัน)ไม่เอา

Nee **after the topic** - nee/nia - *Nee*, or informally *nia*, may be included after the topic to call attention to it. In the second sentence it's put after an entire clause ("When we go traveling").

Gambling - I don't do it at all.

    Gan pha-nan nee - phom mai len leuy.

    การพนันนี่ผมไม่เล่นเลย

When we go traveling, we should take some friends along.

    Way-la rao pai thio nai nia, rao kuan ja ao pheuan pai duay.

    เวลาเราไปเที่ยวไหนเนี่ยเราควรจะเอาเพื่อนไปด้วย

Gaw **after the subject** - gaw - *Gaw* is a common linking word in Thai and one of its functions is to give statements a hypothetical meaning. Here it's included after the subject when the speaker is offering information, making the statement sound less direct and putting it into the context of the conversation. The subject may be omitted and isn't included in the second example ("we").

I've never been to Ko Samui.

    Gaw Sa-mui (chan) gaw mai keuy pai.

    เกาะสมุย(ฉัน)ก็ไม่เคยไป

We have a lot of flowers like this at home. ("Flowers like this...")

    Dawk mai baep nee, thee ban gaw mee yeuh.

    ดอกไม้แบบนี้ที่บ้านก็มีเยอะ

Two subjects ("she and I") - Put "I" first and use *gap* for "and". Phrases like *phaw-mae* ("mother and father") and *phee-nawng* ("brothers and sisters") don't require "and".

My older sister and I live in Pattaya.

    Chan gap phee-sao yoo thee Phat-tha-ya.

    ฉันกับพี่สาวอยู่ที่พัทยา

Noi and a friend are coming tomorrow.

    Noi gap pheuan ja ma phroong-nee.

    น้อยกับเพื่อนจะมาพรุ่งนี้

Repeating "he/she" - "He", "she", and "it" can be repeated after the subject or name.

Jane went to Had Yai already. ("Jane, she went...")

    Jane, kao pai Had Yai laeo.

    เจนเค้าไปหาดใหญ่แล้ว

My friend doesn't want to go. ("My friend he...")

    Pheuan, kao mai yak pai.

    เพื่อนเค้าไม่อยากไป

Objects of sentences - Objects are put after the verb or between two-word verbs (here between *ao* and *ma* for "bring").

I brought some snacks.

    Chan ao ka-nom ma fak duay.

    ฉันเอาขนมมาฝากด้วย

TO BE

There are two words for "to be" in Thai—*pen* and *keu*. They're used to link two nouns or a pronoun and a noun but aren't used with adjectives as in English.

***Pen* for "to be"** - In the first sentence "this" is linked with "house", in the second "this place" with "national park", and in the third "she" with "child".

This is the house I bought five years ago.

    Nee pen ban thee chan seu meua ha pee thee laeo.

    นี่เป็นบ้านที่ฉันซื้อเมื่อห้าปีที่แล้ว

This (place) is a national park.

    Thee-nee pen oot-tha-yan haeng chat.

    ที่นี่เป็นอุทยานแหงชาติ

A: Whose child is she?

    Kao pen look (kawng) krai?

        เค้าเป็นลูก(ของ)ใคร

B: Mine.

    Look phom ayng.

        ลูกผมเอง

Negative of "to be" - mai chai - *Mai chai* (not *mai pen*) is put before nouns for the negative. It's also "not" before nouns as in the fourth sentence.

He's not German.

    Kao mai chai kon Yeuh-ra-mun.

        เค้าไม่ใช่คนเยอรมัน

This (place) isn't a school.

    Thee-nee mai chai rong-rian.

        ที่นี่ไม่ใช่โรงเรียน

Bangkok isn't a dangerous city.

    Groong-thayp mai chai meuang an-ta-rai.

        กรุงเทพไม่ใช่เมืองอันตราย

We're going to Surat, not Korat.

    Rao ja pai Soo-rat, mai chai Ko-rat.

        เราจะไปสุราษฎร์ไม่ใช่โคราช

It wasn't he who said he was a policeman. It was actually his younger brother.

    Mai chai kao rawk thee bawk wa pen tam-ruat. Thee thae pen nawng-chai kao.

        ไม่ใช่เค้าหรอกที่บอกว่าเป็นตำรวจ ที่แท้เป็นน้องชายเค้า

it's not that... - mai chai wa... - "It" (*mun*) is optional, included for emphasis. *Gaw* is also optional, included for indirectness or to indicate that the meaning is hypothetical.

It's not that I don't love her, but that her parents don't like me.

    (Mun) (gaw) mai chai wa phom mai rak theuh, tae (wa) phaw-mae theuh mai

    chawp phom.

        (มัน)(ก็)ไม่ใช่ว่าผมไม่รักเธอแต่(ว่า)พ่อแม่เธอไม่ชอบผม

Short responses - Use *mai pen* or *mai chai* in short responses.

A: Is that person a friend of yours?

    Kon nan pen pheuan koon reu plao?

        คนนั้นเป็นเพื่อนคุณรึเปล่า

B: No.

    Mai pen./Mai chai.

        ไม่เป็น/ไม่ใช่

not as thought - Here *dai* is included to mean "not as thought".

He's a student. He's not a teacher (as we may have thought).

> Kao pen nak-rian. Kao mai dai pen kroo.
>
> เค้าเป็นนักเรียน เค้าไม่ได้เป็นครู

She's not the one who did it. I did it myself.

> Theuh mai dai pen kon tham. Chan tham ayng.
>
> เธอไม่ได้เป็นคนทำ ฉันทำเอง

Keu for "to be" - *Keu* links two things that are equivalent, compared with *pen* which links things that are more descriptive. These pairs of sentences compare the two words. In the first example "this" is the equivalent of "rose" and they're linked with *keu* (which is optional). In the second sentence "these" is linked with "the roses my boyfriend bought me". This is more descriptive and *pen* is used.

This is a rose.

> Nee (keu) dawk goo-lap.
>
> นี่(คือ)ดอกกุหลาบ

These are the roses my boyfriend bought me.

> Nee pen dawk goo-lap thee faen seu hai chan.
>
> นี่เป็นดอกกุหลาบที่แฟนซื้อให้ฉัน

In this example "he" is the equivalent of "my teacher", while "he is a teacher" describes the person. *Keu* isn't optional after "she/he".

He's my teacher.

> Kao keu kroo kawng chan.
>
> เค้าคือครูของฉัน

He's a teacher.

> Kao pen kroo.
>
> เค้าเป็นครู

namely/that is to say - keu/keu wa -

The police concentrate on two things, namely prostitution and gambling.

> Tam-ruat son-jai yoo sawng reuang, keu (reuang) so-phay-nee gap gan pha-nan.
>
> ตำรวจสนใจอยู่สองเรื่อง คือ(เรื่อง)โสเภณีกับการพนัน

I don't like these kinds of problems, that's to say, they're completely boring.

> Phom mai koi chawp pan-ha baep nee leuy. Keu wa, mun na beua, na.
>
> ผมไม่ค่อยชอบปัญหาแบบนี้เลย คือว่ามันน่าเบื่อนะ

to be at a place - This is *yoo* in Thai.

My home is in the South.

>   Ban chan yoo thee phak tai.

>   บ้านฉันอยู่ที่ภาคใต้

Maeo is in the bedroom.

>   Maeo yoo nai hawng-nawn.

>   แมวอยู่ในห้องนอน

Nim's not at home much on weekends.

>   Nim mai koi yoo ban wan sao a-thit.

>   นิ่มไม่ค่อยอยู่บ้านวันเสาร์อาทิตย์

THERE IS/THERE EXISTS/IT HAPPENED

These are formed with *mee* ("have"), *geuht* ("born"), and *geuht keun* ("born-go up").

With *mee* -

There's a party tonight at Noi's house.

>   Mee pa-tee thee ban Noi keun-nee.

>   มีปาร์ตี้ที่บ้านน้อยคืนนี้

Is there a hospital here?/Does this place have a hospital?

>   Thee-nee mee rong-pha-ya-ban mai?

>   ที่นี่มีโรงพยาบาลมั้ย

There's a coffee shop at the beginning of the lane.

>   Trong pak soi mee ran kai ga-fae yoo ran neung.

>   ตรงปากซอยมีร้านขายกาแฟอยู่ร้านหนึ่ง

If there's any water, please buy me a bottle.

>   Tha mee nam, chuay seu hai kuat neung, na.

>   ถ้ามีน้ำช่วยซื้อให้ขวดหนึ่งนะ

A: Does it flood here?

>   Thee-nee (keuy) mee nam thuam mai?

>   ที่นี่(เคย)มีน้ำท่วมมั้ย

B: Yes./No.

>   Mee./Mai mee.

>   มี/ไม่มี

Not very often./Never.

>   Mai koi mee./Mai mee leuy.

>   ไม่ค่อยมี/ไม่มีเลย

With *geuht* - Basic patterns are *mee* followed by the event then by *geuht keun*, or *geuht* alone followed by the event.

There was an accident.

> Mee oo-bat-tee-hayt (geuht keun)./Geuht oo-bat-tee-hayt.
>
> มีอุบัติเหตุ(เกิดขึ้น)/เกิดอุบัติเหตุ

There have been a lot of accidents on this street.

> (Keuy) mee oo-bat-tee-hayt (geuht keun) mak mai bon tha-nong saij nee.
>
> (เคย)มีอุบัติเหตุ(เกิดขึ้น)มากมายบนถนนสายนี้

There's a storm in the South.

> Mee pha-yoo geuht keun thee pak tai.
>
> มีพายุเกิดขึ้นที่ปักษ์ใต้

There aren't many earthquakes in Thailand.

> (Thee) meuang Thai mai koi geuht phaen-din waij. (or mai koi mee)
>
> (ที่)เมืองไทยไม่ค่อยเกิดแผ่นดินไหว

PREFIXES
THE PREFIX *KWAM*

Kwam is put before verbs, adverbs, and adjectives to make nouns that express a concept. "True" becomes "truth", "fast" becomes "speed", and "think" becomes "thought", "idea" or "concept". The basic meaning of *kwam* is "substance", "matter", or "sense". Following are some common words with *kwam*.

cooperation - kwam ruam-meu - This refers to the abstract idea of "cooperation", not to the action of cooperating.

Thank you for your cooperation.

> Kawp-koon thee hai kwam ruam-meu.
>
> ขอบคุณที่ให้ความร่วมมือ

dream - kwam funj -

It's something that's in my dreams.

> Mun pen sing thee yoo nai kwam funj kawng phomj.
>
> มันเป็นสิ่งที่อยู่ในความฝันของผม

importance - kwam samj-kan -

He doesn't see the importance of education.

> Kao mai henj kwam samj-kan kawng gan seuk-saj.
>
> เค้าไม่เห็นความสำคัญของการศึกษา

knowledge - kwam roo -

She has a lot of knowledge./She knows a lot.

   Kao mee kwam roo yeuh.

   เค้ามีความรู้เยอะ

skill/ability - kwam sa-mat -

It's an ability that only she has. ("that only she can do")

   Mun pen kwam sa-mat thee kao tham dai kon dio.

   มันเป็นความสามารถที่เค้าทำได้คนเดียว

truth - kwam jing -

I want to know the truth about who did it.

   Phom yak roo kwam jing wa krai tham.

   ผมอยากรู้ความจริงว่าใครทำ

Other words with *kwam* -

bad/evil	kwam chua	ความชั่ว
beauty	kwam suay-ngam	ความสวยงาม
belief	kwam cheua	ความเชื่อ
confidence	kwam cheua-mun	ความเชื่อมั่น
	kwam mun-jai	ความมั่นใจ
fairness	kwam yoot-tee-tham	ความยุติธรรม
good/goodness	kwam dee	ความดี
happiness	kwam sook	ความสุข
happiness/well-being	kwam sook sa-bai	ความสุขสบาย
heat	kwam rawn	ความร้อน
honesty	kwam seu-sat	ความซื่อสัตย์
intensity	kwam nak-bao	ความหนักเบา
intention	kwam tang-jai	ความตั้งใจ
love	kwam rak	ความรัก
memory	kwam jam	ความจำ
necessity(ies)	kwam jam-pen	ความจำเป็น
patience	kwam ot-thon	ความอดทน
popularity	kwam nee-yom	ความนิยม
possibility/chance	kwam pen pai dai	ความเป็นไปได้
prosperity	kwam ja-reuhn	ความเจริญ
success	kwam sam-ret	ความสำเร็จ
wants/needs/desires	kwam tawng-gan	ความต้องการ

THE PREFIX *GAN*

Gan (pronounced mid/long) is put before verbs to make nouns (or gerunds in English grammar) that are used as the subject or object of sentences. *Gan* is also a suffix in a few words like *wi-thee-gan* ("method") and *gra-buan-gan* ("process"). *Gan* is optional or required in some patterns as follows:

1. in the subject - When *gan* is in the subject it's optional if you're talking about a real action (first two sentences) but needed with concepts (third sentence).

Listening to music is fun.

> (Gan) fang phlayng nee sa-nook mak.
>
> (การ)ฟังเพลงนี้สนุกมาก

Not studying caused him to fail the exam.

> (Gan) mai an nang-seu tham hai kao sawp tok.
>
> (การ)ไม่อ่านหนังสือทำให้เค้าสอบตก

Advertising makes people want to buy things (more).

> Gan kot-sa-na tham hai kon yak seu kawng mak keun.
>
> การโฆษณาทำให้คนอยากซื้อของมากขึ้น

2. in the predicate - *Gan* is almost never included in the predicate when the gerund refers to a real action, but could theoretically be included with "going" ("I like going") in the first example. It's needed after "there is" and verbs like "impressed by" which are followed by concepts rather than actions.

I like going on trips.

> Phom chawp pai thio.
>
> ผมชอบไปเที่ยว

There's a lot of commerce in the Pratunam area.

> Mee gan ka yoo thaeo Pra-too-nam yeuh.
>
> มีการค้าอยู่แถวประตูน้ำเยอะ

I'm very impressed with Ann's work.

> Chan pra-thap-jai gan tham-ngan kawng Ann mak.
>
> ฉันประทับใจการทำงานของแอนมาก

3. with "to be" - Here a noun beginning with *gan* is followed by "is" (*keu* or *pen*). *Keu* links the noun with its equivalent while *pen* links it with something descriptive.

Education is building for the future.

> Gan seuk-sa keu gan sang a-na-kot.
>
> การศึกษาคือการสร้างอนาคต

Traffic is something that's a headache.

> Gan ja-ra-jawn pen reuang puat hua.
>
> การจราจรเป็นเรื่องปวดหัว

3. with the object of the preposition - *Gan* is needed when the gerund is the object of a preposition. Here it's included after "in", "about", and "from".

This is a machine that's used in manufacturing.

> Nee pen kreuang-jak thee chai nai gan pha-lit.
>
> นี่เป็นเครื่องจักรที่ใช้ในการผลิต

They're discussing ("about") investment.

> Kao gam-lang a-phee-prai gan gio-gap gan long thoon.
>
> เค้ากำลังอภิปรายกันเกี่ยวกับการลงทุน

The staff didn't gain anything from that training.

> Pha-nak-ngan mai dai pra-yot a-rai jak gan feuk op-rom nee.
>
> พนักงานไม่ได้ประโยชน์อะไรจากการฝึกอบรมนี้

4. with possessives - *Gan* is needed when the action is followed by a possessive.

Her smile made me feel better. ("her smiling")

> Gan yim kawng kao tham hai phom roo-seuk dee keun.
>
> การยิ้มของเค้าทำให้ผมรู้สึกดีขึ้น

Words with *gan* - Following are common words with *gan*:

acting/show - gan sa-daeng - This word has two meanings.

His acting doesn't look natural.

> Gan sa-daeng kawng kon nee doo mai pen tham-ma-chat.
>
> การแสดงของคนนี้ดูไม่เป็นธรรมชาติ

The elephant show was fun.

> Gan sa-daeng kawng chang sa-nook mak.
>
> การแสดงของช้างสนุกมาก

competition - gan kaeng-kun -

These two schools always compete with each other. ("have competitions")

> Rong-rian sawng haeng nee mee gan kaeng-kun gan ma ta-lawt.
>
> โรงเรียนสองแห่งนี้มีการแข่งขันกันมาตลอด

She won a trophy in the competition.

> Theuh dai thuay jak gan kaeng-kun.
>
> เธอได้ถ้วยจากการแข่งขัน

cooperation/cooperating - gan ruam-meu - This refers to the action of cooperating, as opposed to the concept (*kwam ruam-meu*).

The villagers' cooperation helped finish this bridge.

> Gan ruam-meu kawng chao-ban tham hai sa-phan nee set.
>
> การร่วมมือของชาวบ้านทำให้สะพานนี้เสร็จ

development/developing - gan phat-tha-na -

Developing the countryside is something the government is presently doing.

> Gan phat-tha-na chon-na-bot pen sing thee rat-tha-ban gam-lang tham yoo.

> การพัฒนาชนบทเป็นสิ่งที่รัฐบาลกำลังทำอยู่

education/studying - gan seuk-sa/gan rian - *Seuk-sa* refers to higher-level education.

My daughter is very interested in studying.

> Look-sao chan son-jai (gan) rian mak.

> ลูกสาวฉันสนใจ(การ)เรียนมาก

Parents are starting to be more interested in their children's education.

> Phaw-mae reuhm son-jai gan seuk-sa kawng look mak keun.

> พ่อแม่เริ่มสนใจการศึกษาของลูกมากขึ้น

having - gan mee -

Having a private car makes it very convenient.

> (Gan) mee rot suan tua tham hai sa-duak mak.

> (การ)มีรถส่วนตัวทำให้สะดวกมาก

meeting - gan pra-choom -

Our company will have its annual meeting in March.

> Baw-ree-sat rao ja mee gan pra-choom pra-jam pee nai deuan Mee-na.

> บริษัทเราจะมีการประชุมประจำปีในเดือนมีนา

Other words with *gan* -

advertising	gan kot-sa-na	การโฆษณา
analysis/analyzing	gan wee-kraw	การวิเคราห์
arguing/argument	gan tha-law	การทะเลาะ
cheating (money)	gan gong	การโกง
cheating/deceiving	gan lawk luang	การหลอกลวง
commerce	gan ka	การค้า
communications	gan seu-san	การสื่อสาร
contest	gan pra-guat	การประกวด
corruption	gan kaw-rap-chun	การคอร์รัปชั่น
	gan gong gin	การโกงกิน
helping	gan chuay-leua	การช่วยเหลือ
living/staying	gan yoo	การอยู่
speaking	gan phoot	การพูด
support/supporting	gan sa-nap sa-noon	การสนับสนุน

thinking	gan kit	การคิด
tourism	gan thawng-thio	การท่องเที่ยว
traffic	gan ja-ra-jawn	การจราจร
training	gan feuk op-rom	การฝึกอบรม
travel/traveling	gan deuhn-thang	การเดินทาง

Gan also means "affairs of" or "matters of".

administration	gan baw-ree-han	การบริหาร
electric company	gan fai-fa	การไฟฟ้า
finance	gan ngeuhn	การเงิน
medicine	gan phaet	การแพทย์
municipal water	gan pra-pa	การประปา
phone company	gan tho-ra-sap	การโทรศัพท์
politics	gan meuang	การเมือง

BEING

Kwam pen and *gan pen* both mean "being" but are used in different ways.

kwam pen - This refers to the state/condition of being and makes nouns that refer to the state of a quality.

femininity	kwam pen phoo-ying
justice/fairness	kwam pen tham
maturity	kwam pen phoo-yai
privacy	kwam pen suan tua
reality	kwam pen jing

I like her femininity. ("the being a woman of her")

Chan chawp kwam pen phoo-ying kawng theuh.

ฉันชอบความเป็นผู้หญิงของเธอ

gan pen - This is similar to *kwam pen* but emphasizes the continuous action of a quality, not the state. *Gan* is optional in both examples.

Being a woman is difficult.

(Gan) pen phoo-ying lam-bak.

(การ)เป็นผู้หญิงลำบาก

Being a teacher, you have to use many skills.

(Gan) pen kroo nee, tawng chai kwam sa-mat lai yang.

(การ)เป็นครูนี้ต้องใช้ความสามารถหลายอย่าง

OTHER PREFIXES/SUFFIXES/COMPOUND WORDS

chao (ชาว) - This is used in compound words for "inhabitant of".

chao Ay-sia	an Asian, Asians	ชาวเอเซีย
chao ban	common person, common people, country people	ชาวบ้าน
chao kaoj/chao doi	hill tribe person or people	ชาวเขา/ชาวดอย
chao meuang	city person or people	ชาวเมือง
chao Moot-sa-lim	a Muslim, Muslims	ชาวมุสลิม
chao na	a farmer, farmers	ชาวนา

jai (ใจ) - This means "heart/mind" and is used as a prefix or suffix in words that concern the mind and emotions.

jai-awn	easily influenced, indecisive, yielding	ใจอ่อน
jai dam/jai-rai	mean, nasty, unscrupulous	ใจดำ/ใจร้าย
jai-dee	nice, kind	ใจดี
jai gwang	broad-minded, magnanamous	ใจกว้าง
jai kaeng	strong-minded in an unyielding, hard-hearted way	ใจแข็ง
jai kaep	closed-minded, lacking in generosity	ใจแคบ
jai noi	overly sensitive, easily offended	ใจน้อย
jai rawn	hot-tempered, anxious	ใจร้อน
jing-jai	sincere	จริงใจ
awn-jai	fed up	อ่อนใจ
cheun-jai	happy, pleased, cheered-up	ชื่นใจ
dee-jai	glad, thrilled, pleased	ดีใจ
gam-lang jai	will-power, spirit	กำลังใจ
gloom-jai	unhappy, depressed	กลุ้มใจ
jai-haj	shocked, upset, afraid	ใจหาย
jep-jai	have hurt feelings	เจ็บใจ
kawng-jai	doubtful, suspicious	ข้องใจ
mai sa-bai-jai	upset	ไม่สบายใจ
mun-jai	sure, confident	มั่นใจ
nae-jai	sure, certain	แน่ใจ
noi-jai	feel slighted, unappreciated	น้อยใจ
pra-lat-jai	surprised	ประหลาดใจ

prá-tháp-jai	impressed (by)	ประทับใจ
phaw-jai	satisfied	พอใจ
phoom-jai	proud, pleased	ภูมิใจ
sà-bai-jai	happy, contented	สบายใจ
siaj-jai	unhappy, sorry	เสียใจ

ká (ค่า) - This is a noun meaning "fee (for)", "cost", "price", or "value". It's used in compound words that refer to prices, amounts of money, or charges for things.

ká a-haŋ	the money you pay for food, charge for food	ค่าอาหาร
ká chai jai	expenses	ค่าใช้จ่าย
ká chaó	rent, rental fee	ค่าเช่า
ká fai	charge for electricity	ค่าไฟ
ká jang	wages, pay	ค่าจ้าง
ká kawm-mít-chun	commission	ค่าคอมมิชชั่น
ká nam	charge for water	ค่าน้ำ
ká (kawŋ) ngeuhn	the value of money	ค่า(ของ)เงิน
ká práp	charge paid for a fine	ค่าปรับ
ká raeng	cost of labor, labor charge	ค่าแรง
ká rot	vehicle fare	ค่ารถ
ká thee-phák	housing cost	ค่าที่พัก

-ká-dee (คดี) - This is a suffix that means "the path" or "the way".

bo-ran-ná-ká-dee	archeology	โบราณคดี
saj-rá-ká-dee	documentary film or book	สารคดี
wán-ná-ká-dee	literature	วรรณคดี

kám (คำ) - This means "word" or "words" and is put before verbs to make nouns that refer to worded content—something said or written.

kám bàwk laó	account of an incident	คำบอกเล่า
kám náe-nam	suggestion, advice, instruction	คำแนะนำ
kám nam	preface or forward of a book	คำนำ
kám plae	translation, meaning	คำแปล
kám prèuk-saj	advice, that which is said in a consultation	คำปรึกษา
kám phoot	that which is/was said	คำพูด

kam rawng	application (ie. for a license), formal complaint or petition	คำร้อง
kam sang	order, command, instructions	คำสั่ง
kam sawn	teaching(s)	คำสอน
kam tawp	a response or reply	คำตอบ
kam tham	a question	คำถาม

kaw (ข้อ) - This means "joint" or "node" and makes compound words that refer to a piece of worded content. It's also the classifier for items on a list or points in a discussion.

kaw bang-kap	rule(s), regulation(s) (bang-kap means "to force")	ข้อบังคับ
kaw dee	good point about something	ข้อดี
kaw sia	bad point about something	ข้อเสีย
kaw kian	articles, as in the newspaper (also bot kwam, bot is low/short)	ข้อเขียน
kaw kwam	message	ข้อความ
kaw mae	stipulation, condition	ข้อแม้
kaw moon	information	ข้อมูล
kaw ra-biap	an item in the regulations	ข้อระเบียบ
kaw riak-rawng	request, demand	ข้อเรียกร้อง
kaw sawp	test questions	ข้อสอบ
kaw sun-ya	item in a contract	ข้อสัญญา
kaw tok-long	an agreement	ข้อตกลง
kaw yok wayn	an exception	ข้อยกเว้น

kawng (ของ) - This means "thing" or "things" and is included in the names of objects.

kawng gin	things to eat	ของกิน
kawng chai	things to use, utensils	ของใช้
kawng len	toys	ของเล่น
kao kawng	possessions, commodities	ข้าวของ
sing kawng	plural for "objects", also more formal-sounding	สิ่งของ
kawng suay	beautiful things	ของสวย
kawng plawm	things that are fake or counter-feit	ของปลอม

kee (ขี้) - This is put before adjectives and verbs to describe people as "characterized by" the attribute of the adjective or verb.

kee bon	a complainer	ขี้บ่น
kee gong	a cheater	ขี้โกง
kee heung	a jealous person (in love)	ขี้หึง
kee kaw	a beggar	ขี้ขอ
kee len	a joker	ขี้เล่น
kee leum	a forgetful person, absent-minded	ขี้ลืม
kee mao	a drunkard	ขี้เมา
kee mo-ho	bad-tempered	ขี้โมโห

kee (ขี้) - This means "excrement".

kee hoo	ear wax	ขี้หู
kee mook	mucus	ขี้มูก
kee nio	stingy	ขี้เหนียว
kee ta	eye secretion	ขี้ตา

kreuang (เครื่อง) - This makes compound words that refer to an apparatus, implement, instrument, or paraphernalia.

kreuang chai	utensils, appliances, equipment	เครื่องใช้
kreuang deum	drinks	เครื่องดื่ม
kreuang gaeng	ingredients for making curry	เครื่องแกง
kreuang jak	machine, machinery	เครื่องจักร
kreuang krua	kitchen utensils	เครื่องครัว
kreuang nai	internal body organs	เครื่องใน
kreuang phroong	condiments, garnishes	เครื่องปรุง
kreuang pra-dap	jewelry, ornaments	เครื่องประดับ
kreuang meu	tools	เครื่องมือ
kreuang thayt	spice, spices	เครื่องเทศ
kreuang yon	engine	เครื่องยนต์

ma-ha (มหา) - This means "great".

ma-ha na-kawn	great city	มหานคร
ma-ha sa-moot	ocean	มหาสมุทร
ma-ha sayt-thee	a very rich person	มหาเศรษฐี
ma-ha wit-tha-ya-lai	university	มหาวิทยาลัย

mai (ไม้) - This is both a prefix and a suffix for plants, parts of plants, and things made of wood. It's also used in the names of the Thai tone markers.

mai gwat	broom	ไม้กวาด
mai phai	bamboo	ไม้ไผ่
mai sak	teak wood	ไม้สัก
bai mai	leaf	ใบไม้
dawk mai	flower	ดอกไม้
ton mai	tree, plant	ต้นไม้
phoŋ-la-mai	fruit	ผลไม้

-maiŋ (หมาย) - This is a suffix for things that have meaning.

got-maiŋ	law	กฎหมาย
jot-maiŋ	letter	จดหมาย
kwam-maiŋ	meaning	ความหมาย

moon (มูล) - This means "source", "origin", "root", or "foundation". The same spelling in Thai can also mean "excrement" or "rubbish".

moon-ka/moon-la-ka	worth, value	มูลค่า
moon kwam-jing	basis in truth	มูลความจริง
kaw moon	information	ขอมูล

na (น่า) - This is put before verbs to mean "should" or "worthy of".

na doo	worth seeing	น่าดู
na gin	good to eat, tasty-looking	น่ากิน
na gliat	ugly (both looks and actions)	น่าเกลียด
na glua	frightening	น่ากลัว
na pai	worth going to	น่าไป
na puat huaŋ	confusing	น่าปวดหัว
na soŋ-saŋ	pitiful	น่าสงสาร
na soŋ-jai	interesting	น่าสนใจ
na thio	good for visiting	น่าเที่ยว
na yoo	worth living at/in	น่าอยู่

nam (น้ำ) - This is for the names of liquids. *Nam* may have a short vowel length in compound words, as written here.

nam chai	water to use (for washing, etc)	น้ำใช้
nam gin/nam deum	drinking water	น้ำกิน/น้ำดื่ม
nam mun	oil, gasoline	น้ำมัน
nam ta	tear, tears	น้ำตา
nam phoŋ-la-mai	fruit juice	น้ำผลไม้

na-na (นานา) - This means "various" and is used to make plurals.

na-na chat	races, nations, also the adjective "international"	นานาชาติ
na-na pra-thet	many countries	นานาประเทศ

-phap (ภาพ) - This is a suffix meaning "state" or "condition".

eet-sa-ra-phap	freedom	อิสระภาพ
mit-tra-phap	friendship	มิตรภาพ
sayŋ-ree-phap	liberty	เสรีภาพ
suŋ-tee-phap	peace	สันติภาพ

In these words *phap* is an elegant term for "picture", "image", or "figure".

phap-pha-yon	movie (elegant term)	ภาพยนต์
roop-phap	picture, photo	รูปภาพ

rat (รัฐ) - This is used in words that concern states or nations.

rat-tha-ban	government	รัฐบาล
rat-tha-mon-tree	government minister	รัฐมนตรี
rat-tha-tham-ma-noon	constitution	รัฐธรรมนูญ
sa-ha-rat	federation, united states	สหรัฐ

-sat (ศาสตร์) - This is a suffix for the names of sciences and other academic disciplines.

ga-sayt-sat	agricultural science	เกษตรศาสตร์
ka-nit-sat/lek	mathematics	คณิตศาสตร์
pra-wat-sat	history	ประวัติศาสตร์
phaet-sat/gan phaet	medicine	แพทย์ศาสตร์
phoo-mee-sat	geography	ภูมิศาสตร์

rat-tha-sat	political science	รัฐศาสตร์
saŋ-kom-ma-sat	social science	สังคมศาสตร์
sayt-sat / sayt-tha-sat	economics	เศรษฐศาสตร์
seuk-saj-sat	education	ศึกษาศาสตร์
than-ta-phaet-sat	dentistry	ทันตแพทย์ศาสตร์
wit-sa-wa-gam-ma-sat	engineering	วิศวกรรมศาสตร์
wit-tha-ya-sat	science	วิทยาศาสตร์

2. REFERRING TO THINGS

Classifiers are used in many of the patterns in this chapter including "this/that", numbers, "more", and "other/another". See the appendix for a list of classifiers.

IT

Optional "it" - mun - "It" is commonly omitted in Thai sentences and is included mainly to put emphasis on what you're referring to. "It" can be put after the subject as in the third example.

It was too expensive, so I didn't buy it.

    Mun phaeng mak, phom leuy mai seu (mun).

    มันแพงมาก ผมเลยไม่ซื้อ(มัน)

I don't want to buy it. It's too expensive.

    Mai yak seu. (Mun) phaeng.

    ไม่อยากซื้อ (มัน)แพง

There are a lot of cars.

    Rot (mun) yeuh.

    รถ(มัน)เยอะ

I'm going to exchange it.

    Chan ja ao (mun) pai plian (mai).

    ฉันจะเอา(มัน)ไปเปลี่ยน(ใหม่)

A: Is that a Thai song or a Western song?

    (Mun) pen phlayng Thai reu phlayng fa-rang?

    (มัน)เป็นเพลงไทยหรือเพลงฝรั่ง

B: It's a Thai song.

    (Pen) phlayng Thai./Mun pen phlayng Thai.

    (เป็น)เพลงไทย/มันเป็นเพลงไทย

Gaw after "it" ("it's good that...") - "It" is also optional here where it introduces a longer sentence. Compare the use of _gaw_ after "it" in the following two sentences. _Gaw_, which makes statements hypothetical, isn't included in the first because it's a direct fact, but may be included in the second because what follows has a hypothetical meaning. It's also included to make the suggestion ("you didn't have to come so early") sound understated and more polite.

It's very good that you came on time.

(Mun) dee mak thee koon ma than way-la.

(มัน)ดีมากที่คุณมาทันเวลา

It's very good that you came on time, but you didn't have to come so early.

(Mun) (gaw) dee mak thee koon ma than way-la, tae mai tawng chao ka-nat nee gaw dai.

(มัน)(ก็)ดีมากที่คุณมาทันเวลาแต่ไม่ต้องเช้าขนาดนี้ก็ได้

THIS/THAT

Two different tones are used on "this/that" depending on whether they're pronouns or modifiers: as pronouns they have falling tones and as modifiers they have high tones. Informally *nee* can be pronounced *nia*, *ngee*, or *ngia*. *Nee* is more common in Thai while "that" is more common in English.

As pronouns - Here the single word *nee* or *nan* refers to an object or action. The words have falling tones (*nan* is falling/short) and in writing are marked with the first Thai tone marker (*mai ayk*).

This is very delicious.

Nee a-roi mak.

นี่อร่อยมาก

As modifiers - Here *nee* or *nan* are in phrases like "this shirt" or "that person". They have high tones (*nan* is high/short) and are written with the second Thai tone marker (*mai tho*). There are three patterns: *nee/nan* after both the noun and the classifier ("this shirt" is *seua tua nee*), after the classifier alone (*tua nee*), or after the noun alone (*seua nee*). The third pattern isn't really correct Thai but may be used informally.

This book isn't expensive. It's only 50 baht.

(Nang-seu) lem nee mai phaeng. Kae ha-sip baht ayng.

(หนังสือ)เล่มนี้ไม่แพง แค่ห้าสิบบาทเอง

"that" with adjectives ("that big car") - The adjective is doubled in this kind of phrase, giving it the meaning of "rather" or "-ish". It's put after either the noun or the classifier.

That big car over there is her father's.

Rot yai-yai kun nan kawng phaw theuh.

รถใหญ่ๆ คันนั้นของพ่อเธอ

Rot kun yai-yai nan kawng phaw theuh.

รถคันใหญ่ๆ นั้นของพ่อเธอ

this one/that one - uṅ nee/uṅ nan̄ - *Un* is the general classifier and can refer to any object. The specific classifier for the object may replace *un* in these examples.

Ayk gave me this/this one.

Ayk ao un̄ nee hȧi phŏm̐./Un̄ nee Ayk hȧi (phŏm̐).

เอกเอาอันนี้ให้ผม/อันนี้เอกให้(ผม)

If you eat this you might get sick.

Uṅ nee, gin̄ laeo at̄ jȧ mȧi sȧ-bai.

อันนี้กินแล้วอาจจะไม่สบาย

This isn't the one I wanted.

Uṅ nee mȧi chȧi uṅ thee̅ chan̐ yak̲ dȧi.

อันนี้ไม่ใช่อันที่ฉันอยากได้

A: Which one would Jaeo like?

Jaeoŋ jȧ chawp̄ uṅ naiŋ?/Uṅ naiŋ thee̅ Jaeoŋ (jȧ) chawp̄?

แจ๋วจะชอบอันไหน/อันไหนที่แจ๋ว(จะ)ชอบ

B: What about this one?

Uṅ nee mai?/Uṅ nee dee mai?

อันนี้มั้ย/อันนี้ดีมั้ย

A: Where's that tape?

Thayp̄ uṅ nan̄, na̐, pȧi naiŋ?

เทปอันนั้นน่ะไปไหน

B: What tape?

Thayp̄ uṅ naiŋ?

เทปอันไหน

A: That one, the one I play every day.

Uṅ nan̄ ngȧi, uṅ thee̅ phŏm̐ peuht̲ thook̄ wȧn, na̐.

อันนั้นไง อันที่ผมเปิดทุกวันน่ะ

exactly this one/that one - ayng/ngȧi/lae̲ - In the second sentence *lang* is the classifier for buildings.

That's the table he made.

To̅ tua nan̄ ayng thee̅ kȧo tham̐.

โต๊ะตัวนั้นเองที่เค้าทำ

I live right here.

Yoo lȧngŋ ngee ngȧi.

อยู่หลังงี้ไง

A: This is the ring you bought in Burma, isn't it?

  Nee waenɉ thee koon seu thee Pha-ma, chai mai?

  นี่แหวนที่คุณซื้อที่พม่าใช่มั้ย

B: No. This one my husband bought for me. That's the one I bought in Burma.

  Mai chai. Un nee faen seu hai. Un nan lae thee seu thee Pha-ma.

  ไม่ใช่ อันนี้แฟนซื้อให้ อันนั้นแหละที่ซื้อที่พม่า

Referring to actions - un nee/un nan -

To do this, you have to be strong.

  Tham un nee (koon) tawɉ kaeɉ-raeɉ.

  ทำอันนี้(คุณ)ต้องแข็งแรง

She'll do that tomorrow.

  Un nan, kao ja tham phroong-nee.

  อันนั้นเค้าจะทำพรุ่งนี้

I'll do it later.

  Chan ja tham un nee thee lanɉ.

  ฉันจะทำอันนี้ทีหลัง

Referring to events - Here *nee, un nee*, and *trong nee/nan* are used to refer to things that happened or will happen. *Trong* is "direct" or "directly", meaning "exactly here".

This happened because you weren't careful.

  Nee mun geuht keun phraw koon mai ra-wang.

  นี่มันเกิดขึ้นเพราะคุณไม่ระวัง

Where we go depends on you.

  Ja pai nai, un nee gaw laeo tae koon.

  จะไปไหน อันนี้ก็แล้วแต่คุณ

I can't say much about that because I wasn't there.

  Un nee phomɉ phoot a-rai mai dai mak, phraw phomɉ mai dai yoo thee-nan.

  อันนี้ผมพูดอะไรไม่ได้มากเพราะผมไม่ได้อยู่ที่นั่น

The police shot a student. That was what started the riot.

  Tam-ruat dai ying nak seuk-saɉ. Trong nee lae thee gaw hai geuht gan ja-ra-jon.

  ตำรวจได้ยิงนักศึกษา ตรงนี้แหละที่ก็ให้เกิดการจราจล

The U.N. can't help much with the problems in China because they're internal.

  Pan-haɉ nai meuang Jeen, Sa-haɉ Pra-cha-chat chuay mai dai mak, phraw un nan

    mun pen pan-haɉ phai nai pra-thet.

  ปัญหาในเมืองจีนสหประชาชาติช่วยไม่ได้มากเพราะอันนั้นมันเป็นปัญหาภายในประเทศ

THAT (RELATIVE PRONOUN)

(the shirt) that - thee/seung - These two words are used in the same way, but *seung* is formal and not common in everyday conversation (the third example, with *seung*, is formal). *Thee* can follow either the name of the object you're referring to, the classifier for the object, or both the name of the object and the classifier. In the first example *reua* is "boat" and *lum* is the classifier.

The boat that just arrived came from Ko Pha-ngan.

> Reua lum thee pheung ma theung ma jak Gaw Pha-ngan. (or *reua thee/lum thee*)
>
> เรือลำที่เพิ่งมาถึงมาจากเกาะพงัน

I bought the book that you liked.

> Phom seu nang-seu thee koon chawp ma. (or *lem thee*)
>
> ผมซื้อหนังสือที่คุณชอบมา

The projects that have been completed have been very successful.

> Krong-gan seung set laeo pra-sop kwam sam-ret mak.
>
> โครงการซึ่งเสร็จแล้วประสบความสำเร็จมาก

A common pattern in speaking is to pause after the noun, then say the classifier with *thee*. This pinpoints the object or indicates that there's only one object.

That shirt he's wearing is mine.

> Seua, tua thee kao sai yoo, pen kawng phom.
>
> เสื้อตัวที่เค้าใส่อยู่เป็นของผม

this is the shirt that - There are four variations with the noun (here "shoes") optional in three of them. *Koo* ("pair") is the classifier.

These are the shoes that I like.

> Nee pen (rawng-thao) koo thee phom chawp.
>
> นี่เป็น(รองเท้า)คู่ที่ผมชอบ

> (Rawng-thao) koo nee pen koo thee phom chawp.
>
> (รองเท้า)คู่นี้เป็นคู่ที่ผมชอบ

> Koo nee pen rawng-thao thee phom chawp.
>
> คู่นี้เป็นรองเท้าที่ผมชอบ

> (Rawng-thao) koo nee phom chawp.
>
> (รองเท้า)คู่นี้ผมชอบ

That's not the book that I bought.

> Nan mai chai (nang-seu) lem thee chan seu.
>
> นั่นไม่ใช่(หนังสือ)เล่มที่ฉันซื้อ

> (Nang-seu) lem nan mai chai lem thee chan seu.
>
> (หนังสือ)เล่มนั้นไม่ใช่เล่มที่ฉันซื้อ

Lem̄ nan mai chai nang-seu̯ thee chan seu.

เล่มนั้นไม่ใช่หนังสือที่ฉันซื้อ

(Nang-seu̯) lem̄ nan chan mai dai seu.

(หนังสือ)เล่มนั้นฉันไม่ได้ซื้อ

one that - Here un is optional and *thee* becomes the whole phrase—"one that" or "those that".

I've found one that I want to buy.

Phom̯ jeuh (un) thee yak seu laeo.

ผมเจอ(อัน)ที่อยากซื้อแล้ว

This hotel is better than others I've stayed in.

Rong-raem nee dee gwa thee keuy yoo ma.

โรงแรมนี้ดีกว่าที่เคยอยู่มา

POSSESSIVE

For the possessive put the name of the owner after the name of the object, with *kawng* optional between the two words. The possessive may be omitted when it's obvious who the owner is, as in the fourth sentence.

That's Yawt's bicycle, isn't it?

Nan jak-gra-yan (kawng) Yawt, chai mai?

นั่นจักรยาน(ของ)ยอดใช่มั้ย

This isn't mine. Mine's red.

Un nee mai chai kawng phom̯. Kawng phom̯ see̯ daeng.

อันนี้ไม่ใช่ของผม ของผมสีแดง

Mine's the one without buttons.

Kawng chan un thee mai mee gra-doom.

ของฉันอันที่ไม่มีกระดุม

I forgot my notebook.

Leum ao sa-moot ma.

ลืมเอาสมุดมา

A: Whose pants are those?

Gang-gayng tua nan kawng krai?

กางเกงตัวนั้นของใคร

B: They're mine.

(Kawng) chan ayng.

(ของ)ฉันเอง

NUMBERS OF THINGS

Phrases with numbers include the classifier for the object you're talking about. Numbers are put before the classifier except for "one", which can be put either before or after (after is more informal, and the tone on *neung* may change from low to mid). *Dio* may also be used instead of *neung* for "single", "sole", or "only".

I'd like one plate of fried rice.

   Kaw̌ kao-phat neung jan, krup./Kaw̌ kao-phat jan neung, krup.

   ขอข้าวผัดหนึ่งจานครับ/ขอข้าวผัดจานนึงครับ

I only have one good pair of pants.

   Phǒm mee gang-gayng dee-dee yoo kae̒ tua dio.

   ผมมีกางเกงดีๆ อยู่แค่ตัวเดียว

This company has five vehicles.

   Baw-ree-sat nee mee rot ha̒ kun.

   บริษัทนี้มีรถห้าคัน

Those three shirts aren't clean.

   Seua̒ sǎm tua nan mai sa-at.

   เสื้อสามตัวนั้นไม่สะอาด

These two chairs are mine.

   Gao̒-ee sawng tua nee kawng chan.

   เก้าอี้สองตัวนี้ของฉัน

Steve's two suitcases are missing.

   Gra-pǎo sawng bai kawng Steve hǎi.

   กระเป๋าสองใบของสตีฟหาย

"there are/I have" with numbers - The name of the object can be omitted here if it's known what you're referring to.

There are two vehicles for us to use./I have two vehicles.

   Mee (rot) chai sawng kun.

   มี(รถ)ใช้สองคัน

I have three of them to give you./There are three of them for you.

   Mee hǎi sǎm un.

   มีให้สามอัน

At this time five houses are vacant.

   Tawn-nee mee wang (yoo) ha̒ lǎng.

   ตอนนี้มีว่าง(อยู่)ห้าหลัง

Pluralizers - phuak (noun)/(noun) phuak nee/lao nee - *Phuak* is put before nouns (both people and things) to show that they're plural. *Phuak nee* is put after nouns for "these" and can also be used alone for "these things" or "these people". *Lao nee* is a formal form of *phuak nee*, used to refer to things only.

The motorcycles going by in front of the house are very noisy.

> Phuak maw-teuh-sai thee phan na ban siang dang mak.
>
> พวกมอเตอร์ไซด์ที่ผ่านหน้าบ้านเสียงดังมาก

I don't like those trucks at all.

> Chan mai chawp rot ban-thook phuak nee leuy.
>
> ฉันไม่ชอบรถบรรทุกพวกนี้เลย

Liquor, cigarettes, and coffee - these things have no benefit to the body.

> Lao, boo-ree, ga-fae - lao nee mai mee pra-yot taw rang-gai.
>
> เหล้า บุหรี่ กาแฟ เหล่านี้ไม่มีประโยชน์ต่อร่างกาย

KIND/STYLE

kind/type—general terms - yang/baep - *Yang* is for smaller units of things, like kinds of food, while *baep* is for larger units, categories, or types. *Baep* also means "style". "What kind?" is on page 75.

She ordered two two kinds of food.

> Kao sang a-han sawng yang.
>
> เค้าสั่งอาหารสองอย่าง

It's a Thai-style tradition.

> Pen wat-tha-na-tham baep Thai.
>
> เป็นวัฒนธรรมแบบไทย

kind/type—formal terms - cha-nit/pra-phayt - *Cha-nit* is like *yang*, for smaller units (including species of animals), while *pra-phayt* is for categories or types.

This kind of food isn't very hot.

> A-han cha-nit nee mai phet.
>
> อาหารชนิดนี้ไม่เผ็ด

Thais like cars that save on gas.

> Kon Thai nee-yom rot pra-phayt pra-yat nam-mun.
>
> คนไทยนิยมรถประเภทประหยัดน้ำมัน

this kind/that kind - yang-ngee/yang-ngan/baep nee/baep nan - These also mean "like this/like that" and "this/that style". They can be put after nouns, as in the first two examples, or used as the subjects of sentences, as in the third. *Yang* has two pronunciations: low is more formal, while mid/short (used here) is informal. *Ngee* and *ngan* are informal variations of *nee* and *nan*.

I like this kind of food a lot.

Chan chawp a-han yang-ngee mak.

ฉันชอบอาหารยังงี้มาก

This kind of shirt shrinks easily.

Seua baep nee hot ngai.

เสื้อแบบนี้หดง่าย

This kind doesn't look very nice. That kind looks nicer.

Yang-ngee mai suay. Yang-ngan suay gwa.

ยังงี้ไม่สวย ยังงั้นสวยกว่า

For hair/house styles - song -

Please cut my hair in this style.

Chuay tat phom song nee hai noi.

ช่วยตัดผมทรงนี้ให้หน่อย

For music/movies/writing - naeo -

Rock music is very popular in Thailand. ("is a hit")

Don-tree naeo rawk gam-lang hit mak nai meuang Thai.

ดนตรีแนวร๊อคกำลังฮิตมากในเมืองไทย

For types of medical practices - phaen/sa-mai - The two words are interchangable in these phrases.

traditional medicine	ya phaen bo-ran
modern medicine	ya phaen pat-joo-ban
traditional massage	nuat phaen bo-ran

Old-style medicine is still good to use.

Ya phaen bo-ran yang chai dai dee.

ยาแผนโบราณยังใช้ได้ดี

model - roon - This is for things that are put out regularly in new models such as televisions and cars. It also means "age group" or "generation".

This model came out five years ago.

Roon nee awk meua ha pee thee laeo.

รุ่นนี้ออกเมื่อห้าปีที่แล้ว

brand - yee-haw -

What brand are these jeans?

Gang-gayng yeen (tua nee) yee-haw a-rai?

กางเกงยีน(ตัวนี้)ยี่ห้ออะไร

MORE THINGS/OTHER THINGS

one more/two more - eeg (number) (classifier) - For "one" *neung* is put either before or after the classifier (the tone may be mid if it's put after) or omitted altogether informally. Other numbers are put before the classifier only. "One more" is also "another" in English. "More" is explained further on page 214.

I'd like another can of Coke.

    Kaw Coke eeg neung gra-pawng./Kaw Coke eeg gra-pawng (neung).

    ขอโค้กอีกหนึ่งกระป๋อง/ขอโค้กอีกกระป๋อง(นึง)

Do you have another pen? (classifier and "one" omitted informally)

    Mee pak-ga eeg (dam) mai?

    มีปากกาอีก(ด้าม)มั้ย

A: How many more batteries so you want?

    Ja ao than (fai-chai) eeg gee gawn?

    จะเอาถ่าน(ไฟฉาย)อีกกี่ก้อน

B: One more will be enough.

    Eeg gawn dio gaw phaw.

    อีกก้อนเดียวก็พอ

many more/a lot more - eeg mak/eeg yeuh/eeg lai (classifier) -

He has a lot more amulets.

    Kao mee phra eeg lai ong.

    เค้ามีพระอีกหลายองค์

A: Do you have a lot more sweets like this?

    Mee ka-nom baep nee eeg yeuh mai? (or *eeg mak mai?*)

    มีขนมแบบนี้อีกเยอะมั้ย

A: Yes, I have a lot more.

Mee eeg yeuh

มีอีกเยอะ

another one/the other one (additional) - eeg (classifier) neung -

I live with my father, and my sister lives with my mother in another house.

Chan yoo gap phaw, laeo gaw nawng-sao yoo gap mae thee ban eeg lang neung.

ฉันอยู่กับพ่อแล้วก็น้องสาวอยู่กับแม่ที่บ้านอีกหลังหนึ่ง

A: Did you bring the other book?

Ao (nang-seu) eeg lem (neung) ma reu plao?

เอา(หนังสือ)อีกเล่ม(หนึ่ง)มารึเปล่า

B: The other book? No, I didn't bring it.

Eeg lem reuh? Mai dai ao ma.

อีกเล่มเหรอ ไม่ได้เอามา

another one/the other ones (not this one) - (classifier) eun - This is "another one" when it means "besides this one", not "in addition to this one". *Eun* can be doubled for the plural.

I want to wear another shirt, not this one.

Phom yak sai tua eun, mai chai tua nee.

ผมอยากใส่ตัวอื่น ไม่ใช่ตัวนี้

This house doesn't have electricity, but the others all do.

Ban lang nee mai mee fai-fa, tae lang eun mee mot laeo.

บ้านหลังนี้ไม่มีไฟฟ้าแต่หลังอื่นมีหมดแล้ว

A: Do you have another video? I don't like this one.

Mee wee-dee-o reuang eun mai? Chan mai chawp reuang nee.

มีวิดีโอเรื่องอื่นมั้ย ฉันไม่ชอบเรื่องนี้

B: I don't have any others. I rented only one.

Mai mee eeg laeo. Chao ma kae reuang dio.

ไม่มีอีกแล้ว เช่ามาแค่เรื่องเดียว

another one/something new - (classifier) mai - This is used when "another one" or "something else" refers to something new.

Change it to another movie. This one isn't any good.

Plian reuang mai, na. Reuang nee mai sa-nook.

เปลี่ยนเรื่องใหม่นะ เรื่องนี้ไม่สนุก

OBJECTS— A THING/SOMETHING/NOTHING

Real objects/possessions - kawng -

Noom has a lot of things.

> Noom mee kawng yeuh.
>
> หนุ่มมีของเยอะ

Where are the things I gave you yesterday?

> Kawng thee phom hai meua-wan-nee yoo nai?
>
> ของที่ผมให้เมื่อวานนี้อยู่ไหน

Are these Daeng's things?

> Kawng phuak nee (pen) kawng Daeng reu plao?
>
> ของพวกนี้(เป็น)ของแดงรึเปล่า

You have Noi's things, don't you?/Are Noi's things with you?

> Kawng kawng Noi yoo thee koon chai mai? (or *yoo gap koon*)
>
> ของของน้อยอยู่ที่คุณใช่มั้ย

Which is the new one?/Which are the new things?

> Un nai kawng mai?
>
> อันไหนของใหม่

This watch is fake.

> Na-lee-ga reuan nee pen kawng plawm.
>
> นาฬิกาเรือนนี้เป็นของปลอม

something - kawng/a-rai/sing - These words all mean "something" but they aren't always interchangable. *Kawng* is for real objects, while *arai* is for a more general "something". *Sing* is for specific objects (it's usually followed by a modifier such as "this", a number, or a clause beginning with *thee*) and is also more formal.

I have something to give you.

> Chan mee kawng ja hai./Chan mee a-rai ja hai.
>
> ฉันมีของจะให้/ฉันมีอะไรจะให้

This is something my mother gave me.

> Nee pen kawng thee mae hai ma.
>
> นี่เป็นของที่แม่ให้มา
>
> Nee pen a-rai (yang neung) thee mae hai ma.
>
> นี่เป็นอะไร(อย่างหนึ่ง)ที่แม่ให้มา
>
> Nee pen sing (neung) thee mae hai ma.
>
> นี่เป็นสิ่ง(หนึ่ง)ที่แม่ให้มา

Use *sing* or *arai* here (not referring to a physical object).

It's something that's very useful.

> Mun pen a-rai thee mee pra-yot mak.
>
> มันเป็นอะไรที่มีประโยชน์มาก

Is something bothering you? (making you feel bothered)

> Mee sing thee tham hai koon ram-kan reu plao?
>
> มีสิ่งที่ทำให้คุณรำคาญรึเปล่า

Use only *sing* here. *Arai* is too general and *kawng* is too concrete.

The thing I want to buy most is a car.

> Sing thee phom yak seu (mak) thee-soot keu rot-yon.
>
> สิ่งที่ผมอยากซื้อ(มาก)ที่สุดคือรถยนต์

A vehicle is something that's very important.

> Rot pen sing (thee) sam-kan mak.
>
> รถเป็นสิ่ง(ที่)สำคัญมาก

something/anything/nothing - a-rai - *Kawng* and *sing* aren't used here because you're referring to an undefined "something" or "anything".

I'm looking for something to read.

> Chan gam-lang ha a-rai an yoo.
>
> ฉันกำลังหาอะไรอ่านอยู่

Is there anything you want to buy?

> Mee a-rai thee koon yak seu bang mai?
>
> มีอะไรที่คุณอยากซื้อบ้างมั้ย

I want this one more than anything else.

> Phom yak dai un nee mak gwa a-rai (thook yang).
>
> ผมอยากได้อันนี้มากกว่าอะไร(ทุกอย่าง)

There's nothing special in that cave.

> Nai tham nan mai mee a-rai phee-set.
>
> ในถ้ำนั้นไม่มีอะไรพิเศษ

A: What should I take with me?

> Chan tawng ao a-rai pai bang?
>
> ฉันต้องเอาอะไรไปบ้าง

B: You don't have to take anything.

> Mai tawng ao a-rai pai leuy.
>
> ไม่ต้องเอาอะไรไปเลย

CLASSIFIERS FOR "THINGS" (OBJECTS)

Here you're talking about "things" with patterns that require classifiers such as amounts, "this", "every", and "more". Two words may be used for the classifier—*yang* and *sing*. *Yang* is the general term while *sing* is more specific and also more formal. (Note that *sing* is both the noun "thing" and the classifier for "things".)

Numbers of things - Here *yang* is used as the classifier for unspecified objects. In the second example *sing* may also be used because it's more specific.

She bought a few (two or three) things and took them home.

> Kao seu a-rai sawng-sam yang glap ban.
>
> เค้าซื้ออะไรสองสามอย่างกลับบ้าน

One thing I want is a house.

> Yang neung thee phom yak dai keu ban. (or *sing neung*)
>
> อย่างหนึ่งที่ผมอยากได้คือบ้าน

Yesterday I left three things with you, but one is missing.

> Meua-wan-nee chan fak kawng wai gap koon sam yang, na, tae hai pai yang
>
> neung.
>
> เมื่อวานนี้ฉันฝากของไว้กับคุณสามอย่างนะ แต่หายไปอย่างหนึ่ง

something/some things - a-rai yang neung/a-rai sak yang/a-rai bang yang - These are for a specific, unnamed "something". The first two are singular and the third is plural. The last sentence has *kawng* instead of *arai* for concrete "things".

She brought something with her.

> Theuh theu a-rai yang neung ma duay.
>
> เธอถืออะไรอย่างหนึ่งมาด้วย

I want to buy something in that shop.

> Yak seu a-rai sak yang thee ran nan.
>
> อยากซื้ออะไรซักอย่างที่ร้านนั้น

I have some things to show you.

> Phom mee a-rai bang yang (thee) ja hai koon doo.
>
> ผมมีอะไรบางอย่าง(ที่)จะให้คุณดู

In Had Yai some things are very cheap.

> Thee Had Yai kawng bang yang thook mak.
>
> ที่หาดใหญ่ของบางอย่างถูกมาก

many things - a-rai lai yang -

He keeps a lot of things on the table.

> Kao gep a-rai lai yang wai bon to.
>
> เค้าเก็บอะไรหลายอย่างไว้บนโต๊ะ

this thing - a-rai yang nee/kawng yang nee/kawng sing nee - These phrases refer to a single item or to many items of a single kind. To be more specific use *un nee* for "this" or "this one".

My father sent me this from America.

Kawng sing nee phaw song ma hai jak A-may-ree-ga.

ของสิ่งนี้พ่อส่งมาให้จากอเมริกา

Un nee phaw song ma hai jak A-may-ree-ga.

อันนี้พ่อส่งมาให้จากอเมริกา

these things - kawng phuak nee/a-rai phuak nee -

I'm not using these things anymore. Just throw them away.

Kawng phuak nee mai chai laeo. Thing dai leuy.

ของพวกนี้ไม่ใช้แล้ว ทิ้งได้เลย

These things I want to keep, but you can take those (over there).

A-rai phuak nee chan ja gep, tae koon ao phuak nan pai dai.

อะไรพวกนี้ฉันจะเก็บแต่คุณเอาพวกนั้นไปได้

everything - thook yang - In the second sentence "anything" in English is "everything" or "all of the things" in Thai. *Thook yang* can be expanded to *thook sing thook yang*.

When you move are you taking everything with you?

Tawn yai ban, ja ao kawng thook yang pai duay reu plao?

ตอนย้ายบ้านจะเอาของทุกอย่างไปด้วยรึเปล่า

She doesn't like anything ("everything") I give her.

Kao mai chawp thook sing thook yang thee phom hai leuy.

เค้าไม่ชอบทุกสิ่งทุกอย่างที่ผมให้เลย

more things/other things (additional) - eeg yang -

I want to buy this book and one other thing.

Yak seu nang-seu lem nee, gap a-rai eeg (sak) yang neung.

อยากซื้อหนังสือเล่มนี้กับอะไรอีก(ซัก)อย่างหนึ่ง

Do you want to buy anything else?

Ja seu a-rai eeg sak yang mai?

จะซื้ออะไรอีกสักอย่างมั้ย

Another thing we have to take is a flashlight.

Kawng eeg yang thee tawng ao pai duay keu fai-chai.

ของอีกอย่างที่ต้องเอาไปด้วยคือไฟฉาย

something else/other things (not this one) - <u>yang</u> <u>eun</u> -

Please take this suitcase and I'll take the other things.

 Chuay <u>theuj</u> gra-<u>pao</u> nee, na, laeo <u>phomj</u> ja <u>theuj</u> kawnj <u>yang</u> <u>eun</u>.

 ช่วยถือกระเป๋านี้นะแล้วผมจะถือของอย่างอื่น

It would be better to take him something else.

 Ao a-rai <u>yang</u> <u>eun</u> pai <u>hai</u> kao dee <u>gwa</u>.

 เอาอะไรอย่างอื่นไปให้เค้าดีกว่า

ACTIONS—THINGS/SOMETHING/NOTHING

Patterns here are the same as with objects. *Arai* and *sing* are "thing", "something", or "anything" in sentences like "I have two things to do". *Arai* is general while *sing* is more specific and formal.

With *arai* - In these examples "thing" is general and unmodified, so *arai* or *arai bang yang* are used.

I have something/some things to do.

 <u>Phomj</u> mee a-rai (bang <u>yang</u>) (thee ja) tawnj tham.

 ผมมีอะไร(บางอย่าง)(ที่จะ)ต้องทำ

If something like this happens again, call the police right away.

 Tha mee a-rai yang-ngee <u>geuht</u> keun eeg, riak tam-<u>ruat</u> leuy.

 ถ้ามีอะไรอย่างนี้เกิดขึ้นอีกเรียกตำรวจเลย

With *sing* - Here "thing/something" refers to a more specific action, so *sing* is used.

The things he does aren't good at all.

 (<u>Sing</u>) thee kao tham nee, <u>mai</u> dee leuy.

 (สิ่ง)ที่เค้าทำนี้ไม่ดีเลย

Killing animals is something I don't like.

 Gan <u>ka</u> <u>sat</u> pen <u>sing</u> (neung) thee <u>phomj</u> <u>mai</u> chawp.

 การฆ่าสัตว์เป็นสิ่ง(หนึ่ง)ที่ผมไม่ชอบ

This isn't anything that's illegal.

 Nee <u>mai</u> <u>chai</u> <u>sing</u> thee <u>phit</u> got-<u>maj</u>.

 นี่ไม่ใช่สิ่งที่ผิดกฎหมาย

I have to be responsible for the things I do.

 Chan tawnj rap-<u>phit</u>-chawp nai <u>sing</u> thee chan tham.

 ฉันต้องรับผิดชอบในสิ่งที่ฉันทำ

The thing that's interesting is that the prime minister won't quit.

 <u>Sing</u> thee na <u>sonj</u>-jai keu (<u>wa</u>) na-yok <u>mai</u> yawm la <u>awk</u>.

 สิ่งที่น่าสนใจคือ(ว่า)นายกไม่ยอมลาออก

This is something most people don't know much about.

Un nee pen sing thee kon suan yai mai koi roo reuang.

อันนี้เป็นสิ่งที่คนส่วนใหญ่ไม่ค่อยรู้เรื่อง

doing nothing/not doing anything -

There's nothing else we have to do.

Mai mee a-rai ja tawng tham eeg.

ไม่มีอะไรจะต้องทำอีก

She's never done anything against the law.

Kao mai keuy tham a-rai thee phit got-mai. (or *sing thee*)

เค้าไม่เคยทำอะไรที่ผิดกฎหมาย

A: What would you like me to do?

Yak (ja) hai chan tham a-rai, ka?

อยาก(จะ)ให้ฉันทำอะไรคะ

B: You don't have to do anything. Just relax.

Mai tawng tham a-rai. Yoo cheuy-cheuy, theuh.

ไม่ต้องทำอะไร อยู่เฉยๆ เถอะ

NOTE: Compare these sentences. The first has *sing* for "the things", the second has *arai* for "anything" and the third has *yang* for "as/like" (page 253-254).

He doesn't do the things I tell him.

Kao mai tham sing thee chan bawk.

เค้าไม่ทำสิ่งที่ฉันบอก

He doesn't do anything I tell him.

Kao mai tham a-rai thee chan bawk.

เค้าไม่ทำอะไรที่ฉันบอก

He doesn't do as I say.

Kao mai tham yang thee phom bawk.

เค้าไม่ทำอย่างที่ผมบอก

CLASSIFIERS FOR "THINGS" (ACTIONS)

The same two words used with objects, *yang* and *sing*, are used as classifiers for actions.

Numbers of things (actions) - In the first example *sing* or *arai* is "things" and *yang* is the classifier. The second example has the classifier only.

There are two things I have to do./I have two things to do.

Mee sing thee tawng tham sawng yang. (or *mee arai thee...*)

มีสิ่งที่ต้องทำสองอย่าง

There are two things I'd like to do.

> Mee sawnɠ yang theē phǒmɲ yak tham.

> มีสองอย่างที่ผมอยากทำ

many things - à-rai laiɲ yang - Also *lai sing lai yang* instead of *lai yang* alone.

I have to do a lot of things every day.

> Chǎn tawnɠ tham à-rai laiɲ yang thook wàn. (or *arai yeuh-yae, arai mak mai*)

> ฉันต้องทำอะไรหลายอย่างทุกวัน

I have many things that I have to do.

> Phǒmɲ mee à-rai laiɲ yang tawnɠ tham.

> ผมมีอะไรหลายอย่างต้องทำ

everything - This is usually *thook yang* but *thook sing* may also be used in the third sentence because it's more specific (followed by a clause).

 I did everything myself.

> Chǎn tham ayng thook yang.

> ฉันทำเองทุกอย่าง

 We finished doing everything.

> Rǎo tham sèt mòt thook yang laeo.

> เราทำเสร็จหมดทุกอย่างแล้ว

Everything she does is reasonable.

> Thook sing theē kao tham mee hayt-phonɲ sà-meuhɲ.

> ทุกสิ่งที่เค้าทำมีเหตุผลเสมอ

something else - à-rai yang eun -

I want to do something else. (not this)

> Phǒmɲ yak tham à-rai yang eun.

> ผมอยากทำอะไรอย่างอื่น

3. REFERRING TO PEOPLE

The word *kon* is included in most of the examples in this chapter. *Kon*, which means "person" or "people", is also the classifier for people and is used in patterns that require classifiers like "this/that", "everyone", "more", "other/another", and numbers. The word *farang* is commonly used in Thailand to refer to westerners and shouldn't be thought of as derogatory.

this person/that person - kon nee/kon nan - These may be used alone or combined in phrases, for example, *phoo-chai kon nee* is "this man" and *phoo-ying kon nan* is "that woman" (*phoo* is optional in these phrases). *Kon nee* is often used where "she", "he", or "they" would be used in English.

A: What's that man's name?

 Phoo-chai kon nan cheu a-rai?

 ผู้ชายคนนั้นชื่ออะไร

B: Who?/Which person?

 Kon nai?

 คนไหน

A: That *farang.*

 Fa-rang kon nan.

 ฝรั่งคนนั้น

B: Oh, his name's Steve.

 Aw, kao cheu Steve.

 อ้อ เค้าชื่อสตีฟ

He/she's very good-looking.

 Kon nee na-ta dee mak.

 คนนี้หน้าตาดีมาก

That's not my brother. I don't know him at all.

 Kon nan mai chai phee-chai chan. Chan mai roo-jak kao leuy.

 คนนั้นไม่ใช่พี่ชายฉัน ฉันไม่รู้จักเค้าเลย

That friend of yours, is he still in Thailand?

 Pheuan koon kon nan, (kao) yang yoo meuang Thai reu plao?

 เพื่อนคุณคนนั้น (เค้า)ยังอยู่เมืองไทยรึเปล่า

Informally *nee* or *nan* may be used to refer to a person.

That's your sister, isn't it?

> Nan nawng-saoj, chai mai?
>
> นั่นน้องสาวใช่มั้ย

exactly this/this very person - kon nee ngai/lae/ayng - All three mean "exactly this" or "this very person". With *ayng* the meaning is "he himself" or "she herself".

A: Who gave it to you?

> Krai (ao) hai?
>
> ใคร(เอา)ให้

B: That man right there.

> (Pen) phoo-chai kon nan lae.
>
> (เป็น)ผู้ชายคนนั้นแหละ

It was he/she who came to see you yesterday.

> Kon nee ngai, thee ma haj koon meua-wan-nee.
>
> คนนี้ไงที่มาหาคุณเมื่อวานนี้

It was that woman herself who helped him.

> Pen phoo-yingj kon nan ayng thee chuay kao.
>
> เป็นผู้หญิงคนนั้นเองที่ช่วยเค้า

Doubled adjectives - When using an adjective to identify someone it should be doubled to mean "sort of/-ish".

Where's that skinny guy? ("Where did he go?")

> Kon phawmj-phawmj kon nan pai naij?
>
> คนผอมๆ คนนั้นไปไหน

this kind of person - kon yang-ngee/kon baep nee - Also *yang-ngan* and *baep nan* for "that kind". "That" is more common in English while *nee* is more common in Thai.

People like him have a lot of friends.

> Kon baep nee ja mee pheuan yeuh.
>
> คนแบบนี้จะมีเพื่อนเยอะ

I don't like that kind of person.

> Chan mai chawp kon yang-ngan.
>
> ฉันไม่ชอบคนยังงั้น

Joe's that kind of person. He likes to go home early.

> Joe pen kon yang-ngee lae. Kao chawp glap ban gawn.
>
> โจเป็นคนยังงี้แหละ เค้าชอบกลับบ้านก่อน

person/people (formal) - book-kon -

This person used to be prime minister.

> Book-kon kon nee keuy pen na-yok ma laeo.
>
> บุคคลคนนี้เคยเป็นนายกมาแล้ว

WHO (RELATIVE PRONOUN)

the person who/people who... - kon thee... - *Seung* can replace *thee* but it's more formal and not common in everyday conversation. The examples here all have *thee*.

People who like the ocean should go to the South.

> Kon thee chawp tha-lay tawng pai thang tai.
>
> คนที่ชอบทะเลต้องไปทางใต้

A: Who's your boyfriend/girlfriend?

> Faen koon kon nai?
>
> แฟนคุณคนไหน

B: The one who came with Lek.

> (Kon) thee ma gap Lek.
>
> (คน)ที่มากับเล็ก

the woman who... - *Kon* isn't needed here but may be included to pin-point the person or to emphasize the singular, as in the second two examples.

The woman who came to see him is a friend from school. (or "The women who...")

> Phoo-ying thee ma hai kao pen pheuan ruam rong-rian kawng kao.
>
> ผู้หญิงที่มาหาเค้าเป็นเพื่อนร่วมโรงเรียนของเค้า

That man - the one who came to see her - is her younger brother.

> Phoo-chai, kon thee ma hai kao, pen nawng-chai kawng kao ayng.
>
> ผู้ชายคนที่มาหาเค้าเป็นน้องชายของเค้าเอง

That person - the one who came yesterday - is he a friend of yours?

> Kon nan, (kon) thee ma meua-wan-nee, pen pheuan koon reu plao?
>
> คนนั้น(คน)ที่มาเมื่อวานนี้เป็นเพื่อนคุณรึเปล่า

A: Have you seen her/that person again?

> Jeuh kon nan eeg reu plao?
>
> เจอคนนั้นอีกรึเปล่า

B: Who?

> Krai?
>
> ใคร

A: That woman - who teaches English.

    Phoo-ying kon nan, thee sawn pha-sa Ang-grit.

    ผู้หญิงคนนั้นที่สอนภาษาอังกฤษ

B: She went back to Australia.

    Kao glap pai Aws-tray-lia laeo.

    เค้ากลับไปออสเตรเลียแล้ว

she's someone who... - *Thee* can be omitted here, but not when the second clause refers to a different person.

I'm someone who likes to read.   (*thee* is optional, refers to one person)

    Phom pen kon (thee) chawp an nang-seu.

    ผมเป็นคน(ที่)ชอบอ่านหนังสือ

She's someone who I like a lot.   (*thee* is needed, subjects are "she" and "I")

    Kao pen kon thee chan chawp mak.

    เค้าเป็นคนที่ฉันชอบมาก

He's not a hard-working person./He's not someone who's hard-working.

    Kao mai chai kon (thee) ka-yan.

    เค้าไม่ใช่คน(ที่)ขยัน

this is the person who... - kon nee pen kon thee... - The first *kon* may be omitted and *nee* given a falling tone (it becomes the pronoun "this"). *Nan* may also be used instead of *nee*.

A: Is this the person who's going to be my teacher?

    Kon nee pen kon thee ja ma pen kroo chan reuh? (or "Nee pen kon thee...")

    คนนี้เป็นคนที่จะมาเป็นครูฉันเหรอ

B: No. That person hasn't come yet.

    Mai chai. Kon nan yang mai ma.

    ไม่ใช่ คนนั้นยังไม่มา

NUMBERS OF PEOPLE

Numbers are put before *kon* except for "one", which may be put either before or after.

There's a Japanese person working with me.

    Mee kon Yee-poon kon neung tham-ngan gap phom.

    มีคนญี่ปุ่นคนหนึ่งทำงานกับผม

John went with two women.

    John pai gap phoo-ying sawng kon.

    จอห์นไปกับผู้หญิงสองคน

For numbers of "people" (not men/women) *kon* is needed both before and after the number. *Kon* before the number may be omitted if it's the first word of the sentence, as in the second example.

There are three people who I know here.

> Thee-nee mee kon samɟ kon thee phomɟ roo-jak.
>
> ที่นี่มีคนสามคนที่ผมรู้จัก

The two people we met last week have come back.

> (Kon) sawngɟ kon thee rao jeuh a-thit gawn glap ma laeo.
>
> (คน)สองคนที่เราเจออาทิตย์ก่อนกลับมาแล้ว

Numbers with "there are" - The first *kon* can be omitted if it's known in context what you're referring to, with *mee* ("there is/are") followed directly by the verb.

Five people are going./There are five people going.

> Mee kon (ja) pai ha kon./Mee pai ha kon. (second in context)
>
> มีคน(จะ)ไปห้าคน/มีไปห้าคน

A: How many people are there?

> Mee yoo gee kon?
>
> มีอยู่กี่คน

B: There are three people.

> Mee yoo samɟ kon.
>
> มีอยู่สามคน

in addition to yourself - *Eeg* is included in Thai when you're talking about a person or people in addition to yourself. This isn't done in English.

I'm going with a friend.

> Chan pai gap pheuan eeg kon neung.
>
> ฉันไปกับเพื่อนอีกคนหนึ่ง

I have a wife and three children.

> Phomɟ mee mia gap look eeg samɟ kon.
>
> ผมมีเมียกับลูกอีกสามคน

these/those two people - sawngɟ kon nee/nan -

These three women don't have tickets yet.

> Phoo-yingɟ samɟ kon nee yang mai mee tuaɟ.
>
> ผู้หญิงสามคนนี้ยังไม่มีตั๋ว

Have you seen those two people?

> Jeuh gap sawngɟ kon nan reu plao?
>
> เจอกับสองคนนั้นรึเปล่า

In this example *nan* is put after a whole clause and may have either a high tone (to mean "those") or a falling tone (explained on page 5).

A: Those two men who came yesterday - have they gone to Chiang Mai yet?

  Phoo-chai sawng kon thee ma meua-wan-nee nan, kao pai Chiang Mai reu yang?

  ผู้ชายสองคนที่มาเมื่อวานนี้นั้น เค้าไปเชียงใหม่รึยัง

B: They left last night.

  Kao pai (tang-tae) meua-keun laeo.

  เค้าไป(ตั้งแต่)เมื่อคืนแล้ว

many people - kon mak/kon yeuh/lai kon -

A lot of people come here (traveling).

  Mee kon ma thio thee-nee mak./Thee-nee mee kon ma thio yeuh.

  มีคนมาเที่ยวที่นี่มาก/ที่นี่มีคนมาเที่ยวเยอะ

There are a lot of people in the market now.

  Thee ta-lat tawn-nee kon yeuh.

  ที่ตลาดตอนนี้คนเยอะ

Quite a few people have called you.

  Mee (kon) lai kon tho ma hai koon.

  มี(คน)หลายคนโทรมาหาคุณ

Many Westerners who come here like to eat papaya salad.

  Fa-rang lai kon thee ma thee-nee chawp gin som-tam.

  ฝรั่งหลายคนที่มาที่นี่ชอบกินส้มตำ

few people - kon noi/noi kon - The second is more general, referring to an amount rather than a number.

The party wasn't much fun because there weren't many people.

  Ngan nee mai sa-nook phraw wa (mee) kon noi.

  งานนี้ไม่สนุกเพราะว่า(มี)คนน้อย

Not many people come traveling here.

  Noi kon (thee ja) ma thio thee-nee./Mai koi mee kon ma thio thee-nee.

  น้อยคน(ที่จะ)มาเที่ยวที่นี่/ไม่ค่อยมีคนมาเที่ยวที่นี่

Pluralizer - phuak - *Phuak* indicates or clarifies plurality. It's included in "we", "they", and other phrases that describe groups of people. *Phuak nee* and *phuak nan* are also used alone to refer to groups of people. *Phuak* can also be put before "I"—*phuak chan/phuak phom* is a formal way to refer to yourself.

I went to a bar with them.

  Phom pai thio "ba" gap phuak kao.

  ผมไปเที่ยวบาร์กับพวกเค้า

Rich people like to come and eat here.

    Phuak kon ruay chawp ma gin thee-nee.

        พวกคนรวยชอบมากินที่นี่

They're students of mine.

    Phuak nan pen nak-rian kawng phom.

        พวกนั้นเป็นนักเรียนของผม

I came with those people.

    Chan ma gap phuak nan.

        ฉันมากับพวกนั้น

Doubled nouns - The following phrases are plural:

dek-dek	children (in general)
look-look	children (of mine, yours, etc)
nawng-nawng	people younger than you
phee-phee	people older than you
pheuan-pheuan	friends
noom-noom	young men
sao-sao	young women

I'm going with some friends.

    Chan ja pai gap pheuan-pheuan.

        ฉันจะไปกับเพื่อนๆ

Formal pluralizer - ban-da - This means "all".

Of all the children studying here Moo is the best.

    Nai ban-da dek-dek thee rian thee-nee, Moo rian geng thee-soot.

        ในบรรดาเด็กๆ ที่เรียนที่นี่หมูเรียนเก่งที่สุด

SOMEONE

Include *mee*.

Someone came to see you./Some people came to see you.

    Mee kon ma ha.

        มีคนมาหา

A woman phoned you.

    Mee phoo-ying tho ma ha.

        มีผู้หญิงโทรมาหา

People say that you're very nice. (Someone said/Some people said)

    Mee kon phoot wa koon jai-dee mak.

    มีคนพูดว่าคุณใจดีมาก

Be careful, someone will see us.

    Dioj, ja mee kon ma henj./Dioj, kon (ja) ma henj./Dioj, kon henj.

    เดี๋ยวจะมีคนมาเห็น/เดี๋ยวคน(จะ)มาเห็น/เดี๋ยวคนเห็น

I saw someone - henj mee kon -

I saw someone come to see him yesterday morning.

    Henj mee kon ma haj kao meua-chao-nee.

    เห็นมีคนมาหาเค้าเมื่อเช้านี้

I didn't see anyone there at all.

    Mai henj mee kon yoo leuy./Mai henj mee krai yoo leuy.

    ไม่เห็นมีคนอยู่เลย/ไม่เห็นมีใครอยู่เลย

A specific, unnamed person - kon, kon neung - Here "someone" refers to a specific but unnamed person. The first *kon* may be omitted when the phrase is the subject of the sentence, as in the first example. Other phrases are *phoo-ying kon neung* ("a woman"), *phoo-chai kon neung* ("a man"), etc.

Someone who I love a lot is my mother.

    (Kon) kon neung thee phomj rak mak keu mae.

    (คน)คนหนึ่งที่ผมรักมากคือแม่

He left with someone.

    Kao awk pai gap kon, kon neung.

    เค้าออกไปกับคนคนหนึ่ง

Compare the previous sentence with the following where *kon neung* alone refers to the number of people.

He left with one person.

    Kao awk pai gap kon neung.

    เค้าออกไปกับคนหนึ่ง

An unnamed "someone" - kao -

I have to go and pick up someone at 4 o'clock.

    See mong tawng pai rap kao.

    สี่โมงต้องไปรับเค้า

I gave it to someone already.

    Chan ao hai kao (pai) laeo.

    ฉันเอาให้เค้า(ไป)แล้ว

Indefinite/estimated - krai sak kon - *Sak* indicates that you're referring to an undefined person. It also minimizes or estimates the number of people. Other phrases are *kon sak kon*, *phoo-ying sak kon*, etc. See also "indefinite quantifiers" on page 194.

I'd like to have someone to travel with.

Chan yak mee krai sak kon ma pen pheuan thio.

ฉันอยากมีใครซักคนมาเป็นเพื่อนเที่ยว

Why don't you hire a woman to help clean your house?

Tham-mai mai jang phoo-ying sak kon ma chuay tham kwam sa-at ban?

ทำไมไม่จ้างผู้หญิงซักคนมาช่วยทำความสะอาดบ้าน

ANYBODY/NOBODY

This is *krai* or sometimes *kon*. See "whoever" (pages 177-179) for "anybody/nobody" meaning "no matter who".

Nobody knows.

Mai mee krai roo.

ไม่มีใครรู้

I don't have anyone to help me.

Phom mai mee krai chuay.

ผมไม่มีใครช่วย

I'm not afraid of anyone.

Phom mai glua krai.

ผมไม่กลัวใคร

Do you know anyone here?

Roo-jak krai thee-nee bang mai?

รู้จักใครที่นี่บ้างมั้ย

He doesn't like to talk to anyone.

Kao mai chawp kui gap krai.

เค้าไม่ชอบคุยกับใคร

I don't want to be anybody's mistress.

Chan mai yak pen mia noi (kawng) krai.

ฉันไม่อยากเป็นเมียน้อย(ของ)ใคร

A: Does anyone want to go swimming?

Mee krai yak pai wai-nam mai?

มีใครอยากไปว่ายน้ำมั้ย

B: No, nobody wants to go.

Mai mee krai yak pai.

ไม่มีใครอยากไป

nobody—minimized/estimated - maĭ...kraĭ sak kon -

I don't like any of the people in that office.

    Chan maĭ chawp kraĭ sak kon naĭ awf-fit nan.

    ฉันไม่ชอบใครซักคนในออฟฟิศนั้น

What I've just been talking about, nobody understands at all.

    Theĕ phŏm phoot ma, maĭ mee kraĭ kao-jai sak kon leuy.

    ที่ผมพูดมาไม่มีใครเข้าใจซักคนเลย

Out of a group - Use *kon naĭ* instead of *kraĭ*.

Out of my friends, nobody smokes.

    Naĭ gloom pheuan-pheuan (kawng) phŏm, maĭ mee kon naĭ soop boo-ree.

    ในกลุ่มเพื่อนๆ (ของ)ผม ไม่มีคนไหนสูบบุหรี่

She doesn't know any Western singers at all.

    Kao maĭ roo-jak nak-rawng fa-rang kon naĭ leuy.

    เค้าไม่รู้จักนักร้องฝรั่งคนไหนเลย

more than anyone - (mak) gwa kraĭ/(mak) gwa kon eun - Also *kraĭ-kraĭ* for a more general meaning.

She's more beautiful than anyone.

    Theuh suayy gwa kraĭ.

    เธอสวยกว่าใคร

He should get that job more than anyone.

    Kao na ja daĭ ngan nee mak gwa kraĭ-kraĭ.

    เค้าน่าจะได้งานนี้มากกว่าใครๆ

Ann can read Thai better than anyone else.

    Ann an pha-say Thai daĭ dee gwa kon eun.

    แอนอ่านภาษาไทยได้ดีกว่าคนอื่น

EVERYONE/SOME PEOPLE

everyone - thook kon/thook-thook kon - The second is "each and every person". See page 178 for "everyone" when it means means "whoever".

Everybody wants to go.

    Thook kon yak pai./Yak pai thook kon.

    ทุกคนอยากไป/อยากไปทุกคน

I want to buy a present for everyone.

    Chan yak seu kawng-kwan haĭ thook kon.

    ฉันอยากซื้อของขวัญให้ทุกคน

I only need two people to help me. Not everyone.

    Tawng-gan kon chuay kae sawngj kon. Mai chai thook kon.

      ต้องการคนช่วยแค่สองคน ไม่ใช่ทุกคน

Almost every man likes to watch boxing.

    Phoo-chai thook-thook kon chawp doo muay.

      ผู้ชายทุกทุกคนชอบดูมวย

Not everyone has to go./Everyone doesn't have to go.

    Mai tawng pai thook kon gaw dai.

      ไม่ต้องไปทุกคนก็ได้

Not everyone can play music well./It's not everyone who can play music well.

    Mai chai thook kon (thee) len don-tree dai geng.

      ไม่ใช่ทุกคน(ที่)เล่นดนตรีได้เก่ง

A: Is everyone going?

    Pai (gan) thook kon reu plao?

      ไป(กัน)ทุกคนรึเปล่า

B: Not everybody. Some people want to stay here.

    Mai (chai) thook kon. Bang kon yak yoo thee-nee.

      ไม่(ใช่)ทุกคน บางคนอยากอยู่ที่นี่

everyone in general - kon thook kon - The first *kon* emphasizes "people in general".

Everybody wants to have a house.

    (Kon) thook kon yak mee ban.

      (คน)ทุกคนอยากมีบ้าน

some people - bang kon - "Some" is explained on pages 200-202.

Some people like it, some people don't.

    Bang kon chawp, bang kon (gaw) mai chawp.

      บางคนชอบ บางคน(ก็)ไม่ชอบ

MORE PEOPLE/OTHER PEOPLE/ANOTHER PERSON

more people - Include *eeg* for "more", "other", or "another".

The other two women haven't come yet.

    Phoo-yingj eeg sawngj kon yang mai ma.

      ผู้หญิงอีกสองคนยังไม่มา

Another person is coming./More people are coming.

    (Ja) mee kon ma eeg.

      (จะ)มีคนมาอีก

One more person is coming./One other person is coming.

Jà mee (kon) ma eeg kon neung./(Jà) mee kon, kon neung ma eeg.

จะมี(คน)มาอีกคนหนึ่ง/(จะ)มีคนคนหนึ่งมาอีก

We're going with another person. (or "one other person/someone else")

(Rào jà) pai gàp (kon) eeg kon neung.

(เราจะ)ไปกับ(คน)อีกคนหนึ่ง

Another person wants to go.

Mee kon yak pai eeg kon neung./Mee (kon) eeg kon (neung) yak pai.

มีคนอยากไปอีกคนหนึ่ง/มี(คน)อีกคน(หนึ่ง)อยากไป

the other person (specific) - eeg kon neung -

Where did the other person go?

Eeg kon neung pai naij?

อีกคนหนึ่งไปไหน

One of my children goes to school. The other one hasn't started yet. ("entered school")

Look kon neung kao rong-rian laeo. Eeg kon neung yang mai dai rian.

ลูกคนหนึ่งเข้าโรงเรียนแล้ว อีกคนหนึ่งยังไม่ได้เรียน

another person (not this one) - kon eun - Other meanings are "a different person" and "somebody else".

She's not coming with Daeng. She's coming with someone else.

Theuh jà mai ma gàp Daeng. (Theuh) jà ma gàp kon eun.

เธอจะไม่มากับแดง เธอจะมากับคนอื่น

Someone else is coming./Other people are coming.

(Jà mee) kon eun ma eeg./(Mee) kon eun jà ma eeg.

(จะมี)คนอื่นมาอีก/(มี)คนอื่นจะมาอีก

A: Where's the book? Have you given it to Dam?

Nang-seuŋ yoo naij? Ao hai Dam reu yang?

หนังสืออยู่ไหน เอาให้ดำรึยัง

B: I didn't give it to him. I gave it to someone else.

Chan mai dai ao hai kao. Chan ao hai kon eun.

ฉันไม่ได้เอาให้เค้า ฉันเอาให้คนอื่น

A: Why? I told you not to give it to anyone else.

Ao! Tham-mai là? Chan bawk laeo wà ya ao hai kon eun.

อ้าว! ทำไมล่ะ ฉันบอกแล้วว่าอย่าเอาให้คนอื่น

The plural is *kon eun* or *kon eun-eun*. Another phrase is *phuak thee leua*—"those who are left" or "the rest" (rising tone on *leua*).

I came alone. The others were all sleeping.

Phom̩ ma kon dio. Kon eun lap mot laeo.

ผมมาคนเดียว คนอื่นหลับหมดแล้ว

a new person - kon mai - Use *mai* when "another person" means "someone new".

I'm looking for someone to replace him.

Chan ja hạ̩ kon mai ma thaen kao.

ฉันจะหาคนใหม่มาแทนเค้า

nobody else - mai mee krai eun/eeg - With *eun* it means "no one else besides you", with *eeg* it means "no one in addition to you".

I love only you. There's no one else.

Chan rak koon kon dio. Mai mee krai eun.

ฉันรักคุณคนเดียว ไม่มีใครอื่น

Nobody else wants to go.

Mai mee krai eeg laeo yak ja pai.

ไม่มีใครอีกแล้วอยากจะไป

A: Who else is coming?

Mee krai (thee) ja ma eeg?/Mee krai eeg ja ma?

มีใคร(ที่)จะมาอีก/มีใครอีกจะมา

B: There's nobody else.

Mai mee (eeg) laeo.

ไม่มี(อีก)แล้ว

MYSELF/YOURSELF

There are four ways to say "myself/yourself" in Thai.

1. ayng - This means "oneself" or "by oneself". *Ayng* is put after either the verb or the subject/object with a difference in meaning as follows:

After the verb - The meaning here is that the action was done or is being done alone.

Lek drew it himself. (nobody helped him)

Lek wat ayng.

เล็กวาดเอง

I'm going by myself./I'm going alone.

Phom̩ ja pai ayng. (same as *kon dio*)

ผมจะไปเอง

A: Who did it? Did you do it yourself?

    Krai tham, la? Koon tham ayng reu plao?

        ใครทำล่ะ คุณทำเองรึเปล่า

B: Yes, I did it myself.

    Chan tham ayng.

        ฉันทำเอง

After the subject/object - This emphasizes that it was the person named who did or received the action, not someone else.

She herself was the one who gave it to me.

    Kao ayng (pen kon) hai chan.

        เค้าเอง(เป็นคน)ให้ฉัน

I'm going myself. (I myself am going./I'm the one who's going.)

    Phom ayng ja pai.

        ผมเองจะไป

It was he himself who went and told the police.

    Pen kao ayng thee pai bawk tam-ruat.

        เป็นเค้าเองที่ไปบอกตำรวจ

Joe told me. (he didn't tell another person)

    Joe bawk phom ayng.

        โจบอกผมเอง

2. tua ayng - This is "yourself", etc, when the self is the center or receiver of the action.

If you don't help yourself, then who will help you?

    Tha mai chuay tua ayng, laeo krai ja chuay?

        ถ้าไม่ช่วยตัวเองแล้วใครจะช่วย

She's calling herself *phee*.

    Kao riak tua ayng wa "phee".

        เค้าเรียกตัวเองว่า พี่

The phrase *duay tua ayng* means "by yourself", "by herself", etc.

She fixed the car by herself.

    Theuh sawm rot (duay tua) ayng.

        เธอซ่อมรถ(ด้วยตัว)เอง

Tua may be used alone to emphasize the physical person.

What's he really like?

    Tua kao pen kon yang-ngai bang?

        ตัวเค้าเป็นคนยังไงบ้าง

3. ton - This means "ones self". It's similar to *tua ayng* but not as common.

Children should love their parents.

Look tawng rak phaw-mae kawng ton.

ลูกต้องรักพ่อแม่ของตน

4. suan phom/suan chan - These are "as for me" or "personally".

My friends drank beer, but I just sat and listened to the music.

Phuak pheuan-pheuan deum bia, suan phom nang fang phlayng cheuy-cheuy.

พวกเพื่อนๆ ดื่มเบียร์ ส่วนผมนั่งฟังเพลงเฉยๆ

TOGETHER

There are five ways to say "together". The first is the most common. See also page 350.

1. duay-gan - This can be shortened to *gan*.

Do you want to go with me?/Shall we go together?

Pai duay-gan mai?

ไปด้วยกันมั้ย

We work together.

Rao tham-ngan (yoo) duay-gan.

เราทำงาน(อยู่)ด้วยกัน

Gai and I are going traveling together.

Gai gap chan ja pai thio duay-gan.

ไก่กับฉันจะไปเที่ยวด้วยกัน

Shall we go to a movie tonight?

Keun-nee rao pai doo nang gan mai?

คืนนี้เราไปดูหนังกันมั้ย

A lot of my friends are going (together).

Pheuan pai gan lai kon.

เพื่อนไปกันหลายคน

2. duay-kon - Use *duay-kon* instead of *duay-gan* when you're asking to be included in an activity.

Let me go with you.

> Kawɲ pai duay-kon, na.
>
> ขอไปด้วยคนนะ

3. duay gap/duay-gan gap - These phrases mean "with" and have the same meaning as *gap* alone.

I live with her.

> Phomɲ yoo (duay) gap kao./Phomɲ yoo duay-gan gap kao.
>
> ผมอยู่(ด้วย)กับเค้า/ผมอยู่ด้วยกันกับเค้า

4. phrawm gan/phrawm-phrawm gan - These mean "simultaneously" or "at the same time".

They stopped working at the same time and went out to play golf.

> Phuak kao leuhk ngan phrawm gan laeo awk pai len gawp.
>
> พวกเค้าเลิกงานพร้อมกันแล้วออกไปเล่นกอล์ฟ

I like to drink coffee and smoke cigarettes (together/at the same time).

> Phomɲ chawp deum ga-fae laeo gaw soop boo-ree phrawm-phrawm gan.
>
> ผมชอบดื่มกาแฟแล้วก็สูบบุหรี่พร้อมๆ กัน

5. ruam-gan - *Ruam* with a falling tone means "do together".

He asked me to come and work with him. ("He called me")

> Kao riak ma tham-ngan ruam-gan.
>
> เค้าเรียกมาทำงานร่วมกัน

EACH OTHER/IN A GROUP

Gan (mid/short) means "each other" or "with each other". Here it's put after verbs to indicate an interaction between people or things.

We live near each other. Our rooms are next to each other's.

> Rao yoo glai gan. Hawng tit gan.
>
> เราอยู่ใกล้กัน ห้องติดกัน

These things are heavy. Can you help me?

> Kawng nee nak mak. Chuay gan noi, see.
>
> ของนี้หนักมาก ช่วยกันหน่อยซิ

Actions within a group - gan ayng - Include *ayng* when people in a group are doing an action to or with each other. The phrase *gan ayng* alone means "friendly/casually".

They went alone. They didn't tell anyone.

    (Phuak) kao pai gan ayng. Mai dai bawk krai.

    (พวก)เค้าไปกันเอง ไม่ได้บอกใคร

Sometimes prisoners kill each other.

    Bang thee nak-thot gaw ka gan ayng.

    บางทีนักโทษก็ฆ่ากันเอง

Actions by many people - Include *gan*.

Please close the doors. (asking many people)

    Chuay pit pra-too gan noi.

    ช่วยปิดประตูกันหน่อย

Let's wait to eat until Sue comes.

    Raw Sue ma laeo koi gin gan.

    รอซูมาแล้วค่อยกินกัน

A: What are you all doing?

    Gam-lang tham a-rai gan yoo?

    กำลังทำอะไรกันอยู่

B: Nothing. Just playing cards.

    Mai mee a-rai. Len phai cheuy-cheuy.

    ไม่มีอะไร เล่นไพ่เฉยๆ

it's believed/people believe that - These phrases include *gan* to show that the action or thought is general among many people.

cheua gan wa	it's believed that, people believe that
kao-jai gan wa	it's understood that
pen thee roo gan wa	it's known that
roo-roo gan (yoo) wa	it's known that

People believe that Westerners have more money than Thais.

    Cheua gan wa fa-rang mee ngeuhn yeuh gwa kon Thai.

    เชื่อกันว่าฝรั่งมีเงินเยอะกว่าคนไทย

EXPRESSION: (seung) gan lae gan - This means "each other". When *seung* is included it's more formal.

We have to understand each other.

    Rao tawng kao-jai (seung) gan lae gan.

    เราต้องเข้าใจซึ่งกันและกัน

USING *RUAM*

Ruam has two pronunciations which have similar meanings.

1. do together - ruam - Here *ruam* has a falling tone and is spelled in Thai with a *mai ayk*. It refers to people, countries, etc, actively doing things together and is translated as "do together", "join in", "join together", "participate", "joint" or "co-". *Ruam-gan* means "collaborate", "cooperate", or "jointly". In the last example it's similar to *duay-gan*.

He's come to work with me.

Kao ma ruam tham-ngan gap phom laeo.

เค้ามารวมทำงานกับผมแล้ว

I'm not participating.

Phom mai ruam duay.

ผมไม่รวมด้วย

She's a co-worker.

Kao pen pheuan ruam ngan.

เค้าเป็นเพื่อนร่วมงาน

Thailand and Laos are working together to develop the Mekong River.

Thai gap Lao ruam-gan phat-tha-na mae-nam Kong.

ไทยกับลาวรวมกันพัฒนาแม่น้ำโขง

I live with my father and mother.

Chan yoo ban ruam gap koon phaw koon mae.

ฉันอยู่บ้านรวมกับคุณพ่อคุณแม่

2. be put together - ruam - Here *ruam* has a mid tone and is written in Thai without a tone marker. It's a verb with a more passive meaning referring to things being put together, mixed, gathered, collected, combined, added up, or included. It also means "altogether" or "in all".

Let's put our money together.

Ao ngeuhn ma ruam gan.

เอาเงินมารวมกัน

The entire bill for the food was five hundred baht.

Ka a-han ruam thang-mot ha roi baht.

ค่าอาหารรวมทั้งหมดห้าร้อยบาท

The total time I lived in Libya was ten years.

Ruam way-la thee yoo Lee-bia dai sip pee.

รวมเวลาที่อยู่ลิเบียได้สิบปี

This includes two nights in a hotel and two breakfasts.

Un nee ruam ka rong-raem sawng keun, laeo gaw a-han chao sawng meu.

อันนี้รวมค่าโรงแรมสองคืนแล้วก็อาหารเช้าสองมื้อ

4. QUESTIONS

This chapter describes three kinds of questions. First are questions answered by "yes" or "no" such as "Are you hungry?", second are questions asked to confirm if something is correct such as "You're going, aren't you?", and third are questions that begin with question words like "what" or "who".

YES/NO QUESTIONS

There are four ways to form questions answered by "yes" or "no".

1. mai - *Mai* (pronounced high/short) is put at the end of statements to turn them into questions. To answer "yes" repeat the verb or adjective. For "no" put *mai* (falling/short) before it. This type of question can be interpreted as both a general question and an invitation or suggestion, for example, *Pai mai?* can mean either "Are you going?" or "Do you want to go?"

A: If I go to Phuket will you go with me?

    Tha phom ja pai Phoo-get, koon ja pai duay mai?

    ถ้าผมจะไปภูเก็ตคุณจะไปด้วยมั้ย

B: Sure.

    Pai see.

    ไปซิ

2. reu plao - *Reu plao* at the end of a statement means "or not?", but the meaning isn't as strong as in English and indicates only that you want a definite answer. *Reu plao* is also used when *mai* could be interpreted wrongly as an invitation.

A: Did Lek go to Phuket?

    Lek pai Phoo-get reu plao?

    เล็กไปภูเก็ตรึเปล่า

B: Yes./No.

    Pai./Mai dai pai.

    ไป/ไม่ได้ไป

A: Are you going anywhere, Ann?

    Ann ja pai nai reu plao?

    แอนจะไปไหนรึเปล่า

B: No.

Mai pai.

ไม่ไป

3. reu yang - This is used instead of *reu plao* when "or not" means "or not yet". *Ja* may be included if the action is about to happen.

A: Shall we go?

(Ja) pai reu yang?

(จะ)ไปรึยัง

B: Yes

Pai

ไป

A: Is that enough?

Phaw reu yang?

พอรึยัง

B: No./No, that's not enough.

Yang./Yang mai phaw.

ยัง/ยังไม่พอ

4. reu mai?/reu mai? - These are formal and used mostly to replace *reu plao* in writing. *Reu* can have two different pronunciations. The first is informal while the second emphasizes "or" and is more formal.

Reversed sentence order - A common pattern in Thai is to ask the question first then state what you're referring to.

A: Is Thai food good?   (Is it good - Thai food?)

A-roi mai - a-han Thai?

อร่อยมั้ยอาหารไทย

B: Yes.

A-roi.

อร่อย

A: Do you know how old Noi is?   (Do you know - how old is Noi?)

Koon roo reu plao - Noi a-yoo thao-rai?

คุณรู้รึเปล่า น้อยอายุเท่าไหร่

B: I'm not sure. She's thirty, isn't she?

Mai nae-jai. Sam-sip, chai mai?

ไม่แน่ใจ สามสิบใช่มั้ย

OTHER WAYS TO ANSWER "YES"

There are four ways to answer "yes" in addition to repeating the verb or adjective.

1. respectful - Respond with the single word *ka* (women) or *krup* (men) to sound more polite and respectful. *Ka* can have two pronunciations in responses, and there's also a third pronunciation that's used at the end of questions. *Krup* is always high/short.

ká	for women with responses, statements, commands
kâ	for women with responses, statements, commands; adds emphasis
kā	for women, used at the end of questions
krup	for men, all uses
krup phŏm	"yes sir", as a soldier

2. I agree/that's right - châi -

A: The weather is very good on Ko Samui.

   Gàw Sà-muij a-gàt dee mâk.

       เกาะสมุยอากาศดีมาก

B: I agree.

   Châi.

       ใช่

3. now you understand - châi láeo - This means that the person you're talking to has finally understood or agreed with what you're saying.

A: So, that shows he didn't steal it.

   Ngán, gâw sà-daeng wâ kao mâi dâi kà-moy.

       งั้นก็แสดงว่าเค้าไม่ได้ขโมย

B: That's right.

   Châi láeo.

       ใช่แล้ว

4. informal - euh/ah/uh/mm - These are all informal ways to answer "yes".

OTHER WAYS TO ANSWER "NO"

1. that's not right - mâi châi - This is also translated as "I don't agree".

A: He's English.

   Kao pen kon Ang-grit.

       เค้าเป็นคนอังกฤษ

B: No. He's Australian.

   Mâi châi. Kao pen kon Aws-tray-lia.

       ไม่ใช่ เค้าเป็นคนออสเตรเลีย

2. wrong/it's not as you say - plao - *Plao* is used alone for "no" or "nothing". It means that whatever was brought up is wrong or not pertinent.

A: Are you going?

Jă păi reŭ plao?

จะไปรึเปล่า

 B: No.

Plao.

เปล่า

A: What are you doing?

Tham ă-răi?

ทำอะไร

B: Nothing.

Plao.

เปล่า

3. măi/măi leuy/kit wâ măi - For "definitely not", "no, not at all", and "I don't think so".

A: Do you like snakes?

Koon chawp ngoo măi?

คุณชอบงูมั้ย

B: No./No, not at all.

Măi./Măi leuy.

ไม่/ไม่เลย

A: Do you think it's going to rain?

Kit wâ fŏn jă tòk măi?

คิดว่าฝนจะตกมั้ย

B: I don't think so.

Kit wâ măi, ná.

คิดว่าไม่นะ

CONFIRMATION QUESTIONS

These are asked to confirm an answer that's already expected. Five different words or phrases are added to statements to form them.

1. chai măi - This is the equivalent of "aren't you?", "isn't it?" or "right?", answered by repeating the verb or adjective or with *chai/mai chai*. In this example "John" could mean "you" if you're talking to someone named John. (People's names are often used for "you" in Thai.)

A: John's going with us, isn't he?/You're going with us, aren't you John?

    John jà pai duay, chai mai?

        จอห์นจะไปด้วย ใช่มั้ย

B: Yes.

    Chai./Pai.

        ใช่/ไป

    No.

    Mai chai./Mai pai./Plao.

        ไม่ใช่/ไม่ไป/เปล่า

A: Oot isn't going, is he?

    Oot mai pai, chai mai?

        อู๊ดไม่ไปใช่มั้ย

B: No./He isn't going.

    Chai./Mai pai./Plao. Mai pai.

        ใช่/ไม่ไป/เปล่า ไม่ไป

    No, he's going too.

    Mai chai, kao jà pai duay.

        ไม่ใช่ เค้าจะไปด้วย

2. mai chai reuh - This is used in the same way as *chai mai*.

A: You work today, don't you?

    Koon tham-ngan wan-nee, mai chai reuh?

        คุณทำงานวันนี้ไม่ใช่เหรอ

B: Yes, but I'm going a little late.

    Tham, tae jà pai saj noi.

        ทำ แต่จะไปสายหน่อย

3. chai reu plao - This is higher-level Thai, used when you want a definite answer. *Chai* can be split from *reu plao* as in the the second example.

Is he a doctor?

    Kao pen maw, chai reu plao?

        เค้าเป็นหมอใช่รึเปล่า

Was it that person?

    Chai kon nan reu plao?

        ใช่คนนั้นรึเปล่า

4. naw/na - These mean "isn't it?" or "right?" and are used in the same way as *reuh* or *chai mai*. They're both said quickly with a high tone.

A: It's beautiful, isn't it.

   Suay, naw?/Suay, na?

      สวยเนอะ/สวยนะ

B: Yes.

   Suay.

      สวย

5. reuh - Using *reuh* to form a question is equivalent to putting a rising inflection on a statement in English.

A: This one?

   Un nee reuh?

      อันนี้เหรอ

B: Yes.

   Chai (laeo).

      ใช่(แล้ว)

A: You didn't go?

   Koon mai dai pai reuh?

      คุณไม่ได้ไปเหรอ

B: No.

   Mai dai pai.

      ไม่ได้ไป

A: Not this one?

   Mai chai un nee reuh?

      ไม่ใช่อันนี้เหรอ

B: No. That one (over there).

   Mai chai (un nee). Un noon.

      ไม่ใช่(อันนี้) อันโน้น

REUH—VARIATIONS

Reuh is common in informal Thai and is used in a number of question patterns.

Polite questions - Use *reu ka* or *reu krup* instead of *reuh* alone to be polite.

A: You're not going swimming today?

   Wan-nee mai pai wai-nam reu krup?

      วันนี้ไม่ไปว่ายน้ำรึครับ

B: No.

   Mai, ka.

   ไม่ค่ะ

With *laeo* - *Laeo* is included for "already" (affirmative) or "anymore" (negative).

A: You're leaving? (already/now)

   Pai laeo reuh?/Ja glap laeo reuh?

   ไปแล้วเหรอ/จะกลับแล้วเหรอ

B: Yes.

   Glap laeo./Chai./Ka./Krup.

   กลับแล้ว/ใช่/ค่ะ/ครับ

   No./No, not yet.

   Yang./Plao, yang mai glap.

   ยัง/เปล่า ยังไม่กลับ

A: You don't want it anymore?

   Mai ao laeo reuh?

   ไม่เอาแล้วเหรอ

B: No, I do!

   Ao!

   เอา

With "anywhere/nobody" - Use question words for "anywhere", etc.

A: You're not going anywhere?

   Mai pai nai reuh?

   ไม่ไปไหนเหรอ

B: No, I'm not.

   Mai pai.

   ไม่ไป

A: Nobody's going?

   Mai mee krai pai reuh?

   ไม่มีใครไปเหรอ

B: No, some people are/someone is.

   Mee.

   มี

With wh- questions - *Reuh* can be put at the end of wh- questions to make them sound more polite.

What?

A-rai <u>reuh</u>?

อะไรเหรอ

Where has Gop gone?

Gop pai <u>nai</u> <u>reuh</u>?

กบไปไหนเหรอ

Why did he come again?

Kao ma <u>eeg</u> tham-mai <u>reuh</u>?

เค้ามาอีกทำไมเหรอ

QUESTION WORDS
WHAT?

Following are common questions with *arai*.

What's this?/What's that?

Nee (keu) a-rai?/Nan (keu) a-rai?

นี่(คือ)อะไร/นั่น(คือ)อะไร

What is it? (asking about an object)

Keu a-rai?/Mun keu a-rai?/Nee mun (keu) a-rai?

คืออะไร/มันคืออะไร/นี่มัน(คือ)อะไร

Use *pen* or *mee* with problems.

What's wrong?/Is something wrong?

Pen a-rai?/Pen a-rai pai?/Pen a-rai reu <u>plao</u>?

เป็นอะไร/เป็นอะไรไป/เป็นอะไรรึเปล่า

Pen a-rai <u>reuh</u>?/Mee a-rai <u>reuh</u>?

เป็นอะไรเหรอ/มีอะไรเหรอ

What's wrong with your leg?

<u>Ka</u> pen a-rai?

ขาเป็นอะไร

Is something wrong?/Do you have a problem with that?

Mee a-rai reu <u>plao</u>?/Mee a-rai <u>reuh</u>?

มีอะไรรึเปล่า/มีอะไรเหรอ

Geuht or *geuht keun* is "to happen".

What's wrong with Dam?/What happened to Dam?

Dam pen a-rai?/<u>Geuht</u> a-rai (keun) gap Dam?

ดำเป็นอะไร/เกิดอะไร(ขึ้น)กับดำ

A: What happened? (accident, etc)

Geuht a-rai keun?/Mee a-rai geuht keun?/Geuht a-rai na?

เกิดอะไรขึ้น/มีอะไรเกิดขึ้น/เกิดอะไรนะ

B: Nothing.

Mai mee a-rai (geuht keun).

ไม่มีอะไร(เกิดขึ้น)

Reuang here means "situation", "matter", or "affair".

What's happening?/What's the problem? (a situation)

Geuht reuang a-rai?

เกิดเรื่องอะไร

These include *gan* for something happening in a group.

What's wrong?/What's going on? (problem in a group)

Pen a-rai gan?/Mee a-rai gan?/A-rai gan?/Geuht a-rai gan?

เป็นอะไรกัน/มีอะไรกัน/อะไรกัน/เกิดอะไรกัน

What's the matter? (argument/fight)

Reuang a-rai gan?

เรื่องอะไรกัน

Arai is also used in phrases like "what province" and "what model".

What province is Ko Chang in?

Gaw Chang yoo thee jang-wat a-rai?

เกาะช้างอยู่ที่จังหวัดอะไร

WHICH?

For "which" put *nai* after the classifier for the object you're referring to, or after *kon* if you're referring to a person. "Which shirt?" is *tua nai?*, "which vehicle" is *kun nai?*, and "which person" is *kon nai?* You can also use the general classifier *un* to replace the specific classifier for any object (first example). If the name of the object is included it's put first in the phrase before the classifier (second example). *Nai* usually isn't put directly after the name of an object although an exception is "which house?" where *nai* can be put after *ban* ("house"), *lang* (the classifier) or both, as in the third example.

Which one do you want? (general for any object)

Ao un nai?

เอาอันไหน

Which shirt do you like? (*tua* is the classifier, *seua* is "shirt")

Chawp tua nai?/Chawp seua tua nai?

ชอบตัวไหน/ชอบเสื้อตัวไหน

A: Which house?

    Lǎng nǎi?/Bân nǎi?/Bân lǎng nǎi?

    หลังไหน/บ้านไหน/บ้านหลังไหน

B: That one.

    Lǎng nán./Bân lǎng nán.

    หลังนั้น/บ้านหลังนั้น

WHO?/WHICH PERSON?

Krai is "who" or "whom" while *kon nai* is "which person" or "which people", referring to a person or people from a specific group.

A: Who is this? (pointing to a person in a picture)

    Nêe (keu) krai?

    นี่(คือ)ใคร

B: This is my father.

    Nêe (keu) phâw.

    นี่(คือ)พ่อ

A: Who's going?

    Krai jà pai (bâng)?

    ใครจะไป(บ้าง)

B: Gai and a friend of his.

    Gai gàp pheuan káo.

    ไก่กับเพื่อนเค้า

A: Which person is named Poo? (out of a group)

    Kon nǎi cheu Poo?

    คนไหนชื่อปู

B: She's not here.

    Káo mâi yòo.

    เค้าไม่อยู่

WHY?

There are five ways to ask "why". The first is the most common.

1. thǎm-mǎi - *Thammai* is put at the end of affirmative questions except when *tawng* or a similar modal verb is included. With negative questions it's put at either the beginning or the end.

Why are you going home?   (affirmative, *thammai* at the end)

    (Koon) (jà) pai bân thǎm-mǎi?

    (คุณ)(จะ)ไปบ้านทำไม

Why do you have to go home?   (affirmative with *tawng*, *thammai* at beginning)

    Tham-mai (koon) (ja) tawng glap ban?

    ทำไม(คุณ)(จะ)ต้องกลับบ้าน

Why aren't you going?   (negative, *thammai* at beginning or end)

    Tham-mai (koon) ja mai pai?/Tham-mai mai pai?/Koon ja mai pai tham-mai?

    ทำไม(คุณ)จะไม่ไป/ทำไมไม่ไป/คุณจะไม่ไปทำไม

Why didn't you go?

    Tham-mai (koon) mai dai pai?/Tham-mai mai pai?/Koon mai dai pai tham-mai, la?

    ทำไม(คุณ)ไม่ได้ไป/ทำไมไม่ไป/คุณไม่ได้ไป ทำไมล่ะ

2. tham-mai theung - *Theung* means "arrive" or "reach to", and *thammai theung* is "Why has it happened that", "Why has it come to the point that", or "Why has it become this way?" The subject of the sentence is put before *theung*.

Why does Thailand have so many temples?

    Tham-mai meuang Thai theung mee wat mak?

    ทำไมเมืองไทยถึงมีวัดมาก

3. phraw a-rai - This is literally "because of what?" It's more formal and not as common as *thammai*.

Do you know why he's selling his car?

    Roo mai, kao kai rot phraw a-rai?

    รู้มั้ย เค้าขายรถเพราะอะไร

Why do you like the cool season?

    Phraw a-rai koon theung chawp na naoj?

    เพราะอะไรคุณถึงชอบหน้าหนาว

4. pheua a-rai - This is "for the sake of what?"

Why are you going to the Philippines?

    Koon ja pai Fee-lip-peen pheua a-rai?

    คุณจะไปฟิลิปปินส์เพื่ออะไร

5. tham a-rai - This is literally "do-what" and usually refers to actions.

I told you to stay at home, so why did you come here?

    Bawk hai yoo ban, laeo ma tham a-rai?

    บอกให้อยู่บ้านแล้วมาทำอะไร

Why are you tired?/What did you do to be so tired?

    Tham a-rai theung neuay?

    ทำอะไรถึงเหนื่อย

WHEN?

Meuarai is put at the end of questions in the past, present, and future. With the future it may also be put at the beginning (with *ja* included). Use *wan nai* for "what day".

When did you come?/When are you coming?

Ma meuă-rai?

มาเมื่อไหร่

When is Joe coming? (when *meuarai* is at the beginning *ja* isn't optional)

Joe (jă) ma meuă-rai?/Meuă-rai Joe jă ma?

โจ(จะ)มาเมื่อไหร่/เมื่อไหร่โจจะมา

What day are you coming to meet us?

Koon jă ma phop rao wăn naị?

คุณจะมาพบเราวันไหน

since when? - tang-tae meuă-rai -

A: When did Lek go to Ubon?

Lek pai Oo-bon tang-tae meuă-rai?

เล็กไปอุบลตั้งแต่เมื่อไหร่

B: It must have been on Saturday.

Gaw kong pen wăn Sao.

ก็คงเป็นวันเสาร์

WHERE?

Theenai can be shortened to *nai*.

A: Where have you been?

Pai naị ma bang?

ไปไหนมาบ้าง

B: I went out.

Pai thio ma.

ไปเที่ยวมา

Theenai may be put at the beginning in questions meaning "Where is there...?" or "Where is a place that...?".

A: Where do they sell shoes?

Thee-naị mee rawng-thao kaị bang?/Thee-naị (thee) kaị rawng-thao?

ที่ไหนมีรองเท้าขายบ้าง/ที่ไหน(ที่)ขายรองเท้า

B: They're for sale in the market.

Mee kaị thee tă-lat.

มีขายที่ตลาด

exactly where? - trong naij - This is for asking about locations, fields of work, feelings, and thoughts.

Where exactly does it hurt?

    Jep trong naij?

        เจ็บตรงไหน

In what way do you think she's a good person?

    Kit wa kao dee trong naij?

        คิดว่าเขาดีตรงไหน

HOW MUCH?

Use *thaorai* to ask about amounts and prices.

A: How much did you buy it for?

    Seu ma thao-rai?

        ซื้อมาเท่าไหร่

B: I bought it for three hundred baht.

    Seu ma samj roi baht.

        ซื้อมาสามร้อยบาท

Mak may be included when asking about an amount.

How much sugar should I put in?

    Sai nam-tan (mak) thao-rai, ka?

        ใส่น้ำตาล(มาก)เท่าไหร่คะ

A: How many employees does he have?

    Kao mee kon ngan yoo (mak) thao-rai?

        เค้ามีคนงานอยู่(มาก)เท่าไหร่

B: Around 50 people.

    Mee pra-man ha-sip kon.

        มีประมาณห้าสิบคน

Thaorai is also used to ask about calendar dates.

A: What's the date today?

    Wan-nee wan thee thao-rai?

        วันนี้วันที่เท่าไหร่

B: Today's the seventh.

    Wan-nee wan thee jet.

        วันนี้วันที่เจ็ด

what number? - This is either *lek thee thaorai* or *beuh arai*. *Beuh* comes from the second syllable of "number".

What seat number did you get?

Koon dai thee-nang lek thee thao-rai? (or "beuh a-rai?")

คุณได้ที่นั่งเลขที่เท่าไหร่/เบอร์อะไร

HOW MANY?

To ask about numbers of objects put *gee* before the classifier for the object.

A: How many plates do you want to buy?

Koon tawng-gan seu jan gee bai?

คุณต้องการซื้อจานกี่ใบ

B: Six should be enough.

Hok bai kong phaw.

หกใบคงพอ

A: How many people do you live with? ("How many live together?")

Yoo (gan) gee kon?

อยู่(กัน)กี่คน

B: Three people. (answer includes yourself)

Yoo (gan) samj kon.

อยู่(กัน)สามคน

a lot? - *yeuh mai/mak mai* - These are interchangable.

A: Did a lot of people go?/Are a lot of people going?

Mee kon pai yeuh mai?

มีคนไปเยอะมั้ย

B: Yes, really a lot.

Yeuh mak.

เยอะมาก

TO WHAT EXTENT?/TO WHAT POINT?

There are two phrases.

1. kae naij - This is used to ask about the size or extent of something and is translated as "how" in English. *Kae* means "extent", "level", or "only to the extent of".

How well do you know her?/How long have you known her?

Roo-jak kao dee kae naij?/Roo-jak kao nan kae naij?

รู้จักเค้าดีแค่ไหน/รู้จักเค้านานแค่ไหน

How much money do you make?

    Koon dai ngeuhn mak kae nai?

    คุณได้เงินมากแค่ไหน

2. ka-nat nai - This is "what size" or "to what magnitude".

A: How well can he play football?

    Kao len foot-bawn geng ka-nat nai?

    เค้าเล่นฟุตบอลเก่งขนาดไหน

B: He's the best in this town.

    Geng thee-soot nai meuang nee.

    เก่งที่สุดในเมืองนี้

HOW?/IN WHAT WAY?

Informal/formal - yang-ngai/yang-rai - The first is the common spoken form (used in this book) and the second is formal and written.

How will you go if I don't go?

    (Koon) (ja) pai yang-ngai tha phom mai pai?

    (คุณ)(จะ)ไปยังไงถ้าผมไม่ไป

How do you feel about the weather in Thailand?

    (Koon) roo-seuk yang-ngai gio-gap a-gat (nai) meuang Thai?

    (คุณ)รู้สึกยังไงเกี่ยวกับอากาศ(ใน)เมืองไทย

A: How did the accident happen?

    Oo-bat-tee-hayt (mun) geuht keun dai yang-ngai?

    อุบัติเหตุ(มัน)เกิดขึ้นได้ยังไง

B: The motorcycle cut in front of the car.

    Rot-kreuang tat na rot-yon.

    รถเครื่องตัดหน้ารถยนต์

Characteristics/conditions - pen yang-ngai -

A: How's this hotel?

    Rong-raem nee pen yang-ngai (bang)?

    โรงแรมนี้เป็นยังไง(บ้าง)

B: It's OK.

    Phaw chai dai.

    พอใช้ได้

How are you? - This is asked among friends in Thailand but not with people you've just met. The question can end with *bang* ("some") to show that there could be more than one answer. This makes it sound less demanding (more polite).

A: How are you?/How's everything going?

    (Koon) pen yang-ngai?/Pen yang-ngai bang?

    (คุณ)เป็นยังไง/เป็นยังไงบ้าง

B: Fine.

    Sa-bai dee.

    สบายดี

How to do something - Questions like "How should I do it?" or "How do you do it?" don't include "it" in Thai.

How do you do it?/How should I do it?

    Tham yang-ngai?

    ทำยังไง

How do you eat it?

    Gin yang-ngai?

    กินยังไง

"what" in English/"how" in Thai - These sentences have "what" in English but *yang-ngai* in Thai, for example, "What should we do?" is "How should we do?" in Thai. For "What did he say?" use either *yang-ngai* or *arai*. In the last sentence *wa* alone means "think", "say", or "plan".

What should we do? (having a problem)

    (Rao) ja tham yang-ngai dee?

    (เรา)จะทำยังไงดี

What do you think about this situation/matter/problem?

    Koon kit (wa) yang-ngai gio-gap reuang nee?

    คุณคิด(ว่า)ยังไงเกี่ยวกับเรื่องนี้

What did he say about that situation/matter/problem?

    Kao phoot (wa) yang-ngai gio-gap reuang nan?   (or *phoot wa arai*)

    เค้าพูด(ว่า)ยังไงเกี่ยวกับเรื่องนั้น

What did you say?/What do you think?/How's it going?

    (Koon) wa yang-ngai, na?

    (คุณ)ว่ายังไงนะ

WHAT KIND?

yang naj/baep naj/cha-nit naj/pra-phayt naj - The second two are more formal. *Yang* and *chanit* are for smaller units of things while *baep* and *pra-phayt* are for larger units. *Baep* also means "style". See page 30 for these words in statements.

What kind of food do you like? (refers to a small unit)

    Chawp a-han cha-nit naj? (or *a-han yang nai?*)

       ชอบอาหารชนิดไหน

What kind of ticket are you buying? (small unit)

    Koon ja seu tuaj yang naj? (or *tua cha-nit nai?*)

       คุณจะซื้อตั๋วอย่างไหน

What type of stereo do you want to buy? (large unit)

    Yak seu sa-tay-ree-o pra-phayt naj? (or *baep nai?*)

       อยากซื้อสเตอริโอประเภทไหน

What style of shirt do you want? (clothing style - use *baep*)

    Ja ao seua baep naj?

       จะเอาเสื้อแบบไหน

"SOME" WITH QUESTIONS

Bang with a falling tone means "some", "somewhat", or "in part". Here it's included with questions that could have more than one answer, making them sound more polite because you're asking to hear only some of the possibilities for answers, not all of them. The informal pronunciation is *mang* or *mung*.

With question words -

What do you want to eat?/What shall we eat?

    Ja gin a-rai bang?

       จะกินอะไรบ้าง

What did you buy?

    Seu a-rai (ma) mang?

       ซื้ออะไร(มา)มั้ง

Who has a master's degree?

    Mee krai thee jop prin-ya tho bang? /Mee krai bang thee jop prin-ya tho?

       มีใครที่จบปริญญาโทบ้าง/มีใครบ้างที่จบปริญญาโท

Where did you go traveling?

    Pai thio thee-naj (ma) bang?

       ไปเที่ยวที่ไหน(มา)บ้าง

Who are you going with?

    Ja pai gap krai bang?

       จะไปกับใครบ้าง

Asking for a list - Here the question word is put between *mee* and *bang*.

A: Who's going?

    Mee krai bang thee pai?

    มีใครบ้างที่ไป

B: Mary and Lek.

    Mee Mary gap Lek.

    มีแมรี่กับเล็ก

A: What kinds of Thai food do you like?

    A-han Thai thee chawp mee a-rai mang?

    อาหารไทยที่ชอบมีอะไรมั่ง

B: I like tom yam and barbequed chicken.

    Chawp tom yam gap gai yang.

    ชอบต้มยำกับไก่ย่าง

Yes/no quesions with "any" - Here *bang* or *mang* means "any/some".

Did anybody come?

    Mee krai ma mung mai?

    มีใครมามั่งมั้ย

Do you have anything to eat?

    Mee a-rai gin bang mai?

    มีอะไรกินบ้างมั้ย

Did anyone see him this morning?

    Chao nee mee krai hen kao bang reu plao?

    เช้านี้มีใครเห็นเค้าบ้างรึเปล่า

    Chao nee mee krai bang mai, (thee) hen kao?

    เช้านี้มีใครบ้างมั้ย(ที่)เห็นเค้า

When the object is named follow it with *nai* or *arai* and include *bang*. With *nai* you're asking about any item from a specific group, while *arai* is more general.

Are there any shirts that you like?

    Mee (seua) tua nai thee koon chawp bang reu plao?

    มี(เสื้อ)ตัวไหนที่คุณชอบบ้างรึเปล่า

Is there any medicine that can help me?

    Mee ya a-rai bang thee ja chuay phom dai mai?

    มียาอะไรบ้างที่จะช่วยผมได้มั้ย

5. EXPANDED SENTENCES

This chapter describes longer sentences with clauses introduced by *wa* or *thee*. In general, *wa* is "that" or "if" connecting "I said", "Do you know" and other phrases with what was said, asked about, etc. *Thee* is also "that" in English, but it refers to the fact itself and shows that it's a fact that's existing or true.

I said that/think that - Use only *wa* here.

I think he's coming tomorrow.

Phom kit wa kao ja ma phroong-nee.

ผมคิดว่าเค้าจะมาพรุ่งนี้

Ning said that her mother was ill.

Ning phoot wa mae kao mai sa-bai.

หนิงพูดว่าแม่เค้าไม่สบาย

I told him that I wasn't going.

Phom bawk kao wa (phom) mai pai.

ผมบอกเค้าว่า(ผม)ไม่ไป

Do you know if? - Two question words are needed here—*mai* after "Do you know" and *reu plao* at the end. They may be switched but it's not as common. Use *reu yang* instead of *reu plao* if the meaning is "or not yet".

Do you know if John's going?

Koon roo mai, wa John ja pai reu plao?

คุณรู้มั้ยว่าจอห์นจะไปรึเปล่า

Koon roo reu plao wa John ja pai mai?

คุณรู้รึเปล่าว่าจอห์นจะไปมั้ย

Do you know yet if you got the job?

Koon roo reu yang wa koon dai ngan mai?

คุณรู้รึยังว่าคุณได้งานมั้ย

Do you know if she's left yet?

Koon roo mai, wa kao pai (laeo) reu yang?

คุณรู้มั้ยว่าเค้าไป(แล้ว)รึยัง

Do you know if we're going on Saturday or Sunday?

Roo mai, wa rao ja pai wan Sao reu wan A-thit?

รู้มั้ยว่าเราจะไปวันเสาร์หรือวันอาทิตย์

I don't know if/whether - *Reu plao* at the end can be omitted in informal conversation as in the second example.

I don't know whether I can go or not.

    Chan mai roo wa chan ja pai dai reu plao.

      ฉันไม่รู้ว่าฉันจะไปได้รึเปล่า

It's not for sure that he's coming.

    Mai nae wa kao ja ma.

      ไม่แน่ว่าเค้าจะมา

I don't know if I can sell it or not.

    Chan mai roo wa ja kai dai reu mai dai. (or *reu plao*)

      ฉันไม่รู้ว่าจะขายได้หรือไม่ได้

I'll know tomorrow if I can get the tickets or not.

    Phom ja roo phroong-nee wa ja dai tua reu plao. (or *reu mai*)

      ผมจะรู้พรุ่งนี้ว่าจะได้ตั๋วรึเปล่า

Has he told you if? - *Thee* may also be used here but *wa* is more common. *Thee* refers to something known from the past to be true or certain.

Has she told you if she's coming?

    Kao bawk koon reu plao wa ja ma?

      เค้าบอกคุณรึเปล่าว่าจะมา

    Kao bawk koon reu yang thee kao ja ma? (for sure—"that she's coming")

      เค้าบอกคุณรึยังที่เค้าจะมา

Other beginnings - Following are other first clauses:

I want to know if...	Phom yak roo wa...	ผมอยากรู้ว่า...
I don't know yet if...	Chan yang mai roo wa...	ฉันยังไม่รู้ว่า...
Nobody knows if...	Mai mee krai roo wa...	ไม่มีใครรู้ว่า...
I can't remember if...	Phom jam mai dai wa...	ผมจำไม่ได้ว่า...
I'm not sure if...	Chan mai nae-jai wa...	ฉันไม่แน่ใจว่า...
He didn't tell me if...	Kao mai dai bawk (phom) wa...	เค้าไม่ได้บอก(ผม)ว่า...
She hasn't told me (yet) if...	Kao yang mai dai bawk (chan) wa...	เค้ายังไม่ได้บอก(ฉัน)ว่า...
Please tell me if...	(Chuay) bawk phom noi wa...	(ช่วย)บอกผมหน่อยว่า...
I'll ask him if...	Phom ja tham (kao) wa...	ผมจะถาม(เค้า)ว่า...
I didn't ask her if...	Chan mai dai tham (kao) wa...	ฉันไม่ได้ถาม(เค้า)ว่า...
He asked me if...	Kao tham chan wa...	เค้าถามฉันว่า...

I didn't know before if...   Chan mai roo ma gawn (leuy)   ฉันไม่รู้มาก่อน(เลย)ว่า...
                              wa...

                              (Meua) gawn nee chan mai roo   (เมื่อ)ก่อนนี้ฉันไม่รู้(เลย)ว่า...
                              (leuy) wa...

Combine the first clauses with these sample endings. Subjects can be omitted if they're understood in context.

he'll come or not.	(kao) ja ma reu plao.	(เค้า)จะมารึเปล่า
she will/would like it.	(theuh) ja chawp reu plao.	(เธอ)จะชอบรึเปล่า
I can go or not.	(phom) (ja) pai dai reu plao.	(ผม)(จะ)ไปได้รึเปล่า
he went or not.	(kao) dai pai reu plao.	(เค้า)ได้ไปรึเปล่า
there's any beer.	mee bia reu plao.	มีเบียร์รึเปล่า

Reversed sentence order - Here "I don't know" is at the end and *gaw* links the two clauses. The second subject is often omitted.

I don't know if she's here or not. ("If she's here or not, I don't know")
    Kao yoo reu plao (gaw) mai roo.
        เค้าอยู่รึเปล่า(ก็)ไม่รู้

I don't know ("yet") if I'm going or not.
    Chan pai reu mai pai (gaw) yang mai roo.
        ฉันไปหรือไม่ไป(ก็)ยังไม่รู้

Nobody knows if he's coming or not.
    Kao ja ma reu plao (gaw) mai mee krai roo.
        เค้าจะมาหรือเปล่า(ก็)ไม่มีใครรู้

When will you know if -

When will you know if you can go or not?
    Koon ja roo dai meua-rai wa koon ja pai dai reu plao?
        คุณจะรู้ได้เมื่อไหร่ว่าคุณจะไปได้รึเปล่า

How did you know that he didn't return the car?
    Koon roo dai yang-ngai wa kao mai dai keun rot? (or *mai dai ao rot pai keun*)
        คุณรู้ได้ยังไงว่าเค้าไม่ได้คืนรถ

Confirmation questions - In English these statements have a rising inflection. In Thai use *reuh* or *chai mai*.

You think she doesn't know?
    Kit wa kao mai roo reuh?/Kit reuh, wa kao mai roo?
        คิดว่าเค้าไม่รู้เหรอ/คิดเหรอว่าเค้าไม่รู้

You don't think she'll be unhappy?/You didn't think she'd be unhappy?

Mai kit wa kao ja siaj-jai reuhj?

ไม่คิดว่าเค้าจะเสียใจเหรอ

You didn't know he had a child?

Mai roo wa kao mee look laeo reuhj?/Mai roo reuhj, wa kao mee look laeo?

ไม่รู้ว่าเค้ามีลูกแล้วเหรอ/ไม่รู้เหรอว่าเค้ามีลูกแล้ว

She told you, didn't she, that she was quitting?

Kao bawk koon, chai mai, wa kao ja la awk?

เค้าบอกคุณใช่มั้ยว่าเค้าจะลาออก

DO YOU KNOW WHO/WHAT/WHY?

Here "I don't know" is followed by a question word in English. In Thai the question word is generally put at the end of the sentence but there are exceptions with "who", "why", and "when".

I don't know...	Chan mai roo (wa)...	ฉันไม่รู้(ว่า)...
Do you know...	(Koon) roo mai (wa)...	(คุณ)รู้มั้ย(ว่า)...
I know...	Chan roo (laeo) (wa)...	ฉันรู้(แล้ว)(ว่า)...
where he went.	kao pai thee-naij.	เค้าไปที่ไหน
where her house is.	ban kao yoo thee-naij.	บ้านเค้าอยู่ที่ไหน
which house she lives in.	kao yoo ban lanj naij.	เค้าอยู่บ้านหลังไหน
how many people are going.	ja mee kon pai gee kon.	จะมีคนไปกี่คน
what this is.	nee (keu) a-rai.	นี่(คือ)อะไร
	nee pen a-rai.	นี่เป็นอะไร
what happened.	mee a-rai geuht keun.	มีอะไรเกิดขึ้น
what he said.	kao phoot (wa) a-rai.	เค้าพูด(ว่า)อะไร
how to say it.	ja phoot yang-ngai.	จะพูดยังไง
how to do it/what to do.	ja tham yang-ngai.	จะทำยังไง
how I can go.	ja pai dai yang-ngai.	จะไปได้ยังไง
what kind of person he is.	kao pen kon yang-ngai.	เค้าเป็นคนยังไง

With *dee* - *Dee* is included when asking for a suggestion or talking about a choice.

I don't know...	Phomj mai roo (wa)...	ผมไม่รู้(ว่า)...
where to go.	ja pai thee-naij dee.	จะไปที่ไหนดี

what we should do.	já tham a-rai dee.	จะทำอะไรดี
what to say.	já phoot yang-ngai dee.	จะพูดยังไงดี
which shirt to wear.	já sai seua tua nai dee.	จะใส่เสื้อตัวไหนดี

I don't know whether to go to the North or South first.

Mai roo wa ja pai phak neuaj reuj phak tai gawn dee.

ไม่รู้ว่าจะไปภาคเหนือหรือภาคใต้ก่อนดี

With "who" - *Krai* or *kon nai* are put after *wa* when they're the subject of the sentence (first two examples) but at the end when they're the object (last three).

I don't know...	Phomj mai roo (wa)...	ผมไม่รู้ว่า...
who is going.	krai ja pai (bang).	ใครจะไป(บ้าง)
which person is Pla.	kon nai cheu Pla.	คนไหนชื่อปลา
who she gave it to.	kao ao hai krai pai.	เค้าเอาให้ใครไป
who he is.	kao pen krai.	เค้าเป็นใคร
who to tell.	ja bawk krai.	จะบอกใคร

With "why" - *Thammai* is put after *wa* with negatives ("he didn't come" in the first example) and either after *wa* or at the end with affirmatives (second example).

Do you know why he didn't come?   (negative—after *wa*)

Koon roo mai (wa) tham-mai kao mai dai ma?

คุณรู้มั้ย(ว่า)ทำไมเค้าไม่ได้มา

Do you know why we're going there?   (affirmative—after *wa* or at the end)

Koon roo mai (wa) tham-mai rao ja pai thee-nan?

คุณรู้มั้ย(ว่า)ทำไมเราจะไปที่นั่น

Koon roo mai (wa) rao ja pai thee-nan tham-mai?

คุณรู้มั้ย(ว่า)เราจะไปที่นั่นทำไม

With "when" - *Meuarai* is put after *wa* or at the end. When it's after *wa*, *thee* may be included which makes "when" more specific ("the time that...").

I don't know when she's coming.

Chan mai roo (wa) theuh ja ma meua-rai.   (at end)

ฉันไม่รู้(ว่า)เธอจะมาเมื่อไหร่

Chan mai roo (wa) meua-rai (thee) theuh ja ma.   (after *wa*, *thee* optional)

ฉันไม่รู้(ว่า)เมื่อไหร่(ที่)เธอจะมา

More examples -

She didn't tell me why we're not going.

Theuh mai dai bawk (phŏm) wa tham-mai (theung) mai pai.

เธอไม่ได้บอก(ผม)ว่าทำไม(ถึง)ไม่ไป

I'm not interested in what other people think of me.

Chan mai keuy sŏn-jai wa krai ja kit yang-ngai gap chan.

ฉันไม่เคยสนใจว่าใครจะคิดยังไงกับฉัน

Ask him first, then we'll know when we're going.

Thamj kao gawn, laeo ja roo wa ja pai meua-rai.

ถามเค้าก่อนแล้วจะรู้ว่าจะไปเมื่อไหร่

Reversed sentence order -

I don't know what she's saying. ("What she's saying I don't know.")

Kao phoot a-rai (gaw) mai roo.

เค้าพูดอะไร(ก็)ไม่รู้

He hasn't told me yet what day he's going.

Kao ja pai wan naij, kao (gaw) yang mai bawk.

เค้าจะไปวันไหนเค้า(ก็)ยังไม่บอก

When/Where do you think? - The question word is at the end in Thai.

Where do you think he went?

Koon kit wa kao pai naij?

คุณคิดว่าเค้าไปไหน

When did Gai say she was coming?

Gai phoot wa ja ma meua-rai?

ไก่พูดว่าจะมาเมื่อไหร่

Where did she tell you she was going?

Kao bawk wa (kao) ja pai thee-naij?

เค้าบอกว่า(เค้า)จะไปที่ไหน

Why do you think? - There are two meanings. In the first type you want to know the reason why the person did what you're asking about. *Thammai* is at the end or after *wa*.

Why do you think he did that? (what's the reason he did it?)

Koon kit wa kao tham yang-ngan tham-mai?

คุณคิดว่าเค้าทำยังงั้นทำไม

Koon kit wa tham-mai kao tham yang-ngan?

คุณคิดว่าทำไมเค้าทำยังงั้น

The second type means "What makes you think he did that?" *Thammai* is at the beginning. In practice this may also be used generally for the first meaning.

Why do you think he did that? (what makes you think so?)

    Tham-mai koon kit wa kao tham (yang-ngan)?

    ทำไมคุณคิดว่าเค้าทำ(ยังงั้น)

Why do you think he's the one who did it?

    Tham-mai koon kit wa kao pen kon tham?

    ทำไมคุณคิดว่าเค้าเป็นคนทำ

Confirmation questions - Use *reuh* or *chai mai*.

He told you when he was coming?

    Kao bawk reuh, wa kao ja ma meua-rai?

    เค้าบอกเหรอว่าเค้าจะมาเมื่อไหร่

She didn't tell you where her house was?

    Kao mai bawk wa ban kao yoo nai reuh?

    เค้าไม่บอกว่าบ้านเค้าอยู่ไหนเหรอ

Do you know where there's a house for rent?

    Koon roo reuh, wa mee ban hai chao thee-nai?

    คุณรู้เหรอว่ามีบ้านให้เช่าที่ไหน

I haven't told you where we're going yet, have I?

    Chan yang mai dai bawk, chai mai, wa rao ja pai thio thee-nai?

    ฉันยังไม่ได้บอกใช่มั้ยว่าเราจะไปเที่ยวที่ไหน

OTHER PATTERNS

I don't know when - Put the question word after *mai roo*.

A: When are you going to visit your parents again?

    Ja pai yiam phaw-mae eeg meua-rai?

    จะไปเยี่ยมพ่อแม่อีกเมื่อไหร่

B: I don't know when.

    (Chan) mai roo (wa) meua-rai.

    (ฉัน)ไม่รู้(ว่า)เมื่อไหร่

I don't know her name - Put the noun right after "know" or use *wa* as in the second example.

I don't know her name.

    Phom mai roo cheu kao.

    ผมไม่รู้ชื่อเค้า

I know his phone number.

    Chan roo beuh tho-ra-sap (kawng) kao.

    ฉันรู้เบอร์โทรศัพท์(ของ)เค้า

    Chan roo wa beuh tho-ra-sap (kawng) kao beuh a-rai.

    ฉันรู้ว่าเบอร์โทรศัพท์(ของ)เค้าเบอร์อะไร

    Chan roo wa beuh tho-ra-sap (kawng) kao keu a-rai.

    ฉันรู้ว่าเบอร์โทรศัพท์(ของ)เค้าคืออะไร

I don't know either - Include *meuan-gan* for "either/too"

I don't know (either) if they have cars for rent.

    Phom mai roo meuan-gan wa mee rot hai chao reu plao.

    ผมไม่รู้เหมือนกันว่ามีรถให้เช่ารึเปล่า

Polite language - Use *sap* instead of *roo* and put *ka/krup* after the first question.

Do you know where Bangkok Bank is?

    Koon sap mai krup, wa Tha-na-kan Groong-thayp yoo thee-nai?

    คุณทราบมั้ยครับ ว่าธนาคารกรุงเทพอยู่ที่ไหน

USING *THEE*

Here *wa, thee,* or *thee wa* are interchangable for "that". *Wa* connects the clauses, *thee* refers to and represents the fact itself, while *thee wa* is expanded from *thee* or has the separate meaning of "that people say that" (shortened from *thee kon phoot wa*).

It's not true that I love him.

    Mun mai jing leuy wa chan rak kao.   (*wa*—general "that")

    มันไม่จริงเลยว่าฉันรักเค้า

    Mun mai jing leuy thee chan rak kao.   (*thee*—"the fact that")

    มันไม่จริงเลยที่ฉันรักเค้า

    Mun mai jing leuy thee wa chan rak kao. (*thee wa*—"that"/"that people say that")

    มันไม่จริงเลยที่ว่าฉันรักเค้า

More examples -

It's good that Nok didn't buy that car.

    Mun dee na, thee Nok mai dai seu rot kun nan.

    มันดีนะ ที่นกไม่ได้ซื้อรถคันนั้น

It's impossible that he forgot the time of the appointment.

    Pen pai mai dai wa kao ja leum way-la nat.

    เป็นไปไม่ได้ว่าเค้าจะลืมเวลานัด

Nobody knows that she's married.

Mai mee krai roo thee kao mee faen laeo.

ไม่มีใครรู้ที่เค้ามีแฟนแล้ว

I'm happy that you were able to finish the work.

Phom dee-jai thee koon tham ngan nee set dai.

ผมดีใจที่คุณทำงานนี้เสร็จได้

I don't like it that he's so jealous of me. ("too jealous")

Chan mai chawp thee kao heung chan geuhn pai.

ฉันไม่ชอบที่เค้าหึงฉันเกินไป

It's important for everyone to come to the meeting. ("that everyone has to come")

Mun sam-kan mak thee thook kon tawng ma pra-choom.

มันสมควรมากที่ทุกคนต้องมาประชุม

Switching clauses—"the story that" - The clauses can also be switched with *nan* in-cluded after the first. *Reuang* is "the story that", "the rumor that", or "saying that".

The rumor that I love her isn't true at all.

(Reuang) thee (wa) chan rak kao nan, mun mai jing leuy.

(เรื่อง)ที่(ว่า)ฉันรักเค้านั่น มันไม่จริงเลย

Saying that he stole my money was a misunderstanding.

(*Thee wa* needed for "that people say that".)

(Reuang) thee wa kao ka-moy ngeuhn phom nan pen reuang kao-jai phit.

(เรื่อง)ที่ว่าเค้าขโมยเงินผมนั่นเป็นเรื่องเข้าใจผิด

USING *GAN THEE*

Here *gan* forms a noun (or gerund) clause which is the subject or object of the sentence. For example, "I didn't come because I was sick" is stated as "My not coming is because I was sick". *(Gan) thee* is also translated as "the fact that", "the fact being that", "the story that", or "the rumor that".

It's not certain that she's coming. (Her coming/The fact that she's coming...)

(Gan) thee kao ja ma nan, yang mai nae.

(การ)ที่เค้าจะมานั่นยังไม่แน่

I didn't tell you because I didn't know. (My not telling you...)

    (Gan) thee phŏm mâi bawk (nêe), gâw phráw phŏm mâi roo jing-jing.

    (การ)ที่ผมไม่บอก(นี่)ก็เพราะผมไม่รู้จริงๆ

He doesn't like it that his girlfriend lies. (He doesn't like the fact that...)

    Kao mâi chawp (gan) thee faen chawp go-hŏk.

    เค้าไม่ชอบ(การ)ที่แฟนชอบโกหก

With prepositions - Here *gan thee* begins a clause that's the object of a preposition. *Gan* isn't optional because there must be a noun following the preposition.

This problem might come from his being nervous. ("from" is the preposition)

    Reuang nee at jà ma jàk gan thee kao krîat.

    เรื่องนี้อาจจะมาจากการที่เค้าเครียด

She's not satisfied that the hotel's service isn't good.

    ("about the hotel's service not being good")

    Kao mâi phaw-jai (gìo-gàp gan) thee rong-raem baw-ree-gan mâi dee.

    เค้าไม่พอใจ(เกี่ยวกับการ)ที่โรงแรมบริการไม่ดี

I agree that we should reduce the amount of staff. ("with"/*gap* is the preposition)

    Phŏm hĕn dûay (gàp gan) thee wâ tawng lót jam-nuan phá-nák-ngan.

    ผมเห็นด้วย(กับการ)ที่ว่าต้องลดจำนวนพนักงาน

I was very impressed that she would come to see me. ("in her coming")

    Chan prà-tháp-jai (nai gan) thee kao jà ma hǎ chan.

    ฉันประทับใจ(ในการ)ที่เค้าจะมาหาฉัน

With "to be" - Here the *gan thee* clause is after "to be" (*keu*).

One thing I don't like is having to pay more because I'm a foreigner.

    Sing nèung thee chan mâi chawp keu gan thee chan tawng jài mâk gwa phráw

    chan pen kon tang chât.

    สิ่งหนึ่งที่ฉันไม่ชอบคือการที่ฉันต้องจ่ายมากกว่าเพราะฉันเป็นคนต่างชาติ

With "I don't know if" -

I don't know if helping my friend will cause me any problems.

    Phŏm mâi roo (wâ) (gan thee wâ) phŏm chûay pheuan jà tham hâi phŏm mee

    pan-hǎ rěu plào.

    ผมไม่รู้(ว่า)(การที่ว่า)ผมช่วยเพื่อนจะทำให้ผมมีปัญหารึเปล่า

6. TENSES

Expressing time in Thai is simpler than in Western languages because there are no changes in verb form. A basic sentence like *Kao pai Chiang Mai* can mean "He went to Chiang Mai", "He goes to Chiang Mai" or "He's going to Chiang Mai" depending on the time of the action. Some optional words called "tense markers" (such as *gamlang*, *ja*, and *dai*) are included to emphasize or clarify meanings.

PRESENT

There are two tense markers for continuous actions happening in the present. *Gamlang* (which means "power" or "energy") is put before the verb to emphasize that the action is going on at the present time, and *yoo* ("to be at") is put after the verb to show that the state of the action exists. They can be used together on either side of the verb, which emphasizes that the action is in the process of happening.

Lek's eating. (general)	Lek gin kao.
(the action is going on)	Lek gam-lang gin kao.
(the state of the action exists)	Lek gin kao yoo.
(he's in the process of eating)	Lek gam-lang gin kao yoo.

Thailand is developing.
   Meuang Thai gam-lang phat-tha-na.
      เมืองไทยกำลังพัฒนา

He's a teacher.
   Kao pen kroo yoo.
      เขาเป็นครูอยู่

I have ten baht.
   Phom mee yoo sip baht.
      ผมมีอยู่สิบบาท

A: She's sleeping?
   Kao lap yoo reuh?
      เค้าหลับอยู่เหรอ

B: No. She's taking a bath.
   Plao. Kao ab-nam yoo.
      เปล่า เค้าอาบน้ำอยู่

happening now/existing now - (verb) laeo/yoo laeo - *Laeo* is put after verbs and adjectives to show that an action or condition is happening or existing now/already. With *yoo* the action or condition has had some duration.

It's raining./It's started raining now.

    Fonj tok laeo.

        ฝนตกแล้ว

I know.

    Phomj roo (yoo) laeo.

        ผมรู้(อยู่)แล้ว

He's doing well in school now. (before he wasn't)

    Kao rian geng yoo laeo.

        เค้าเรียนเก่งอยู่แล้ว

FUTURE

The tense marker for the future is *ja*. It's put before verbs and like other tense markers can be omitted if the meaning is understood in context. Basically *ja* gives a hypothetical meaning to what's being said.

A: Are you going tomorrow?

    Koon ja pai phroong-nee reuhj?

        คุณจะไปพรุ่งนี้เหรอ

B: No. I'm going the day after tomorrow.

    Plao. Ja pai ma-reun-nee.

        เปล่า จะไปมะรืนนี้

I don't think she's going out tonight.

    Phomj kit wa kao ja mai pai thio keun-nee.

        ผมคิดว่าเค้าจะไม่ไปเที่ยวคืนนี้

If you eat it all you'll be really full.

    Tha gin mot ja im mak.

        ถ้ากินหมดจะอิ่มมาก

He told me that he would drive. ("be the driver")

    Kao bawk chan wa kao ja pen kon kap ayng.

        เค้าบอกฉันว่าเค้าจะเป็นคนขับเอง

I won't be a teacher in the city.

    Chan ja mai pen kroo nai meuang.

        ฉันจะไม่เป็นครูในเมือง

If you walk in the rain you can get a fever.

    Deuhn tak fonj dio ja pen kai.

        เดินตากฝนเดี๋ยวจะเป็นไข้

just about to happen - There are six ways to say this.

1. ja (verb) laeo - *Gamlang* and *yoo* may also be included here with their respective meanings. *Gamlang* isn't used with adjectives (third sentence). In the fourth sentence *ja* and *laeo* are used with an action that you were about to do in the past.

I'm finishing it./I'm almost finished.

    Gam-lang ja set (yoo) laeo.

    กำลังจะเสร็จ(อยู่)แล้ว

I'm just about to get my visa.

    Chan gam-lang ja dai wee-sa (laeo).

    ฉันกำลังจะได้วีซ่า(แล้ว)

The coffee's getting cold.

    Ga-fae ja yen laeo.

    กาแฟจะเย็นแล้ว

I was about to go to bed but I hadn't locked the door yet.

    Phom ja nawn (yoo) laeo, (tae) yang mai dai lawk pra-too leuy.

    ผมจะนอน(อยู่)แล้ว (แต่)ยังไม่ได้ล็อคประตูเลย

2. glai (ja) - *Glai* (falling/short) means "near".

The job/work is nearly done.

    Ngan nee glai (ja) set laeo.

    งานนี้ใกล้(จะ)เสร็จแล้ว

3. juan (ja) - With *ja* the action is nearer to happening.

The bus is about to leave.

    Rot juan (ja) awk laeo.

    รถจวน(จะ)ออกแล้ว

Time's almost up.

    Juan (ja) mot way-la laeo.

    จวน(จะ)หมดเวลาแล้ว

4. geuap (ja) - The meaning of this and the following phrase concern the circumstances of the action more than the time.

The fish sauce is almost gone. Please buy another bottle.

    Nam pla geuap mot laeo. Chuay seu eeg kuat, na.

    น้ำปลาเกือบหมดแล้ว ช่วยซื้ออีกขวดนะ

I almost couldn't come.

    Chan geuap ja ma mai dai laeo.

    ฉันเกือบจะมาไม่ได้แล้ว

5. $\overline{\text{thaep}}$ (jȧ) -

I'm so hungry, I feel like I'm going to die.

$\overline{\text{Chan}}$ hiuɯ $\overline{\text{thaep}}$ (jȧ) tai.

ฉันหิวแทบ(จะ)ตาย

6. dioɯ - This means "just a moment" and indicates that an action will happen in a short time. It's also used with warnings.

A: Are you going to the ordination party?

Jȧ pȧi ngan $\overline{\text{buat-nak}}$ $\overline{\text{mai}}$?

จะไปงานบวชนาคมั้ย

B: Yes, I'm leaving soon. I'll see you there.

Dioɯ $\overline{\text{phom}}$ $\overline{\text{gaw}}$ jȧ pȧi. Laeo jeuh gȧn $\overline{\text{thee-nan}}$, nȧ.

เดี๋ยวผมก็จะไป แล้วเจอกันที่นั่นนะ

happen by then - $\overline{\text{gaw}}$ jȧ (verb) $\overline{\text{laeo}}$ - *Gaw* is a common linking word that gives sentences a hypothetical or understated meaning. It also has several distinct meanings of its own. Here it means "subsequently" and links a time with an action that will have happened "by then". *Ja* may be used in the same way here, and *gaw*, *ja*, or *gaw ja* are interchangable in these examples (or optional—they may also be left out). The words are put after the subject of the sentence or after the time phrase if the subject is omitted.

In a week it'll be finished.

$\overline{\text{Eeg}}$ neung a-$\overline{\text{thit}}$ ($\overline{\text{gaw}}$) sȩt.

อีกหนึ่งอาทิตย์(ก็)เสร็จ

By Friday she'll be back.

Wȧn $\overline{\text{Sook}}$ ($\overline{\text{kao}}$) ($\overline{\text{gaw}}$) (jȧ) glȧp ma $\overline{\text{laeo}}$.

วันศุกร์(เค้า)(ก็)(จะ)กลับมาแล้ว

By tomorrow I'll be gone.

$\overline{\text{Phroong-nee}}$ ($\overline{\text{gaw}}$) (jȧ) pȧi $\overline{\text{laeo}}$.

พรุ่งนี้(ก็)(จะ)ไปแล้ว

Only one more kilometer and we'll be home.

Kae gee-lo dio $\overline{\text{gaw}}$ jȧ $\underline{\text{theung}}$ bȧn $\overline{\text{laeo}}$.

แค่กิโลเดียวก็จะถึงบ้านแล้ว

-in the past - These sentences are in the past and don't include *ja*.

By 11 P.M. I was already sleeping.

$\overline{\text{Ha}}$ $\overline{\text{thoom}}$ ($\overline{\text{gaw}}$) nawn $\overline{\text{laeo}}$.

ห้าทุ่ม(ก็)นอนแล้ว

When we got to Krabi it was already 1 A.M.

(Tawn thee) pai theung Gra-bee (gaw) tee neung laeo.

(ตอนที่)ไปถึงกระบี่(ก็)ตีหนึ่งแล้ว

She came to tell me, but I'd already gone.

Kao ma bawk, phom (gaw) pai laeo.

เค้ามาบอก ผม(ก็)ไปแล้ว

After only an hour he said that he was tired.

Kae chua-mong dio kao gaw bawk wa neuay.

แค่ชั่วโมงเดียวเค้าก็บอกว่าเหนื่อย

PAST

With time phrases - The simplest way to state the past is to include a past time phrase or clause. Time phrases are usually put first in the sentence in Thai.

I was a teacher in Yala last year. ("last year" is first)

(Meua) pee thee laeo chan pen kroo thee Ya-la.

(เมื่อ)ปีที่แล้วฉันเป็นครูที่ยะลา

I bought some food when I went to the market.

Phom seu a-han tawn (thee) pai ta-lat.

ผมซื้ออาหารตอน(ที่)ไปตลาด

With "already" - Laeo may be included to emphasize that an action has already or recently happened. Compare these sentences.

She went to Ubon.

Kao pai Oo-bon.

เค้าไปอุบล

She's gone to Ubon (already).

Kao pai Oo-bon laeo.

เค้าไปอุบลแล้ว

With "come" and "go" - "Come" (ma) and "go" (pai) are commonly put after verbs to show that the action (or the person/object) has come or gone. These words may also show the direction of the action ("secondary verbs" on pages 102 and 103).

She sold it./She's sold it.

Kao kai pai laeo.

เค้าขายไปแล้ว

I told her./I've told her already.

Phom bawk theuh pai laeo.

ผมบอกเธอไปแล้ว

I've already gone there (and come back).

Chan pai ma laeo.

ฉันไปมาแล้ว

I've worked for many companies.

Phom tham-ngan ma lai baw-ree-sat laeo.

ผมทำงานมาหลายบริษัทแล้ว

I've seen this movie before.

Nang reuang nee phom doo ma laeo.

หนังเรื่องนี้ผมดูมาแล้ว

Past continuous - *Gamlang* and/or *yoo* are included with the past as with the present. *Gamlang* emphasizes that the action was continuous and *yoo* that the state existed.

I was sleeping when he came.

Chan gam-lang lap yoo tawn kao ma.

ฉันกำลังหลับอยู่ตอนเค้ามา

I was farming for two years, then I came to Bangkok. ("enter-Bangkok")

Phom tham na yoo sawng pee, laeo kao Groong-thayp.

ผมทำนาอยู่สองปีแล้วเข้ากรุงเทพฯ

Yes/no questions - Three phrases are used to make yes/no questions in the past. *Reu yang* may be expanded to *laeo reu yang* or *ma laeo reu yang*.

Did he finish washing the clothes?

Kao sak pha set reu plao?   (Did he finish?)

เค้าซักผ้าเสร็จรึเปล่า

Kao sak pha set (laeo) reu yang?   (Has he finished yet?)

เค้าซักผ้าเสร็จ(แล้ว)รึยัง

Kao sak pha set laeo, chai mai?   (He has finished, hasn't he?)

เค้าซักผ้าเสร็จแล้วใช่มั้ย

A: Has Lek gone to Phuket yet?

Lek pai Phoo-get (laeo) reu yang?

เล็กไปภูเก็ต(แล้ว)รึยัง

B: Yes, she's gone already.

Pai laeo.

ไปแล้ว

A: The bus hasn't left yet, has it?

Rot yang mai awk, chai mai?

รถยังไม่ออกใช่มั้ย

B: No.

    Yang./Chai.

    ยัง/ใช่

DAI BEFORE VERBS

A common pattern is to put *dai* (with a falling tone) before verbs. *Dai* has two basic meanings: "can/able to" and "get/obtain/acquire". It's used in five different patterns before verbs with one or both meanings in each.

1. did/didn't - *Dai* before the verb in the past affirmative emphasizes that you did the action (meaning "got" or "acquired").

I sent the letter to Germany this morning.

    Phom dai song jot-maj pai Yeuh-ra-mun meua chao nee.

    ผมได้ส่งจดหมายไปเยอรมันเมื่อเช้านี้

I've thrown out the garbage already.

    Phom dai ao ka-ya pai thing laeo.

    ผมได้เอาขยะไปทิ้งแล้ว

I rested completely/got a complete rest.

    Chan dai phak-phawn tem-thee laeo.

    ฉันได้พักผ่อนเต็มที่แล้ว

Did you go running?

    (Dai) pai wing reu plao?

    (ได้)ไปวิ่งรึเปล่า

With the negative, *dai* makes it clear that the action was in the past. The meaning is "didn't" or "didn't get to".

Today I didn't eat breakfast.

    Wan-nee phom mai dai gin kao chao.

    วันนี้ผมไม่ได้กินข้าวเช้า

2. do/get to/can—present/future - *Dai* is also put before verbs in the present and future to emphasize "doing", "getting to do", "getting the chance to do" or "being able to do" the action.

If I get to go to Cambodia, I'll go to Angkor Wat.

    Tha dai pai Gum-phoo-ja, phom ja pai Na-kawn Wat.

    ถ้าได้ไปกัมพูชา ผมจะไปนครวัด

I hope I'll (get to) meet him again.

    Chan wang wa ja dai phop kao eeg.

    ฉันหวังว่าจะได้พบเค้าอีก

She wrote it down so she wouldn't forget it.

Kao kian wai pheua (thee) kao ja dai mai leum.

เค้าเขียนไว้เพื่อ(ที่)เค้าจะได้ไม่ลืม

Nowadays I don't study Thai much.

Tawn-nee mai koi dai rian pha-sa Thai.

ตอนนี้ไม่ค่อยได้เรียนภาษาไทย

These days I don't go to see him anymore.

Dio-nee mai dai pai ha kao laeo.

เดี๋ยวนี้ไม่ได้ไปหาเค้าแล้ว

I don't know if I can go or not.

Mai roo (ja) dai pai reu piao.

ไม่รู้(จะ)ได้ไปรึเปล่า

Please help me so I can get it done quickly.

Chuay gan tham noi, na, ja dai set reo-reo.

ช่วยกันทำหน่อยนะจะได้เสร็จเร็วๆ

I have to study hard so I can be a doctor.

Chan ja tawng ka-yan rian theung ja dai pen maw.

ฉันจะต้องขยันเรียนถึงจะได้เป็นหมอ

Read this handbook well, then you'll understand.

An koo-meu lem nee hai dee, ja dai kao-jai.

อ่านคู่มือเล่มนี้ให้ดีจะได้เข้าใจ

When will you (be able to) come back?

Meua-rai koon (theung) ja dai glap ma eeg?

เมื่อไหร่คุณ(ถึง)จะได้กลับมาอีก

Dai pen is translated as "become".

I've become a pilot.

Chan dai pen nak-bin laeo.

ฉันได้เป็นนักบินแล้ว

3. have/haven't—present perfect - Here *dai* is included to emphasize that an action or state that began in the past is still going on. Compare these two sentences. The first, without *dai,* means only that the person went to work in Bangkok—he may still be there but it isn't stated. Including *dai*, as in the second, shows that he's still there.

He went to work in Bangkok.

Kao pai tham-ngan thee Groong-thayp (laeo).

เค้าไปทำงานที่กรุงเทพฯ (แล้ว)

He's gone to work in Bangkok. (he's still there)

Kao dai pai tham-ngan thee Groong-thayp (laeo).

เค้าได้ไปทำงานที่กรุงเทพฯ (แล้ว)

Negative - The negative is translated as "haven't" or "haven't yet". Don't include *dai* with adjectives (last sentence).

I haven't ironed the clothes yet.

Phom yang mai dai reet seua-pha leuy.

ผมยังไม่ได้รีดเสื้อผ้าเลย

I haven't seen him for three months.

Chan mai dai jeuh kao ma sam deuan laeo.

ฉันไม่ได้เจอเค้ามาสามเดือนแล้ว

I'm not hungry yet.

Phom yang mai hiw.

ผมยังไม่หิว

yang mai or *yang mai dai* - *Dai* is included or omitted in "haven't yet" with a difference in meaning. *Yang mai dai* (before the verb) means that you're not going to do the action yet but intend to do it in the future. *Yang mai* alone, without *dai*, means only that you're not going to do the action now. You're not saying anything about the future. Compare these sentences.

I haven't bought it yet.   (with *dai*—means "but I intend to")

Chan yang mai dai seu.

ฉันยังไม่ได้ซื้อ

I'm not going to buy it yet.   (without *dai*—you're going to wait, not sure)

Chan yang mai seu.

ฉันยังไม่ซื้อ

A: Have you cut your hair yet?

Tat phom reu yang?

ตัดผมรึยัง

B: I haven't cut it yet.   (with *dai*—you're planning to get it cut)

Yang mai dai tat leuy.

ยังไม่ได้ตัดเลย

A: Are you going to cut your hair?

Ja tat phom reu yang?

จะตัดผมรึยัง

B: I'm not going to cut it yet.   (without *dai*—you're not planning to cut it now)

Yang mai tat.

ยังไม่ตัด

4. not as thought - Here *mai dai* is included before the verb when stating something that's the opposite of what was thought.

I'm not lying to you.

    (Chan) mai dai go-hok koon.

    (ฉัน)ไม่ได้โกหกคุณ

Not everybody's going.

    Mai dai pai thook kon.

    ไม่ได้ไปทุกคน

5. as you told me to do - *Dai* is also included when you're reporting that you've done something you've been told to do.

I bought it. (as you told me to)

    Phom dai seu laeo.

    ผมได้ซื้อแล้ว

EVER/NEVER/USED TO

"Have you ever", "I've never", and "I have (done something)" are formed with *keuy*. *Keuy* also means "used to" referring to something you once did habitually but don't do anymore.

I have/I haven't ever - keuy/mai keuy -

I've seen a volcano.

    Chan keuy heng phoo-kao fai (laeo).

    ฉันเคยเห็นภูเขาไฟ(แล้ว)

She's been married three times.

    Theuh keuy taeng-ngan ma sam krang laeo.

    เธอเคยแต่งงานมาสามครั้งแล้ว

I've never done this before.

    Phom mai keuy tham yang-ngee (ma gawn) leuy.

    ผมไม่เคยทำยังงี้(มาก่อน)เลย

Dai may be included to emphasize "getting" the action, or *dai* can replace *keuy* to show that you "got" the action in the past. Compare the two ways to say the first sentence.

I've been to Hong Kong once.

> Chan keuy (dai) pai Hawng Gong ma laeo (krang neung).
>
> ฉันเคย(ได้)ไปฮ่องกงมาแล้ว(ครั้งหนึ่ง)
>
> Chan dai pai Hawng Gong ma laeo (krang neung).
>
> ฉันได้ไปฮ่องกงมาแล้ว(ครั้งหนึ่ง)

I've never tried Vietnamese food.

> Chan mai keuy dai lawng a-han Wiat Nam leuy.
>
> ฉันไม่เคยได้ลองอาหารเวียดนามเลย

Yang may also be included with *keuy*. There's no change in meaning, although in English it would seem to mean "haven't yet"—that you plan to do the action in the future (it doesn't have this meaning).

I haven't been to Burma.

> Chan yang mai keuy pai Pha-ma.
>
> ฉันยังไม่เคยไปพม่า

used to - This is also *keuy*.

She used to be a teacher./She's been a teacher.

> Kao keuy pen kroo (ma gawn).
>
> เค้าเคยเป็นครู(มาก่อน)

I used to smoke, but I quit.

> Chan keuy soop boo-ree tae leuhk pai laeo.
>
> ฉันเคยสูบบุหรี่แต่เลิกไปแล้ว

This place is better than where we used to live.

> Thee-nee dee gwa thee deuhm thee rao keuy yoo.
>
> ที่นี่ดีกว่าที่เดิมที่เราเคยอยู่

Questions with *keuy* - For yes/no questions put *mai*, *reu plao*, or *chai mai* at the end. Answer with *keuy/mai keuy*.

A: Have you ever been to Hua Hin?

> Keuy pai Huai Hin mai?
>
> เคยไปหัวหินมั้ย

B: Yes.

> Keuy (laeo)./Keuy pai ma laeo.
>
> เคย(แล้ว)/เคยไปมาแล้ว

A: You've been to Chiang Rai, haven't you?

    Keuy pai Chiang Rai laeo, chai mai?

        เคยไปเชียงรายแล้วใช่มั้ย

B: No.

    (Yang) mai keuy.

        (ยัง)ไม่เคย

Questions may also be formed with *reu yang*. Again, this has the same meaning and doesn't mean that you plan to do the action in the future.

A: Have you ever been to Rangoon?

    Keuy pai Yang-goong reu yang?

        เคยไปย่างกุ้งหรือยัง

B: No.

    Yang./Yang mai keuy./Yang mai keuy pai.

        ยัง/ยังไม่เคย/ยังไม่เคยไป

7. USING VERBS

In this chapter the straightforward character of Thai sentence structure can be seen with words placed in a direct, logical order and complex actions stated as separate verbs in the order they occur.

GENERAL PATTERNS

Verbs connected by "and" - In English "and" is needed to connect the verbs in these sentences. In Thai they just follow one another.

Sit down and talk with me awhile.

> Nang kui gan noi.
>
> นั่งคุยกันหน่อย

Naming each action - Verbs are often strung together in Thai with each action named in the order it happens.

Lek borrowed my tape recorder.

> Lek yeum thayp pai fang.
>
> ("Lek-borrow-tape recorder-go-listen")
>
> เล็กยืมเทปไปฟัง

My (younger) sister is moving to Bangkok.

> Nawng-sao ja yai (kao) ma yoo Groong-thayp.
>
> ("younger sister-will-move-enter-come-live in-Bangkok")
>
> น้องสาวจะย้าย(เขา)มาอยู่กรุงเทพฯ

Infinitives - The verbs follow each other in phrases like "came to tell". The second two sentences have objects which are put between the verbs.

Joe came to tell me that my younger brother wasn't well.

> Joe ma bawk wa nawng-chai phom mai sa-bai.
>
> โจมาบอกว่าน้องชายผมไม่สบาย

I don't have anywhere to go.

> Chan mai mee thee ja pai.
>
> ฉันไม่มีที่จะไป

What are you making to eat?

> Tham a-rai gin?
>
> ทำอะไรกิน

Here there's a second action which may not be expressed in English.

Noi went to buy some food (to eat).

> Noi pai seu a-hanɲ gin.
>
> น้อยไปซื้ออาหารกิน

With adjectives - Verbs may be included before adjectives in Thai in sentences where they wouldn't be expressed in English.

This food is delicious ("to eat").

> A-hanɲ nee gin a-roi.
>
> อาหารนี้กินอร่อย

This shirt isn't comfortable ("to wear").

> Seua tua nee sai mai sa-bai.
>
> เสื้อตัวนี้ใส่ไม่สบาย

With adverbs—already/negative - Words that modify verbs in Thai like "finished" are put after the verb. With negative actions that haven't or cannot be done *mai* is put in between (and also "cause to be" where *hai* is put between—pages 138 and 143).

I finished it./I've finished doing it.

> (Phomɲ) tham set laeo (krup).
>
> (ผม)ทำเสร็จแล้ว(ครับ)

I haven't finished it yet. Is tomorrow OK?

> Chan yang tham mai set. Phroong-nee dai mai?
>
> ฉันยังทำไม่เสร็จ พรุ่งนี้ได้มั้ย

We've eaten it all, but I'm not full yet.

> Gin mot laeo, tae phomɲ yang mai im.
>
> กินหมดแล้วแต่ผมยังไม่อิ่ม

We (probably) can't eat it all. We bought too much.

> Kong gin mai mot. Rao seu ma yeuh (geuhn) pai.
>
> คงกินไม่หมด เราซื้อมาเยอะ(เกิน)ไป

We didn't eat it all. There's a little left.

> Rao mai dai gin mot. Yang leuaɲ yoo nit noi.
>
> เราไม่ได้กินหมด ยังเหลืออยู่นิดหน่อย

to/in order to - Use *pheua* (expanded to *pheua thee ja*) when "to" means "in order to" or "for the purpose of". *Pheua* is explained more under "in order to cause" (page 138), "so that" (pages 164-165), and "for the sake of" (pages 273-274).

I'm saving money to buy a house.

> Chan gep ngeuhn pheua (thee ja) seu ban.
>
> ฉันเก็บเงินเพื่อ(ที่จะ)ซื้อบ้าน

When talking about going to a place for the purpose of doing something the first sentence here is more common (*pheua* sounds more formal).

I'm going to Chatuchak to buy some clothes. (I'm going to buy clothes at Chatuchak.)

    Phŏm ja pai seu seua-pha thee Ja-too-jak.

    ผมจะไปซื้อเสื้อผ้าที่จตุจักร

    Phŏm ja pai Ja-too-jak pheua seu seua-pha. (formal/emphasizes "in order to")

    ผมจะไปจตุจักรเพื่อซื้อเสื้อผ้า

Doubling the verb - Verbs are doubled to show that an action is happening many times or with many different people.

I've talked to my wife about it already.

    Phŏm gaw kui-kui gap faen doo laeo.

    ผมก็คุยๆ กับแฟนดูแล้ว

DON'T

"Don't" is *ya* (sounds strong) or *mai tawng* (similar to "you don't have to" in English).

You don't have to do that. I'll do it.

    Mai tawng tham. Dio, chan tham ayng.

    ไม่ต้องทำ เดี๋ยวฉันทำเอง

Don't do that. It looks bad.

    Ya tham yang-ngan. Na-gliat, na.

    อย่าทำยังงั้น น่าเกลียดนะ

Don't worry./You don't have to worry.

    Ya huang leuy./Mai tawng (pen) huang, na.

    อย่าห่วงเลย/ไม่ต้อง(เป็น)ห่วงนะ

Don't lie to me.

    Ya go-hok phŏm, na.

    อย่าโกหกผมนะ

Three verbs may be included with *ya* — *ma*, *pai*, and *dai*.

1. ya ma - This means "don't come and do that in front of me".

Don't do that/act like that (in front of me).

    Ya ma tham yang-ngan, na.

    อย่ามาทำยังงั้นนะ

2. ya pai - This is "don't go (doing that)".

Don't believe him./Don't go believing him.

    Ya pai cheua kao leuy.

    อย่าไปเชื่อเค้าเลย

3. ya dai - This emphasizes "getting" the action.

Don't tell him.

> Ya dai bawk kao, na.
>
> อย่าได้บอกเค้านะ

I'D RATHER/LET'S

Dee gwa is put after verbs for "I'd rather", "let's", or "it would be better if". *Dee* alone in the second question asks for a suggestion.

A: Do you want to go out?

> Yak pai thio kang nawk mai?
>
> อยากไปเที่ยวข้างนอกมั้ย

B: I'd rather watch TV.

> Doo thee-wee dee gwa.
>
> ดูทีวีดีกว่า

A: Where shall we go?

> Pai naij dee?
>
> ไปไหนดี

B: Let's just go home.

> Glap ban dee gwa.
>
> กลับบ้านดีกว่า

For encouragement - gan theuh - This is put at the end of the sentence. *Gan* is "each other".

Let's go to the North together.

> Rao pai phak neuaj gan theuh.
>
> เราไปภาคเหนือกันเถอะ

SECONDARY VERBS

In Thai action verbs called "secondary verbs" are put after the main verb of a sentence to show the direction of the action. A similar use in English is in phrases like "burn down". See also pages 91-92 where "come" and "go" are included with past actions "coming by" and "going by".

go - pai - This shows that the action is moving away from the speaker.

Gaeo went home.

> Gaeo glap pai ban laeo.
>
> แก้วกลับไปบ้านแล้ว

Jane went downstairs.

Jane long pai chan lang.

เจนลงไปชั้นล่าง

Moo's gone outside (already).

Mooj awk pai kang nawk laeo.

หมูออกไปข้างนอกแล้ว

come - ma - Here the action is toward the speaker.

Please come inside.

Cheuhn kao ma kang-nai, ka.

เชิญเข้ามาข้างในค่ะ

When are you coming back to Thailand?

Ja glap ma meuang Thai (eeg) meua-rai?

จะกลับมาเมืองไทย(อีก)เมื่อไหร่

return/go back - glap -

Kaek walked home already.

Kaek deuhn glap pai ban laeo.

แขกเดินกลับไปบ้านแล้ว

I answered back "no".

Chan tawp glap (pai) wa "mai".

ฉันตอบกลับ(ไป)ว่าไม่

go out - awk -

Nok ran out of the house.

Nok wing awk jak ban.

นกวิ่งออกจากบ้าน

enter/go in - kao -

She walked in to see me.

Kao deuhn kao ma haj phomj.

เค้าเดินเข้ามาหาผม

go up - keun -

I'm going to run upstairs and look.

Chan ja wing keun pai doo kang bon.

ฉันจะวิ่งขึ้นไปดูข้างบน

go down/descend - lŏng -

The people here always throw trash in the street.

    Kon theé-neé chawp thing ka-yá long bon thǎ-nǒn.

    คนที่นี่ชอบทิ้งขยะลงบนถนน

play - lên - "Play" is combined with many verbs to show that an action is being done for fun and not with a serious purpose in mind.

I'm just joking.

    Chǎn phoot lên, na.

    ฉันพูดเล่นนะ

I'll buy this for a snack. ("eat-play")

    Un neé ja séu pai gin lên.

    อันนี้จะซื้อไปกินเล่น

keep/leave - wai/thing wai - These are included to show that an object is being left or kept in a place or that something is being kept in mind. *Wai* means "to keep", "leave", or "place", and *thing* is "to leave", "desert", or "abandon". The first example uses only *wai* but the others can use both *wai* and *thing wai*.

Keep in mind that he broke my heart once.

    Jam wai, na, wa kao keuy tham chan ok-hak.

    จำไว้นะว่าเค้าเคยทำฉันอกหัก

Where did you park the car?

    Jawt rot (thing) wai theé-nǎi?

    จอดรถ(ทิ้ง)ไว้ที่ไหน

I'll order the food first, then come back and pick it up later.

    Phǒm ja sǎng a-han (thing) wai gawn, laeo ja ma ao theé lang.

    ผมจะสั่งอาหาร(ทิ้ง)ไว้ก่อน แล้วจะมาเอาทีหลัง

take - ao - There are two uses: first for telling someone to do something one way rather than another way (with *dee gwa, gaw dai* or *theuh* at the end) and second to mean "take" or "get".

Let's go by bus. The airplane is too expensive.

    Pai rot-may ao theuh. Kreuang-bin mun phaeng.

    ไปรถเมล์เอาเถอะ เครื่องบินมันแพง

If you want it, buy it. It's not expensive.

    Yak dai gaw séu ao. Mai phaeng rawk.

    อยากได้ก็ซื้อเอา ไม่แพงหรอก

Be careful, the knife can cut you.

    Ra-wang, meet ja bat ao.

    ระวังมีดจะบาดเอา

look at - doo - *Doo* is included to show that something is being considered or judged.

Ask him about it.

Tham̌ kao doo gaw̄ daî.

ถามเค้าดูก็ได้

Taste it. It's delicious.

Chim doo see. À-roi, na.

ชิมดูซิ อร่อยนะ

be lost - siaȷ - This adds the meaning of "lose", "gone" or "be lost", or with commands means that you want something done completely or as soon as possible. It can be shortened to *sa,* which is common at the end of commands. See also *sak/sia,* pages 294-296.

Go away!/Get away!

Pai sa!

ไปซะ

Throw it away. It's spoiled.

Thing sa. Mun boot laeo.

ทิ้งซะ มันบูดแล้ว

I want to forget about her.

Chan yak leum theuh siaȷ.

ฉันอยากลืมเธอเสีย

STILL/NOT YET

"Still" is *yang,* and "not yet" is *yang mai.* Both are put before the verb (a short answer "not yet" is just *yang*). *Yoo* can be included to emphasize that the state exists, and *gaw* may be included after the subject as a linking word and to emphasize "still" or "also" (two of the basic meanings of *gaw*).

I'm not hungry yet.

Chan yang mai hiuȷ.

ฉันยังไม่หิว

You can still use it.

Yang chai daî (yoo).

ยังใช้ได้(อยู่)

I can't go yet./I still can't go.

Phom̌ yang pai mai daî.

ผมยังไปไม่ได้

I thought he'd gone already, but he's still here.

Kit wa kao pai laeo tae kao gaw̄ yang yoo.

คิดว่าเค้าไปแล้วแต่เค้าก็ยังอยู่

McDonald's is more expensive over there, but it's still cheap.

Maek-do-nawl thee-nan phaeng gwa, tae gaw yang thook yoo.

แมคโดนัลล์ที่นั่นแพงกว่า แต่ก็ยังถูกอยู่

There are still a lot of quiet places on Ko Samui.

Yang mee thee ngiap-ngiap lai thee bon Gaw Sa-mui.

ยังมีที่เงียบๆ หลายที่บนเกาะสมุย

A: You used to play the guitar.

Koon keuy len gee-ta, nee.

คุณเคยเล่นกีต้าร์นี่

B: I still do.

Gaw yang len yoo.

ก็ยังเล่นอยู่

With _gaw_ alone - _Yang_ can be omitted in these examples; _gaw_ alone expresses "still".

Whether it's clean or not I'll still wear it.

Sa-at reu mai sa-at gaw ja sai.

สะอาดหรือไม่สะอาดก็จะใส่

A: There was a show here before.

Meua-gawn keuy mee "cho" thee-nee.

เมื่อก่อนเคยมีโชว์ที่นี่

B: There still is.

Tawn-nee gaw (yang) mee.

ตอนนี้ก็(ยัง)มี

A: Are you going or not?

Ja pai reu plao?

จะไปรึเปล่า

B: I'm still going, but I'm waiting for the rain to stop first.

Chan gaw pai, tae raw hai fon yoot gawn.

ฉันก็ไป แต่รอให้ฝนหยุดก่อน

With _eeg_ - Here _eeg_ means that you still can't do something even after several tries or a duration of time. Compare these pairs of sentences:

You're not going to bed yet?

Yang mai nawn reuh?

ยังไม่นอนเหรอ

You're still not going to bed yet?

    Yang mai nawn eeg reuhj?

      ยังไม่นอนอีกเหรอ

The train isn't leaving yet./The train hasn't left yet.

    Rot-fai yang mai awk.

      รถไฟยังไม่ออก

The train still isn't leaving. (after waiting)

    Rot-fai yang mai awk eeg.

      รถไฟยังไม่ออกอีก

With *yoo eeg* - Here *eeg* is included with *yang* to mean "more" in the first sentence and "still, again" in the second. *Yoo* shows that the action or state exists.

I'm going to work here longer./I'm still going to work here.

    Chan ja yang tham-ngan thee-nee yoo eeg.

      ฉันจะยังทำงานที่นี่อยู่อีก

I told you to wash the clothes, but you're still watching TV.

    Bawk hai pai sak pha, yang ma doo thee-wee yoo eeg.

      บอกให้ไปซักผ้ายังมาดูทีวีอยู่อีก

ANYWAY

"Anyway" has three meanings in English which are formed in different ways in Thai.

1. I'll still...anyway - This means that you'll still do something even though circumstances have made the situation different from usual or from what was expected. *Yang* is included for "still". See pages 150-151 for "even though".

It's a holiday, but he has to work anyway.

  (It's a holiday but he still has to work./Even though it's a holiday he has to work.)

    Mun pen wan yoot, tae kao gaw yang tawng tham-ngan.

      มันเป็นวันหยุดแต่เค้าก็ยังต้องทำงาน

She didn't have much money, but she gave me some anyway.

    Kao mai mee ngeuhn mak, tae kao gaw yang hai phom.

      เค้าไม่มีเงินมากแต่เค้าก็ยังให้ผม

2. it will happen anyway - The meaning here is "already"—you've already thought or planned something and another circumstance won't affect it. The meaning isn't "still", so *yang* isn't included. Instead, *yoo laeo* is put at the end for "already" or "definitely".

Come with me. I have to go in that direction anyway. (go that way/take that route)

    Pai duay-gan, na. Chan tawng phan thang nan yoo laeo.

      ไปด้วยกันนะ ฉันต้องผ่านทางนั้นอยู่แล้ว

A: Sorry, the tickets were sold out.

    Siaɹ-jai, tuaɹ kaiɹ mot laeo.

        เสียใจ ตั๋วขายหมดแล้ว

B: That's OK. I didn't want to go anyway.

    Mai pen rai. Phomɹ mai yak pai yoo laeo.

        ไม่เป็นไร ผมไม่อยากไปอยู่แล้ว

3. anyway/whatever/despite all - This is *yang-ngai* or *yang-ngai gaw tam* meaning "however", "no matter what happens" or "at any rate".

But anyway, you have to wash the dishes.

    Tae yang-ngai (gaw tam), theuh ja tawngɹ lang jan.

        แต่ยังไง(ก็ตาม)เธอจะต้องล้างจาน

Anyway, he can pass the test.

    Yang-ngai gaw tam, kao sawp dai.

        ยังไงก็ตาม เค้าสอบได้

"AGAIN/MORE" WITH ACTIONS

Three words are put after verbs to say that you're doing an action "more" or "again"—*eeg*, *mai*, and *taw*. *Eeg* is also "more" with quantities (as in "more sugar").

1. with *eeg/eeg laeo* - *Eeg* is both "more" with continuous actions (*len eeg* is "play more") and "again" with actions that start and stop (*pai eeg* is "go again"). When *laeo* is included it means that something has started again soon after stopping.

Do it more./Do it again.

    Tham eeg.

        ทำอีก

When I have free time I'll come again. ("If I'm free I'll come again.")

    Tha wang chan ja ma eeg.

        ถ้าว่างฉันจะมาอีก

He won't come again.

    Kao ja mai ma eeg.

        เค้าจะไม่มาอีก

It's started raining again.

    Fonɹ tok eeg laeo.

        ฝนตกอีกแล้ว

You want to eat again already?

    Yak gin eeg laeo reuhɹ?

        อยากกินอีกแล้วเหรอ

2. with *mai* - *Mai* ("new/newly/anew") is "again" when the same action is done over.

This one isn't sewn right. Could you sew it again?

> Tua nee yep mai dee. Chuay yep mai, dai mai?
>
> ตัวนี้เย็บไม่ดี ช่วยเย็บใหม่ได้มั้ย

I want to come and study again.

> Yak ma rian eeg./Yak ma rian mai.
>
> อยากมาเรียนอีก/อยากมาเรียนใหม่

A: Are you coming again tomorrow?

> Phroong-nee ja ma eeg mai?
>
> พรุ่งนี้จะมาอีกมั้ย

B: I can't come tomorrow. I'll come again next week.

> Phroong-nee ma mai dai. A-thit na ja ma mai.
>
> พรุ่งนี้มาไม่ได้ อาทิตย์หน้าจะมาใหม่

3. with *taw* - This is for actions being done "further". A variation is *taw eeg*. The examples here compare *eeg* and *taw*.

What else shall we do?/What shall we do next?

> Tham a-rai eeg?/Tham a-rai taw?
>
> ทำอะไรอีก/ทำอะไรต่อ

I want to play more./I want to continue playing.

> Yak len eeg./Yak len taw (eeg).
>
> อยากเล่นอีก/อยากเล่นต่อ(อีก)

A: Where are you going next?

> Koon ja pai nai taw?
>
> คุณจะไปไหนต่อ

B: I don't want to go anywhere else. Let's go home.

> Mai yak pai nai taw (eeg) laeo. Glap ban dee gwa.
>
> ไม่อยากไปไหนต่ออีกแล้ว กลับบ้านดีกว่า

***taw pai* (continue to)** - *Taw pai* means "continue to" or "do further". It has three other meanings: "next/later on" (page 338), "from now on" (page 339), and "the next/the following" (pages 348 and 386).

Tam will continue teaching here for another year.

> Tam ja sawn thee-nee taw pai eeg pee neung.
>
> ต้มจะสอนที่นี่ต่อไปอีกปีหนึ่ง

I can't run anymore.

> Chan wing taw pai mai dai laeo.
>
> ฉันวิ่งต่อไปไม่ได้แล้ว

NOT ANYMORE/NEVER AGAIN

There are three patterns: the first for a situation that has stopped, the second for a situation that won't continue, and the third for a situation that won't happen again.

1. has stopped - mai...laeo -

I don't want to go anymore. (wanted to go before but changed your mind)

Mai yak pai laeo.

ไม่อยากไปแล้ว

I don't like it anymore.

Chan mai chawp laeo.

ฉันไม่ชอบเลย

I thought you weren't coming. (thought you had changed your mind)

Chan kit wa koon mai ma laeo.

ฉันคิดว่าคุณไม่มาแล้ว

Gai isn't going anymore? (she had planned to go before)

Gai mai pai laeo reuh?

ไก่ไม่ไปแล้วเหรอ

2. won't continue - mai...eeg laeo - *Eeg* adds the meaning that the action won't continue anymore.

I can't stay here any longer. I have to go back to work.

Chan yoo thee-nee mai dai eeg laeo. Tawng glap pai tham-ngan laeo.

ฉันอยู่ที่นี่ไม่ได้อีกแล้ว ต้องกลับไปทำงานแล้ว

It's not a small town anymore.

Mun mai chai meuang lek-lek eeg (taw pai) laeo.

มันไม่ใช่เมืองเล็กๆ อีก(ต่อไป)แล้ว

These examples can have either meaning so *eeg* is optional.

She doesn't work here anymore.

Kao mai dai tham-ngan thee-nee (eeg) laeo.

เค้าไม่ได้ทำงานที่นี่(อีก)แล้ว

I don't want to stay here anymore.

Mai yak yoo thee-nee (eeg) laeo.

ไม่อยากอยู่ที่นี่(อีก)แล้ว

If I get married I won't be a student anymore.

Tha chan taeng-ngan chan ja mai pen nak-rian (eeg) laeo.

ถ้าฉันแต่งงานฉันจะไม่เป็นนักเรียน(อีก)แล้ว

3. won't happen again - mai...eeg/mai...eeg laeo - Here you're referring to an action that won't be repeated. *Eeg* is needed for "not again" but *laeo* is optional, although including it makes the meaning stronger ("never again").

I don't want to eat here again.

    Mai yak gin thee-nee eeg (laeo).

    ไม่อยากกินที่นี่อีก(แล้ว)

I'm never going to Penang again./I'm not going to Penang anymore.

    Chan ja mai pai Pee-nang eeg (laeo).

    ฉันจะไม่ไปปีนังอีก(แล้ว)

"Wanting" here can be seen as either a continuous or a repeated action so any of the patterns can be used (*laeo, eeg,* or *eeg laeo*).

I don't want this one anymore.

    Un nee mai ao laeo./Un nee mai ao eeg laeo./Un nee mai ao eeg.

    อันนี้ไม่เอาแล้ว/อันนี้ไม่เอาอีกแล้ว/อันนี้ไม่เอาอีก

-in the past - mai...eeg leuy - *Leuy* is used with the past instead of *laeo* to emphasize that the action was never repeated.

I never saw her again.

    Phom mai keuy jeuh theuh eeg leuy.

    ผมไม่เคยเจอเธออีกเลย

I wanted to go and eat there again but never did.

    Chan yak ja pai gin thee-nan, tae mai dai pai eeg leuy.

    ฉันอยากจะไปกินที่นั่นแต่ไม่ได้ไปอีกเลย

WANT TO/WOULD LIKE TO

Use *yak* or *tawng-gan* for wanting to do an action. Wanting an object is also *tawng-gan*, plus *ao* and *yak dai* ("want to get").

Informal - yak - *Ja* or *thee ja* are optional after *yak* in these examples.

Ann wants to go too.

    Ann yak (ja) pai duay.

    แอนอยาก(จะ)ไปด้วย

I'd like to be a manager.

    Phom yak (ja) pen phoo jat-gan.

    ผมอยาก(จะ)เป็นผู้จัดการ

I want to be tall. I don't like being short like this.

    Phom yak soong. Mai chawp tia baep nee leuy.

    ผมอยากสูง ไม่ชอบเตี้ยแบบนี้เลย

A: If I go and play football this afternoon do you want to go with me?

 (Tha) phom̯ ja pai len foot-bawn yen nee, yak pai (duay) mai?

 (ถ้า)ผมจะไปเล่นฟุตบอลเย็นนี้ อยากไปด้วยมั้ย

B: Yes./No.

 Yak (pai)./Mai yak (pai).

 อยาก(ไป)/ไม่อยาก(ไป)

This exchange includes *yang* for "yet/still".

A: When do you want to go back to France?

 Yak glap Fa-rang-set meua-rai?

 อยากกลับฝรั่งเศสเมื่อไหร่

B: I don't want to go yet.

 Yang mai yak pai leuy.

 ยังไม่อยากไปเลย

A: Why don't you want to go yet?

 Tham-mai mai yak pai, la?

 ทำไมไม่อยากไปล่ะ

B: I still want to travel more.

 Yang yak thio taw.

 ยังอยากเที่ยวต่อ

Formal - tawng-gan - *Tawng-gan* is more polite than *yak* and also means "to need". *Ja* or *thee ja* are optional.

I don't want to have problems with anyone.

 Chan mai tawng-gan (ja) mee reuang gap krai.

 ฉันไม่ต้องการ(จะ)มีเรื่องกับใคร

Gai still wants to go to school, but she can't get the money.

 Gai yang tawng-gan rian taw, tae kao yang hai thoon mai dai.

 ไก่ยังต้องการเรียนต่อแต่เค้ายังหาทุนไม่ได้

CAN/COULD/ABLE TO

"Can" refers to three things: having the ability or skill to do something, having permission to do something, and being available/having the opportunity to do something. *Dai* is used for all three, while *pen* is used for the first only (ability/skills).

Dai—have the ability/permission/availability - dai - The pronunciation of *dai* may be drawn out a little when it's at the end of the sentence so that it doesn't sound abrupt.

You can come and stay here.

 Koon ma phak thee-nee dai.

 คุณมาพักที่นี่ได้

Women can be soldiers (too).

    Phoo-ying gaw pen tha-han dai.

    ผู้หญิงก็เป็นทหารได้

Sorry I couldn't call you last night.

    Kaw-thot na, thee meua-keun-nee tho pai hai koon mai dai.

    ขอโทษนะที่เมื่อคืนนี้โทรไปหาคุณไม่ได้

With the future *kong* ("probably") may be included to understate the meaning.

He can probably go tomorrow, but he can't go today.

    Phroong-nee kao kong (ja) pai dai, tae wan-nee pai mai dai.

    พรุ่งนี้เค้าคง(จะ)ไปได้แต่วันนี้ไปไม่ได้

Questions with *dai* -

Can you eat hot food yet?

    Gin a-han phet dai (laeo) reu yang?

    กินอาหารเผ็ดได้(แล้ว)รึยัง

When can we go?

    Rao ja pai dai meua-rai?

    เราจะไปได้เมื่อไหร่

Where can we stay?

    Phak dai thee-nai?/Phak thee-nai dai?

    พักได้ที่ไหน/พักที่ไหนได้

Who can go?

    Krai pai dai bang?

    ใครไปได้บ้าง

Why can't you go, Nit?

    Tham-mai Nit pai mai dai, la?

    ทำไมนิดไปไม่ได้ละ่

If I want to go on a different day I can change it, can't I?

    Tha chan yak pai wan eun, plian dai, chai mai?

    ถ้าฉันอยากไปวันอื่นเปลี่ยนได้ใช่มั้ย

Nim doesn't have a car. How can she go home?/How could she have gone home?

    Nim mai mee rot. Kao glap ban dai yang-ngai?

    นิ่มไม่มีรถ เค้ากลับบ้านได้ยังไง

Why can other people do it but I can't?

    Tham-mai kon eun tham dai tae phom tham mai dai?

    ทำไมคนอื่นทำได้แต่ผมทำไม่ได้

***Dai/pen*—be able to do a skill** - dai/pen - *Dai* and *pen* are interchangable here but there's a difference in meaning. *Dai* refers to having the ability to do something, while *pen* is for knowing how or being accustomed to doing something (the action is an innate part of you—it "is" you).

I'm able write Thai now.

Chan kiang pha-sa Thai dai laeo.

ฉันเขียนภาษาไทยได้แล้ว

Steve isn't able to cook Thai food yet.

Steve tham a-han Thai yang mai pen.

สตีฟทำอาหารไทยยังไม่เป็น

Use *dai* only here, referring to a physical ability.

You can swim well.

Koon wai-nam dai geng.

คุณว่ายน้ำได้เก่ง

He's 50 but he can still play takraw.

Kao a-yoo ha-sip laeo, tae yang len ta-graw dai.

เค้าอายุห้าสิบแล้วแต่ยังเล่นตะกร้อได้

To say that you can't smoke, eat, or drink certain things use *mai dai* if it's for a specific reason (medical, religious) and *mai pen* if it's something you don't do as a habit or that's not part of your diet (you "don't know how" to eat/drink/smoke it).

Thank you, I don't drink.

Kawp-koon ka. Chan gin lao mai pen.

ขอบคุณค่ะ ฉันกินเหล้าไม่เป็น

Physically able - wai - Saying *mai wai* instead of *mai dai* emphasizes that you're not physically able to do the action. *Wai* is most common in the negative, but it's also used in the affirmative as in the second example.

I can't walk anymore. I'm really tired.

Chan deuhn mai wai laeo. Mot raeng leuy.

ฉันเดินไม่ไหวแล้ว หมดแรงเลย

A: I don't think I can lift this box.

Phom kong yok glawng nee mai wai.

ผมคงยกกล่องนี้ไม่ไหว

B: Yes you can.

Wai yoo laeo.

ไหวอยู่แล้ว

Formal - sa-mat - Use *samat* when you're speaking formally or elaborately. It's put before the verb, and *dai* or another word is included after the verb to complete the phrase (here *ayng* and *mot* are used). The informal version is included in parentheses.

I can do it.

Sa-mat tham dai. (informal is *Phom tham dai/Chan tham dai.*)

สามารถทำได้

Pla can take you to Ayuthaya.

Pla sa-mat pha koon pai A-yoot-tha-ya dai. (leave out *samat* informally)

ปลาสามารถพาคุณไปอยุธยาได้

I can go by myself.

Phom sa-mat pai ayng. (*Phom pai ayng dai.*)

ผมสามารถไปเอง

I can eat all of it.

Chan sa-mat gin mot. (*Chan gin dai mot./Chan gin mot dai.*)

ฉันสามารถกินหมด

The negative is used formally only.

I can't lie to my parents.

Chan mai sa-mat go-hok phaw-mae dai. (*Chan go-hok phaw-mai mai dai.*)

ฉันไม่สามารถโกหกพ่อแม่ได้

EXPRESSIONS WITH *DAI*

keep doing - yoo dai - Said when wondering how someone can keep doing something.

How can you keep complaining?

Bon yoo dai.

บนอยู่ได้

doing it wrong - dai laeo - This is for giving a command to inferiors or for telling someone they're doing something wrong. The example here also has the usual meaning of "you can stop doing that".

Stop it!

Yoot dai laeo!

หยุดได้แล้ว

until successful - jon dai - This means "until finally successful in the end".

Her father was strict, but she managed to go out with her friends.

Phaw theuh doo, tae theuh gaw nee awk pai thio gap pheuan jon dai.

พ่อเธอดุ แต่เธอก็หนีออกไปเที่ยวกับเพื่อนจนได้

MUST/HAVE TO

There are three words/phrases: *tawng, jam-pen tawng,* or *jam-pen*. The second two have stronger meanings than the first.

1. general/informal - tawng -

I have some work that I must do.

Phom mee ngan tawng tham.

ผมมีงานต้องทำ

You don't have to go./It's alright if you don't go.

Koon mai tawng pai gaw dai.

คุณไม่ต้องไปก็ได้

You can go, but you'll have to go alone.

Koon pai dai, tae tawng pai kon dio, na.

คุณไปได้แต่ต้องไปคนเดียวนะ

You have to be able to speak English to get this job.

Koon tawng phoot Ang-grit dai, theung ja dai ngan nee.

คุณต้องพูดอังกฤษได้ถึงจะได้งานนี้

You (Jack) will have to spend a long time before you can speak Thai well.

Jack ja tawng chai way-la nan, gwa ja phoot pha-sa Thai dai geng.

แจ็คจะต้องใช้เวลานาน กว่าจะพูดภาษาไทยได้เก่ง

With suggestions -

A mosquito bit you? You should put on some tiger balm.

(Don) yoong gat reuh? Tawng tha ya mawng, na. (*tha* means "spread on")

(โดน)ยุงกัดเหรอ ต้องทายาหม่องนะ

supposed to - *Tawng* is "supposed to" when the meaning is that you're obligated to do something, but not when the meaning is that you expect something to happen (second example).

You're supposed to call him this evening. (obligated to)

Koon tawng tho pai ha kao yen nee.

คุณต้องโทรไปหาเค้าเย็นนี้

There's supposed to be a meeting today. (just "There's a meeting today.")

Wan-nee ja mee pra-choom.

วันนี้จะมีประชุม

Questions - *Ja* is included in the third question because the meaning is hypothetical.

Should I take anything with me?

Chan tawng ao a-rai pai mai?

ฉันต้องเอาอะไรไปมั้ย

Do we have to go to the bank tomorrow?

> Phroong-nee tawng pai tha-na-kan reu plao?
>
> พรุ่งนี้ต้องไปธนาคารรึเปล่า

Why do I have to go?/Why would I have to go?

> Tham-mai ja tawng pai duay?
>
> ทำไมจะต้องไปด้วย

2. to emphasize "must" - jam-pen tawng - This phrase is a little more formal.

He has to ask his father for permission first.

> Kao jam-pen tawng kaw a-noo-yat phaw gawn.
>
> เค้าจำเป็นต้องขออนุญาตพ่อก่อน

3. meaning "necessary" - jam-pen - *Tawng* is included except when *jam-pen* is at the end of the sentence (last example).

It's necessary that I sell my car.

> Mun jam-pen (thee phom) tawng kai rot.
>
> มันจำเป็น(ที่ผม)ต้องขายรถ

It's not necessary that I do it myself.

> Mun mai jam-pen (wa chan) tawng tham ayng.
>
> มันไม่จำเป็น(ว่าฉัน)ต้องทำเอง

I don't like having problems if it's not really necessary.

> Phom mai chawp mee pan-ha tha mai jam-pen jing-jing.
>
> ผมไม่ชอบมีปัญหาถ้าไม่จำเป็นจริงๆ

SHOULD/SHOULD HAVE

There are three words for "should"—*na*, *kuan*, and *som-kuan*. Suggestions with "should" or "shall" are formed with *dee* in Thai

1. least strong - na (ja) - Also *na thee ja*. Other translations are "ought to", "had better", and "supposed to". *Ja* is optional but usually included with future actions or to emphasize hypothetical meanings with "should have". Because *na* is also used to make adjectives from verbs (*na rak* is "lovable/cute" and *na gin* is "good to eat") *ja* should be included if there could be confusion with this meaning.

I should tell her first./I should have told her first.

> Chan na ja bawk kao gawn.
>
> ฉันน่าจะบอกเค้าก่อน

You should do better in school than this.

> Koon na ja rian geng gwa nee.
>
> คุณน่าจะเรียนเก่งกว่านี้

You should get a haircut.

    Koon nâ jà tàt phǒmɲ, ná.

    คุณน่าจะตัดผมนะ

I should have gone last year, but I didn't.

    Phǒmɲ nâ jà pai meua pee thee laeo, tae phǒmɲ gaw mâi dâi pai.

    ผมน่าจะไปเมื่อปีที่แล้วแต่ผมก็ไม่ได้ไป

I think we should be able to do it. (or "should have been able")

    Kit wâ rao nâ jà thǎm dâi.

    คิดว่าเราน่าจะทำได้

Moo should be able to go by himself. (or "should have been able")

    Mooɲ nâ jà pai ayng dâi.

    หมูน่าจะไปเองได้

Negative - *Ja* is optional with "shouldn't" but needed with "shouldn't have" because of the hypothetical meaning. *Leuy* ("at all") is also included with "shouldn't have".

You shouldn't do that./You shouldn't have done that.

    Koon mâi nâ jà thǎm yàng-ngan (leuy).

    คุณไม่น่าจะทำอย่างนั้น(เลย)

We shouldn't have any trouble./We shouldn't have had any trouble.

    Rao mâi nâ jà mee pan-hǎɲ à-rai (leuy).

    เราไม่น่าจะมีปัญหาอะไร(เลย)

should be able to - Include *dai*.

You can get a ticket if you hurry./You could have got a ticket if you'd hurried.

    Koon nâ jà hǎɲ séu tuaɲ dâi, thâ rêep pai.

    คุณน่าจะหาซื้อตั๋วได้ถ้ารีบไป

2. stronger form - kuan - *Kuan* is stronger and more formal than *na*. *Ja* is optional when it means "should" but needed with "should have". The phrase can be extended to *kuan thee ja*. Include *dee gwa* with *kuan* or *na* for "would be better".

You should quit smoking.

    Koon kuan jà léuhk sòop boo-ree dee gwà.

    คุณควรจะเลิกสูบบุหรี่ดีกว่า

He eats more than he should./He ate more than he should have.

    Kao gin mâk gwà thee kao kuan jà gin.

    เค้ากินมากกว่าที่เค้าควรจะกิน

Negative - *Mai kuan* is "shouldn't" or "ought not", meaning that it's improper or inappropriate to do the action. *Ja* and *leuy* are included with "shouldn't have".

He shouldn't talk like that./He shouldn't have said that.

Kao mai kuan ja phoot baep nan (leuy).

เค้าไม่ควรจะพูดแบบนั้น(เลย)

She shouldn't believe the things they say. (or "She shouldn't have believed")

Theuh mai kuan cheua (sing) thee (phuak) kao phoot (leuy).

เธอไม่ควรเชื่อ(สิ่ง)ที่(พวก)เค้าพูด(เลย)

it's likely that - Both *kuan ja* and *na ja* may be used.

She dresses neatly. It's likely that she's a teacher.

Theuh taeng tua sa-at. Kuan ja pen kroo, na.

เธอแต่งตัวสะอาด ควรจะเป็นครูนะ

3. formal - som-kuan - This is the formal form of *kuan* and means "fitting", "proper", "appropriate", or "suitable".

You should rest a lot.

Koon som-kuan ja phak-phawn mak-mak.

คุณสมควรจะพักผ่อนมากๆ

Women shouldn't wear shorts to a temple.

Phoo-ying mai som-kuan sai gang-gayng kaj-sun pai wat.

ผู้หญิงไม่สมควรใส่กางเกงขาสั้นไปวัด

4. "should/shall" with *dee* - To ask for advice put *dee* at the end of the question. Statements ("you'd better", "I'd rather", "let's") end in *dee gwa* (page 102).

What should I do? I lost my billfold.

Tham yang-ngai dee? Phom tham gra-pao ngeuhn hai.

ทำยังไงดี ผมทำกระเป๋าเงินหาย

Is it good to travel alone? (means "should I do it?")

Pai thio kon dio, nia, dee reuh?

ไปเที่ยวคนเดียวเนี่ยดีเหรอ

Shouldn't we go to Chiang Mai first?

Rao pai Chiang Mai (gan) gawn mai dee reuh?

เราไปเชียงใหม่(กัน)ก่อนไม่ดีเหรอ

I don't know if I should go or not.

Mai roo wa ja pai reu mai pai dee.

ไม่รู้ว่าจะไปหรือไม่ไปดี

A: Shall we go to a movie?

Pai doo nang (gan) dee mai?

ไปดูหนัง(กัน)ดีมั้ย

B: I'd rather not./No, let's not.

Mai pai dee gwa.

ไม่ไปดีกว่า

A: Should I go to Phuket with him?

Chan pai Phoo-get gap kao dee mai?

ฉันไปภูเก็ตกับเค้าดีมั้ย

B: It would be better if you didn't.

Ya pai dee gwa.

อย่าไปดีกว่า

A: Would if be good if I called her?

Mun ja dee mai, tha phom ja tho pai ha theuh?

มันจะดีมั้ย ถ้าผมจะโทรไปหาเธอ

B: It's likely to help.

Mun kong ja chuay dai.

มันคงจะช่วยได้

SURE/NOT SURE

There are three ways to say "sure", "surely", or "definitely".

1. nae/nae-nawn/nae-nae - These words are translated as "sure", "certain", "certainly", or "for sure". *Kong* ("probably") may be included for understatement.

Today it will rain for sure./It will surely rain.

Wan-nee fon ja tawng tok nae-nae./Fon kong ja tok nae-nawn.

วันนี้ฝนจะต้องตกแน่แน่/ฝนคงจะตกแน่นอน

You'll pass the test for sure.

Koon sawp dai nae-nawn.

คุณสอบได้แน่นอน

That's the way it has to be.

Mun kong pen baep nan nae.

มันคงเป็นแบบนั้นแน่

Negative - mai nae/mai nae-jai -

I might come again, but I'm not sure (yet).

Phom kong ja ma eeg, tae yang mai nae.

ผมคงจะมาอีกแต่ยังไม่แน่

She should stay in school, but she's not sure if she will. She might get a job.

> Kao na ja rian taw, tae kao mai nae-jai. Kao at ja haj ngan tham gaw dai.

> เค้าน่าจะเรียนต่อแต่เค้าไม่แน่ใจ เค้าอาจจะหางานทำก็ได้

2. yawm - This means "surely", "likely to", or "apt to". The general pattern is "if something happens, then something else will surely happen".

If you do good you'll surely receive good in return.

> Tham dee yawm (ja) dai dee.

> ทำดีย่อม(จะ)ได้ดี

3. yoo laeo - This is put after verbs or used alone to mean "definitely".

A: Are you going?

> Pai mai?

> ไปมั้ย

B: Yes, definitely.

> Pai yoo laeo.

> ไปอยู่แล้ว

PROBABLY

Kong (ja) is "probably", "most likely" or "sure to". *Ja* is optional in all examples.

I can probably go to work again tomorrow.

> Phroong-nee phom kong pai tham-ngan dai laeo.

> พรุ่งนี้ผมคงไปทำงานได้แล้ว

Noo probably went home.

> Noo kong glap ban laeo.

> หนูคงกลับบ้านแล้ว

He probably has to tell his wife first.

> Kao kong tawng bawk faen kao gawn.

> เค้าคงต้องบอกแฟนเค้าก่อน

I hope it won't be long.

    Chan wangˇ wâ kong mâi nan.

       ฉันหวังว่าคงไม่นาน

There probably won't be time.

    Kong mâi mee way-la.

       คงไม่มีเวลา

This room probably isn't very expensive.

    Hawngˇ nee kong mâi phaeng.

       ห้องนี้คงไม่แพง

MIGHT/MAY/MAYBE

There are five ways to say "might" or "maybe".

1. at (jà) - This is put before verbs. *Ja* is optional and *gaw dai* can be included at the end.

Someone might come to see me./Someone might have come to see me.

    At (jà) mee kon ma haˇ.

       อาจ(จะ)มีคนมาหา

I might not go.

    Chan at (jà) mâi pai (gaw dâi).

       ฉันอาจ(จะ)ไม่ไป(ก็ได้)

He might not have sold it yet.

    Kaoˆ at jà yang mâi kaiˇ.

       เค้าอาจจะยังไม่ขาย

It might be in this building.

    Mun at jà yoo nai teuk nee laê.

       มันอาจจะอยู่ในตึกนี้แหละ

What John said is probably true.

    Thee John phoot at jà jing gawˇ dâi.

       ที่จอห์นพูดอาจจะจริงก็ได้

might be able to - Put *dai* at the end.

Daeng might be able to go.

    Daeng at jà pai dâi.

       แดงอาจจะไปได้

Dam might not be able to go.

    Dam at jà pai mâi dâi.

       ดำอาจจะไปไม่ได้

2. na̅ (ja̅) - *Na ja* means "should" and makes a guess more certain than *at ja*.

He might come today./He should come today.

    Kao na̅ ja̅ ma wan-nee.

    เค้านาจะมาวันนี้

She might get that job./She should get that job.

    Theuh na̅ ja̅ dai̅ ngan nan̅.

    เธอนาจะได้งานนั่น

3. dioჟ - *Dio* means "just a moment" and is used for warnings—"be careful or you might...".

Be careful, if you drink that water you could get diarrhea.

    (Tha̅) gin nam nan̅, dioჟ thawng gaw siaჟ rawk.

    (ถ้า)กินน้ำนั้นเดี๋ยวท้องก็เสียหรอก

4. bang-thee - This is used together with *at*. *Thee* here means "time/instance" and has a mid tone. *Bang-thee* also means "sometimes" (page 381).

Maybe I'll open a store.

    Bang-thee pho̅mჟ at ja̅ peuht ran kaiჟ kawngჟ.

    บางทีผมอาจจะเปิดร้านขายของ

A: Will she come?

    Kao ja̅ ma mai?

    เค้าจะมามั้ย

B: Maybe she'll come, maybe she won't.

    Bang-thee at ja̅ ma. Bang-thee at ja̅ mai̅ (ma).

    บางทีอาจจะมา บางทีอาจจะไม่(มา)

5. mung/la-mung - These are put at the end of sentences for "perhaps" or "I guess". There are more examples and other uses of *mung* on pages 289-290.

Maybe Gai's gone already.

    Gai (kong) pai laeo mung.

    ไก่(คง)ไปแล้วมั้ง

Phet might not go.

    Phet kong ja̅ mai̅ pai la-mung.

    เพชรคงจะไม่ไปล่ะมั้ง

A: Why hasn't Lek come?

    Tham-mai Lek yang mai ma?

    ทำไมเล็กยังไม่มา

B: Maybe the traffic's bad.

    Rot tit mung.

    รถติดมั้ง

A: I think she's Japanese.

    Kit wa kon nan pen kon Yee-poon, na.

    คิดว่าคนนั้นเป็นคนญี่ปุ่นนะ

B: That might be so.

    At ja pen yang-ngan, mung.

    อาจจะเป็นยังงั้นมั้ง

MIGHT HAVE/MUST HAVE/COULD HAVE

Here you're guessing about something that might have happened in the past. Four words—*at, kong, na,* and *tawng*—are used depending on the degree of certainty (from least to most). "Surely" is often included at the end.

With *at (ja)* (least certain) -

He might have done that because he was afraid.

    Kao at ja tham yang-ngan phraw wa kao glua gaw dai.

    เค้าอาจจะทำยังงั้นเพราะว่าเค้ากลัวก็ได้

I'm going to the repair shop. My car should be fixed by now.

    Chan ja pai thee oo. Rot at ja (sawm) set laeo.

    ฉันจะไปที่อู่ รถอาจจะ(ซ่อม)เสร็จแล้ว

With *kong (ja)* -

It must have been Piak who took it.

    Kong ja pen Piak thee (pen kon) ao pai.

    คงจะเป็นเปี้ยกที่(เป็นคน)เอาไป

With *na (ja)* -

He must have told her already.

    Kao na ja bawk theuh laeo.

    เค้านาจะบอกเธอแล้ว

With *tawng* (most certain) -

She must be the one who wrote it./She must have been the one who wrote it.

    Theuh tawng pen kon kiang nae-nawn.

    เธอต้องเป็นคนเขียนแน่นอน

Negative - This is "couldn't have" or "might not have". *Kong, at,* and *na* all have the same general meaning.

It couldn't have been Nit who took it.

> Mun mai na ja pen Nit thee ao pai.

> มันไม่น่าจะเป็นนิดที่เอาไป

She might not understand./She might not have understood.

> Kao at ja mai kao-jai gaw dai.

> เค้าอาจจะไม่เข้าใจก็ได้

Ayk couldn't have sold his house. Where will he live? (or "He probably won't...")

> Ayk kong ja mai kaij ban rawk. Kao ja pai yoo thee-naij?

> เอกคงจะไม่ขายบ้านหรอก เค้าจะไปอยู่ที่ไหน

HYPOTHETICAL MEANINGS

There are three ways to state that something is indefinite or conjectural.

1. with *ja* - *Ja* makes statements hypothetical and also understated by suggesting that the action or condition isn't always necessary or true.

You could study computers or whatever - it depends on you.

> Koon ja rian kawm-phiu-teuh reuj a-rai - gaw laeo tae koon.

> คุณจะเรียนคอมพิวเตอร์หรืออะไร ก็แล้วแต่คุณ

At the end of the week I'm usually very tired.

> (Tawn) plai sap-da chan ja neuay mak.

> (ตอน)ปลายสัปดาห์ฉันจะเหนื่อยมาก

If you do it, it's alright. If you don't do it, it's OK too.

> Koon ja tham gaw dai, mai tham gaw dai.

> คุณจะทำก็ได้ ไม่ทำก็ได้

People who like good food will like Thailand.

> Kon thee chawp a-hanj a-roi a-roi ja (tawnj) chawp meuang Thai.

> คนที่ชอบอาหารอร่อยๆ จะ(ต้อง)ชอบเมืองไทย

2. with *gaw* - *Gaw* also makes meanings hypothetical, uncertain, and indirect but it's more informal than *ja*. In the first example either *gaw* or *ja* (or both) can be put after the subject. With *gaw* the sentence sounds more informal.

I'll go if I have someone to travel with.

> Chan ja pai tha mee pheuan./Chan gaw (ja) pai tha mee pheuan.

> ฉันจะไปถ้ามีเพื่อน/ฉันก็(จะ)ไปถ้ามีเพื่อน

A: Are you at home on weekends?

> Wan Saoj A-thit yoo ban mai?

> วันเสาร์อาทิตย์อยู่บ้านมั้ย

B: Yes, usually.

 Gâw̄ yòo.

 ก็อยู่

3. with *wa* (thought/said/planned) - *Wa* here means "thought that", "thought I would", "said that", "planned to", or "plan to".

I'd planned to go, but I didn't have time.

 Phǒm̄ wâ jà pāi, tae̱ mâī mee way-la.

 ผมว่าจะไปแต่ไม่มีเวลา

POSSIBLE/IMPOSSIBLE

These phrases are used alone or in sentences. *Thee* or *wa* are put after them for "that".

possible	pèn pāi dāī
impossible	pèn pāi mâī dāī
might be possible	a̱t (jà) pèn pāi dāī

It's possible that I can get a job.

 Pèn pāi dāī wâ phǒm̱ jà dâī ngan.

 เป็นไปได้ว่าผมจะได้งาน

It's impossible that he'll return the money to you.

 Pèn pāi mâī dāī thêe̱ kao jà keun ngeuhn hâī koon.

 เป็นไปไม่ได้ที่เค้าจะคืนเงินให้คุณ

It might be that Bob didn't know we had a meeting.

 A̱t pèn pāi dāī wâ Bob mâī roo wâ mee prà-choom.

 อาจเป็นไปได้ว่าบ๊อบไม่รู้ว่ามีประชุม

there's no way - mâī mee thang -

There's no way at all that I can help her.

 (Chǎn) mâī mee thang thêe jà chuay kao dâī leuy.

 (ฉัน)ไม่มีทางที่จะช่วยเค้าได้เลย

A: Will he cheat me?

 Kao jà gong chǎn reu p̱lao?

 เค้าจะโกงฉันรึเปล่า

B: No way. He's very honest.

 Mâī mee thang ra̱wk. Kao pèn kon seu-sa̱t mak.

 ไม่มีทางหรอก เค้าเป็นคนซื่อสัตย์มาก

there won't be a day - mai mee wan - This is an expression meaning "never".
You'll never understand her.

> Mai mee wan thee koon ja kao-jai theuh dai rawk.
>
> ไม่มีวันที่คุณจะเข้าใจเธอได้หรอก
>
> Koon mai mee wan (thee ja) kao-jai theuh dai.
>
> คุณไม่มีวัน(ที่จะ)เข้าใจเธอได้

WILL/WOULD

Ja alone is "will" or "would" because of the hypothetical and indefinite meaning it gives.
Going by bus will be too slow./Going by bus would be too slow.

> Keun rot-may ja cha pai noi.
>
> ขึ้นรถเมล์จะช้าไปหน่อย

He'd like a towel.

> Kao ja ao pha chet tua.
>
> เค้าจะเอาผ้าเช็ดตัว

I didn't think she'd come, but she did.

> Phom kit wa kao ja mai ma laeo, tae kao gaw ma.
>
> ผมคิดว่าเค้าจะไม่มาแล้วแต่เค้าก็มา

If I were you, I'd take that job right away.

> Tha chan pen theuh, chan ja rap ngan nan than-thee.
>
> ถ้าฉันเป็นเธอฉันจะรับงานนั้นทันที

"Might" or "probably" are included to show unsureness or understatement.
If I have the money I'll buy a car./If I had the money I'd buy a car.

> Tha mee ngeuhn chan at ja seu rot.
>
> ถ้ามีเงิน ฉันอาจจะซื้อรถ

It probably won't help./It probably wouldn't have helped.

> Mun kong ja chuay a-rai mai dai.
>
> มันคงจะช่วยอะไรไม่ได้

would have to be - ja tawng -
If it were air-conditioned it would be more expensive than this.

> Tha tit ae duay mun (gaw) ja tawng phaeng (mak) gwa nee.
>
> ถ้าติดแอร์ด้วยมัน(ก็)จะต้องแพง(มาก)กว่านี้

You'd surely like this place if you stayed here a long time. (or "You'll...")

> Koon ja tawng chawp thee-nee nae-nawn, tha dai yoo nan-nan.
>
> คุณจะต้องชอบที่นี่แน่นอนถ้าได้อยู่นานๆ

WOULD HAVE

Here you're describing an event that would have taken place if conditions had been different. Hypothetical words included are are *kong*, *gaw*, and *ja*.

I would have gone if I'd heard from you. ("received news")

> Phom̌ kong ja pai laeo, tha phom̌ dai kao jak koon.

> ผมคงจะไปแล้วถ้าผมได้ข่าวจากคุณ

If it had been you, she wouldn't have dared say that.

> Tha pen koon, kao kong mai gla phoot yang-ngan.

> ถ้าเป็นคุณเค้าคงไม่กล้าพูดยังงั้น

It would have been a good game if it hadn't rained.

> Mun kong pen "game" thee sa-nook, tha fon mai tok.

> มันคงเป็นเกมส์ที่สนุกถ้าฝนไม่ตก

If you hadn't come I would have been unhappy./If you don't come I'll be unhappy.

> Tha koon mai ma phom̌ ja roo-seuk siaj-jai mak.

> ถ้าคุณไม่มาผมจะรู้สึกเสียใจมาก

I wouldn't have told him if he hadn't asked.

> Tha kao mai dai thamj, chan gaw kong mai (dai) bawk.

> ถ้าเค้าไม่ได้ถามฉันก็คงไม่(ได้)บอก

OTHER AUXILIARY VERBS

beginning to - chak ja - Also translated as "getting to be" or "starting to be".

Talking to him was starting to get boring.

> Phoot gap kao chak ja beua laeo, na.

> พูดกับเค้าชักจะเบื่อแล้วนะ

I'm starting not to believe him anymore.

> Phom̌ chak ja mai yak cheua kao laeo, la.

> ผมชักจะไม่อยากเชื่อเค้าแล้วละ

do instead - glap - Here something was done other than expected, with *glap* before the unexpected action.

I told her the truth but she (unexpectedly) didn't believe me.

> Chan bawk kwam-jing tae theuh glap mai cheua.

> ฉันบอกความจริงแต่เธอกลับไม่เชื่อ

do prematurely - pheung -

Don't go yet. The food is almost ready.

> Ya pheung pai, na. Gap kao ja set laeo.

> อย่าเพิ่งไปนะ กับข้าวจะเสร็จแล้ว

Let's watch the movie for awhile. Don't go to sleep right away.

> Doo năng nŏi, na. Ya pheung nawn.

> ดูหนังหน่อยนะ อย่าเพิ่งนอน

Don't do that just now.

> Ya pheung, na.

> อย่าเพิ่งนะ

do something wrong - keun - This is for an action you know is wrong or prohibited.

If you drink again the doctor won't be able to help you.

> Tha keun deum lao eeg, maw kong ja chuay mai dai eeg laeo.

> ถ้าขืนดื่มเหล้าอีกหมอคงจะช่วยไม่ได้อีกแล้ว

Why would she be going? (when she shouldn't)

> Kao ja keun pai tham-mai?

> เค้าจะขืนไปทำไม

later - kŏi - *Koi* before a verb (in the future) means "later", "after having waited awhile", "wait to do it later", or "not until then". *Koi* is also an adverb meaning "gradually" or "softly" and is put before adjectives in "not very" (*mai koi...*). There are more examples under "then" on page 335.

I'll come again tomorrow.

> Phroong-nee kŏi ma mai.

> พรุ่งนี้ค่อยมาใหม่

Wait awhile, then we'll go.

> Dio kŏi pai.

> เดี๋ยวค่อยไป

Wait five minutes, then we'll eat.

> Raw eeg hă na-thee kŏi gin.

> รออีกห้านาทีค่อยกิน

Let's eat first, then go shopping.

> Gin gawn, na, laeo kŏi pai chawp-ping.

> กินก่อนนะ แล้วค่อยไปชอปปิ้ง

Let John speak first, then Steve will speak.

> Hai John phoot gawn, laeo Steve kŏi phoot (thee lang).

> ให้จอห์นพูดก่อนแล้วสตีฟค่อยพูด(ทีหลัง)

must - jong - This is an imperative used by superiors to inferiors.

My child, you must behave well.

> Jong tham tua hai dee, na look.

> จงทำตัวให้ดีนะลูก

stray into wrong - long - This means "go astray" or "become lost".

Don't believe him.

    Ya long cheua kao.

    อย่าหลงเชื่อเค้า

Ann (wrongly) fell in love with someone who was already married.

    Ann pai long rak kon thee mee mia laeo.

    แอนไปหลงรักคนที่มีเมียแล้ว

Don't think you're the only one who's great.

    Ya long wa tua ayng geng kon dio.

    อย่าหลงว่าตัวเองเก่งคนเดียว

PASSIVE VOICE

With the passive voice a person or object is the receiver of the action. "A dog bit me" (active voice) is stated as "I was bitten by a dog". In Thai, passive voice sentences are formed by putting either *thook* ("touch/hit") or *don* ("hit/touch/strike/come in contact with") before the verb. *Thook* sounds more polite than *don*.

Following are some verbs that are common in the passive voice. *Don* and *thook* are interchangable, and some active voice sentences are included for comparison.

arrest/catch - jap -

He was arrested.

    Kao thook jap.

    เค้าถูกจับ

Someone was arrested.

    Mee kon don jap.

    มีคนโดนจับ

The police arrested him.

    Tam-ruat jap kao.

    ตำรวจจับเค้า

bump into/hit - chon -

I was hit/bumped into. (by a vehicle/person)

    (Chan) don chon.

    (ฉัน)โดนชน

A car hit me.

    Rot chon chan.

    รถชนฉัน

My car was hit.

    Rot don chon.

        รถโดนชน

A truck ran into my car.

    Rot sawng-thaeo (ma) chon rot phom.

        รถสองแถว(มา)ชนรถผม

Two cars crashed into each other.

    (Mee) rot chon gan.

        (มี)รถชนกัน

cheat - gong - This refers to being cheated for money or an object, not for love.

I was cheated.

    Chan don gong.

        ฉันโดนโกง

He cheated me.

    Kao gong chan.

        เค้าโกงฉัน

cut/injure - bat/bat jep -

I was cut/injured.

    Phom don bat.

        ผมโดนบาด

A knife cut my hand.

    Meet bat meu (phom).

        มีดบาดมือ(ผม)

I received an injury.

    Phom dai rap bat jep.

        ผมได้รับบาดเจ็บ

deceive - lawk - This concerns love, relationships, or schemes.

I was deceived.

    Chan thook lawk.

        ฉันถูกหลอก

He deceived me.

    Kao lawk chan.

        เค้าหลอกฉัน

fine (for an infraction) - pràp -

I was fined for speeding.

    Phǒmj don pràp phraw káp rót réo.

    ผมโดนปรับเพราะขับรถเร็ว

The police fined me for littering.

    Tam-ruàt pràp chan phraw thíng ka-yà.

    ตำรวจปรับฉันเพราะทิ้งขยะ

fire (from a job) - lâi awk -

She was fired.

    Kao thook lâi awk.

    เค้าถูกไล่ออก

The boss fired him. (*thao-gae* refers to the boss/owner of a small business)

    Thaô-gae lâi kao awk.

    เถ้าแก่ไล่เค้าออก

hit - tee -

He was hit. (by someone)

    Kao thook tee.

    เค้าถูกตี

Someone hit him.

    Mee kòn (ma) tee kao.

    มีคน(มา)ตีเค้า

kill - kâ - *Tai*, "to die", can be included.

He was killed.

    Kao thook kâ (tai).

    เค้าถูกฆ่า(ตาย)

She killed him.

    Theuh kâ kao (tai).

    เธอฆ่าเค้า(ตาย)

shoot - yíng -

Someone was shot.

    Mee kòn don yíng.

    มีคนโดนยิง

He was shot.

    Kao thook yíng.

    เค้าถูกยิง

He shot a friend of his.

   Kao ying pheuan (kao).

   เค้ายิงเพื่อน(เค้า)

steal - ka-moy -

My things were stolen.

   Kawng phom thook ka-moy.

   ของผมถูกขโมย

A foreigner had his things stolen.

   Mee fa-rang kon neung thook ka-moy kawng.

   มีฝรั่งคนหนึ่งถูกขโมยของ

He stole my money.

   Kao ka-moy ngeuhn chan.

   เค้าขโมยเงินฉัน

Someone stole my money.

   Mee kon ka-moy ngeuhn chan.

   มีคนขโมยเงินฉัน

Naming the agent - Here the person, animal, or object that did the action is named. In Thai it's put between *thook/don* and the verb.

I was bitten by a dog.

   Chan thook ma gat.

   ฉันถูกหมากัด

I was hit by a car.

   Chan thook rot chon.

   ฉันถูกรถชน

I was cut by a knife.

   Phom don meet bat.

   ผมโดนมีดบาด

Questions in the passive voice -

A: Was he arrested?

   (Kao) don jap reu plao?/(Kao) don jap mai?

   (เค้า)โดนจับรึเปล่า/(เค้า)โดนจับมั้ย

B: Yes.

   Don./Don jap.

   โดน/โดนจับ

No.

Mai don./Mai don jap./Mai.

ไม่โดน/ไม่โดนจับ/ไม่

A: Have you ever had anything stolen?

Keuy don ka-moy kawng mai?

เคยโดนขโมยของมั้ย

B: It's happened to me twice.

Keuy don ma sawng krang laeo.

เคยโดนมาสองครั้งแล้ว

A: Have you ever been scolded by your father?

Keuy don phaw da mai?

เคยโดนพ่อด่ามั้ย

B: Yes, often.

Don boi.

โดนบ่อย

8. USING *HAI*/REQUESTS

Hai, meaning "to give", is common in requests and has the following extended meanings:
- let/allow
- cause
- have/make someone do something
- for (for me/for you)

LET/ALLOW

Hai before a pronoun or noun is "let me", "allow her", etc.

He won't let me go anywhere.

Kao mai hai chan pai naj.

เค้าไม่ให้ฉันไปไหน

Will you let me go?

Koon ja hai phomj pai reu plao?

คุณจะให้ผมไปรึเปล่า

Can we let him go too?

Hai kao pai duay dai reu plao?

ให้เค้าไปด้วยได้รึเปล่า

Let Daeng go first./Daeng should go first.

Hai Daeng pai gawn dee gwa.

ให้แดงไปก่อนดีกว่า

Who let the dog in?

Krai hai maj kao ma?

ใครให้หมาเข้ามา

want to let/have to let - These include *yak* for "want to" or *tawng* for "have to".

I want to let him see that I'm hard-working.

Chan yak hai kao henj wa chan pen kon ka-yanj.

ฉันอยากให้เค้าเห็นว่าฉันเป็นคนขยัน

My mother doesn't want me to go out.

Mae mai yak hai chan awk pai thio.

แม่ไม่อยากให้ฉันออกไปเที่ยว

I don't want you to think I lied to him.

    Phomj mai yak hai koon kit wa phomj go-hok kao.

    ผมไม่อยากให้คุณคิดว่าผมโกหกเค้า

You have to let him think that he's important. ("that he has importance")

    Koon tawnj hai kao kit wa kao mee kwam samj-kan.

    คุณต้องให้เค้าคิดว่าเค้ามีความสำคัญ

allow/agree to let - yawm hai -

They agreed to let her get married.

    Kao yawm hai theuh taeng-ngan dai.

    เค้ายอมให้เธอแต่งงานได้

He can't let her take a vacation.

    Kao yawm hai theuh la phak mai dai.

    เค้ายอมให้เธอลาพักไม่ได้

The police won't let anyone go in there.

    Tam-ruat mai yawm hai krai kao nai nan.

    ตำรวจไม่ยอมให้ใครเข้าในนั้น

allow (formal) - a-noo-yat hai -

My mother is allowing me to go.

    Mae a-noo-yat hai phomj pai dai.

    แม่อนุญาตให้ผมไปได้

My father won't let me live with my friends.

    Phaw mai a-noo-yat hai phomj yoo gap pheuan.

    พ่อไม่อนุญาตให้ผมอยู่กับเพื่อน

"release" and allow - ploi hai - *Ploi* means "to release" or "to let go" and is commonly included with "let".

Her parents won't let her go on trips with her friends.

    Phaw-mae theuh mai ploi hai theuh pai thio gap pheuan. (or *ploi theuh hai pai*)

    พ่อแม่เธอไม่ปล่อยให้เธอไปเที่ยวกับเพื่อน

allow it to happen/let happen - Use *hai* with *mee* or *geuht keun.*

I don't want anyone to know.

    Mai yak hai mee kon roo. (or *hai kon roo/hai krai roo*)

    ไม่อยากให้มีคนรู้

I don't want there to be another war.

    Chan mai yak hai mee songj-kram (geuht keun) eeg.

    ฉันไม่อยากให้มีสงคราม(เกิดขึ้น)อีก

One thing that shouldn't be allowed to happen is tourists being cheated.

Sing neung thee mai na hai geuht keun keu gan lawk luang nak thawng-thio.

สิ่งหนึ่งที่ไม่น่าให้เกิดขึ้นคือการหลอกลวงนักท่องเที่ยว

"let" meaning "until" - Here *hai* is translated as "until", literally "and let".

Leave the water on until the tank is full.

Peuht hai nam tem thang leuy, na./Peuht nam jon tem thang leuy, na.

เปิดให้น้ำเต็มถังเลยนะ/เปิดน้ำจนเต็มถังเลยนะ

Wait until everyone has come, then we'll go. ("Wait and let..")

Koi hai thook kon ma gawn, laeo koi pai.

คอยให้ทุกคนมาก่อนแล้วค่อยไป

CAUSE

Put either *tham* or *tham hai* before verbs for "cause". In general *tham hai* has a stronger and more direct meaning.

Who made this place so dirty?

Krai tham (hai) thee-nee sok-ga-prok?

ใครทำให้ที่นี่สกปรก

I don't want to cause anyone to get into trouble.

Phom mai yak tham (hai) krai deuat-rawn.

ผมไม่อยากทำ(ให้)ใครเดือดร้อน

What made you so tired?

A-rai tham (hai) koon neuay?

อะไรทำ(ให้)คุณเหนื่อย

Stronger actions - *Hai* is needed in these examples because "make/cause" involves a direct or intentional action.

You have to make her believe that you didn't do it.

Koon tawng tham hai kao cheua wa koon mai dai tham.

คุณต้องทำให้เค้าเชื่อว่าคุณไม่ได้ทำ

He doesn't have any experience. That's why he wasn't made boss.

Kao mai mee pra-sop-gan leuy. Un nan thee tham hai kao mai dai pen huay-na.

เค้าไม่มีประสบการณ์เลย อันนั้นที่ทำให้เค้าไม่ได้เป็นหัวหน้า

Love makes people blind.

Kwam-rak tham hai kon ta bawt.

ความรักทำให้คนตาบอด

cause to happen -

Corruption causes problems to occur.

> Gan kaw-rap-chun tham hai pan-ha geuht keun. (or *geuht panha keun*)
>
> การคอรัปชั่นทำให้ปัญหาเกิดขึ้น

Naming the object - If there's no object use *tham* only, not *tham hai*. Compare these sentences. The first has an object ("watch") so *hai* can be included. In the second and third there's no object in Thai ("it" is the object in English) so only *tham* is used.

I broke my watch.

> Chan tham (hai) na-lee-ga sia.
>
> ฉันทำ(ให้)นาฬิกาเสีย

I broke it.

> Phom tham sia.
>
> ผมทำเสีย

I lost it.

> Chan tham hai.
>
> ฉันทำหาย

With adverbs - Here *hai* means "to make it this way".

I'm going to travel all over Thailand.

> Chan ja thio hai thua meuang Thai leuy.
>
> ฉันจะเที่ยวให้ทั่วเมืองไทยเลย

I'm going far away (intentionally).

> Phom ja pai hai glai leuy.
>
> ผมจะไปให้ไกลเลย

I'll finish my homework first.

> Chan ja tham gan-ban hai set gawn.
>
> ฉันจะทำการบ้านให้เสร็จก่อน

in order to cause - *pheua hai/pheua tham hai* - *Pheua hai* is "so that (something will happen)" and *pheua tham hai* is "in order to cause (something to happen)". These phrases may be shortened to *hai* alone when they're in the middle of the sentence, as in the second example. For more uses of *pheua* see "to/in order to" (page 100), "so that/in order to" (pages 164-165) and "for the sake of" (page 273).

To make it (the work) come out well, I have to work very hard.

> Pheua (tham) hai ngan awk ma dee, chan tawng tham-ngan nak mak.
>
> เพื่อ(ทำ)ให้งานออกมาดีฉันต้องทำงานหนักมาก

Bob painted the walls to make them look better.

Bob tha seej faj ban (pheua tham) hai (mun) doo dee keun.

บ๊อบทาสีฝาบ้าน(เพื่อทำ)ให้(มัน)ดูดีขึ้น

HAVE/MAKE SOMEONE DO SOMETHING

Other translations are "wants me to", "asked me to", and "forced me to".

I had him go and buy something.

Phomj hai kao pai seu kawngj.

ผมให้เค้าไปซื้อของ

I'd like you to visit my house.

(Chan) yak hai koon pai thio ban chan.

(ฉัน)อยากให้คุณไปเที่ยวบ้านฉัน

She had me (be the person to) do it.

Kao hai phomj pen kon tham.

เค้าให้ผมเป็นคนทำ

Someone came and asked me to help them.

Mee kon ma hai chan chuay.

มีคนมาให้ฉันช่วย

If you have any problems, please call me to talk about them.

Mee pan-haj a-rai, hai tho pai kui gap chan dai.

มีปัญหาอะไรให้โทรไปคุยกับฉันได้

Do you want me to pay?/Shall I pay?

Hai phomj jai mai?

ให้ผมจ่ายมั้ย

A: When do you want me to start working?

(Yak) hai phomj reuhm tham-ngan meua-rai?

(อยาก)ให้ผมเริ่มทำงานเมื่อไหร่

B: How about right now?

Tawn-nee leuy pen ngai?

ตอนนี้เลยเป็นไง

A: What do you want your child to study?

Koon ja hai look rian a-rai?

คุณจะให้ลูกเรียนอะไร

B: I'd like her to study business, but it's up to her.

Yak hai kao rian (thang) thoo-ra-git, tae gaw laeo tae kao.

อยากให้เค้าเรียน(ทาง)ธุรกิจแต่ก็แล้วแต่เค้า

Offering help - Use these questions to ask if someone needs help.

Do you want me to help you?

Hai chan chuay mai?/(Ja) hai chuay mai?/Yak hai chuay reu plao?

ให้ฉันช่วยมั้ย/(จะ)ให้ช่วยมั้ย/อยากให้ช่วยรึเปล่า

Do you want me to iron the clothes?

(Ja) hai chan reet pha mai?

(จะ)ให้ฉันรีดผ้ามั้ย

I'll help you wash the dishes, OK? (*hai koon* is "for you")

Phom chuay lang jan hai (koon), ao mai?

ผมช่วยล้างจานให้(คุณ)เอามั้ย

Do you want me to do it for you?

Hai phom tham hai mai?

ให้ผมทำให้มั้ย

Following are responses:

No thanks. I can do it myself.

Mai tawng, ka. Chan tham ayng (gaw) dai.

ไม่ต้องค่ะ ฉันทำเอง(ก็)ได้

No thanks. I'll do it myself.

Mai tawng, krup. Kaw tham ayng dee gwa.

ไม่ต้องครับ ขอทำเองดีกว่า

That would be nice.

Chuay gaw dee.

ช่วยก็ดี

That would be nice. Thanks.

Gaw dee, na. Kawp-koon mak.

ก็ดีนะ ขอบคุณมาก

FOR ME/FOR YOU

"You", "me", etc. can be omitted if understood in context. See also "for", pages 272-274.

My father bought it for me.

Phaw seu hai (phom).

พ่อซื้อให้(ผม)

I'll do it for you.

Chan ja tham hai.

ฉันจะทำให้

Who cut your hair?

> Krai tat phom̌ hai (koon)?
>
> ใครตัดผมให้(คุณ)

A: Who are you buying this for?

> Un nee seu hai krai?
>
> อันนี้ซื้อให้ใคร

B: For my (older) sister.

> Hai phee-sao̧.
>
> ให้พี่สาว

A: Who did it for you?/Who made it for you?

> Krai tham hai (koon)?
>
> ใครทำให้(คุณ)

B: A friend did it for me/made it for me.

> Pheuan tham hai.
>
> เพื่อนทำให้

EXPRESSIONS WITH *HAI*

must try to - hai dai - For the past use *jon dai*, page 346.

I have to go, no matter what.

> Tawnǧ pai hai dai.
>
> ต้องไปให้ได้

do it well - hai dee -

Before you leave the house, don't forget to lock the door.

> Gawn awk jak ban, ya leum lawk pra-too hai dee, na.
>
> ก่อนออกจากบ้านอย่าลืมล็อกประตูให้ดีนะ

try to - ao hai - This is used in the same way as *tham hai* but emphasizes "try to".

Try to finish it.

> Ao hai set, na.
>
> เอาให้เสร็จนะ

let it be - hai pen pai -

Forget it./Let it be.

> Ploi hai mun pen pai./Chang mun, theuh.
>
> ปล่อยให้มันเป็นไป/ช่างมันเถอะ

REQUESTS

Requests or commands usually begin with *chuay* and end with one or more of these phrases. "Don't" is *ya* or *mai tawng* (the first is stronger).

put before the action -	chuay	("help")
put after the action -	noi/noi see	("a little")
	duay	("also")
	dai mai?	("can you?")
	hai chan/hai phom	("for me")
	hai noi	("for me a little")
	ka/krup	(polite words)
	na	(OK?)

Please watch the children.

Chuay doo dek hai noi.

ช่วยดูเด็กให้หน่อย

Please buy some food for me ("to eat").

Chuay seu a-han hai chan gin noi.

ช่วยซื้ออาหารให้ฉันกินหน่อย

You don't have to wash the clothes today.

Mai tawng sak pha wan-nee, na.

ไม่ต้องซักผ้าวันนี้นะ

Asking for objects/actions - kaw - Use *kaw* to request an object or for permission to perform an action.

Could I have some money to go to school?

Kaw ngeuhn pai rong-rian noi see krup.

ขอเงินไปโรงเรียนหน่อยซิครับ

Could I try to ride your motorcycle?

Kaw lawng kap maw-teuh-sai noi dai mai, ka?

ขอลองขับมอเตอร์ไซด์หน่อยได้มั้ยค่ะ

He asked to use the computer.

Kao kaw chai kreuang kawm-phiu-teuh.

เค้าขอใช้เครื่องคอมพิวเตอร์

bring the/use the - ao...ma... - This is for asking someone to do an action involving an object, literally "bring the (object) and...".

Bring a knife and cut up these vegetables./Use a knife to cut up these vegetables.

Ao meet ma hun phak phuak nee noi.

เอามีดมาหั่นผักพวกนี้หน่อย

Could you fry the fish?

Ao pla ma thawt noi, dai mai?

เอาปลามาทอดหน่อยได้มั้ย

let/don't let - These include *hai*.

Bring the book and let me see it.

Ao nang-seu ma hai (chan) doo noi.

เอาหนังสือมาให้(ฉัน)ดูหน่อย

Don't let the candle go out.

Ya hai thian dap, na.

อย่าให้เทียนดับนะ

With adjectives/adverbs - Include *hai* for "make it" or "cause it to be".

Can you finish it today?

Tham hai (mun) set wan-nee dai mai?

ทำให้(มัน)เสร็จวันนี้ได้มั้ย

Please do it well.

Tham hai (mun) dee, na.

ทำให้(มัน)ดีนะ

Please write it beautifully.

Kian hai suay, na.

เขียนให้สวยนะ

Please finish eating./Eat it all.

Gin hai set, na./Gin hai mot, na.

กินให้เสร็จนะ/กินให้หมดนะ

Here *tham* ("make") is the verb. It can be omitted if the action isn't emphasized.

Don't make it hot/spicy.

Ya tham hai phet, na./Ya hai phet, na.

อย่าทำให้เผ็ดนะ/อย่าให้เผ็ดนะ

Make it sweet.

Tham hai wan, na./Hai wan-wan, na.

ทำให้หวานนะ/ให้หวานๆ นะ

have someone (do something) - Put *hai* before the name of the person.

Please have Moo clean the bathroom.

Chuay hai Moo lang hawng-nam duay.

ช่วยให้หมูล้างห้องน้ำด้วย

tell him to.../ask her to... - These include verbs like "tell" and "ask" (*kaw* for asking someone to perform an action). *Hai* can be put either before or after the name.

Tell Jane to go (first).

    Bawk hai Jane pai gawn leuy. (or *Bawk Jane hai pai...*)

    บอกให้เจนไปก่อนเลย

Please have Bob come here./Please call Bob.

    Riak Bob hai ma nee noi. (or *Riak hai Bob ma...*)

    เรียกบ๊อบให้มานี่หน่อย

Can you let Jack know?

    Chuay bawk hai Jack roo dai mai?

    ช่วยบอกให้แจ๊คๆรู้ได้มั้ย

Please tell Lek to wash the car.

    Chuay bawk Lek hai lang rot.

    ช่วยบอกเล็กให้ล้างรถ

Please tell Daeng to bring me the newspaper.

    Chuay bawk hai Daeng ao nang-seu phim ma hai noi.

    ช่วยบอกให้แดงเอาหนังสือพิมพ์มาให้หน่อย

Please ask Toom to go and see me at home tomorrow morning.

    Chuay kaw hai Toom pai ha chan thee ban phroong-nee chao, na.

    ช่วยขอให้ตุ่มไปหาฉันที่บ้านพรุ่งนี้เช้านะ

Did you ask Nim to buy some food?

    Koon kaw hai Nim seu gap kao reu plao?

    คุณขอให้นิ่มซื้อกับข้าวรึเปล่า

    Koon (dai) bawk Nim hai seu gap kao ma reu plao?

    คุณ(ได้)บอกนิ่มให้ซื้อกับข้าวมารึเปล่า

A: Please tell Noom to go to the school tomorrow.

    Chuay bawk Noom hai pai rong-rian phroong-nee duay.

    ช่วยบอกหนุ่มให้ไปโรงเรียนพรุ่งนี้ด้วย

B: I'll tell him (for you).

    (Phom) ja bawk (kao) hai.

    (ผม)จะบอก(เค้า)ให้

Negative (tell her not to) - *Mai hai pai* is "don't go" or "not allowed to go", *mai tawng pai* is "no need to go/doesn't have to go", and *ya pai* is "don't go" (the strongest).

Please tell Ann not to go/that she doesn't need to go.

    Chuay bawk (hai) Ann (wa) mai tawng pai.

    ช่วยบอก(ให้)แอน(ว่า)ไม่ต้องไป

Please tell Ann that I don't allow her to go.

> Chuay bawk Ann wa (chan) mai hai pai./Chuay bawk wa chan mai hai Ann pai.
>
> ช่วยบอกแอนว่า(ฉัน)ไม่ให้ไป/ช่วยบอกว่าฉันไม่ให้แอนไป

Please tell Lek there's no need for Moo to go.

> Chuay bawk Lek (wa) mai tawng hai Moo pai. (or *mai hai Moo pai/ya hai moo pai*)
>
> ช่วยบอกเล็ก(ว่า)ไม่ต้องให้หมูไป

Please tell Lek to tell Moo not to go.

> Chuay bawk Lek hai (pai) bawk Moo wa mai tawng pai. (or *wa ya pai*)
>
> ช่วยบอกเล็กให้(ไป)บอกหมู(ว่า)ไม่ต้องไป

Formal requests - kaw hai - *Kaw hai* is used to make requests meaning "I'd like to ask you to" or "I'd like to have you". This is more formal than *chuay*. It's also used in speeches as in the last sentence.

I'd like to ask you to come early tomorrow morning.

> Phroong-nee kaw hai (koon) ma chao-chao, na.
>
> พรุ่งนี้ขอให้(คุณ)มาเช้าๆ นะ

I'd like to ask everyone to be quiet.

> Phom kaw hai thook kon ngiap-ngiap noi, krup.
>
> ผมขอให้ทุกคนเงียบๆ หน่อยครับ

Please do it as well as you can.

> Kaw hai tham hai dee thee-soot.
>
> ขอให้ทำให้ดีที่สุด

I wish continued happiness to all the staff.

> Kaw hai pha-nak-ngan thook kon mee kwam-sook ta-lawt pai.
>
> ขอให้พนักงานทุกคนมีความสุขตลอดไป

Reporting a request (I told him to/etc.) -

I told John to go instead of me.

> Phom bawk hai John pai thaen phom. (or *Phom bawk John hai pai...*)
>
> ผมบอกให้จอห์นไปแทนผม

She invited me to visit her at her house.

> Kao chuan hai chan pai ha thee ban. (or *Kao chuan chan hai pai...*)
>
> เค้าชวนให้ฉันไปหาที่บ้าน

He wants you to go to a party at his house.

> Kao yak hai koon pai ngan pa-tee thee ban kao.
>
> เค้าอยากให้คุณไปงานปาร์ตี้ที่บ้านเค้า

He asked me to help him fix the car.

    Kao kaw̆ (hai) phŏm̆ chuay sawm̆ rot hai.

    เค้าขอ(ให้)ผมช่วยซ่อมรถให้

I had him tell Phet to come and see me here.

    Chan hai kao pai bawk Phet hai ma haj chan thee-nee.

    ฉันให้เค้าไปบอกเพชรให้มาหาฉันที่นี่

He had me come and tell you again.

    Kao hai phŏm̆ ma bawk koon eeg krang.

    เค้าให้ผมมาบอกคุณอีกครั้ง

A: What did she ask you to do?

    Kao kaw̆ hai tham a-rai?

    เค้าขอให้ทำอะไร

B: She asked me to watch the children for a while.

    Kao kaw̆ hai chan chuay doo(lae) dek-dek hai sak kroo.

    เค้าขอให้ฉันช่วยดู(แล)เด็กๆ ให้สักครู่

Negative ("I told him not to...") - The negative is *mai hai/ya* ("don't/not allowed to") or *mai tawng* ("no need to").

I had Dam go and tell him not to go.

    Phŏm̆ hai Dam pai bawk kao wa mai pai. (or *wa ya pai/wa mai tawng pai*)

    ผมให้ดำไปบอกเค้าว่าไม่ไป

She told me not to buy jackfruit.

    Kao bawk phŏm̆ (wa) mai hai seu ka-noon.

    เค้าบอกผม(ว่า)ไม่ให้ซื้อขนุน

    Kao bawk (wa) mai hai phŏm̆ seu ka-noon.

    เค้าบอก(ว่า)ไม่ให้ผมซื้อขนุน

He asked me not to make dinner.

    Kao kaw̆ hai chan mai tawng tham a-han̆ yen.

    เค้าขอให้ฉันไม่ต้องทำอาหารเย็น

9. CONJUNCTIONS

Patterns with conjunctions in Thai are similar to those in English, but in Thai clauses are often reversed and words omitted if they're understood in context. There are also formal/written versions of some words. *Gaw* is common in examples in this chapter. It's included as a general linking word (subject-predicate) and to mean "too/also", "subsequently", or "consequently".

AND

To connect words and phrases - *gap/laeo (gaw)/lae* - These are interchangable for joining words and phrases. The first also means "with", and the second also means "then". The third is more formal. *Duay* may be included at the end for "also".

I bought a shirt and some shoes.

    Phom seu seua gap rawng-thao.

    ผมซื้อเสื้อกับรองเท้า

This place is quiet and also clean.

    Thee-nee ngiap laeo (gaw) sa-at (duay).

    ที่นี่เงียบแล้ว(ก็)สะอาด(ด้วย)

To connect clauses - *laeo (gaw)* - Gaw is optional, put after either *laeo* or the subject of the second clause.

If you go to see her and she's not there, please call and let me know.

    Tha koon pai haj theuh, laeo (gaw) theuh mai yoo, chuay tho ma bawk phom duay.

    ถ้าคุณไปหาเธอแล้ว(ก็)เธอไม่อยู่ ช่วยโทรมาบอกผมด้วย

Last night it rained and the wind blew hard.

    Meua-keun-nee fon tok, laeo lom (gaw) phat raeng duay.

    เมื่อคืนนี้ฝนตกแล้วลม(ก็)พัดแรงด้วย

In this sentence *yang* means "and still something else". *Eeg* emphasizes "also".

He's a good student, and he's also hardworking.

    Kao rian geng, laeo yang ka-yan (eeg) duay.

    เค้าเรียนเก่งแล้วยังขยัน(อีก)ด้วย

ALSO/TOO/EITHER

"Also" has two meanings which are expressed differently in Thai.

Meaning "in addition" - duay/eeg tang hak - *Tang hak* alone means "instead" or "separately" (under "instead" on page 159). *Duay* may be put after both items, as in the last sentence.

I'm going to Had Yai, and ("then") I'm also going to Songkla.

Phom ja pai Had Yai, laeo leuy pai Song-kla duay.

ผมจะไปหาดใหญ่แล้วเลยไปสงขลาด้วย

This house isn't only big, it's cheap.

Ban lang nee mai chai tae yai thao-nan, yang thook eeg tang hak.

บ้านหลังนี้ไม่ใช่แต่ใหญ่เท่านั้น ยังถูกอีกต่างหาก

A: Are you attending school now, Moo?

Tawn-nee Moo rian nang-seu yoo reu plao?

ตอนนี้หมูเรียนหนังสืออยู่รึเปล่า

B: I go to school and I also work.

Rian duay. Tham-ngan duay.

เรียนด้วย ทำงานด้วย

Meaning "likewise"—*gaw* alone - gaw...(meuan-gan/duay) - Here the subjects are different—"I like it and John likes it too" not "I like Coke and I like Pepsi too". *Gaw* alone is "also", put after the second subject. Variations are to put *gaw* after both subjects and to include *meuan-gan* or *duay* (or *meuan-gan duay*) at the end.

Thai food is delicious, and so is Chinese food.

A-han Thai (gaw) a-roi. A-han Jeen gaw a-roi (meuan-gan/duay).

อาหารไทย(ก็)อร่อย อาหารจีนก็อร่อย(เหมือนกัน/ด้วย)

A: I don't have any money at all.

Chan mai mee ngeuhn leuy.

ฉันไม่มีเงินเลย

B: I don't have any either.

Chan gaw mai mee (meuan-gan/duay).

ฉันก็ไม่มี(เหมือนกัน/ด้วย)

A: Over there they have windsurfers for rent.

Thee-noon mee win-seuhf hai chao.

ที่โน่นมี วินเซิฟให้เช่า

B: But they have them here too.

Tae thee-nee gaw mee, na.

แต่ที่นี่ก็มีนะ

A: I've been a soldier.

    Phom keuy pen tha-hang ma gawn.

    ผมเคยเป็นทหารมาก่อน

B: So have I.

    Phom gaw keuy (meuang-gan/duay).

    ผมก็เคย(เหมือนกัน/ด้วย)

A: When you go to Germany I'll ("probably") miss you.

    Pai Yeuh-ra-mun laeo chan kong kit theung (koon).

    ไปเยอรมันแล้วฉันคงคิดถึง(คุณ)

B: Me too.

    Phom gaw meuang-gan.

    ผมก็เหมือนกัน

NOTES ON "ALSO":

1. "Also" and "either" are used more generally in Thai than in English, for example, in the response here *meuan-gan* is included even though the first person didn't say directly that he didn't know. This is inferred because the question was asked.

A: Is he coming?

    Kao ma mai?

    เค้ามามั้ย

B: I don't know ("either").

    Chan gaw mai roo meuang-gan.

    ฉันก็ไม่รู้เหมือนกัน

Meuan-gan in this sentence compares this shop to other shops which may have been previously referred to or not.

This shop has some shirts that are cheap (also).

    Ran nee gaw mee seua bang tua thee thook meuang-gan.

    ร้านนี้ก็มีเสื้อบางตัวที่ถูกเหมือนกัน

2. *Duay* (or *sa duay*) at the end of statements can express surprise.

Oh, your house has a swimming pool ("also").

    Oh, ban koon mee sa wai-nam duay.

    โอ บ้านคุณมีสระว่ายน้ำด้วย

3. *Chen dio-gan* is a formal/written form of "also". It means "like/in the same way".

My girlfriend doesn't like this room, and I don't like it either.

    Faen (phom) mai chawp hawng nee, laeo phom gaw mai chawp chen dio-gan.

    แฟน(ผม)ไม่ชอบห้องนี้แล้วผมก็ไม่ชอบเช่นเดียวกัน

ALTHOUGH/EVEN THOUGH/EVEN IF

The following phrases are used interchangably for "although", "even though", and "even if". *Ja* may be included to show that the meaning is future or hypothetical, and *gaw* can be placed between the subject and verb of the second clause (or the clause that doesn't have "even though/even if") with the meaning of "still".

1. theung (wa)/mae (wa)/theung mae (wa) - *Theung* and *mae* have different meanings. *Theung* means "arrive/reach to" and here refers to a situation reaching a certain point ("even if it reaches this point"). *Mae* separates out a condition ("even if this happens"). "But" may be included as in the fourth example. Don't confuse *mae wa* with *mai wa* ("whether or not").

Even if you notify the police, you'll (probably) never get your camera back.

    Theung koon ja jaeng tam-ruat, koon gaw kong ja mai dai glawng keun.

    ถึงคุณจะแจ้งตำรวจคุณก็คงจะไม่ได้กล้องคืน

Even if he doesn't go, I'll go.

    Mae (wa) kao mai pai, chan gaw ja pai.

    แม่(ว่า)เค้าไม่ไปฉันก็จะไป

Even though she can't speak Thai, she can still have a good time.

    Mae kao ja phoot Thai mai dai, kao gaw yang sa-nook dai.

    แม้เค้าจะพูดไทยไม่ได้เค้าก็ยังสนุกได้

Even though it's raining, ("but") he still wants to go.

    Theung fon (ja) tok, tae kao gaw yang yak ja pai.

    ถึงฝน(จะ)ตกแต่เค้าก็ยังอยากจะไป

2. thang thee/thang-thang thee - These phrases are used in the same way as *theung* and *mae*.

He gave me some money, although he didn't have much.

    Kao hai ngeuhn phom, thang-thang thee kao (gaw) mai koi mee.

    เค้าให้เงินผมทั้งๆ ที่เค้า(ก็)ไม่ค่อยมี

Even though it's the rainy season ("but") they're going to Phuket.

    Thang thee pen na fonj, tae kao gaw ja pai Phoo-get.

    ทั้งที่เป็นหน้าฝนแต่เค้าก็จะไปภูเก็ต

3. ka-nat - Here "even though" is stronger, having the meaning that even if something very strong happens the action will still go through. *Kanat* means "size", "extent" or "magnitude" and here means "even though it's reached the extent that...".

Dam is so stubborn. Even if you don't let her, she'll go.

    Dam nia deu, na. Ka-nat koon mai hai theuh pai, theuh gaw yang ja pai eeg.

    ดำเนียดื้อนะ ขนาดคุณไม่ให้เธอไปเธอก็ยังจะไปอีก

despite - In English, "despite" is followed by a noun. The word doesn't exist in Thai and sentences are stated with "although". ("Despite the weather" is "although the weather was bad").

Despite the weather, the fair was (still) fun.

    Theung a-gat (ja) mai dee, ngan gaw (yang) sa-nook.

    ถึงอากาศ(จะ)ไม่ดีงานก็(ยัง)สนุก

BECAUSE

There are four ways to say "because".

1. phraw (wa) - This is the most common. *Gaw* can be included before *phraw (wa)* to make the reason sound hypothetical and understated.

He had to leave because his contract was over.

    Kao tawng glap phraw wa mot sunj-ya laeo.

    เค้าต้องกลับเพราะว่าหมดสัญญาแล้ว

If Noi doesn't come, it's (probably) because she doesn't have time.

    Tha Noi mai ma, kong pen phraw wa kao mai mee way-la jing-jing.

    ถ้าน้อยไม่มาคงเป็นเพราะว่าเค้าไม่มีเวลาจริงๆ

I like it because it's so cheap.

    Chawp gaw phraw wa mun thook dee.

    ชอบก็เพราะว่ามันถูกดี

I'm unhappy because of her.

    Phomj siaj-jai phraw theuh.

    ผมเสียใจเพราะเธอ

A: Why isn't Gai planning to go (anymore)?

    Tham-mai Gai mai pai eeg.

    ทำไมไก่ไม่ไปอีก

B: It might be because she's already started school.

 At jà pèn phraw wâ kao peuht theuhm laeo.

 อาจจะเป็นเพราะว่าเค้าเปิดเทอมแล้ว

A: Why didn't he come?

 Tham-mai kao mâi ma?

 ทำไมเค้าไม่มา

B: It's because he's forgetful.

 (Thee kao mâi ma) nee gaw phraw wâ kao kee leum.

 (ที่เค้าไม่มา)นี่ก็เพราะว่าเค้าขี้ลืม

With "therefore" - When the "because" clause is first, "therefore" (*leuy, theung,* or *jeung*) is included in the second clause. *Gaw* is used alone in the same way with the meaning of "subsequently" (third sentence).

Because she's exceptional, she ("therefore") became the boss quickly.

 Phraw kao geng, gaw leuy dâi pèn huaŋ-nâ reo.

 เพราะเค้าเก่งก็เลยได้เป็นหัวหน้าเร็ว

We can't go because the car is broken down.

 Phraw wâ rot siaŋ, rao theung pai mâi dâi.

 เพราะว่ารถเสียเราถึงไปไม่ได้

Because I failed the entrance exam I quit going to school.

 Phraw wâ phom sawp "en-thran" mâi dâi, phom gaw mâi rian taw.

 เพราะว่าผมสอบเอนทรานส์ไม่ได้ผมก็ไม่เรียนต่อ

2. neuang jak - This is more formal than *phraw (wa)* and can be translated as "owing to", "on account of", "due to", or "because of the fact that" (followed by clause or noun).

Because there aren't enough teachers, the school can't open.

 Neuang jak (gan thee) kroo mâi phaw, rong-rian leuy peuht mâi dâi.

 เนื่องจาก(การที่)ครูไม่พอโรงเรียนเลยเปิดไม่ได้

3. (duay) kwam thee - This is also more formal and means "because" or "because of the fact that". *Duay* isn't optional when it's in the middle of the sentence as in the second example.

Because I wanted to know, I bought a book.

 (Duay) kwam thee yak roo, (chan) leuy seu nang-seu ma an.

 (ด้วย)ความที่อยากรู้(ฉัน)เลยซื้อหนังสือมาอ่าน

He drove very fast because he was late.

 Kao kàp rot reo mak duay kwam thee mun sai laeo.

 เค้าขับรถเร็วมากด้วยความที่มันสายแล้ว

Here *thee* is optional before *pen* with the phrase *kwam pen kon jai-rawn* (without *thee*) meaning "being a hot-tempered person". This is explained under "being" on page 15.

Because he was hot-tempered, he hit his boss.

Duay kwam thee kao pen kon jai-rawn, kao chok huaɟ-na kao.

ด้วยความที่เค้าเป็นคนใจร้อนเค้าชกหัวหน้าเค้า

Duay kwam (thee) pen kon jai-rawn, kao chok huaɟ-na kao.

ด้วยความ(ที่)เป็นคนใจร้อนเค้าชกหัวหน้าเค้า

4. because/in that - thee/trong thee -

You and I are the same in that we like to take it easy.

Koon gap phomɟ meuaŋ-gan (trong) thee chawp sa-bai sa-bai.

คุณกับผมเหมือนกัน(ตรง)ที่ชอบสบายๆ

The discussion wasn't very good because not many people participated.

Gan a-phee-prai krang nee mai koi dee (trong) thee mee kon ruam (sa-daeng kwam henɟ) noi.

การอภิปรายครั้งนี้ไม่ค่อยดี(ตรง)ที่มีคนร่วม(แสดงความเห็น)น้อย

BUT

tae/tae wa/tae gaw - These are interchangable. *Gaw* is put after the subject of the clause beginning with "but" (if the subject isn't omitted). It means "still" or "also" and makes the sentence understated.

I thought he wasn't coming, but he came.

Kit wa kao (ja) mai ma, tae kao gaw ma.

คิดว่าเค้า(จะ)ไม่มาแต่เค้าก็มา

This house is small, but it's nice.

Ban langɟ nee lek, tae gaw suayɟ.

บ้านหลังนี้เล็กแต่ก็สวย

He thought I was rich but I'm not.

Kao kit wa phomɟ ruay tae mai chai.

เค้าคิดว่าผมรวยแต่ไม่ใช่

We could go by bus, but if we took a car it would be better.

Keun rot-may gaw dai, tae tha ao rot pai gaw (ja) dee gwa.

ขึ้นรถเมล์ก็ได้แต่ถ้าเอารถไปก็(จะ)ดีกว่า

It's not that I don't like him, but I already have a boyfriend.

(Mun) mai chai wa chan mai chawp kao, tae wa chan mee faen laeo.

(มัน)ไม่ใช่ว่าฉันไม่ชอบเค้าแต่ว่าฉันมีแฟนแล้ว

"But" wouldn't be included in this response in English.

A: Are you on vacation?

> Koon <u>yoot</u> phak rawn <u>reuh</u>?
>
> คุณหยุดพักร้อนเหรอ

B: I'm not on vacation. I'm sick. ("but I'm sick")

> Mai (dai) <u>yoot</u> ngan, <u>tae</u> (wa) mai sa-bai.
>
> ไม่(ได้)หยุดงานแต่(ว่า)ไม่สบาย

Gaw alone for "but" - *Tae* may be omitted and *gaw* (meaning "subsequently") used alone when one action follows another and the meaning is clear in context. The last example is reduced to the fewest possible words.

I went to see them but no one was there.

> <u>Phom</u> pai <u>ha</u> gaw mai mee krai <u>yoo</u>.
>
> ผมไปหาก็ไม่มีใครอยู่

I went to see it, but it wasn't really that beautiful.

> Chan pai doo ma laeo, (<u>tae</u>) gaw mai <u>suay</u> thao-<u>rai</u>.
>
> ฉันไปดูมาแล้ว(แต่)ก็ไม่สวยเท่าไหร่

I told her but she wouldn't believe me. (can also mean "whenever I tell her things...")

> <u>Bawk</u> gaw mai cheua.
>
> บอกก็ไม่เชื่อ

EXCEPT/BESIDES/UNLESS

except - nawk-<u>jak</u>/yok wayn - These are interchangable for "except". The first, meaning "besides", is more common at the beginning of sentences. The second, referring to something omitted or skipped, is usually put within the sentence.

Everyone is going except Lek.

> Nawk-<u>jak</u> Lek laeo, thook kon pai <u>mot</u>.
>
> นอกจากเล็กแล้วทุกคนไปหมด

> Thook kon ja pai, yok wayn Lek.
>
> ทุกคนจะไปยกเว้นเล็ก

except that/only that - nawk-<u>jak</u> wa/phiang <u>tae</u> (wa) -

It would be nice to live here, except that there's no place to swim.

> <u>Yoo</u> nee gaw dee, nawk-<u>jak</u> wa (mun) mai mee thee wai-nam.
>
> อยู่นี่ก็ดีนอกจากว่า(มัน)ไม่มีที่ว่ายน้ำ

I want it a lot, it's only that I don't have the money to buy it.

> Yak dai mak, phiang <u>tae</u> (wa) mai mee ngeuhn seu.
>
> อยากได้มากเพียงแต่(ว่า)ไม่มีเงินซื้อ

-only that (something small) - phiang kae wa - Here the condition you're referring to is small or unimportant, compared with *phiang tae (wa)* where there's only one condition which hasn't been met.

They're different only in that one wears glasses and the other one doesn't.

>   Kao mai meuan-gan phiang kae wa kon neung sai waen-ta (tae) eeg kon mai sai.
>   เค้าไม่เหมือนกันเพียงแค่ว่าคนหนึ่งใส่แว่นตา(แต่)อีกคนหนึ่งไม่ใส่

-only one thing wrong - sia yang dio/sia tae wa -

The party was fun except that there wasn't enough beer.

>   Ngan liang sa-nook mak, sia yang dio bia mai phaw.
>   งานเลี้ยงสนุกมากเสียอย่างเดียวเบียร์ไม่พอ

This island is beautiful, it's just a little too far away.

>   Gaw nee suay mak, sia tae wa glai pai noi.
>   เกาะนี้สวยมากเสียแต่ว่าไกลไปหน่อย

-only one thing left - leua tae (wa) -

We're ready to go except that we haven't paid for the room yet.

>   Rao phrawm ja pai gan laeo, leua tae wa rao yang mai dai jai ka hawng leuy.
>   เราพร้อมจะไปกันแล้วเหลือแต่ว่าเรายังไม่ได้จ่ายค่าห้องเลย

unless - nawk-jak (wa)/(yok) wayn tae (wa) - These phrases mean "unless" but they're not used much in conversational Thai. The pattern is more often formed with "if" as in the second way to say the first example.

I'm not going unless you go./I'm not going if you you don't go.

>   Phom mai pai, nawk-jak (wa) koon ja pai./Phom mai pai tha koon mai pai.
>   ผมไม่ไปนอกจาก(ว่า)คุณจะไป/ผมไม่ไปถ้าคุณไม่ไป

It will definitely flood unless it stops raining tonight.

>   Nam ja thuam nae-nawn, wayn tae (wa) fon ja yoot tok keun-nee.
>   น้ำจะท่วมแน่นอนเว้นแต่(ว่า)ฝนจะหยุดตกคืนนี้

I'll quit this job unless they give me my salary.

>   Phom gaw ja la awk jak ngan yok wayn tae kao ja keun ngeuhn deuan hai.
>   ผมก็จะลาออกจากงานยกเว้นแต่เค้าจะขึ้นเงินเดือนให้

besides/other than - nawk-jak - Other translations are "apart from", "in addition to", and "but".

I've never worked any place but here.

>   Chan mai keuy tham-ngan thee-nai nawk-jak thee-nee.
>   ฉันไม่เคยทำงานที่ไหนนอกจากที่นี่

Besides teaching, what other work are you doing now?

Tawn-nee, nawk-jak sawn nang-seu (laeo), koon tham-ngan a-rai eeg?

ตอนนี้นอกจากสอนหนังสือ(แล้ว)คุณทำงานอะไรอีก

besides this/that - nawk-jak nee/nan - Another translation is "in addition to this/that".

A: Nan Province has a lot of old temples, doesn't it?

Jang-wat Nan nia, mee wat gao-gao yeuh mak, chai mai?

จังหวัดน่านเนี่ยมีวัดเก่าๆ เยอะมากใช่มั้ย

B: Yes. And besides that there are ("still") a lot of other interesting things.

Chai. Nawk-jak nan yang mee a-rai na song-jai eeg lai yang.

ใช่ นอกจากนั้นยังมีอะไรน่าสนใจอีกหลายอย่าง

IF

tha - "Probably" (kong) may be included with "if" to make the meaning less direct, as in the first example. Use wa for "if" in sentences like "I don't know if he's coming".

If it hadn't flooded we (probably) would have been there by now.

Tha nam mai thuam rao kong pai theung laeo.

ถ้าน้ำไม่ท่วมเราคงไปถึงแล้ว

If I go, you can go with me.

Tha chan pai, koon (ja) pai duay gaw dai.

ถ้าฉันไปคุณ(จะ)ไปด้วยก็ได้

If I go, I'll call you. ("then I'll call you")

Tha (ja) pai, laeo phom ja tho bawk.

ถ้า(จะ)ไปแล้วผมจะโทรบอก

If you don't take your umbrella and it rains, what will you do?

Tha koon mai ao rom pai duay, laeo (gaw) fon tok, koon ja tham yang-ngai?

ถ้าคุณไม่เอาร่มไปด้วยแล้ว(ก็)ฝนตกคุณจะทำยังไง

Gaw is often included with "if" to link the first and subsequent states or actions. It also reinforces the hypothetical meaning and can mean "consequently".

If I speak Thai well I can probably get a job.

Tha chan phoot Thai geng, (chan) gaw kong dai ngan tham.

ถ้าฉันพูดไทยเก่ง(ฉัน)ก็คงได้งานทำ

Chan gaw kong dai ngan tha chan phoot Thai geng.

ฉันก็คงได้งานถ้าฉันพูดไทยเก่ง

If he went, he didn't tell me.

Tha kao dai pai, kao gaw mai dai bawk phom.

ถ้าเค้าได้ไปเค้าก็ไม่ได้บอกผม

If I go, I'll go a little late.

Tha pai, gaw ja pai cha nit noi.

ถ้าไปก็จะไปช้านิดหน่อย

If you eat it all you'll be full.

Tha gin mot gaw ja im.

ถ้ากินหมดก็จะอิ่ม

"If" is used in Thai for "when" in the future.

I'll go home when I'm out of money.

Phom ja glap ban, tha ngeuhn glai ja mot.

ผมจะกลับบ้านถ้าเงินใกล้จะหมด

Meaning "then/after" - Here the second action or state is a consequence of the first. *Tha* may be omitted and *laeo* or *laeo gaw* used for "then". This pattern is explained under "after" on page 336.

If you take this medicine you'll feel better. (Take this medicine then you'll feel better.)

Gin ya nee laeo (gaw) (ja) roo-seuk dee keun.

กินยานี้แล้ว(ก็)(จะ)รู้สึกดีขึ้น

Commands with "if"—*gaw* alone - In commands *tha* may be omitted and *gaw* used alone to mean "consequently".

If you don't understand, please ask me.

(Tha) koon mai kao-jai, gaw tham chan, na.

(ถ้า)คุณไม่เข้าใจก็ถามฉันนะ

If you have a headache you should take some medicine.

Puat hua gaw gin ya, see.

ปวดหัวก็กินยาซิ

If it's really far then take the car.

Glai mak gaw ao rot pai see.

ไกลมากก็เอารถไปซิ

If you don't have anything else to do, you can just go home.

Mai mee thoo-ra a-rai, gaw glap ban dai leuy.

ไม่มีธุระอะไรก็กลับบ้านได้เลย

If/when you leave please lock the door.

Awk jak ban gaw lawk pra-too hai dee, na.

ออกจากบ้านก็ล็อคประตูให้ดีนะ

If it's yours, take it./Whatever is yours you can take.

(Tha pen) kawng kawng koon, koon gaw ao pai.

(ถ้าเป็น)ของของคุณ คุณก็เอาไป

Longer forms - thă hak (wă)/thă pheua - The first means "if, supposing that" or "if, in the event that" and the second is "if, in case".

If I go, will you go?

    Thă hak (wă) phŏm pai, koon jă pai măi?

    ถ้าหาก(ว่า)ผมไปคุณจะไปมั้ย

If he comes back, please tell him. (not likely that he'll come back)

    Thă pheua kao glăp ma, bawk kao duay, na.

    ถ้าเผื่อเค้ากลับมาบอกเค้าด้วยนะ

IN CASE

pheua - *Pheua* here has a low tone and means "as a surplus" or "to have more than needed as a contingency". In English it's translated as "in case" or "for". See also "extra" on pages 217-218.

Take an umbrella in case it rains.

    Ao rom pai duay pheua fŏn tŏk.

    เอาร่มไปด้วยเผื่อฝนตก

Take your flashlight in case Lek forgot his.

    Ao fai-chai pai duay pheua Lek leum (ao kawng kao pai).

    เอาไฟฉายไปด้วยเผื่อเล็กลืม(เอาของเค้าไป)

In case I'm not there, take these to give to everyone.

    Pheua chan măi dăi pai thee-nan, ao un nee pai hăi thook kon duay.

    เผื่อฉันไม่ได้ไปที่นั่นเอาอันนี้ไปให้ทุกคนด้วย

We'd better call him again in case she didn't tell him.

    Rao na jă tho hai kao eeg pheua theuh măi dăi bawk kao.

    เราน่าจะโทรหาเค้าอีกเผื่อเธอไม่ได้บอกเค้า

Please buy me a pen. (in addition to what else you're doing)

    Seu pak-ga ma pheua (phŏm) duay, na.

    ซื้อปากกามาเผื่อ(ผม)ด้วยนะ

INSTEAD

There are three words/phrases.

1. thaen (noun)/thaen thee jă (verb) - *Thaen* alone is used with nouns or pronouns ("instead of me") and *thaen thee ja* is used with verbs ("instead of walking"). *Thaen* is also a verb meaning "replace" or "substitute".

They changed their minds and went to Phuket instead of Chiang Mai.

    Phuak kao plian-jai, pai Phoo-get thaen Chiang Mai.

    พวกเค้าเปลี่ยนใจไปภูเก็ตแทนเชียงใหม่

Please go to work for me. ("instead of me/and substitute for me")

    Chuay pai tham-ngan thaen chan duay.

    ช่วยไปทำงานแทนฉันด้วย

Instead of going home he went drinking with some friends.

    Thaen thee ja glap ban, kao (glap) pai gin lao gap pheuan.

    แทนที่จะกลับบ้านเค้า(กลับ)ไปกินเหล้ากับเพื่อน

Instead of being sad ("but") she laughed.

    Thaen thee ja siaj-jai, tae kao (glap) huaj-raw.

    แทนที่จะเสียใจแต่เค้า(กลับ)หัวเราะ

2. mai chai - *Mai chai* is "not", translated here as "instead".

School stops at two today instead of at three. (or "at two, not at three")

    Wan-nee rong-rian leuhk bai sawnɤ, mai chai bai samɤ.

    วันนี้โรงเรียนเลิกบ่ายสองไม่ใช่บ่ายสาม

You should play sports instead of cards.

    Koon kuan ja pai len gee-la. Mai chai len phai.

    คุณควรจะไปเล่นกีฬา ไม่ใช่เล่นไพ่

If we take the bus it will be ten baht, not a hundred baht.

    Tha rao keun rot-may mun ja pen sip baht, mai chai roi baht.

    ถ้าเราขึ้นรถเมล์มันจะเป็นสิบบาทไม่ใช่ร้อยบาท

3. tang hak - This means "on the contrary" or "contrary to what you think" and is used when stating something different from what was said or thought. *Tang hak* also means "separately" and *eeg tang hak* is "also".

It's he, instead, who has to work.

    Pen kao, tang hak, thee tawnɤ tham-ngan.

    เป็นเค้าต่างหากที่ต้องทำงาน

OR

reuɤ/reuɤ wa - The second has the meanings "or, alternatively" and "or if not, then".

Do you want to take a walk, or rest at the hotel?

    Koon ja pai deuhn len, reuɤ (wa) ja nawn phak thee rong-raem?

    คุณจะไปเดินเล่นหรือว่าจะนอนพักที่โรงแรม

Will you go, or do you want me to go?

    Theuh ja pai, reuɤ wa, ja hai chan pai?

    เธอจะไปหรือว่าจะให้ฉันไป

A: Do you want coffee, or what?

    Jă ăo ga-fae reuɲ a-rai dee?

        จะเอากาแฟหรืออะไรดี

B: Coffee, or anything else would be fine.

    Ga-fae reuɲ a-rai gaw dai.

        กาแฟหรืออะไรก็ได้

or if not - reuɲ mai -

You can give it to me or ("if not") you can leave it with someone else.

    Koon ăo hai phŏmɲ, reuɲ mai, gaw fak pheuan wai gaw dai.

        คุณเอาให้ผมหรือไม่ก็ฝากเพื่อนไว้ก็ได้

EXPRESSION: reuɲ ngai - This means "or what?".

You don't like it or what?

    Mai chawp reuɲ ngai?

        ไม่ชอบหรือไง

OR ELSE/OTHERWISE

(tha) mai yang-ngan/mee-cha-nan - The first is literally "if it's not like that" and the second is formal. This is often expressed in English as "or" alone.

Lek should leave now, otherwise he won't get to see her.

    Lek kuan ja pai dioɲ-nee, tha mai yang-ngan, kao ja mai jeuh theuh.

        เล็กควรจะไปเดี๋ยวนี้ ถ้าไม่ยังงั้นเค้าจะไม่เจอเธอ

Finish it now, or we won't be able to send it today.

    Tham hai set na, mai yang-ngan rao ja song mai than wan-nee.

        ทำให้เสร็จนะ ไม่ยังงั้นเราจะส่งไม่ทันวันนี้

Give me ("send") your money, or you die.

    Song ngeuhn ma, mee-cha-nan koon tai.

        ส่งเงินมามิฉะนั้นคุณตาย

SO/THEREFORE

There are seven ways to say "so" or "therefore" in Thai.

1. (gaw) leuy - This is put after the subject of the clause beginning with "so/therefore", although the subject may be omitted. *Gaw* here means "consequently". In the last sentence the phrase is expanded to *laeo gaw leuy*.

It's very difficult, so people don't understand it. (or "didn't understand it")

    Mun yak mak, kon (gaw) leuy mai kao-jai.

        มันยากมาก คน(ก็)เลยไม่เข้าใจ

I studied Thai a lot, so then I was able to speak it.

    Chan rian pha-saj Thai yeuh, (gaw) leuy phoot dai.

    ฉันเรียนภาษาไทยเยอะ(ก็)เลยพูดได้

My father won't let me go, so I'm not going. ("Because my father..")

    Phraw wa phaw mai hai pai, chan (gaw) leuy (ja) mai pai.

    เพราะว่าพ่อไม่ให้ไปฉัน(ก็)เลย(จะ)ไม่ไป

I don't have enough money so I'd better not go.

    Phomj mai mee ngeuhn phaw, phomj (gaw) leuy ja mai pai dee gwa.

    ผมไม่มีเงินพอ ผม(ก็)เลยจะไม่ไปดีกว่า

The car was old so I sold it.

    Rot gao laeo, gaw leuy kaij.

    รถเก่าแล้ว ก็เลยขาย

It was very expensive so I didn't buy it.

    Mun phaeng, laeo gaw leuy mai dai seu.

    มันแพงแล้วก็เลยไม่ได้ซื้อ

2. jeung - This is the same as *leuy* but less common. It's put after the subject of the second clause.

The movie wasn't very good, so we left early.

    Nangj mai sa-nook, rao jeung glap ban gawn.

    หนังไม่สนุกเราจึงกลับบ้านก่อน

3. (leuy) theungj - *Theung*, meaning "arrive/reach to", is used for "therefore" when the actions or states are more closely related—the first action or state caused you to "arrive" at the second. In the next section *gaw* is used alone with the same meaning. *Leuy* and *jeung* may also be used in these sentences with less meaning of consequence.

I got so hungry that I went out.

    Hiuj kao, leuy theungj awk pai.

    หิวข้าวเลยถึงออกไป

There wasn't any paper so I went out and bought some.

    Mai mee gra-dat leuy, theungj awk pai seu.

    ไม่มีกระดาษเลยถึงออกไปซื้อ

I was angry, so I told her.

    Chan grot, theungj dai bawk kao.

    ฉันโกรธถึงได้บอกเค้า

It's because of some business that I'm calling you.

    Phraw wa mee thoo-ra, na see, phomj theungj tho ma.

    เพราะว่ามีธุระนะซิผมถึงโทรมา

4. gaw - Here *gaw* alone is like *theung*—the first action causes the second to happen. *Gaw* is informal and the meaning ("consequently") is understood in context.

I didn't know, so I asked him.

> Phom mai roo, phom gaw tham./Phom mai roo, phom theung tham.
>
> ผมไม่รู้ผมก็ถาม/ผมไม่รู้ผมถึงถาม

He didn't give it to me so I just took it.

> Kao mai hai, chan gaw ao ma leuy.
>
> เค้าไม่ให้ฉันก็เอามาเลย

5. stronger form - theung gap - When *gap* is included the meaning is even stronger—the first action or state was so strong that you had to arrive at the second. *Theung gap* can be expanded to *theung gap wa*, but this isn't as common. *Gaw* alone can also be used here except in the last example, which is a question. This pattern is similar to "so...that/up to the point that" on page 223.

I was so angry that I had to tell her.

> Chan grot mak theung (gap) tawng bawk kao.
>
> ฉันโกรธมากถึง(กับ)ต้องบอกเค้า
>
> Chan grot mak gaw tawng bawk kao.
>
> ฉันโกรธมากก็ต้องบอกเค้า

I had some urgent business, so I had to call you.

> Phom mee thoo-ra duan, na see, phom theung (gap) tawng tho ma.
>
> ผมมีธุระด่วนนะซิ ผมถึง(กับ)ต้องโทรมา

Because it rained yesterday I got a fever.

> Phraw fon tok meua-wan phom (gaw) theung (gap) pen kai leuy.
>
> เพราะฝนตกเมื่อวานผม(ก็)ถึง(กับ)เป็นไข้เลย

What's wrong with her that she can't tell you?

> Kao pen a-rai theung (gap) bawk mai dai?
>
> เค้าเป็นอะไรถึง(กับ)บอกไม่ได้

6. (phraw) cha-nan - This is formal and mostly written, but can be used in speaking to emphasize "so/therefore". *Leuy* or *jeung* are included with it.

I've been thinking of you, so I'm writing to you.

> Phom kit theung koon, (phraw) cha-nan phom jeung kian ma hai koon.
>
> ผมคิดถึงคุณ(เพราะ)ฉะนั้นผมจึงเขียนมาหาคุณ

7. dang-nan - This is the most formal and is usually only written.

You didn't come, so I went home.

> Koon mai ma, dang-nan phom jeung glap ban pai.
>
> คุณไม่มาดังนั้นผมจึงกลับบ้านไป

"SO/THEREFORE/THEN" IN RESPONSES

The following words and phrases are used in responses. The first three are used when the action in the response is a consequence of what the first person said. The fourth, *laeo*, is used when the action in the response simply follows what was first said, not when it's a consequence.

ngan/yang-ngan	means "therefore"
gaw	means "consequently", put after the subject
leuy/gaw leuy	stronger meaning of consequence, put after the subject
laeo	with the second action follows the first

Don't use *laeo* in these examples because "therefore" must be expressed.

A: He's not coming.

Kao mai ma.

เค้าไม่มา

B: Then I'm not going.

Ngan phom ja mai pai./Phom gaw mai pai./Phom leuy mai pai.

งั้นผมจะไม่ไป/ผมก็ไม่ไป/ผมเลยไม่ไป

A: I really like this watch.

Chan chawp na-lee-ga reuan nee mak.

ฉันชอบนาฬิกาเรือนนี้มาก

B: Then take it.

Ngan (gaw) ao pai leuy./Yang-ngan (gaw) ao pai leuy.

งั้น(ก็)เอาไปเลย/ยังงั้น(ก็)เอาไปเลย

A: There's no food at all.

Mai mee a-han leuy.

ไม่มีอาหารเลย

B: Then we have to go out and buy some.

Ngan tawng awk pai seu./Gaw tawng awk pai seu.

งั้นต้องออกไปซื้อ/ก็ต้องออกไปซื้อ

A: I don't have to work on Monday.

Chan mai tawng tham-ngan wan Jan.

ฉันไม่ต้องทำงานวันจันทร์

B: So we don't have to go back today.

(Rao) leuy mai tawng glap wan-nee.

เราเลยไม่ต้องกลับวันนี้

Any of the four may be used here, with *leuy* having the strongest meaning.

A: He didn't return the money.

    Kao mai dai keun ngeuhn.

    เค้าไม่ได้คืนเงิน

B: So don't give him any more.

    Gaw, mai tawng hai eeg./Laeo ya hai kao eeg, na./Rao leuy mai tawng hai eeg.

    ก็ไม่ต้องให้อีก/แล้วอย่าให้เค้าอีกนะ/เราเลยไม่ต้องให้อีก

Laeo, gaw, or *ngan* can be used in these responses, but not *leuy* because the meaning of consequence isn't strong enough.

A: I'll finish washing the clothes at around 5 P.M.

    Chan ja sak pha hai set pra-man ha mong yen.

    ฉันจะซักผ้าให้เสร็จประมาณห้าโมงเย็น

B: So I'll come and pick them up then.

    Laeo phom ja ma rap tawn-nan./Phom gaw ja ma rap tawn-nan.

    แล้วผมจะมารับตอนนั้น/ผมก็จะมารับตอนนั้น

A: It's not a money problem.

    Mun mai chai pan-ha reuang ngeuhn rawk.

    มันไม่ใช่ปัญหาเรื่องเงินหรอก

B: So what kind of a problem is it?

    Laeo mee pan-ha a-rai, la?/Ngan mee pan-ha a-rai, la?

    แล้วมีปัญหาอะไรล่ะ/งั้นมีปัญหาอะไรล่ะ

SO THAT/IN ORDER TO

There are three words or phrases—*pheua, theung,* and *gan thee ja...dai. Pheua* (with a falling tone) is also under "to/in order to (page 100), "in order to cause" (page 138), and "for" meaning "for the sake of" (page 273).

1. in order to/for the purpose of - pheua (thee) (ja) - Also *pheua wa.* In the second sentence *hai dai* is included for "in order to be able to".

Press this button to turn off the machine.

    Got poom nee pheua pit kreuang.

    กดปุ่มนี้เพื่อปิดเครื่อง

Maeo agreed to get up early so we could take the first bus.

    Maeo yawm teun chao pheua ja keun rot thio raek hai dai.

    แมวยอมตื่นเช้าเพื่อจะขึ้นรถเที่ยวแรกให้ได้

in order to cause/so that - pheua (tham) hai - *Hai* or *tham hai* are included after *pheua* for "cause". With *tham hai* the meaning is stronger than with *hai* alone. *Hai* may also be used alone for "in order to" when the phrase is in the middle of the sentence.

To get there on time we have to take a taxi.

Pheua (tham) hai rao pai theung trong way-la, rao tawng keun thaek-see.

เพื่อ(ทำ)ให้เราไปถึงตรงเวลาเราต้องขึ้นแท็กซี่

Please write the letters big so I can read them easily.

Chuay kian tua to-to, na, (pheua) hai chan an dai ngai.

ช่วยเขียนตัวโตๆ นะ(เพื่อ)ให้ฉันอ่านได้ง่าย

so that a condition will exist - pheua ja dai - Here *dai* refers to "getting" an action or state.

So I won't forget, I have to write it down in a notebook.

Pheua ja dai mai leum, chan tawng jot sai sa-moot wai.

เพื่อจะได้ไม่ลืมฉันต้องจดใส่สมุดไว้

I won't say anything, so she'll feel happy.

Chan mai phoot a-rai pheua kao ja dai sa-bai jai.

ฉันไม่พูดอะไรเพื่อเค้าจะได้สบายใจ

In this sentence *pheua* is omitted informally.

To be thin you have to eat less and exercise.

Ja phawm dai tawng ot a-han lae awk gam-lang gai.

จะผอมได้ต้องอดอาหารและออกกำลังกาย

With "if" - Sentences with "in order to" in English are commonly phrased with "if" in Thai.

To fix it you have to call the mechanic. ("If you want to fix it")

Tha tawng-gan sawm tawng riak chang. (or *Tha ja sawm...*)

ถ้าต้องการซ่อมต้องเรียกช่าง

2. theung (ja) - Here *theung* means "in order to arrive at a state or situation" and emphasizes that the first action must happen before the second can. This is similar to "before" (page 331) and "then" (page 335) but with a stronger meaning of consequence.

You have to be able to speak English in order to get this job.

Koon tawng phoot (pha-sa) Ang-grit dai, theung ja dai ngan nee.

คุณต้องพูด(ภาษา)อังกฤษได้ถึงจะได้งานนี้

If you work hard you'll have a lot of money.

Tham-ngan nak theung ja dai ngeuhn mak.

ทำงานหนักถึงจะได้เงินมาก

What did he do to be so rich?/What can I do to be rich?

    Tham yang-ngai theung ruay?/Tham yang-ngai (theung) ja ruay dai?

      ทำยังไงถึงรวย/ทำยังไง(ถึง)จะรวยได้

3. gan thee ja...dai - *Gan thee* is explained on pages 85-86.

In order to buy things cheaply, Westerners should be able to speak Thai.

    Gan thee ja seu kawng thook dai, fa-rang tawng phoot pha-sa Thai dai.

      การที่จะซื้อของถูกได้ฝรั่งต้องพูดภาษาไทยได้

WHETHER (OR NOT)

mai wa - "Or not" is *reu plao* or *reu mai* (the second is more formal). *Mai wa* is also used with "whatever", "whenever", etc, pages 174-182. Another meaning of "whether" is "if" in sentences like "I don't know whether he's coming". This is *wa* in Thai, explained in chapter 5. *Gaw* in these examples means "still" or "also".

Whether he comes or not, I'm (still) going.

    Mai wa kao ja ma reu plao, phom gaw ja pai.

      ไม่ว่าเค้าจะมารึเปล่าผมก็จะไป

I like going to the beach whether the sun is out or not.

    Chan chawp thio chai-hat mai wa daet awk reu mai (awk).

      ฉันชอบเที่ยวชายหาดไม่ว่าแดดออกรึไม่(ออก)

Whether he comes or not it's all the same.

    Mai wa kao ja ma reu mai ma gaw meuang-gan.

      ไม่ว่าเค้าจะมาหรือไม่มาก็เหมือนกัน

10. USING *GAW*

Meanings and functions - *Gaw* (pronounced falling/short) is used in many ways in spoken Thai. Basically it's a linking word that gives a hypothetical, indirect, and understated meaning to sentences, making them sound less emphatic and putting them into the context of the conversation. *Gaw* has five specific meanings for which it may be used alone, explained on the following pages:

1. hypothetical, 125-126

2. still, 106

3. also, 148-149

4. subsequently: happen by then, 90-91, 319; but, 154; before, 332; then, 335; after, 336

5. consequently: commands with "if", 157; so/therefore, 162; "so/therefore/then" in responses, 163-164; as soon as, 341

Gaw is also used, with one or more of the five meanings, in the following patterns:

- after the subject (offering information), 5-6
- with "it", 23-24
- reversed sentence order, 79, 82
- at the beginning of sentences, 168-169
- with repeated words, 169-171
- with "whatever", "whoever", 174-182
- with conjunctions:
  and, 147
  although, 150-151
  because, 151-153
  but, 153-154
  if, 156-157
  so/therefore, 160-164
  whether or not, 166
- with time:
  linking, after subject, 301
  before, 331-333
  then, 334-336
  after, 336-341
  as soon as, 341
  whenever/any time, 380
  sometimes, 381-382
- expressions with *gaw* , 171-174

GAW AT THE BEGINNING OF SENTENCES

When *gaw* is the first word of a sentence or reply (followed by a pause) it shows that you're reflecting on a thought and makes what you're about to say sound hypothetical, uncertain, understated, and also more polite because it's not stated abruptly.

To show uncertainty or to downplay answers -

A: Does this place have a lot of restaurants?

Thee-nee mee ran-a-han yeuh mai?

ที่นี่มีร้านอาหารเยอะมั้ย

B: It has around five or six.

Gaw, pra-man ha hok thee.

ก็ประมาณห้าหกที่

A: Is this restaurant good?

Ran-a-han nee dee mai?

ร้านอาหารนี้ดีมั้ย

B: Well, it's pretty good.

Gaw, dee (meuan-gan).

ก็ดี(เหมือนกัน)

Here *gaw* is put after the pronoun with the same meaning (or at the beginning of the sentence if the pronoun is omitted).

I don't know./I don't know either.

(Phom) gaw, mai roo meuan-gan.

(ผม)ก็ไม่รู้เหมือนกัน

We'll talk to Steve (about it).

Rao gaw ja kui gap Steve.

เราก็จะคุยกับสตีฟ

With a contradictory reply - Here *gaw* softens the reply. *Na* may be included at the end for the same reason.

A: This hotel is expensive.

Rong-raem nee phaeng.

โรงแรมนี้แพง

B: No, it's not really that expensive.

Gaw mai phaeng, na.

ก็ไม่แพงนะ

A: They don't have foreign liquor here, do they?

Thee-nee mai mee lao fa-rang, chai mai?

ที่นี่ไม่มีเหล้าฝรั่งใช่มั้ย

B: Yes, they do.

    Gaw mee, na.

    ก็มีนะ

With "because" - With *gaw* the reason sounds understated.

A: Why didn't John come?

    Tham-mai John mai ma?

    ทำไมจอห์นไม่มา

B: Because he was still working.

    Gaw, phraw wa kao yang tham-ngan yoo.

    ก็เพราะว่าเค้ายังทำงานอยู่

GAW WITH REPEATED WORDS

A common pattern in Thai is to say a word twice, first to bring it up and then to state it or comment on it. *Gaw* is put between the two words and can have various meanings depending on the sentence ("also", "still", "subsequently", or "consequently"). It also makes the sentence hypothetical.

Repeated adjectives - The adjective is first brought up, then stated again as a fact.

She's both rich and beautiful.

    Theuh ruay gaw ruay, suay gaw suay.

    เธอรวยก็รวย สวยก็สวย

He's not tall and he's not short.

    Kao soong gaw mai soong, tia gaw mai tia.

    เค้าสูงก็ไม่สูง เตี้ยก็ไม่เตี้ย

It's hot and there's also a lot of dust.

    Rawn gaw rawn, foon gaw yeuh.

    ร้อนก็ร้อน ฝุ่นก็เยอะ

Repeated verbs -

If I fall I fall./If it falls it falls.

    Tok gaw tok.

    ตกก็ตก

When I eat I eat a lot.

    Gin gaw gin yeuh.

    กินก็กินเยอะ

When/if I study I study hard.

    Rian laeo gaw rian jing.

    เรียนแล้วก็เรียนจริง

I drink and I smoke.

    (Gin) lao gaw gin. Boo-<u>ree</u> gaw <u>soop</u>.

    (กิน)เหล้าก็กิน บุหรี่ก็สูบ

If there's anything to do I'll do it.

    Mee a-rai tham gaw tham.

    มีอะไรทำก็ทำ

If we're going then let's go.

    Pai gaw pai <u>see</u>./Pai gaw pai leuy.

    ไปก็ไปซิ/ไปก็ไปเลย

If we're going to break up then let's just do it.

    Tha ja leuhk gan gaw leuhk (dai).

    ถ้าจะเลิกกันก็เลิก(ได้)

Here the verb is repeated in the second sentence with *gaw* for "also" or "still".

If it's cheap I'll buy it. If it's expensive I'll still buy it.

    <u>Thook</u> gaw seu. Phaeng gaw seu.

    ถูกก็ซื้อ แพงก็ซื้อ

These sentences are negative.

I can't go.

    Pai gaw pai mai dai.

    ไปก็ไปไม่ได้

I can't cook.

    Tham a-<u>han</u> gaw tham mai pen.

    ทำอาหารก็ทำไม่เป็น

I still can't remember your name.

    Jam cheu koon gaw yang jam mai dai.

    จำชื่อคุณก็ยังจำไม่ได้

When she should go to school she doesn't go.

    Pai rong-rian gaw mai pai.

    ไปโรงเรียนก็ไม่ไป

When it's time to eat he won't eat.

    Way-la gin, kao gaw mai gin.

    เวลากินเค้าก็ไม่กิน

The answer here is "if I go I go" and shows some indifference or understated politeness.

A: Do you want to go?

    <u>Yak</u> pai mai?

    อยากไปมั้ย

B: OK.

    Pai gaw pai.

    ไปก็ไป

Repeated verbs with "whatever/whoever" - Here the verb is repeated on either side of a question word. Examples with "whenever" are on page 380.

Anywhere he goes, he goes late.

    Pai thee-nai gaw pai sai.

    ไปที่ไหนก็ไปสาย

There's no way to get there. ("Anyway you go...")

    Pai yang-ngai gaw pai mai dai.

    ไปยังไงก็ไปไม่ได้

If I love someone I love him/her truly.

    Chan rak krai gaw rak jing.

    ฉันรักใครก็รักจริง

I can do anything.

    Tham a-rai gaw tham dai.

    ทำอะไรก็ทำได้

Nothing I eat tastes good.

    Chan gin a-rai gaw gin mai a-roi.

    ฉันกินอะไรก็กินไม่อร่อย

EXPRESSIONS WITH *GAW*

is alright/that would be alright - gaw dai -

Going today would be alright. Going tomorrow would be alright too.

    Pai wan-nee gaw dai. Pai phroong-nee gaw dai (meuang-gan).

    ไปวันนี้ก็ได้ ไปพรุ่งนี้ก็ได้เหมือนกัน

It's OK if you don't go to work today.

    Wan-nee mai pai tham-ngan gaw dai.

    วันนี้ไม่ไปทำงานก็ได้

Gaw dai is also used with "might/may" and "have to".

He might like it.

    Kao at ja chawp gaw dai.

    เค้าอาจจะชอบก็ได้

You don't have to come tomorrow.

    Phroong-nee koon mai tawng ma gaw dai.

    พรุ่งนี้คุณไม่ต้องมาก็ได้

let it be - gaw chang - This is similar to *gaw dai*. Other meanings are "OK", "alright", and "I don't care". *Chang* is a verb that means "let it go" or "let it be".

I don't care what he does.

> Kao ja tham a-rai gaw chang.
>
> > เค้าจะทำอะไรก็ช่าง

would be good/a good idea - gaw dee - This phrase is also used alone as a response meaning "that would be good" or "that would be fine".

Any time would be good.

> Meua-rai gaw dee.
>
> > เมื่อไหร่ก็ดี

It would be good to go tomorrow.

> Pai phroong-nee gaw dee.
>
> > ไปพรุ่งนี้ก็ดี

it's alright/it's OK - gaw mai pen rai -

Whether she goes or not makes no difference.

> Kao pai reu mai pai gaw mai pen rai.
>
> > เค้าไปหรือไม่ไปก็ไม่เป็นไร

It's alright if you're not free.

> Gaw mai pen rai tha koon mai wang.
>
> > ก็ไม่เป็นไรถ้าคุณไม่ว่าง

If the quality is good it doesn't matter if it's expensive.

> Tha koon-na-phap dee, ra-ka phaeng gaw mai pen rai.
>
> > ถ้าคุณภาพดีราคาแพงก็ไม่เป็นไร

never mind - gaw laeo pai -

She took it, but never mind.

> Kao ao pai, gaw laeo pai.
>
> > เค้าเอาไปก็แล้วไป

and be done with it - gaw laeo gan - This is for suggestions, agreeing to things, and ending disputes. Other meanings are "it's the same to me", "that's it", and "that's all there is to it". It can indicate indifference.

Let's just go.

> Pai gaw laeo gan.
>
> > ไปก็แล้วกัน

Let's make it 100 baht.

    Roi baht gaw laeo gan.

      ร้อยบาทก็แล้วกัน

How about your doing it today?

    Wan-nee koon tham gaw laeo gan.

      วันนี้คุณทำก็แล้วกัน

Forget about it and be done with it.

    Ploi mun pai gaw laeo gan.

      ปล่อยมันไปก็แล้วกัน

it's true, but - gaw jing (yoo) - This can be put before or after the fact.

It's true that the train is slow, but it's good for sleeping.

    Rot-fai cha gaw jing yoo, tae mun nawn sa-bai.

      รถไฟช้าก็จริงอยู่แต่มันนอนสบาย

It's true that she's cute, but she's not a nice person.

    Gaw jing yoo wa kao pen kon na-rak, tae gaw pen kon mai dee.

      ก็จริงอยู่ว่าเค้าเป็นคนน่ารักแต่เค้าเป็นคนไม่ดี

so... - gaw laeo -

So, why didn't you tell me first?

    Gaw laeo, tham-mai mai bawk gan gawn, la?

      ก็แล้วทำไมไม่บอกกันก่อนละ

So, who was the person who did it?

    Gaw laeo, krai, la, pen kon tham?

      ก็แล้วใครละเป็นคนทำ

so what? - gaw laeo ngai, la? - Also "What difference does it make?" and "Forget it!"

A: Don't go alone.

    Koon ya pai kon dio, na.

      คุณอย่าไปคนเดียวนะ

B: What difference does it make?

    Gaw laeo ngai, la?

      ก็แล้วไงละ

what else could it be? - gaw a-rai sia eeg, la? -

A: She must like him.

    Theuh tawng chawp kao nae-nae.

      เธอต้องชอบเค้าแน่ๆ

B: What else could it be?

    Gaw̄ a-rai <u>siaj</u> <u>eeg</u>, <u>la</u>?

    ก็อะไรเสียอีกล่ะ

I agree with that - gaw̄ wā ngan, lae -

A: Things in this shop are too expensive.

    <u>Kawnj</u> nai ran nee phaeng geuhn pai, na.

    ของในร้านนี้แพงเกินไปนะ

B: I agree.

    Gaw̄ wā ngan, lae.

    ก็ว่างั้นแหละ

WHATEVER/ANYWHERE/NO MATTER WHO

Phrases like *arai gaw dai* ("anything is alright") and *meuarai gaw dai* ("any time is OK") are common in basic Thai. Here they're used for "whatever", "whenever", etc., as the subject or object of the sentence. Most sentences here can be stated in more than one way and, typically in Thai, may be reduced to a few words in the context of the conversation. *Gaw* is usually included to show that the meaning is hypothetical.

    Gaw dai can be replaced with *gaw tam*, which is more formal and refers to everything/anything at all rather than just to things that "can" happen as with *gaw dai*. Other phrases that may be included are *mai wa* ("whether"), and *theung* ("even if"). For "whatever", *mai wa arai* means "whether it's this or that thing", and *theung pen arai* means "even if it's this or that thing". They may or may not be interchangable depending on the meaning of the sentence.

    These examples can be said in more than one way in English as well as in Thai, for example, "Whoever wants it can have it" can be "Anyone who wants it can have it" or "No matter who wants it can have it".

WHATEVER

This is *arai gaw dai*, usually shortened to *arai* alone unless *gaw dai* is needed at the end of the sentence or for the meaning of "will be alright" (as in the first example).

I'll do anything you want.

    Koon ja hai chan tham a-rai gaw̄ dai.   ("You can have me do anything")

    คุณจะให้ฉันทำอะไรก็ได้

    Koon hai tham a-rai gaw̄ dai, chan ja tham. ("Whatever you have me do, I'll do")

    คุณให้ทำอะไรก็ได้ ฉันจะทำ

I like to eat anything that isn't hot.

    Chan chawp gin a-rai (gaw̄ dai) thee mai <u>phet</u>.

    ฉันชอบกินอะไร(ก็ได้)ที่ไม่เผ็ด

A-rai thee mai phet gaw chawp (gin).

อะไรที่ไม่เผ็ดก็ชอบ(กิน)

Eat whatever you want.

Gin a-rai (gaw dai) thee koon yak gin./Yak gin a-rai gaw gin.

กินอะไร(ก็ได้)ที่คุณอยากกิน/อยากกินอะไรก็กิน

He does whatever he wants.

Kao tham a-rai thee kao yak ja tham./Yak tham a-rai (kao) gaw tham.

เค้าทำอะไรที่เค้าอยากจะทำ/อยากทำอะไร(เค้า)ก็ทำ

(Mai wa) a-rai thee kao yak ja tham, kao gaw tham. ("whether it's this or that")

(ไม่ว่า)อะไรที่เค้าอยากจะทำเค้าก็ทำ

Theung ja pen yang-ngai, kao gaw ja tham. ("even if it's this or that")

ถึงจะเป็นยังไงเค้าก็จะทำ

Anything you have could get stolen.

(Mai wa/theung) mee a-rai gaw haij./A-rai gaw haij.

(ไม่ว่า/ถึง)มีอะไรก็หาย/อะไรก็หาย

No matter what happens she won't go home.

(Mai wa/theung) geuht a-rai keun, kao gaw mai glap ban.

(ไม่ว่า/ถึง)เกิดอะไรขึ้นเค้าก็ไม่กลับบ้าน

Meaning "everything" - Include *mot* or *thook yang* to emphasize "everything".

Whatever it is, it will be delicious.

(Mai wa) a-rai gaw a-roi (mot/thook yang).

(ไม่ว่า)อะไรก็อร่อย(หมด/ทุกอย่าง)

Everything he buys is expensive.

A-rai thee kao seu gaw phaeng thook yang.

อะไรที่เค้าซื้อก็แพงทุกอย่าง

Meaning "nothing/not anything" -

Nothing I eat tastes good. ("Whatever I eat isn't delicious.")

A-rai thee chan gin gaw mai a-roi./(Chan) gin a-rai gaw mai a-roi.

อะไรที่ฉันกินก็ไม่อร่อย/(ฉัน)กินอะไรก็ไม่อร่อย

(Mai wa) a-rai gaw mai a-roi.

(ไม่ว่า)อะไรก็ไม่อร่อย

She won't eat anything./No matter what it is, she won't eat it.

Mai wa a-rai gaw mai gin.

ไม่ว่าอะไรก็ไม่กิน

Nothing can wash it out.

A-rai gaw sak mai awk.

อะไรก็ซักไม่ออก

I don't want anything old.

A-rai thee gao gaw mai ao.

อะไรที่เก่าก็ไม่เอา

Nothing is as relaxing as traditional massage.

(Mai wa/theung) a-rai gaw mai sa-bai thao nuat phaeng bo-ran.

(ไม่ว่า/ถึง)อะไรก็ไม่สบายเท่านวดแผนโบราณ

WHICHEVER

"Which" is formed by putting *nai* after the classifier.

Meaning "any" -

Buy any one of them.

Seu un naij gaw dai.

ซื้ออันไหนก็ได้

We can eat at any restaurant that's cheap.

Rao pai gin ran naij gaw dai thee thook.

เราไปกินร้านไหนก็ได้ที่ถูก

Whichever one you like you can take. (with *tua* as the classifier for clothing)

Chawp tua naij gaw ao pai (dai) leuy.

ชอบตัวไหนก็เอาไป(ได้)เลย

Tua naij gaw dai thee chawp, ao pai leuy.

ตัวไหนก็ได้ที่ชอบเอาไปเลย

Arai for "any/whatever" has a more general meaning. Compare these two sentences:

We can take any vehicle.

Pai rot a-rai gaw dai.   (with *arai*—any kind of vehicle)

ไปรถอะไรก็ได้

Pai rot kun naij gaw dai.   (with *nai*—any of the vehicles that are available)

ไปรถคันไหนก็ได้

We can eat at any kind of restaurant you like.

Rao pai gin ran a-rai thee koon chawp.

เราไปกินร้านอะไรที่คุณชอบ

No kind of medicine will help.

Ya a-rai gaw chuay mai dai.

ยาอะไรก็ช่วยไม่ได้

Meaning "all/every" - *Gaw dai* isn't included here. See also "neither/none/not any" on pages 199-200.

All of the shops are closed. ("whichever shop")

> Ran nai gaw pit (mot) laeo.
>
> ร้านไหนก็ปิด(หมด)แล้ว

Every province (in Thailand) has interesting places to visit.

> Jang-wat nai (nai Thai) gaw mee thee-thio na song-jai.
>
> จังหวัดไหน(ในไทย)ก็มีที่เที่ยวน่าสนใจ

WHOEVER

This is *krai gaw dai, kon nai gaw dai* (for a person or people from a specific group), or *krai gaw tam* (more general and formal).

A: Who should I give it to?

> Ao hai krai?
>
> เอาให้ใคร

B: Give it to anyone.

> Ao hai krai gaw dai.
>
> เอาให้ใครก็ได้

Give it to anyone who's in the office.

> Ao hai krai gaw dai thee yoo nai awf-fit.
>
> เอาให้ใครก็ได้ที่อยู่ในออฟฟิศ

I can work with anyone as long as he can speak English.

> Chan tham-ngan gap kon nai gaw dai, tha kao phoot pha-sa Ang-grit dai.
>
> ฉันทำงานกับคนไหนก็ได้ถ้าเค้าพูดภาษาอังกฤษได้

People who don't want to go don't have to go.

> Krai mai yak pai gaw mai tawng pai.
>
> ใครไม่อยากไปก็ไม่ต้องไป

Whoever's interested come this way. (or "Anyone who's...")

    Krai soṅ-jai ma thang nee.

    ใครสนใจมาทางนี้

He can't live with anyone./There's no one he can live with.

    Kao yoo gap krai gaw mai dai.

    เค้าอยู่กับใครก็ไม่ได้

These examples can include *mai wa* ("whether") or *theung* ("even if"). In the first sentence, if *mai wa* is used the meaning is "whether it's this person or that person who tells her". If *theung* is used it's "even if it's this person or that person who tells her".

No matter who tells her, she won't believe it.

    (Mai wa/theuṅ) krai bawk, (kao) gaw mai cheua.

    (ไม่ว่า/ถึง)ใครบอก(เค้า)ก็ไม่เชื่อ

No matter who you are, they won't let you go in.

    (Mai wa/theuṅ) koon ja pen krai, kao gaw mai hai kao.

    (ไม่ว่า/ถึง)คุณจะเป็นใครเค้าก็ไม่ให้เข้า

"everyone/anyone" in the subject - Here "whoever" means "everyone". Many phrases may be used for the subject. See "everyone", pages 50-51, for more examples with *thook kon* and *thook-thook kon*.

    krai/krai-krai/kon naiṅ/krai kon naiṅ/

    krai gaw dai/krai gaw tam (formal)/

    thook kon/thook-thook kon/

    mai wa krai/theuṅ pen krai.

Everyone is beautiful.

    Kon naiṅ gaw suaỵ./Krai gaw suaỵ./Krai-krai gaw suaỵ./Krai kon naiṅ gaw suaỵ.

    คนไหนก็สวย/ใครก็สวย/ใครๆ ก็สวย/ใครคนไหนก็สวย

    Thook kon (gaw) suaỵ./Thook-thook kon (gaw) suaỵ./Suaỵ (mot) thook kon.

    ทุกคน(ก็)สวย/ทุกๆ คน(ก็)สวย/สวย(หมด)ทุกคน

Anybody can do it.

    Krai gaw tham dai. (or any of the phrases in place of *krai*)

    ใครก็ทำได้

Everybody likes the food here.

    A-haṅ thee-nee - krai-krai gaw chawp./Krai-krai gaw chawp a-haṅ thee-nee.

    อาหารที่นี่ใครๆ ก็ชอบ/ใครๆ ก็ชอบอาหารที่นี่

"nobody" in the subject - Use the same phrases. "Nobody" can also be formed with *mai mee krai* and *mai mee kon nai*. There are more examples on pages 49-50.

Nobody can do it.

(Mai wa) krai gaw tham mai dai./Mai mee krai tham dai.

(ไม่ว่า)ใครก็ทำไม่ได้/ไม่มีใครทำได้

Kon naij gaw tham mai dai./Mai mee kon naij tham dai.

คนไหนก็ทำไม่ได้/ไม่มีคนไหนทำได้

With *thook kon* you're referring to everyone from a specific group.

Nobody can do it.

Thook kon tham mai dai.

ทุกคนทำไม่ได้

WHENEVER

"Whenever" is *meuarai gaw dai*, often shortened to *meuarai* only.

You can come whenever you're free./You can come any time you're free.

Koon ja ma meua-rai gaw dai thee koon wang.

คุณจะมาเมื่อไหร่ก็ได้ที่คุณว่าง

Meua-rai (thee koon) wang, koon gaw ma dai.

เมื่อไหร่(ที่คุณ)ว่างคุณก็มาได้

Tha koon wang meua-rai, koon gaw ma (dai)./Wang meua-rai gaw ma (dai).

ถ้าคุณว่างเมื่อไหร่คุณก็มา(ได้)/ว่างเมื่อไหร่ก็มา(ได้)

Whenever you go, I'll go with you.

(Mai wa) meua-rai thee koon pai, phomj gaw ja pai duay.

(ไม่ว่า)เมื่อไหร่ที่คุณไปผมก็จะไปด้วย

(Mai wa/theungj) koon pai meua-rai, phomj gaw ja pai duay.

(ไม่ว่า/ถึง)คุณไปเมื่อไหร่ผมก็จะไปด้วย

Pai meua-rai gaw ja pai duay./Pai gaw pai duay.

ไปเมื่อไหร่ก็จะไปด้วย/ไปก็ไปด้วย

These sentences have *wan nai* for "whichever day/whatever day".

Whatever day you want to go is fine.

Wan naij thee yak pai gaw pai dai.

วันไหนที่อยากไปก็ไปได้

Whatever day I go back, my parents won't say anything.

(Mai wa/theungj) chan ja glap ban wan naij, phaw-mae gaw mai wa (a-rai).

(ไม่ว่า/ถึง)ฉันจะกลับบ้านวันไหนพ่อแม่ก็ไม่ว่า(อะไร)

Meaning "any time/always" - Here *meuarai* or *deuan nai* (*wan nai*, etc) are used for "always". See page 380 for more examples and ways to say "whenever/always".

Whenever you go, there will be people selling noodles.

Meua-rai (gaw tam) thee koon pai, gaw ja mee kon kai guay-tioj.

เมื่อไหร่(ก็ตาม)ที่คุณไปก็จะมีคนขายก๋วยเตี๋ยว

(Mai wa/theungj) pai meua-rai, gaw ja mee kon kaij guayj-tioj.

(ไม่ว่า/ถึง)ไปเมื่อไหร่ก็จะมีคนขายก๋วยเตี๋ยว

(Pai) meua-rai gaw mee kon kaij guayj-tioj.

(ไป)เมื่อไหร่ก็มีคนขายก๋วยเตี๋ยว

Here it's hot every month./Whatever month it is, it's hot.

Thee-nee (mai wa) deuan naij a-gat gaw rawn./Deuan naij gaw rawn.

ที่นี่(ไม่ว่า)เดือนไหนอากาศก็ร้อน/เดือนไหนก็ร้อน

WHEREVER

This is *theenai gaw dai*, shortened to *theenai*.

I'll go wherever you like./I'll go anywhere you like.

Chan ja pai thee-naij gaw dai thee koon tawnj-gan.

ฉันจะไปที่ไหนก็ได้ที่คุณต้องการ

Thee-naij gaw dai thee koon tawnj-gan, chan gaw ja pai.

ที่ไหนก็ได้ที่คุณต้องการฉันก็จะไป

We can stay anywhere that's near the beach.

Phak thee-naij gaw dai thee yoo glai chai-hat.

พักที่ไหนก็ได้ที่อยู่ใกล้ชายหาด

Meaning "everywhere/nowhere" -

Wherever I went in Switzerland it was beautiful.

(Anywhere I went.../Everywhere is beautiful in Switzerland.)

(Mai wa/theungj) chan pai thee-naij nai Sa-wit gaw suayj mot.

(ไม่ว่า/ถึง)ฉันไปที่ไหนในสวิสก็สวยหมด

(Mai wa) thee-naij (gaw dai) nai Sa-wit suayj mot.

(ไม่ว่า)ที่ไหน(ก็ได้)ในสวิสสวยหมด

Nai Sa-wit, thee-naij gaw suayj (mot).

ในสวิสที่ไหนก็สวย(หมด)

Nowhere I go is any fun.

    Thee-naij thee chan pai gaw mai sa-nook.

    ที่ไหนที่ฉันไปก็ไม่สนุก

    Pai thee-naij gaw mai sa-nook./Pai naij gaw mai sa-nook.

    ไปที่ไหนก็ไม่สนุก/ไปไหนก็ไม่สนุก

It's hard to go anywhere here. The roads aren't good.

    Thee-nee pai naij gaw lam-bak. Tha-nonj mun mai dee.

    ที่นี่ไปไหนก็ลำบาก ถนนมันไม่ดี

Another way to say "everywhere" is *thook thee*.

In this town it's clean everywhere.

    Meuang nee thee-naij gaw sa-at./Meuang nee sa-at thook thee.

    เมืองนี้ที่ไหนก็สะอาด/เมืองนี้สะอาดทุกที่

HOWEVER

however much (amounts) - This is *thaorai gaw dai*, shortened to *thaorai*.

A: How much water should I put in?

    Sai nam thao-rai?

    ใส่น้ำเท่าไหร่

B: Any amount is OK.

    Thao-rai gaw dai.

    เท่าไหร่ก็ได้

You have to pay 300 baht but you can eat as much as you want. There's no limit.

    Jai samj roi baht, tae ja gin thao-rai gaw dai. Mai mee jam-gat.

    จ่ายสามร้อยบาทแต่จะกินเท่าไหร่ก็ได้ ไม่มีจำกัด

Take as much as you want.

    Ao pai leuy, thao-rai gaw dai thee koon tawng-gan.

    เอาไปเลยเท่าไหร่ก็ได้ที่คุณต้องการ

No matter how much she eats she won't get fat.

    (Mai wa/theung) kao ja gin sak thao-rai gaw mai uan.

    (ไม่ว่า/ถึง)เค้าจะกินซักเท่าไหร่ก็ไม่อ้วน

    Gin thao-rai gaw mai uan.

    กินเท่าไหร่ก็ไม่อ้วน

No matter how much they sell it for, I'll buy it.

    (Mai wa) kao kaij thao-rai, phomj gaw ja seu./(Mai wa) thao-rai gaw ja seu.

    (ไม่ว่า)เค้าขายเท่าไหร่ผมก็จะซื้อ/(ไม่ว่า)เท่าไหร่ก็จะซื้อ

With *gaw dee* you're saying that any amount is a good idea.

Any amount you give them is fine.

    Koon hai thao-rai gaw dee.

    คุณให้เท่าไหร่ก็ดี

to whatever extent - Put *kae nai* after the the quality.

No matter how hot it is, I have to work.

    (Mai wa/theung) (a-gat) rawn kae nai, chan gaw tawng tham-ngan.

    (ไม่ว่า/ถึง)(อากาศ)ร้อนแค่ไหนฉันก็ต้องทำงาน

However long I'd have waited, he wouldn't have come.

    (Mai wa/theung) phom ja koi kao nan kae nai, gaw mai hen kao ma.

    (ไม่ว่า/ถึง)ผมจะคอยเค้านานแค่ไหนก็ไม่เห็นเค้ามา

    Koi kae nai gaw mai hen ma./Koi kae nai gaw mai ma.

    คอยแค่ไหนก็ไม่เห็นมา/คอยแค่ไหนก็ไม่มา

in whatever way - This is *yang-ngai gaw dai*. In the third sentence "what" in English is translated as "how" in Thai.

Do it any way you like, but please do it well.

    Tham yang-ngai gaw dai, (tae) hai mun dee gaw laeo gan.

    ทำยังไงก็ได้(แต่)ให้มันดีก็แล้วกัน

Any way he dresses he looks good.

    (Mai wa/theung) kao taeng tua yang-ngai gaw doo dee.

    (ไม่ว่า/ถึง)เค้าแต่งตัวยังไงก็ดูดี

No matter what I do the car won't start.

    (Mai wa/theung) phom tham yang-ngai, rot gaw sa-tat mai tit.

    (ไม่ว่า/ถึง)ผมทำยังไงรถก็สต๊าทไม่ติด

whatever happens - Here *yang-ngai gaw tam* is "no matter what happens", "anyway", "despite all", or "at any rate".

Whatever happens, I'll go./I'll go no matter what.

    Yang-ngai (gaw tam), phom gaw ja pai.

    ยังไง(ก็ตาม)ผมก็จะไป

11. QUANTIFIERS

VERY

There are many words and phrases for "very" which can also be used with the verbs "want" and "like" for "I really want" and "I like (something) a lot".

mak/mak-mak	the general way to say "very"
mak mai	common in patterns with "so"
nak	means "really", "extremely", or "excessively"
jang	means "extremely", "very much", or "a great deal"
leuaj geuhn/la geuhn	"very" or "exceedingly", literally "with too much left over"
na doo	literally "should be seen", used for "extremely" or "really"
thee dio	"very" or "quite", with "like" and "want" use *mak thee dio*
chio	"very" or "quite"
jat	"strong" or "extreme", used in the phrases *rawn jat* ("extremely hot"), *phet jat* ("extremely hot/spicy"), and *rot jat* ("strong tasting/strong flavor")

There are also combinations with *mak*, including *mak nak, mak leua geuhn, mak na doo, mak jing-jing,* and *mak leuy.*

You're extremely beautiful.

Koon suayj jang (leuy).

คุณสวยจัง(เลย)

It's extremely hot.

Rawn na doo.

ร้อนน่าดู

I really want to go home.

Chan yak glap ban mak leuy.

ฉันอยากกลับบ้านมากเลย

Hotels in Hong Kong are very expensive.

Rong-raem nai Hawng Gong phaeng mak leuaj geuhn.

โรงแรมในฮ่องกงแพงมากเหลือเกิน

If she gets up really late you don't have to wait for her.

Tha theuh teun saij nak, gaw mai tawng raw gaw dai.

ถ้าเธอตื่นสายนักก็ไม่ต้องรอก็ได้

I didn't think he would be so tall.

> Maí keuy kit waˋ kao jaˋ soonɟ makˋ mai yaŋ-ŋee. (*mak mai* with "so")
>
> ไม่เคยคิดว่าเค้าจะสูงมากมายยังงี้

not very/not much - maí...thaoˋ-raí/maí koˋi...(thaoˋ-raí) - *Thao-rai* can be replaced with *nak, mak, mak nak, thao-rai nak,* or *mak thao-rai.*

I don't like pork much.

> Chan maí (koˋi) chawp mooɟ thaoˋ-raí.
>
> ฉันไม่(ค่อย)ชอบหมูเท่าไหร่

It's not very far.

> (Mun) maí glai makˋ nakˋ.
>
> (มัน)ไม่ไกลมากนัก

not a lot/not much - maí makˋ -

It's cold here, but not really cold.

> Thee-nee naoɟ, tae maí makˋ.
>
> ที่นี่หนาวแต่ไม่มาก

It's not very hot today.

> Wan-nee rawn maí makˋ./Wan-nee maí rawn makˋ.
>
> วันนี้ร้อนไม่มาก/วันนี้ไม่ร้อนมาก

not a little - maí noi -

I'd be very happy if I saw her again. ("I wouldn't be a little happy")

> Phomɟ jaˋ dee-jai maí noi thaˋ daiˋ jeuh kao eeg.
>
> ผมจะดีใจไม่น้อยถ้าได้เจอเค้าอีก

OTHER QUANTIFYING ADVERBS

a little/a bit - nit noˋi/nit dio/nit neung/nit-nit - *Noi* is low/short when it's a modifier (it modifies *nit* here), and *neung* is mid/short rather than low/short in *nit neung.*

I'm a person who's a little short-tempered.

> Chan pen kon jai-rawn nit noˋi.
>
> ฉันเป็นคนใจร้อนนิดหน่อย

I only went a little late.

> Phomɟ pai cha nit dio ayng.
>
> ผมไปช้านิดเดียวเอง

It's a little too long.

> Mun yao pai nit neung, naˋ.
>
> มันยาวไปนิดหนึ่งนะ

A: Do you like him a lot?

    Chawp kao mak reuhj?

       ชอบเค้ามากเหรอ

B: A little.

    Nit-nit.

       นิดๆ

about/approximately/around - pra-man/rao/rao-rao -

Around ten people are going.

    Pai pra-man sip kon.

       ไปประมาณสิบคน

Now I have a little over 200,000 baht.

    Tawn-nee chan mee ngeuhn yoo rao sawnj saenj gwa.

       ตอนนี้ฉันมีเงินอยู่ราวสองแสนกว่า

almost - geuap - *Dai* can be included after quantities, as in the second example.

Yesterday I wrote almost ten letters.

    Meua-wan-nee chan kianj jot-maj geuap sip cha-bap.

       เมื่อวานนี้ฉันเขียนจดหมายเกือบสิบฉบับ

She spent almost five thousand baht.

    Kao chai ngeuhn geuap ha phan dai.

       เค้าใช้เงินเกือบห้าพันได้

completely - tem-thee/tem-thee - *Thee* in *tem-thee* can have either a mid tone or a falling tone. With a mid tone it means "very" or "extremely" and is put after adjectives or adverbs as in the first example. With a falling tone it means "completely", "to the fullest extent", or "to the utmost", and is put after verbs as in the second example.

He's very hard to understand.

    Kao pen kon kao-jai yak tem-thee.

       เค้าเป็นคนเข้าใจยากเต็มที

She ran as fast as she could so she'd be first.

    Kao wing tem-thee, hai dai thee neung.

       เค้าวิ่งเต็มที่ให้ได้ที่หนึ่ง

exactly - phaw dee/thuan - *Phaw dee* also means "just right" (page 208) and "at that very moment" (page 350). *Thuan* is for exact amounts in round numbers. A common expression is *nap mai thuan* which means "countless" (high/short on *nap*).

That's exactly 100 baht.

    Roi baht phaw dee.

       ร้อยบาทพอดี

This umbrella cost exactly 200 baht.

> Rom kun nee ra-ka sawng roi baht thuan.
>
> ร่มคันนี้ราคาสองร้อยบาทถ้วน

nice and... - Include *dee* after the adjective or adverb.

Your house is nice and big.

> Ban koon yai dee.
>
> บ้านคุณใหญ่ดี

Playing sports is fun.

> Len gee-la sa-nook dee.
>
> เล่นกีฬาสนุกดี

really/truly - jing-jing - In the second sentence *jing-jing* with a verb means "truly/not a lie".

Daeng smiles really beautifully.

> Daeng yim suay jing-jing.
>
> แดงยิ้มสวยจริงๆ

He really ate it.

> Kao gin jing-jing.
>
> เค้ากินจริงๆ

rather/fairly - meuang-gan/kawn-kang/phaw somj-kuan - The third phrase is literally "enough as appropriate" or "as it should be".

A: Is it difficult?

> Yak mai?
>
> ยากมั้ย

B: It's pretty difficult.

> Gaw, yak meuang-gan.
>
> ก็ยากเหมือนกัน

My father's rather thin.

> Phaw kawn-kang phawmj.
>
> พ่อค่อนข้างผอม

Quite a few people came to the concert.

> Kawn-seuht nee mee kon ma mak phaw somj-kuan.
>
> คอนเสิร์ตนี้มีคนมามากพอสมควร

I like beer. (rather/sort of)

> Phomj chawp bia meuang-gan.
>
> ผมชอบเบียร์เหมือนกัน

somewhat/to some extent - bang/mung - The second is a colloquial pronunciation of the first. The meaning may be extended to "sometimes". See also pages 202 and 289-290.

A: Do you like watching videos?

    Chawp doo wee-dee-o mai?

      ชอบดูวีดีโอมั้ย

B: I like it pretty much.

    Gaw chawp mung.

      ก็ชอบมั่ง

A: Is it cold at Kao Yai?

    Thee Kao Yai nao mai?

      ที่เขาใหญ่หนาวมั้ย

B: It's a little cold.

    Gaw nao bang meuan-gan./Gaw nao bang nit noi.

      ก็หนาวบ้างเหมือนกัน/ก็หนาวบ้างนิดหน่อย

utterly/absolutely - leuy -

It's really hot.

    Rawn jang leuy.

      ร้อนจังเลย

They ate it all.

    Kao gin mot leuy.

      เค้ากินหมดเลย

I don't swim well at all.

    Chan wai-nam mai geng leuy.

      ฉันว่ายน้ำไม่เก่งเลย

whole/a complete - tem/tem-tem -

It took us three whole hours to walk up the mountain.

    Rao chai way-la sam chua-mong tem-tem deuhn keun kao.

      เราใช้เวลาสามชั่วโมงเต็มๆ เดินขึ้นเขา

DOUBLING ADJECTIVES AND ADVERBS

Adjectives and adverbs may be doubled with two different meanings.

1. rather/sort of - For this meaning the word has the usual tone both times it's said.

The rather tall person is named Phet.

    Kon soong-soong (nan) cheu Phet.

      คนสูงๆ (นั่น)ชื่อเพชร

2. very - For this meaning the word has a high tone the first time it's said and the usual tone the second. In the second example, because the usual tone of *rawn* is high, it's held out longer the first time and stressed with a slight rising sound. This pattern is used by women more than by men.

Such beautiful hair!

    Phom̃ suay-suay.

    ผมสวย สวย

Today it's so hot!

    Wan-nee rawn-rawn. (first *rawn* is held out longer)

    วันนี้ร้อน ร้อน

MANY/A LOT

For "many/a lot" with people see also chapter 3, page 46.

a lot/many/much - mak - Variations are *mak-mak, mak mai, mak nak, mak leua geuhn*, and *mak na doo*.

He bought a lot of food.

    Kao seu a-han̥ ma mak.

    เค้าซื้ออาหารมามาก

yeuh/yeuh-yae/yeuh-yeuh - The first is general, the second is for having a lot of things, and the third is for commands.

Joe eats a lot, but he's not fat.

    Joe gin yeuh, tae mai uan.

    โจกินเยอะแต่ไม่อ้วน

I've heard that story many times, but I don't believe it.

    Chan fang reuang nee ma yeuh, tae chan mai cheua.

    ฉันฟังเรื่องนี้มาเยอะแต่ฉันไม่เชื่อ

Why did you bring so many things?

    Tham-mai ao kawng̥ ma yeuh-yae yang-ngee?

    ทำไมเอาของมาเยอะแยะยังงี้

I like sour food. Put in a lot of lemon.

    Chan chawp gin prio. Sai ma-nao yeuh-yeuh noi.

    ฉันชอบกินเปรี้ยว ใส่มะนาวเยอะๆ หน่อย

lai̥ (classifier)/lai̥-lai̥ (classifier) - These are put before classifiers so they're used only with things you can count like shirts and bottles (as opposed to things you can't count like water and rice). For "a lot of water" use *mak/yeuh* or the name of a container with *lai* ("many bottles of water" is *nam lai kuat*).

She has a lot of plants.

> Kao mee ton-mai laij ton.
>
> เค้ามีต้นไม้หลายต้น

A lot of my shirts are old.

> Seua phomj laij tua gao laeo.
>
> เสื้อผมหลายตัวเก่าแล้ว

Many people want to go.

> Laij-laij kon yak pai.
>
> หลายๆ คนอยากไป

not a little/not a few - mai noi -

More than a few people come to eat here.

> Mee kon mai noi ma than a-hanj thee-nee.
>
> มีคนไม่น้อยมาทานอาหารที่นี่

there's a lot - mee yeuh/mee mak/mee laij (classifier) -

There's a lot of Western food for sale in Bangkok.

> A-hanj fa-rang mee kaij yeuh nai Groong-thayp.
>
> อาหารฝรั่งมีขายเยอะในกรุงเทพฯ

There are a lot of good Thai musicians.

> Mee nak don-tree Thai yoo laij kon thee geng mak.
>
> มีนักดนตรีไทยอยู่หลายคนที่เก่งมาก

A: Do people go to those islands?

> Mee kon pai thio gaw phuak nan mai?
>
> มีคนไปเที่ยวเกาะพวกนั้นมั้ย

B: Yes, really a lot.

> Mee, mee yeuh leuy.
>
> มี มีเยอะเลย

many thousands - laij phan - This indicates a large number; also with *meun, lan*, etc.

A: How many millions did this house cost?

> Ban langj nee ra-ka gee lan, ka?
>
> บ้านหลังนี้ราคากี่ล้านคะ

B: Many millions.

> Laij lan.
>
> หลายล้าน

With *pen* - This is put before an amount to emphasize that it's large.

A: How many people came here last year?

    Mee kon ma thio thee-nee pee thee laeo gee kon?

      มีคนมาเที่ยวที่นี่ปีที่แล้วกี่คน

B: It must have been a million!

    Pen lan!

      เป็นล้าน

With verbs - mak/yeuh - *Nak* (low/short) can also be used in this example for working "hard".

I've worked a lot this week so I don't want to do anything this weekend.

    A-thit nee tham-ngan mak, leuy mai yak tham a-rai (nai) wan a-rai sao a-thit (eeg)

      อาทิตย์นี้ทำงานมาก เลยไม่อยากทำอะไร(ใน)วันเสาร์อาทิตย์(อีก)

A LITTLE/A FEW

Here nouns are divided into two groups—those you can count ("a few people", "not many books") and those you can't count ("a little water", "not much rice"). Some of the words or phrases for "a little/a few" are used with only one of the groups. For "few people" see page 46. *Noi* has a high tone when it states an amount.

With any noun - noi/nit dio/noi mak - The last means "a very little" or "a very few".

This shop has only a few things for sale.   ("things" is countable)

    Ran nee mee kawng kai nit dio.

      ร้านนี้มีของขายนิดเดียว

Moo's thin because he eats so little.   ("rice" is uncountable)

    Moo phawm phraw kao gin (kao) noi mak.

      หมูผอมเพราะเค้ากิน(ข้าว)น้อยมาก

With uncountable nouns - nit noi/nit neung/lek noi - These refer to the size of an amount, not to a number of things. *Noi* is low/short when it's a modifier (modifies *nit*).

There's only a little gas left in my car.

    Rot chan leua nam-mun (eeg) lek noi./Rot chan mee nam-mun leua (eeg) lek noi.

      รถฉันเหลือน้ำมัน(อีก)เล็กหน่อย/รถฉันมีน้ำมันเหลือ(อีก)เล็กหน่อย

With countable nouns - mai gee (classifier) - Classifiers are used with things you can count only.

We didn't drink much. ("not many bottles")

    Rao deum mai gee kuat.

      เราดื่มไม่กี่ขวด

not a lot/not many/not much - mai mak/mai yeuh/mai koi mak - Also *mai mak thaorai* and *mai yeuh thaorai*.

Don't put much pepper in mine.

    Kawng phom sai phrik mai yeuh, na.

    ของผมใส่พริกไม่เยอะนะ

This factory doesn't have many female workers.

    Rong-ngan nee mee kon ngan phoo-ying mai koi mak.

    โรงงานนี้มีคนงานผู้หญิงไม่ค่อยมาก

A: Are there a lot of mosquitoes here?

    Thee-nee yoong yeuh mai?

    ที่นี่ยุงเยอะมั้ย

B: No, not many.

    Mai koi yeuh thao-rai.

    ไม่ค่อยเยอะเท่าไหร่

Mak or *yeuh* aren't included in these sentences because they express a degree, not a quantity.

I don't understand it much.

    Chan mai kao-jai thao-rai (rawk).

    ฉันไม่เข้าใจเท่าไหร่(หรอก)

She ate just a little and felt full.

    Kao gin mai thao-rai gaw im.

    เค้ากินไม่เท่าไหร่ก็อิ่ม

With verbs ("run a little") - nit dio/nit noi/nit neung - These refer to the amount of the activity.

I ran just a little and got tired.

    Phom wing nit dio gaw neuay laeo.

    ผมวิ่งนิดเดียวก็เหนื่อยแล้ว

not much (verbs) - mai mak/mai yeuh - For the amount of an activity.

She doesn't read much, but she likes to listen to other people talk.

    Kao an nang-seu mai mak, tae kao chawp fang kon (eun) phoot.

    เค้าอ่านหนังสือไม่มากแต่เค้าชอบฟังคน(อื่น)พูด

mai koi (verb) - Here *mai koi* is put before a verb to mean "not much" or "not often". *Ja* is optional between *koi* and the verb. *Mai koi* may also be put between two-word negative verbs as in the last two examples. See also page 372 where *mai koi* is used for "not often".

Noi doesn't stay at home much.

> Noi mai koi (ja) yoo ban./Noi mai koi dai yoo ban.
>
> น้อยไม่ค่อย(จะ)อยู่บ้าน/น้อยไม่ค่อยได้อยู่บ้าน

Some people don't get to go to school much.

> Bang kon mai koi dai rian rawk.
>
> บางคนไม่ค่อยได้เรียนหรอก

I couldn't sleep very well.

> Phomj nawn mai koi lap.
>
> ผมนอนไม่ค่อยหลับ

I can't understand much. (of what someone's saying)

> (Chan) fang mai koi roo reuang.
>
> (ฉัน)ฟังไม่ค่อยรู้เรื่อง

there are few - mee noi - In the third sentence *noi kon* refers to a small amount of people (see page 46).

In Bangkok there aren't many old cars.

> Thee Groong-thayp mee rot gao noi.
>
> ที่กรุงเทพมีรถเก่าน้อย

In Thailand there are few people who like American football.

> Thee meuang Thai kon thee chawp A-may-ree-gan foot-bawn mee noi.
>
> ที่เมืองไทยคนที่ชอบอเมริกันฟุตบอลมีน้อย
>
> Thee meuang Thai mee noi kon thee chawp A-may-ree-gan foot-bawn.
>
> ที่เมืองไทยมีน้อยคนที่ชอบอเมริกันฟุตบอล

NOT ANY AT ALL

mai...leuy - *Koi* may be included for understatement as in the first sentence.

These days I don't play golf at all.

> Chuang nee mai koi dai len gawp leuy.
>
> ช่วงนี้ไม่ค่อยได้เล่นกอล์ฟเลย

A: What did he bring?

> Kao ao a-rai ma?
>
> เค้าเอาอะไรมา

B: He didn't bring anything at all.

> Kao mai dai ao a-rai ma leuy.
>
> เค้าไม่ได้เอาอะไรมาเลย

TOO/TOO MUCH

"Too" is *geuhn* or *pai* alone, together, or in combinations with *mak*.

With adjectives/adverbs - pai/geuhn pai/mak pai/mak geuhn pai - Put any of these after the adjective or adverb.

I want to walk, but it's too far.

Yak deuhn, tae glai geuhn pai.

อยากเดินแต่ไกลเกินไป

This room is too small for four people.

Hawŋ nee lek pai sam̥-rap see kon.

ห้องนี้เล็กไปสำหรับสี่คน

With verbs - mak pai/geuhn pai/mak geuhn pai - *Pai* can't be used alone with verbs.

I think you work too much. You should relax more.

Chan wa koon tham-ngan mak pai. Koon kuan ja phak-phawn bang.

ฉันว่าคุณทำงานมากไป คุณควรจะพักผ่อนบ้าง

He's too fussy. (a verb in Thai—"He fusses too much")

Kao joo-jee mak geuhn pai.

เค้าจู้จี้มากเกินไป

With nouns - mak pai/mak geuhn pai - Or with *yeuh* instead of *mak*. *Mak* or *yeuh* are needed to show that there's an amount of something. *Mak pai* is also used alone as an expression meaning "you're going too far" or "that's too much", said when someone is doing or saying something exaggerated.

This boat has too many people in it.

Reua lum nee mee kon mak pai.

เรือลำนี้มีคนมากไป

This neighborhood has too many dogs.

Thaeŋ nee mee soo-nak yeuh (geuhn) pai.

แถวนี้มีสุนัขเยอะ(เกิน)ไป

too (big) to (lift) - There are four patterns, as in the first example.

It's too big to lift.

Mun yai pai thee ja yok (dai)./Mun yai geuhn (thee) ja yok (dai).

มันใหญ่ไปที่จะยก(ได้)/มันใหญ่เกิน(ที่)จะยก(ได้)

Mun yai geuhn pai thee ja yok (dai)./Mun yai geuhn gwa thee ja yok (dai).

มันใหญ่เกินไปที่จะยก(ได้)/มันใหญ่เกินกว่าที่จะยกได้

He's too little to work here.

Kao lek geuhn pai thee ja tham-ngan thee-nee.

เค้าเล็กเกินไปที่จะทำงานที่นี่

INDEFINITE QUANTIFIERS

The words *tang* and *sak* are used in many patterns. Their basic meanings are as follows:

Large amounts - tang - This shows that the amount you're referring to is considered large. It's the opposite of *kae*, "only".

Fifty people came!

    Mee kon ma tang ha-sip kon.

    มีคนมาตั้งห้าสิบคน

Small amounts/estimating - sak - This minimizes the amount or shows that it's being estimated. Meanings are "as little as", "merely", "just", or "about".

They have around ten vehicles.

    Kao mee rot sak sip kun.

    เค้ามีรถซักสิบคัน

I'm going to buy a book. (estimating that it's one)

    Phom ja seu nang-seu sak lem (neung).

    ผมจะซื้อหนังสือซักเล่ม(นึง)

There's nobody.

    Mai mee krai sak kon.

    ไม่มีใครซักคน

I don't have even a single pair.

    Chan mai mee sak koo leuy.

    ฉันไม่มีสักคู่เลย

A: Do you know how many people came to apply?

    Roo mai wa mee kon ma sa-mak sak gee kon?

    รู้มั้ยว่ามีคนมาสมัครซักกี่คน

B: No, I don't know how many.

    Mai roo wa sak gee kon.

    ไม่รู้ว่าซักกี่คน

ALL/EVERY

There are six basic words. "All/every" is also expressed with "whatever" (page 175), "whichever" (page 177), "whoever" (page 178), "whenever", and "wherever" (page 180).

1. thang - This is used in the following phrases for "all", "all of", or "the whole of":

all/altogether - thang-mot - Also "all of it", "all of them", and "the whole lot".

All of us are going.

    Rao ja pai gan thang-mot.

    เราจะไปกันทั้งหมด

I'll pay for everything/all of these.

    Thang-mot nee, chan ja jai ayng.

    ทั้งหมดนี้ฉันจะจ่ายเอง

Altogether I'll be here for five days.

    Ja yoo thang-mot ha wan.

    จะอยู่ทั้งหมดห้าวัน

She doesn't want any of it/them.

    Kao mai tawng-gan thang-mot.

    เค้าไม่ต้องการทั้งหมด

He can't take all of it/them.

    Kao ao pai thang-mot mai dai./Kao ao pai mai mot.

    เค้าเอาไปทั้งหมดไม่ได้/เค้าเอาไปไม่หมด

all/the whole group - (noun) thang-laij - This is put after nouns or pronouns.

All of them are soldiers.

    Kao thang-laij pen tha-hanj.

    เค้าทั้งหลายเป็นทหาร

together with/including - ruam thang (noun) -

She's going there with her family.

    Kao ja pai thee-nan ruam thang krawp-krua kao duay.

    เค้าจะไปที่นั่นรวมทั้งครอบครัวเค้าด้วย

If you include the cost of housing it's around 15,000 baht per month.

    Tha ruam thang ka thee-phak duay, gaw pra-man deuan la meun ha phan baht.

    ถ้ารวมทั้งค่าที่พักด้วยก็ประมาณเดือนละ 15,000 บาท

all of it - thang-nan/thang-nee - The meaning here is more general. Translations are "all of that/them", "any of that/them", and "anything and everything".

If I'm hungry I can eat anything.

    Tha phomj hiuj, phomj gin dai thang-nan (lae).

    ถ้าผมหิวผมกินได้ทั้งนั้น(แหละ)

Today they all went to the temple together.

    Wan-nee kao pai wat gan thang-nan.

    วันนี้เค้าไปวัดกันทั้งนั้น

I'm not eating anything.

    Chan mai gin (a-rai) thang-nan.

    ฉันไม่กิน(อะไร)ทั้งนั้น

This all happened because I didn't understand.

Thang-nee phraw phomɲ kaô-jai phit ayng.

ทั้งนี้เพราะผมเข้าใจผิดเอง

2. mot - This is "completely", "entirely", "exhaustively", and also "used up". *Hai* is included in the last example for "cause to be all" or "make to be all".

I've spent (used) all the money.

Chan chai ngeúhn mot laeo.

ฉันใช้เงินหมดแล้ว

All of my friends went home.

Pheuan-pheuan glap mot laeo.

เพื่อนๆ กลับหมดแล้ว

Where did all the kids go?

Dek pai naiɲ mot?

เด็กไปไหนหมด

Time's up.

Mot way-la./Way-la mot laeo.

หมดเวลา/เวลาหมดแล้ว

They're all beautiful. I'd like to buy all of them.

Suayɲ mot leuy. Yak seu thang-mot leuy.

สวยหมดเลย อยากซื้อทั้งหมดเลย

Please tell me the whole story. (*hai* is "cause to be")

Chuay laô reuang nee (ma) haî mot, seê.

ช่วยเล่าเรื่องนี้(มา)ให้หมดซิ

Here *mot* is put before the name of a container (a box) to refer to the entire container.

She burned the whole box of paper. ("until the whole box was burned")

Kaô phaoɲ gra-dat jon mai mot glawng.

เค้าเผากระดาษจนไหม้หมดกล่อง

3. thook (classifier) - *Thook* before a classifier means "every" or "each". When doubled, as in the third sentence, it means "each and every". See also pages 37 and 40 ("everything"), pages 50-51 ("everybody"), and chapter 18 ("every day", "every time").

Every shirt is dirty.

Seua thook tua sok-ga-prok./Seua sok-ga-prok thook tua.

เสื้อทุกตัวสกปรก/เสื้อสกปรกทุกตัว

When you move are you taking everything with you?

Tawn yai ban ja aô kawngɲ thook yang pai duay reu plaô?

ตอนย้ายบ้านจะเอาของทุกอย่างไปด้วยรึเปล่า

I'd like to go everywhere in Bangkok.

> Chan yak pai thio thook-thook haeng nai Groong-thayp.

> ฉันอยากไปเที่ยวทุกๆ แห่งในกรุงเทพ

I'd like to go and see every place. (*hai* is "cause to be")

> Chan yak pai doo hai thook thee.

> ฉันอยากไปดูให้ทุกที่

I can eat anything/any kind.

> Phom gin dai thook yang./Phom gin thook yang dai./Thook yang, phom gin dai.

> ผมกินได้ทุกอย่าง/ผมกินทุกอย่างได้/ทุกอย่างผมกินได้

4. thua - This is "throughout", "all over", or "pervading". It's used in phrases as follows:

I've traveled all over Thailand.

> Pra-thet Thai, chan thio ma thua (pra-thet) laeo.

> ประเทศไทย ฉันเที่ยวมาทั่ว(ประเทศ)แล้ว

People watch CNN news all over the world.

> Kao CNN mee kon doo thua lok.

> ข่าว CNN มีคนดูทั่วโลก

The whole city is flooded.

> Nam thuam thua meuang.

> น้ำท่วมทั่วเมือง

My whole body hurts.

> Chan jep pai thua tua leuy.

> ฉันเจ็บไปทั่วตัวเลย

in general - thua pai/thua-thua pai -

Everyone likes this song.

> Kon thua pai chawp fang phlayng nee.

> คนทั่วไปชอบฟังเพลงนี้

I'm the same as other women.

> Chan gaw meuan gap phoo-ying thua-thua pai.

> ฉันก็เหมือนกับผู้หญิงทั่วๆ ไป

5. tang - This is "all" or "each and every" with people and things, usually referring back to something already mentioned. *Tang* with this pronunciation also means "different" or "varied" and the meaning here may be interpreted as "each different one".

Everything is getting more expensive these days.

> Kao-kawng sa-mai nee, tang gaw phaeng keun pai mot.

> ข้าวของสมัยนี้ต่างก็แพงขึ้นไปหมด

6. ta-lawt - This means "throughout" or "the whole time/always". Common phrases are *talawt wayla* ("all the time") and *talawt cheewit* ("my whole life"). In this example it's "completely", referring to a hotel being empty throughout.

This hotel is completely empty.

Rong-raem nee wang ta-lawt.

โรงแรมนี้ว่างตลอด

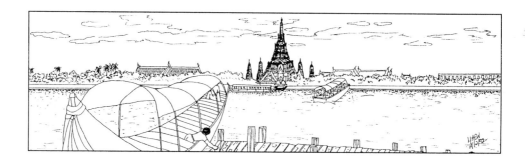

BOTH/ALL THREE

thang (number) (classifier) - The classifier is needed when the phrase includes "this". Compare the two ways to say the first example (*kon* is the classifier).

Both of these people are from Canada./Both of them are from Canada.

Thang sawng kon nee ma jak Kae-na-da.

ทั้งสองคนนี้มาจากแคนาดา

(Kao) thang sawng (kon) ma jak Kae-na-da.

(เค้า)ทั้งสอง(คน)มาจากแคนาดา

You both might like it.

Koon thang sawng (kon) at ja chawp gaw dai.

คุณทั้งสอง(คน)อาจจะชอบก็ได้

All three models are about the same price. (referring to cars)

Rot thang sam roon nee ra-ka thao-thao gan.

รถทั้งสามรุ่นนี้ราคาเท่าๆ กัน

The classifier is also needed when the phrase is at the end of the sentence as in the response here.

A: Do you like Phuket or Ko Samui more?

Chawp Phoo-get reu Gaw Sa-muij mak gwa gan?

ชอบภูเก็ตหรือเกาะสมุยมากกว่ากัน

B: I like both places.

Chawp thang sawng haeng. (or "thee" instead of *haeng*)

ชอบทั้งสองแห่ง

both...and... - thang...lae/gap... - Use either *lae* or *gap* for "and".

Both my mother and father like you (Jill) a lot.

> Thang phaw lae mae chawp Jill mak.
>
> ทั้งพ่อและแม่ชอบจิลมาก

A: What language does your child speak?

> Look phoot pha-saj a-rai?
>
> ลูกพูดภาษาอะไร

B: Both Thai and English.

> Thang pha-saj Thai gap pha-saj Ang-grit.
>
> ทั้งภาษาไทยกับภาษาอังกฤษ

thang...thang... - Put one of the things you're talking about after each *thang*.

I both love him and hate him.

> Chan thang rak, thang gliat kao.
>
> ฉันทั้งรักทั้งเกลียดเค้า

There are both difficult ones and easy ones./Some are difficult and some are easy.

> Mee thang thee yak (lae) thang thee ngai.
>
> มีทั้งที่ยาก(และ)ทั้งที่ง่าย

Both the staffmembers who are staying and those who are leaving, please come.

> Pha-nak-ngan thang thee ja yoo lae thang thee ja awk, ga-roo-na ma duay.
>
> พนักงานทั้งที่จะอยู่และทั้งที่จะออกกรุณามาด้วย

EXPRESSION: thang nee thang nan - This means "all in all".

All in all, it's up to you to decide for yourself.

> Thang nee thang nan gaw laeo tae koon ja tat-sinj-jai ayng.
>
> ทั้งนี้ทั้งนั้นก็แล้วแต่คุณจะตัดสินใจ

NEITHER/NONE/NOT ANY

neither/none - mai mee (classifier) naij - Here no distinction is made between "neither" (for two things) and "none" (for more than two).

Neither/none of these tape recorders works.

> Thayp phuak nee mai mee kreuang naij chai dai leuy.
>
> เทปพวกนี้ไม่มีเครื่องไหนใช้ได้เลย

Of those three islands, none was more beautiful than Ko Phi-Phi.

> Mai mee gaw naij leuy, nai samj gaw nan, thee suayj gwa Gaw Phee-Phee.
>
> ไม่มีเกาะไหนเลยในสามเกาะนั้นที่สวยกว่าเกาะพีพี

Of the houses around here, none is for rent.

    Ban thaeoŋ nee, mai mee laŋ naiŋ hai chao leuy.

       บ้านแถวนี้ไม่มีหลังไหนให้เช่าเลย

For people - mai mee krai/mai mee kon naiŋ - This is "neither" (for two people) or "none" (for more than two). "Nobody" is explained on pages 49-50 and 179.

Neither/none of them has a car.

    Phuak kao, mai mee krai mee rot leuy.

       พวกเค้าไม่มีใครมีรถเลย

neither/"not both" - This is "both of them haven't/both of them aren't".

Neither of these motorcycles has a registration.

    Rot thang sawnŋ kun nee mai mee tha-bian.

       รถทั้งสองคันนี้ไม่มีทะเบียน

not any - This is literally "not which" with *nai* or *arai* after the classifier (*arai* is more general). See also "yes/no questions with *any*" (page 76) and "whichever" (page 176).

He doesn't like any of the songs.

    Kao mai chawp phlayng naiŋ leuy.

       เค้าไม่ชอบเพลงไหนเลย

I don't have any problems.

    Chan mai mee pan-haŋ a-rai.

       ฉันไม่มีปัญหาอะไร

SOME

With countable nouns - (noun) bang (classifier) - *Bang* has a mid tone before classifiers. The noun can be omitted if it's understood in context.

Some of the shrimp are rotten.

    (Goonŋ) bang tua nao laeo.

       (กุ้ง)บางตัวเน่าแล้ว

pen bang (classifier) - *Pen* may be included when the phrase is at the end.

A: Did everyone come?

    Ma thook kon mai?

       มาทุกคนมั้ย

B: Some people came.

    Ma (pen) bang kon.

       มา(เป็น)บางคน

With uncountable nouns - bang/sak nit neung/sak noi - *Bang* with a falling tone means "some", "in part", "to some extent", or "somewhat".

There's some rice in the cupboard.

Mee kao yoo nai too (yoo) bang.

มีข้าวอยู่ในตู้อยู่บ้าง

I want to give the children some food.

Chan yak ao a-han hai dek-dek sak nit neung.

ฉันอยากเอาอาหารให้เด็กๆ ซักนิดนึง

there are some - mee bang (classifier)/mee bang -

Some people complain that the bathroom over there is dirty.

Mee bang kon bon wa hawng-nam thee-nan mai sa-at.

มีบางคนบ่นว่าห้องน้ำที่นั่นไม่สะอาด

A: Is there a lot of money left?

Mee ngeuhn leua yeuh mai?

มีเงินเหลือเยอะมั้ย

B: There's some.

Gaw mee yoo bang.

ก็มีอยู่บ้าง

A: Do you like Western food?

Chawp a-han fa-rang mai?

ชอบอาหารฝรั่งมั้ย

B: There are some kinds I like. (*yang* is the classifier for "kinds")

Gaw mee bang yang thee chawp./Gaw mee thee chawp bang.

ก็มีบางอย่างที่ชอบ/ก็มีที่ชอบบ้าง

"a part of" for "some" - suan neung/jam-nuan neung/bang suan -

Some of the money is missing.

Ngeuhn suan neung hai pai./Ngeuhn hai pai jam-nuan neung.

เงินส่วนหนึ่งหายไป/เงินหายไปจำนวนหนึ่ง

Some of the rice we keep and some of it we sell.

Kao suan neung ja gep wai. Eeg suan neung ja kai.

ข้าวส่วนหนึ่งจะเก็บไว้ อีกส่วนหนึ่งจะขาย

Thai men who are over 25, some of them have been monks.

Phoo-chai Thai thee a-yoo geuhn yee-sip pee, bang suan keuy pen phra (ma laeo).

ผู้ชายไทยที่อายุเกิน 25 ปี บางส่วนเคยเป็นพระ(มาแล้ว)

With verbs ("study some") - bang/mung - Put *bang* or *mung* after the verb to mean "some", "somewhat" or "sometimes". *Mung* (also pronounced *mang*) is informal. A common pattern is to say two things that have the opposite meaning and put *bang* after each (as in the response in the examples). See also pages 75-76 ("*some* with questions") 289-290 ("uses of *mung*"), and 382 ("*bang* for *sometimes*").

I can read some of it.

> Phǒmj an dai bang.
>
> ผมอ่านได้บ้าง

A: Do you cook your own food?

> Tham gap kao gin ayng reu plao?
>
> ทำกับข้าวกินเองรึเปล่า

B: We cook some and buy some.

> Gaw tham gin ayng bang, seu gin bang.
>
> ก็ทำกินเองบ้าง ซื้อกินบ้าง

THE GREATER PART/THE SMALLER PART

most/mostly/the greater part - suan mak/suan yai - *Suan* means "part" or "portion", and these phrases mean "the greater part", "the majority", or "mostly". *Suan mak* also means "usually", "mostly", or "most of the time" (pages 384-385).

Most of the clothes around Pratunam are cheap.

> Seua-pha thaeoj Pra-too-nam suan mak ra-ka thook.
>
> เสื้อผ้าแถวประตูน้ำส่วนมากราคาถูก

Some women like to watch boxing, but mostly it's men.

> Gaw mee phoo-yingj bang kon thee chawp doo muay, tae suan mak pen phoo-chai.
>
> ก็มีผู้หญิงบางคนที่ชอบดูมวย แต่ส่วนมากเป็นผู้ชาย

A: Why doesn't the traffic improve?

> Tham-mai gan ja-ra-jawn mai dee keun?
>
> ทำไมการจราจรไม่ดีขึ้น

B: Mostly because there are too many cars.

> Suan yai gaw phraw wa mee rot mak geuhn pai.
>
> ส่วนใหญ่ก็เพราะว่ามีรถมากเกินไป

pen suan mak - This is used at the end of sentences.

Most of the people here do their farm work together.

> Chao-ban thee-nee tham na gan pen suan mak.
>
> ชาวบ้านที่นี่ทำนากันเป็นส่วนมาก

the smaller part/few - <u>suan</u> <u>noi</u> - This also means "the minority".

There are few people who don't like rice.

    Kon <u>suan</u> <u>noi</u> <u>mai</u> <u>chawp</u> <u>kao</u>.

    คนส่วนน้อยไม่ชอบเค้า

Some people don't agree, but they're in the minority.

    Mee kon <u>mai</u> <u>heny</u> duay, tae (mun) (pen) <u>suan</u> <u>noi</u>.

    มีคนไม่เห็นด้วยแต่(มัน)(เป็น)ส่วนน้อย

especially - doy <u>cha-phaw</u> (<u>yang ying</u>) - This is also translated as "particularly" or "in particular". Here you're referring to one thing that stands out from others.

I like hot food, especially "phat phet".

    <u>Chan</u> <u>chawp</u> a-<u>hany</u> <u>phet</u>, doy <u>cha-phaw</u> (<u>yang ying</u>) <u>phat</u> <u>phet</u>.

    ฉันชอบอาหารเผ็ด โดยเฉพาะ(อย่างยิ่ง)ผัดเผ็ด

There are many reasons why he quit, but it was mostly because he didn't like the boss.

    Mee <u>lai</u> <u>hayt-phony</u> <u>thee</u> <u>kao</u> la <u>awk</u>, doy <u>cha-phaw</u> (phraw wa) <u>kao</u> <u>mai</u> <u>chawp</u>

    <u>huay-na</u>.

    มีหลายเหตุผลที่เค้าลาออก โดยเฉพาะ(เพราะว่า)เค้าไม่ชอบหัวหน้า

EACH/EVERY/PER

(so much) per (month/person) - There are two ways to form this pattern.

1. (classifier) <u>la</u> (amount) - Put *la*, meaning "each", between the month, person, etc, and the amount. In the first example *phaeng* is the classifier for medicine sold in small, flat packages.

This medicine is sold at ten baht a package.

    Ya <u>nee</u> <u>kai</u> <u>phaeny</u> <u>la</u> <u>sip</u> <u>baht</u>.

    ยานี้ขายแผงละสิบบาท

I'd like one of each (kind).

    <u>Chan</u> <u>ao</u> <u>yang</u> <u>la</u> <u>un</u>, <u>ka</u>.

    ฉันเอาอย่างละอันค่ะ

Give them each 100 baht.

    <u>Hai</u> <u>kao</u> <u>kon</u> <u>la</u> <u>roi</u> <u>baht</u>.

    ให้เค้าคนละร้อยบาท

Give each child two pieces of candy.

    <u>Hai</u> <u>look</u>-om <u>dek</u> <u>kon</u> <u>la</u> <u>sawny</u> <u>met</u>.

    ให้ลูกอมเด็กคนละสองเม็ด

There are two houses left that are three million each.

    <u>Ban</u>, <u>lany</u> <u>la</u> <u>samy</u> <u>lan</u>, mee <u>leua</u> <u>yoo</u> <u>sawny</u> <u>lany</u>.

    บ้านหลังละสามล้านมีเหลืออยู่สองหลัง

2. (amount) <u>taw</u> (classifier) - With *taw* the words are switched. *Deuan la meun baht* ("ten thousand baht a month") becomes *meun baht taw deuan*.

Farmers around here plant rice twice a year.

    Chao-na <u>thaeo</u> nee <u>plook</u> kao sawng krang <u>taw</u> pee.

    ชาวนาแถวนี้ปลูกข้าวสองครั้งต่อปี

They pay us each 100 baht a day.

    Kao <u>jai</u> hai rao roi <u>baht</u> taw kon taw wan.

    เค้าจ่ายให้เราร้อยบาทต่อคนต่อวัน

He drove at 150 kilometers per hour.

    Kao <u>kap</u> rot roi ha-<u>sip</u> gee-lo-met <u>taw</u> chua-mong.

    เค้าขับรถร้อยห้าสิบกิโลเมตรต่อชั่วโมง

each (one)/every (one) - <u>tae</u> la (classifier) - This also means "each and every" or "every single".

Every year I stay with my parents for one week.

    Nai <u>tae</u> la pee phom ja <u>yoo</u> gap phaw-mae neung a-thit.

    ในแต่ละปีผมจะอยู่กับพ่อแม่หนึ่งอาทิตย์

Each time I go to Bangkok I spend more than 1,000 baht.

    Pai Groong-thayp <u>tae</u> la krang tawng chai ngeuhn <u>gwa</u> phan <u>baht</u>.

    ไปกรุงเทพฯ แต่ละครั้งต้องใช้เงินกว่าพันบาท

Each person can eat two.

    <u>Tae</u> la kon gin dai <u>sawng</u> un.

    แต่ละคนกินได้สองอัน

The Chinese government stipulates that no family can have more than one child.

    Rat-tha-ban Jeen gam-<u>not</u> wa <u>tae</u> la krawp-krua mee look dai mai geuhn kon

    (<u>neung</u>).

    รัฐบาลจีนกำหนดว่าแต่ละครอบครัวมีลูกได้ไม่เกินคน(หนึ่ง)

ENOUGH

There are many patterns and expressions with *phaw* ("enough").

With nouns ("enough money") - *Mak* is optional between the noun and *phaw*.

I have enough money.

    Chan mee ngeuhn (mak) phaw.

    ฉันมีเงิน(มาก)พอ

I don't have enough money.

    <u>Phom</u> mai mee ngeuhn phaw./<u>Phom</u> mee ngeuhn mai phaw.

    ผมไม่มีเงินพอ/ผมมีเงินไม่พอ

Three million baht should be enough.

> Sam̄y lán baht kong (mak̄) phaw.

> สามล้านบาทคง(มาก)พอ

With verbs and adjectives -

I've played enough. I'm tired.

> Chan̄ len̄ phaw laeo. Neuay.

> ฉันเล่นพอแล้ว เหนื่อย

A: Is it big enough?

> Yai phaw mai?

> ใหญ่พอมั้ย

B: Yes./No.

> (Yai) phaw./(Yai) mai phaw.

> (ใหญ่)พอ/(ใหญ่)ไม่พอ

enough to... - phaw (thee) (ja)... -

I have enough medicine to take for three days.

> Chan̄ mee ya phaw (thee) (ja) gin dai sam̄y wan.

> ฉันมียาพอ(ที่)(จะ)กินได้สามวัน

I don't have enough money to buy it.

> Phom̄y mai mee ngeuhn phaw (thee ja) seu. (or *phaw ja seu* in all)

> ผมไม่มีเงินพอ(ที่จะ)ซื้อ

> Phom̄y mee ngeuhn mai phaw (thee ja) seu.

> ผมมีเงินไม่พอ(ที่จะ)ซื้อ

> Ngeuhn (phom̄y) mai mee phaw (thee ja) seu.

> เงิน(ผม)ไม่มีพอ(ที่จะ)ซื้อ

I haven't had time to finish it.

> Yang mai mee way-la phaw (thee) ja tham̄ hai set.

> ยังไม่มีเวลาพอ(ที่)จะทำให้เสร็จ

There's not enough to eat./I don't have enough to eat.

> Mai mee phaw gin./Mee mai phaw gin.

> ไม่มีพอกิน/มีไม่พอกิน

Following are examples with adjectives, verbs, and adverbs.

She's tall enough to play basketball.

> Kao soonḡy phaw (thee) ja len̄ bas-get-bawn dai.

> เค้าสูงพอ(ที่)จะเล่นบาสเก็ตบอลได้

I'm not tall enough to be a soldier.

> Phŏm soong mâi phaw (thee) jà pen thá-han.

> ผมสูงไม่พอ(ที่)จะเป็นทหาร

I've studied enough to pass the test.

> Chán rian ma (mâk) phaw thee jà sawp phan dâi.

> ฉันเรียนมา(มาก)พอที่จะสอบผ่านได้

I still can't speak Thai well enough to use it to teach.

> Phŏm yang phôot pha-sa Thai mâi geng phaw thee jà chai sawn dâi.

> ผมยังพูดภาษาไทยไม่เก่งพอที่จะใช้สอนได้

An alternative with verbs is to put *phaw ja* or *phaw-phaw ja* first, before the verb.

I know enough already. You don't have to say anymore.

> Chán phaw-phaw jà roo laeo. Mâi tawng phôot eeg laeo.

> ฉันพอๆ จะรู้แล้ว ไม่ต้องพูดอีกแล้ว

OTHER PHRASES WITH "ENOUGH"

sufficient/sufficiently - phiang phaw - This is more formal than *phaw* alone.

I've slept enough.

> Phŏm dâi láp (phiang) phaw laeo.

> ผมได้หลับ(เพียง)พอแล้ว

enough for - phaw sam-ràp/phaw gàp/phaw hai - The last is "enough to give".

This is enough for me.

> Kae nee gaw phaw laeo sam-ràp chán.

> แค่นี้ก็พอแล้วสำหรับฉัน

This isn't enough food for everyone.

> A-han nee mâi (phiang) phaw sam-ràp thook kon.

> อาหารนี้ไม่(เพียง)พอสำหรับทุกคน

There's only enough for one person.

> Mee phaw (sam-ràp) kae neung kon.

> มีพอ(สำหรับ)แค่หนึ่งคน

There aren't enough police here for the needs of the people.

> Tam-ruat thee-nee mâi phaw gàp kwam tawng-gan kawng chao-ban.

> ตำรวจที่นี่ไม่พอกับความต้องการของชาวบ้าน

We have enough shirts for/to give to everyone.

> Rao mee seua (phiang) phaw (thee) jà hai thook kon.

> เรามีเสื้อ(เพียง)พอ(ที่)จะให้ทุกคน

fairly good to (verb) - phaw (verb) dai - Put the verb between *phaw* and *dai*. Following are some common phrases:

phaw chai dai	adequate, adequately, passable, fair, good enough to use
phaw doo dai	fairly good to see (for movies, tourist spots)
phaw fang dai	alright to listen to (for music)
phaw gin dai	fairly good to eat
phaw kao-jai dai	can understand well enough
phaw tham dai	can do it well enough

He doesn't play really well, but he's alright.

Kao len mai geng mak, tae gaw phaw chai dai.

เค้าเล่นไม่เก่งมากแต่ก็พอใช้ได้

A: Is it good?

Dee mai?

ดีมั้ย

B: It's good enough.

Dee phaw chai dai.

ดีพอใช้ได้

can do adequately - (verb) phaw dai/phaw ja (verb) dai -
John can speak Thai pretty well.

John phoot pha-sa Thai phaw dai.

จอห์นพูดภาษาไทยพอได้

I can fix cars fairly well, but not really well.

Phom phaw ja sawm rot dai bang, tae mai geng.

ผมพอจะซ่อมรถได้บ้างแต่ไม่เก่ง

I have enough - phaw mee -
I have some friends, but we're not that close.

Phaw mee pheuan yoo bang, tae gaw mai koi sa-nit thao-rai.

พอมีเพื่อนอยู่บ้างแต่ก็ไม่ค่อยสนิทเท่าไหร่

A: Do you have enough money?

Mee ngeuhn phaw mai?

มีเงินพอมั้ย

B: Yes. about enough.

Gaw phaw mee./Phaw mee bang.

ก็พอมี/พอมีบ้าง

a fair amount - phaw sŏm-kuan - This is also under "rather/fairly" on page 186.

I've studied a fair amount.

Phŏm rian ma phaw sŏm-kuan.

ผมเรียนมาพอสมควร

just right - phaw dee - With quantities this means "exactly", "precisely", or "just the right size/amount", and with time it means "just then" or "at that very moment".

This room is just right for two people.

Hawng nee yoo dai sawng kon phaw dee.

ห้องนี้อยู่ได้สองคนพอดี

This dress is just right for me.

Choot nee phaw dee (sǎm-ráp) chan leuy.

ชุดนี้พอดี(สำหรับ)ฉันเลย

it's complete - krop - This is "fully", "completely", or "in full", meaning that something is complete or has everything that should be there. A waiter in a restaurant might say *mai krop* if you haven't given him enough money. (The "r" may not be pronounced.)

A: Is it enough? (to cover the bill)

Krop mai, krup?

ครบมั้ยครับ

B: No. I need 50 more baht.

Yang mai krop, ka. Kat eeg ha-sip baht.

ยังไม่ครบค่ะ ขาดอีกห้าสิบบาท

A: Are all of your things there?

Kawng yoo krop mai?

ของอยู่ครบมั้ย

B: No. Two or three things are missing.

Mai krop. Kat pai sawng-sam yang.

ไม่ครบ ขาดไปสองสามอย่าง

ONLY/JUST

There are at least eleven ways to say "only/just" in Thai. "Only" has two meanings—"only a small amount" and "only one thing/exclusively". In Thai the first is *kae, ayng,* or *phiang* and the second is *yang dio, leuy, tae, cha-phaw, dio,* or *cheuy-cheuy. Thao-nan* is used for both, and *pheung* is used with time ("I just came").

1. kae - This word means "level", "point", "as far as", or "up to" and has the extended meaning of "only".

I only have 500 baht. Is that enough?

> Chan mee ngeuhn kae ha roi baht. Phaw mai?
>
> ฉันมีเงินแค่ห้าร้อยบาท พอมั้ย

The company only gave me two shirts.

> Baw-ree-sat hai seua kae sawng tua.
>
> บริษัทให้เสื้อแคสองตัว

On this trip to Thailand Bob's only staying in Bangkok.

> Kao ma thio meuang Thai krang nee, Bob ja yoo kae nai Groong-thayp.
>
> เข้ามาเที่ยวเมืองไทยครั้งนี้บ๊อบจะอยู่แค่ในกรุงเทพฯ

I just want to try.

> Phom kae yak ja lawng doo.
>
> ผมแค่อยากจะลองดู

only this much/only to here - kae nee -

I can only help you this much.

> Phom chuay koon dai kae nee, lae.
>
> ผมช่วยคุณได้แค่นี้แหละ

Have I turned the air conditioner up far enough?/Is this the right level?

> Peuht ae kae nee phaw mai?
>
> เปิดแอร์แค่นี้พอมั้ย

2. thao-nan - This is literally "equal to that" and means both "only a small amount" (first example) and "only one thing" (second example). *Kae* can be included with the first meaning.

I have only five baht.

> Phom mee kae ha baht thao-nan.
>
> ผมมีแค่ห้าบาทเท่านั้น

This restroom is for women only.

> Hawng-nam nee sam-rap phoo-ying thao-nan.
>
> ห้องน้ำนี้สำหรับผู้หญิงเท่านั้น

3. ayng - This is used with numbers to emphasize that an amount is small and can be used along with *kae* or *thao-nan* (or all three words at once).

Only two or three people are going.

> Pai pra-man sawng-sam kon ayng.
>
> ไปประมาณสองสามคนเอง

Gai only comes up to (the level of) my shoulders.

> Gai soong kae lai phom thao-nan ayng.
>
> ไกสูงแค่ไหลผมเท่านั้นเอง

4. only to the level of - phiang/phiang kae/phiang tae - *Phiang* and *phiang tae* are "only/just" and *phiang kae* is "only to the level of". See also "except that", pages 154-155.

It's sold for only 500 baht.

Kai̯ ra-ka phiang (kae) ha roi baht thao-nan.

ขายราคาเพียง(แค่)ห้าร้อยบาทเท่านั้น

I just looked at his eyes and knew he was lying.

Phiang tae mawng ta, chan gaw roo wa kao go-hok. (or use *phiang kae*)

เพียงแค่มองตาฉันก็รู้ว่าเค้าโกหก

The negative *mai phiang tae* can include *eeg tang hak* or *duay* at the end for "also".

She's not only beautiful, she's rich.

Theuh mai phiang tae suay̯, yang ruay eeg tang hak.

เธอไม่เพียงแต่สวยยังรวยอีกต่างหาก

5. only one kind/thing - yang dio - This is used with actions for "does only one thing" and with objects for "one kind" or "the only kind". *Ahan yang dio* means both "one kind of food" and "the only kind of food".

I only want fried rice.

Ao kao-phat yang dio, na.

เอาข้าวผัดอย่างเดียวนะ

I only asked him his name.

Phom̯ tham̯ cheu̯ yang dio.

ผมถามชื่ออย่างเดียว

The only thing my mother wants me to do is study.

Mae yak hai chan rian yang dio.

แม่อยากให้ฉันเรียนอย่างเดียว

EXPRESSION: look dio - This is an informal phrase that refers to a strong feeling of wanting to do only one thing.

He's not interested in anyone. He just likes to play with his computer.

Kao mai son̯-jai krai. Ao tae len kawm-phiu-teuh look dio.

เค้าไม่สนใจใคร เอาแต่เล่นคอมพิวเตอร์ลูกเดียว

6. "only/just/recently" with time - pheung̯ (ja) -

I just bought it today.

Pheung seu wan-nee ayng.

เพิ่งซื้อวันนี้เอง

I've just learned that she used to be a teacher.

Chan pheung ja roo wa kao keuy pen kroo ma gawn.

ฉันเพิ่งจะรู้ว่าเค้าเคยเป็นครูมาก่อน

7. just/simply - leuy -

Just do it!

    Tham pai leuy!

       ทำไปเลย

If he wants to take a vacation, the only thing he can do is quit.

    Tha kao yak yoot ngan, kao gaw tawng la awk pai leuy.

       ถ้าเค้าอยากหยุดงานเค้าก็ต้องลาออกไปเลย

8. "but" meaning "only" - tae - This is "nothing but" or "only this exclusively" with things, amounts, and actions.

I'm only going to Korat.

    Phom ja pai tae Ko-rat (thao-nan). (or *kae* instead of *tae*)

       ผมจะไปแต่โคราช(เท่านั้น)

She only likes to watch TV.

    Theuh chawp tae doo tho-ra-that./Theuh chawp doo tae tho-ra-that.

       เธอชอบดูแต่โทรทัศน์/เธอชอบแต่ดูโทรทัศน์

Why does the manager just stay in his office?

    Tham-mai phoo-jat-gan yoo tae nai awf-fit?

       ทำไมผู้จัดการอยู่แต่ในออฟฟิศ

He's only good at talking.

    Kao geng tae phoot.

       เค้าเก่งแต่พูด

I'm just thinking about what place would be nice to go to.

    Chan kit tae wa ja pai nai dee.

       ฉันคิดแต่ว่าจะไปไหนดี

there's only/it only happens - mee tae -

In this house there are only women, no men.

    Ban nee mee tae phoo-ying, mai mee phoo-chai leuy.

       บ้านนี้มีแต่ผู้หญิง ไม่มีผู้ชายเลย

In that place it just rains every day.

    Thee-noon mee tae fon tok thook wan.

       ที่โน่นมีแต่ฝนตกทุกวัน

EXPRESSION: ao tae - This means that someone persists in doing only one thing.

Study! Don't just go out.

    An nang-seu bang see. Ya ao tae thio.

       อ่านหนังสือบ้างซิ อย่าเอาแต่เที่ยว

9. exclusively - cha-phaw - This is "only", "exclusively", "particularly", "only for", or "exclusively for". *Doy cha-phaw* is "especially/in particular".

I go to school on Sundays only.

Chan rian cha-phaw wan a-thit.

ฉันเรียนเฉพาะวันอาทิตย์

Service here is for members only.

Thee-nee baw-ree-gan cha-phaw sa-ma-chik.

ที่นี่บริการเฉพาะสมาชิก

10. single/sole - (classifier) dio -

He's the only Westerner who lives in this village.

Kao pen fa-rang kon dio thee yoo nai moo-ban nee.

เค้าเป็นฝรั่งคนเดียวที่อยู่ในหมู่บ้านนี้

11. meaning "indifferently" - cheuy-cheuy - *Cheuy-cheuy* means "indifferent" or "indifferently" and here has the extended meaning of "only".

I'm just looking.

Phom doo cheuy-cheuy.

ผมดูเฉยๆ

QUANTIFIERS WITH REQUESTS & SUGGESTIONS

These are included to make requests and suggestions sound more polite.

"a little" with requests (for politeness) - Include *noi* generally at the end of any request (page 142). *Nit dio*, *nit neung*, and *nit noi* are included when requesting an amount of something to show that the amount is small, thereby minimizing the request.

Let me see it.

Kaw doo noi, na.

ขอดูหน่อยนะ

Please put in a little milk.

Sai nom nit dio, na.

ใส่นมนิดเดียวนะ

May I try a little of that?

Kaw chim nit neung, na.

ขอชิมนิดนึงนะ

"a little" with requests (for an amount) - nit noi/nit dio/nit neung/noi-noi -

Put a little more water in the curry and that will be enough.

Gaeng nee sai nam nit dio gaw phaw laeo.

แกงนี้ใส่น้ำนิดเดียวก็พอแล้ว

A: Should I put in a lot? How much should I put in?

    Sai mak mai? Sai thao-rai dee.

        ใส่มากมั้ย ใส่เท่าไหร่ดี

B: Just a little.

    Sai noi-noi, na.

        ใส่น้อยๆ นะ

"a little" with *sak* - sak noi/sak nit -

Could I have some water?

    Kaw nam sak noi, see./Kaw nam sak gaeo, see.

        ขอน้ำสักหน่อยซิ/ขอน้ำสักแก้วซิ

I'd like to take a little walk.

    Phom yak deuhn len sak noi.

        ผมอยากเดินเล่นซักหน่อย

"more" with requests and offers - Use *eeg noi, eeg nit noi, eeg nit dio, eeg sak noi, eeg nit neung,* or *eeg sak nit neung.*

Could I have a little more rice?

    Kaw kao eeg nit neung.

        ขอข้าวอีกนิดนึง

Would you like more rice?

    Ao kao eeg sak noi mai?

        เอาข้าวอีกซักหน่อยมั้ย

Please let me sleep a little more.

    Kaw nawn (taw) eeg noi.

        ขอนอน(ต่อ)อีกหน่อย

"a little" with warnings - *Noi* tones down the meaning.

It's pretty far.

    Glai noi, na.

        ไกลหน่อยนะ

My car is pretty hard to drive.

    Rot chan kap yak noi, na.

        รถฉันขับยากหน่อยนะ

"some" with requests - *Bang* minimizes the amount.

Share the candy with your brother.

    Baeng ka-nom hai nawng bang see.

        แบ่งขนมให้น้องบ้างซิ

"some" with suggestions - Include *bang see* to make suggestions sound less forceful and direct.

She might want some time to herself.

> Kao kong yak mee way-la suan tua bang see.
>
> เค้าคงอยากมีเวลาส่วนตัวบ้างซิ

MORE/LESS

more/additional - eeg - *Eeg* also means "again" (page 108). For "one more/two more" and "a lot more" see page 32.

I can still eat more.

> Yang gin dai eeg.
>
> ยังกินได้อีก

left/leftover - Use *leua* when "more" means "remaining".

I still have more money.

> Chan yang mee ngeuhn leua (eeg).
>
> ฉันยังมีเงินเหลือ(อีก)

I don't have any money left./I don't have any more money.

> Chan mai mee ngeuhn leua (eeg) laeo. (or *leua leuy*)
>
> ฉันไม่มีเงินเหลือ(อีก)แล้ว

There are still a lot of people.

> Yang leua eeg lai kon.
>
> ยังเหลืออีกหลายคน

Only Lek is left.

> Leua (tae) Lek kon dio.
>
> เหลือ(แต่)เล็กคนเดียว

For the two days that are left I'm going to Mae Hong Song.

> Eeg sawng wan thee leua phom ja pai Mae Hawng Sawng.
>
> อีกสองวันที่เหลือผมจะไปแม่ฮ่องสอน

a little more - eeg noi/eeg nit noi/eeg nit dio - The last is "only a little more".

A: How much more water is there?

Mee nam eeg thao-rai?

มีน้ำอีกเท่าไหร่

B: There's a little more.

Mee eeg nit noi.

มีอีกนิดหน่อย

some more - eeg bang (nit noi) -

I have some more money.

Phom mee ngeuhn eeg bang nit noi.

ผมมีเงินอีกบ้างนิดหน่อย

more than - mak gwa/soong gwa - The first is for amounts, and the second means "higher than" or "taller than" and is used with prices.

There are more students this year than last year.

Pee nee mee nak-rian mak gwa pee gawn.

ปีนี้มีนักเรียนมากกว่าปีก่อน

Before, money was worth more than it is now.

Meua-gawn ngeuhn mee ka mak gwa nee.

เมื่อก่อนเงินมีค่ามากกว่านี้

Prices in Sydney are a lot higher than in Bangkok.

Ra-ka kawng thee Sid-nee soong gwa thee Groong-thayp mak.

ราคาของที่ซิดนีย์สูงกว่าที่กรุงเทพมากๆ

less than/fewer than/lower than - tam gwa/noi gwa - *Tam gwa* refers to a level while *noi gwa* is for amounts. The first two sentences can use both.

Children who are under fifteen can't see this movie.

Dek a-yoo tam gwa sip-ha pee doo nang reuang nee mai dai.

เด็กอายุต่ำกว่า 15 ปีดูหนังเรื่องนี้ไม่ได้

Two hundred an hour. If it's less than that I won't take it.

Sawng roi taw chua-mong. Tha noi gwa nee chan mai ao.

สองร้อยต่อชั่วโมง ถ้าน้อยกว่านี้ฉันไม่เอา

Don't use *tam gwa* here because "less" refers to an amount.

Fewer people are coming to Pattaya this year than in the past.

Pee nee mee kon ma Phat-tha-ya noi gwa deuhm.

ปีนี้มีคนมาพัทยาน้อยกว่าเดิม

over (an amount) - Words/phrases are put either before or after the amount.

1. after the amount - gwa/gwa-gwa - The monetary unit (here *baht*) or classifier (*kon*) may be put after *gwa* but not after *gwa-gwa*.

This class has over thirty students.

    Hawng-rian nee mee nak-rian samj-sip gwa kon.

    ห้องเรียนนี้มีนักเรียนสามสิบกว่าคน

A: How much did you buy it for?

    Seu ma thao-rai?

    ซื้อมาเท่าไหร่

B: A little over a thousand baht.

    Phan gwa baht./Phan gwa-gwa.

    พันกว่าบาท/พันกว่าๆ

2. before the amount - gwa/geuhn/mak gwa/geuhn gwa - When *gwa* is put before numbers it refers to a greater amount than when it's put after. *Gwa roi baht*, as here, refers to 200 or 300 baht while *roi gwa baht* refers to 120 or 130 baht.

More than 200 people died.

    Mee kon siaj chee-wit gwa sawngj roi kon.

    มีคนเสียชีวิตกว่าสองร้อยคน

I was waiting for over two hours.

    Phomj koi yoo mak gwa sawngj chua-mong.

    ผมคอยอยู่มากกว่าสองชั่วโมง

We made more profit than we expected.

    Rao dai gam-rai geuhn gwa thee kat wai.

    เราได้กำไรเกินกว่าที่คิดไว้

not over/not more than - mai geuhn -

A: How much is a taxi to Silom Rd?

    Ka thaek-see pai tha-nonj Seej-lom thao-rai?

    ค่าแท็กซี่ไปถนนสีลมเท่าไหร่

B: Around 80 baht. Not over 100.

    Kong rao paet-sip baht. Mai geuhn roi.

    คงราว 80 บาท ไม่เกินร้อย

not more than this - mai mak gwa nee/mai geuhn gwa nee -

I'll stay here for two or three nights. Not more than that.

    Chan ja phak thee-nee sawngj-samj keun. Mai mak gwa nee.

    ฉันจะพักที่นี่สองสามคืน ไม่มากกว่านี้

not higher/taller than - mãi soongǰ gwa - This is for height and prices.

The price of this car isn't over 100,000 baht.

Ra-ka rot kun nee mãi soongǰ gwa saenǰ baht.

ราคารถคันนี้ไม่สูงกว่าแสนบาท

not less than - mãi noi gwa/mãi tam gwa - These are interchangable with prices, quantities, and height.

To be a policeman, you can't be less than 160 cm tall.

Jà pen tam-ruat dãi, tawngǰ soongǰ mãi tam gwa roi hok-sip sen.

จะเป็นตำรวจได้ต้องสูงไม่ต่ำกว่า 160 เซน

If you sold this house it wouldn't be for less than five million baht.

Ban langǰ nee, thã (jà) kaiǰ, (ra-ka) kong (jà) mãi noi gwa hã lan baht.

บ้านหลังนี้ถ้า(จะ)ขาย(ราคา)คง(จะ)ไม่น้อยกว่าห้าล้านบาท

extra - There are at least seven ways to say "extra", depending on the meaning.

wang	when the meaning is "free"
leuaǰ	"leftover" or "in excess of what's needed"
sam-rawng	"reserve" or "in reserve"
seuhmǰ	"to supplement"
phee-set	means "special"
pheua	"as a surplus for a contingency"; this word also means "in case" and has that meaning in the last example here
geuhn	means "over" or "in excess"

We have an extra room. You can stay there.

Rao mee hawngǰ wang yoo hawngǰ neung. Koon phak thee-nan gaw dãi.

เรามีห้องว่างอยู่ห้องหนึ่ง คุณพักที่นั่นก็ได้

Do you have an extra shirt I could wear?

Mee seuaǰ leuaǰ hãi phomǰ sai mãi?

มีเสื้อเหลือให้ผมใส่มั้ย

This is an extra light bulb. Use it if one burns out.

Neeǰ pen lawt-fai sam-rawng. Chai meua lawt-fai siaǰ.

นี่เป็นหลอดไฟสำรอง ใช้เมื่อหลอดไฟเสีย

They have extra buses during rush hours.

Mee rot seuhmǰ nai chuang chua-mong rengǰ duan.

มีรถเสริมในช่วงชั่วโมงเร่งด่วน

This month I had extra expenses, so I had to ask my parents for some money.

Deuan neeǰ mee kã chai-jai phee-set, leuy tawngǰ kawǰ ngeuhn phaw-maeǰ.

เดือนนี้มีค่าใช้จ่ายพิเศษเลยต้องขอเงินพ่อแม่

Please take an extra jacket for me. I didn't bring one.

Ao seua-gan-naoჯ pai pheua chan duay, na. Chan mai dai ao ma duay leuy.

เอาเสื้อกันหนาวไปเผื่อฉันด้วยนะ ฉันไม่ได้เอามาด้วยเลย

I brought some extra money in case we're here longer than we expected.

Phomჯ ao ngeuhn ma geuhn, wai pheua rao yoo nan gwa thee kat wai.

ผมเอาเงินมาเกิน ไว้เผื่อเราอยู่นานกว่าที่คาดไว้

give as a bonus - thaemჯ - This is a verb meaning "to add to for good measure". It may be used in stores and advertising to refer to a free gift you receive when you buy something.

Buy a large tube of toothpaste and get a free plate.

Seu ya seeჯ funჯ lawt yai thaemჯ jan neung bai.

ซื้อยาสีฟันหลอด ใหญ่แถมจานหนึ่งใบ

INCREASE/DECREASE

increased/gone up - pheuhm/keun/pheuhm keun - These are verbs with the passive meaning that something has increased or gone up. With prices use only *keun* or *pheuhm keun*, not *pheuhm* alone.

My weight has gone up to 50 kilos.

Nam-nak pheuhm pen ha-sip gee-lo laeo.

น้ำหนักเพิ่มเป็น 50 กิโลแล้ว

Noi's complaining that the rent has gone up again.

Noi bon wa ka chao (pheuhm) keun eeg laeo.

น้อยบ่นว่าค่าเช่า(เพิ่ม)ขึ้นอีกแล้ว

raise/increase (actively) - pheuhm/seuhmჯ - The first is a verb meaning "to increase", "raise", or "augment", referring to adding something to what was already there. It can be expanded to *pheuhm eeg* or *pheuhm keun eeg*. *Seuhm* is a verb meaning "to add to" or "to supplement".

I want to gain ten kilos.

Yak pheuhm nam-nak (keun) eeg sak sip gee-lo.

อยากเพิ่มน้ำหนัก(ขึ้น)อีกซักสิบกิโล

My pay is too low. I'd like to make more.

Ngeuhn deuan noi pai. Yak dai pheuhm (keun eeg).

เงินเดือนน้อยไป อยากได้เพิ่ม(ขึ้นอีก)

The factory is adding more machinery.

Rong-ngan gam-lang ja pheuhm jam-nuan kreuang-jak.

โรงงานกำลังจะเพิ่มจำนวนเครื่องจักร

Some Thais add to their noses, while Westerners have some taken off.

Kon Thai bang kon seuhmj ja-mook, suan fa-rang bang kon tat ja-mook awk.

คนไทยบางคนเสริมจมูก ส่วนฝรั่งบางคนตัดจมูกออก

With prices - Compare these pairs of sentences. The first in each has *keun* and refers to a person or agency actively raising or increasing a price. The second has *keun* or *pheuhm keun* and refers to a price being increased.

The government has raised the tax on cigarettes.

Rat-tha-ban keun pha-seej boo-ree.

รัฐบาลขึ้นภาษีบุหรี่

The tax on liquor will go up. (will be increased)

Pha-seej soo-ra ja (pheuhm) keun.

ภาษีสุราจะ(เพิ่ม)ขึ้น

This station has increased its gasoline prices again.

Pum nee keun ra-ka nam-mun eeg laeo.

ปั๊มนี้ขึ้นราคาน้ำมันอีกแล้ว

The price of gasoline has gone up. (has been increased)

Nam-mun keun ra-ka./Ra-ka nam-mun (pheuhm) keun.

น้ำมันขึ้นราคา/ราคาน้ำมัน(เพิ่ม)ขึ้น

become more - mak keun/pheuhm (mak) keun - Here you're describing an amount so *mak* is included. *Keun* isn't a verb here; it's included for the comparative. (The opposite of *mak keun* is *noi long*.)

Working here has given me more experience.

Tham-ngan thee-nee tham hai chan mee pra-sop-gan mak keun.

ทำงานที่นี่ทำให้ฉันมีประสบการณ์มากขึ้น

More people will go to Phuket this year.

Pee nee ja mee kon pai Phoo-get pheuhm keun.

ปีนี้จะมีคนไปภูเก็ตเพิ่มขึ้น

gone down/decreased - long - This is the opposite of *pheuhm* or *(pheuhm) keun*.

The price of this car has come down to 500,000.

Ra-ka rot kun nee long ma pen ha saenj.

ราคารถคันนี้ลงมาเป็นห้าแสน

noi long - This is both a verb (*noi* meaning "become less") as in the first example and an adverb meaning "decreasingly/less" as in the second (where *noi long* modifies the verb "work" and is the opposite of *mak keun*). *Long* is included to show the direction of the action or to compare the amounts.

The tax on cars will decrease.

 Pha-seej rot ja noi long.

 ภาษีรถจะน้อยลง

Daeng's been working less since she had her baby.

 Daeng tham-ngan noi long tang-tae theuh mee look.

 แดงทำงานน้อยลงตั้งแต่เธอมีลูก

reduce/decrease (prices/amounts) - lot - This is for actively reducing an amount or price.

If Joe lost a little weight he'd ("probably") be better looking.

 Tha Joe lot kwam-uan sak noi, kao kong ja doo dee keun.

 ถ้าโจลดความอ้วนซักหน่อยเค้าคงจะดูดีขึ้น

Please reduce the price.

 Chuay lot hai noi, see.

 ช่วยลดให้หน่อยซิ

lot long - This is for reductions being done to something and also for something going down or becoming less.

Reduce it by one inch.

 Ao lot long neung niu.

 เอาลดลงหนึ่งนิ้ว

The temperature will go down to ten degrees.

 Oon-ha-phoom ja lot long pen sip ong-saj.

 อุณหภูมิจะลดลงเป็นสิบองศา

add on - buak -

The price includes tax doesn't it? ("adds on tax")

 Ra-ka nee buak pha-seej laeo, chai mai?

 ราคานี้บวกภาษีแล้วใช่มั้ย

subtract/deduct - hak awk/lop - *Hak awk* is "take off" and *lop* is for mathematical subtractions. *Lop* can be used in the first example but not in the second.

I get a discount. Please subtract ten percent.

 Phomj dai suan lot. Chuay hak awk sip peuh-sen duay. (or use *lop*)

 ผมได้ส่วนลด ช่วยหักออก 10 เปอร์เซนต์ด้วย

They should deduct the price of the elephant ride we didn't take.

 Kao kuan ja hak ka kee chang awk, rao mai dai kee.

 เค้าควรจะหักค่าขี่ช้างออก เราไม่ได้ขี่

UP TO AN AMOUNT/TO THIS EXTENT

up to/to the extent of - theung/theung gap - Use the first with amounts and the second with verbs or adjectives.

I have some small bills, but not 100 baht worth.

Phom mee baeng yoi, tae mai theung roi baht.

ผมมีแบงค์ย่อยแต่ไม่ถึงร้อยบาท

Taking a trip to Europe will cost a lot. ("up to many hundreds of thousands")

Deuhn-thang pai Yoo-rop tawng chai ngeuhn theung lai saeng.

เดินทางไปยุโรปต้องใช้เงินถึงหลายแสน

He wasn't really angry, just a little annoyed.

Kao mai theung gap grot, phiang tae ngoot-ngit nit noi.

เค้าไม่ถึงกับโกรธเพียงแต่หงุดหงิดนิดหน่อย

only up to - theung kae -

It's great that you were able to do this much.

Koon tham dai theung kae nee, gaw yiam laeo.

คุณทำได้ถึงแค่นี้ก็เยี่ยมแล้ว

If you can find just twenty workers, I'll give you five thousand baht.

Tha koon ha kon ngan dai theung kae yee-sip kon, chan ja jai hai koon ha phan baht.

ถ้าคุณหาคนงานได้ถึงแค่ยี่สิบคนฉันจะจ่ายให้คุณห้าพันบาท

this much/this extent - ka-nat nee - Also *kanat nan* for "that much" or "that extent". *Kanat* means "size" or "magnitude".

A: Is it OK to drive this fast/at this speed?

Kap ka-nat nee, dee mai?

ขับขนาดนี้ดีมั้ย

B: It's too fast.

Reo geuhn pai.

เร็วเกินไป

A: Do you have a million baht in the bank?

Mee ngeuhn nai tha-na-kan theung lan mai?

มีเงินในธนาคารถึงล้านมั้ย

B: No, not that much.

Mai theung ka-nat nan rawk.

ไม่ถึงขนาดนั้นหรอก

to this extent/so - (adj/adv) yang-ngee/ka-nat nee - Also with *nan*. *Yang-ngee* describes a condition while *kanat nee* is for things that are measured.

My house isn't hot like this.   (describes a condition)

Ban phom mai rawn yang-ngee.

บ้านผมไม่ร้อนยังงี้

My house isn't this hot/so hot. (describes the amount of heat)

Ban phom mai rawn ka-nat nee.

บ้านผมไม่ร้อนขนาดนี้

With test questions this easy anyone can pass.

Kaw sawp ngai yang-ngee krai-krai gaw sawp dai.

ข้อสอบง่ายยังงี้ใครๆ ก็สอบได้

I don't want to travel that far.

Phom mai yak pai glai ka-nat nan.

ผมไม่อยากไปไกลขนาดนั้น

It's never been so clean.

Mai keuy sa-at yang-ngee ma gawn.

ไม่เคยสะอาดยังงี้มาก่อน

Mak, mak mai, or *yeuh* may also be included after the adjective to add emphasis.

I didn't think it would be so expensive.

Mai kit wa ja phaeng mak yang-ngee.

ไม่คิดว่าจะแพงมากยังงี้

Following are examples with adverbs.

If you drive this fast you could have an accident.

Tha kap reo yang-ngee, dio gaw geuht oo-bat-tee-hayt (rawk).

ถ้าขับเร็วยังงี้เดี๋ยวก็เกิดอุบัติเหตุ(หรอก)

Someone who speaks English this well should be able to get a job easily.

Kon thee phoot Ang-grit geng (mak) ka-nat nee na ja ha ngan dai ngai.

คนที่พูดอังกฤษเก่ง(มาก)ขนาดนี้น่าจะหางานได้ง่าย

so much/that much - (noun/verb) mak yang-ngee/mak ka-nat nee - *Mak* is needed here because you're referring to an amount of a thing or activity.

I don't have that much money.

Chan mai mee ngeuhn mak yang-ngan.

ฉันไม่มีเงินมากยังงั้น

Someone with so many children probably has a lot of money problems.

Kon thee mee look mak ka-nat nee kong ja mee pan-ha reuang ngeuhn.

คนที่มีลูกมากขนาดนี้คงจะมีปัญหาเรื่องเงิน

I can't run so much./I can't run that much.

Phǒmɉ wîng mâk kà-nàt nán mâi dâi ràwk.

ผมวิ่งมากขนาดนั้นไม่ได้หรอก

Generalized statements (hypothetical) - These sentences have *ja* to show that they're generalized and hypothetical. *Kanat nee* and *yang-ngee* aren't needed.

Big apartments are expensive./Such big apartments are expensive.

Hâwng thêe yài jà phaeng.

ห้องที่ใหญ่จะแพง

People with so much money should give some to charity.

Kon thêe mee ngeuhn mâk-mâk kuan jà baw-rée-jàk sǐaɉ bâng.

คนที่มีเงินมากๆ ควรจะบริจาคเสียบ้าง

so little - nói yang-ngee - This also means "such a small amount as this".

I don't know why they gave me so little money.

Chǎn mâi róo wâ thám-mai káo hâi ngeuhn (chǎn) nói yang-ngee.

ฉันไม่รู้ว่าทำไมเค้าให้เงิน(ฉัน)น้อยยังงี้

so...that/up to the point that - jon/theunɉ gàp/jon theunɉ gàp - *Theung* is "arrive" or "reach to" and *jon* or *jon theung* mean "until". Here they refer to something happening up to the point of causing something else to occur. This is similar to "so/therefore" with *theung gap* (page 162). The difference here is that the meaning includes "until", so *jon* can also be used.

He was so drunk that he couldn't walk.

Káo mao (jon) theunɉ gàp deuhn mâi dâi.

เค้าเมา(จน)ถึงกับเดินไม่ได้

They have so many children that some of them can't go to school.

Káo mee lôok mâk jon lôok bang kon theunɉ gàp mâi dâi rian náng-seuɉ.

เค้ามีลูกมากจนลูกบางคนถึงกับไม่ได้เรียนหนังสือ

He made me wait so long that I was completely bored.

Káo hâi chǎn raw jon beua leuy.

เค้าให้ฉันรอจนเบื่อเลย

Was she so angry that she was going to hit him?

Theuh gròt jon jà tee káo reuɉ?

เธอโกรธจนจะตีเขาเหรอ

EXPRESSION: sǐaɉ jon - This has the same meaning but exphasizes "so".

You're so much more beautiful now, we didn't recognize you.

Koon suayɉ keûn (sǐaɉ) jon phûak rao jam mâi dâi.

คุณสวยขึ้น(เสีย)จนพวกเราจำไม่ได้

only...resulting in - k̄ae...theung gap -

Her boyfriend only forgot to buy toothpaste and she got angry.

    Kae faen kao leum seu ya-seej-fun, kao theung gap grot.

       แค่แฟนเค้าลืมซื้อยาสีฟัน เค้าถึงกับโกรธ

to the extent that - (theung) ka-nat (gap) - This refers to a size or magnitude. Compare it with *kanat* meaning "even if" on page 151.

It was so cold that people died. ("that people could die")

    Mun naoj ka-nat (gap) mee kon tai dai.

       มันหนาวขนาด(กับ)มีคนตายได้

She's so good at computers that a lot of companies are fighting to get her.

    Kao geng kawm-phiu-teuh theung ka-nat mee laij baw-ree-sat yaeng tua kao.

       เค้าเก่งคอมพิวเตอร์ถึงขนาดมีหลายบริษัทแย่งตัวเค้า

He goes drinking with friends, but not to the point of being delinquent.

    Kao gin lao gap pheuan bang, tae mai theung ka-nat gay-ray.

       เค้ากินเหล้ากับเพื่อนบ้างแต่ไม่ถึงขนาดเกเร

USING NUMBERS

The word "number" - There are four terms:

1. lek thee - This is for house and account numbers.

Nui lives in house number 21.

    Nui yoo ban lek thee yee-sip et.

       หนุ่ยอยู่บ้านเลขที่ 21

I can't remember my account number.

    Chan jam lek thee ban-chee mai dai.

       ฉันจำเลขที่บัญชีไม่ได้

2. maij lek - This is for official numbers such as registrations and ID's.

Her car license number is Chiang Mai 0658.

    Maij lek tha-bian rot (kawngj) kao keu Chiang Mai soonj hok ha paet.

       หมายเลขทะเบียนรถ(ของ)เค้าคือ เชียงใหม่ 0658

3. beuh - This comes from the second syllable of "number". It's used for phone numbers, seat numbers, and clothing sizes. In this example *tho* is used on the phone for the number "two" instead of *sawng*.

My phone number is 246-2200.

    Beuh tho-ra-sap phomj keu tho see hok, tho tho soonj soonj.

       เบอร์โทรศัพท์ผมคือ 246-2200

4. lek̃/tua lek̃ - These are for written number symbols.

Thais like to use Western numerals.

    Kon Thai nee-yom chai (tua) lek̃ baep fa-rang.

    คนไทยนิยมใช้(ตัว)เลขแบบฝรั่ง

Ordinal numbers - Put *thee* before the cardinal number.

the first	thee neung
the second	thee sawng
the first person	kon thee neung
Which person? (in a sequence)	kon thee thao-rai?

My first child is a doctor.

    Look kon thee neung pen maw.

        ลูกคนที่หนึ่งเป็นหมอ

I bought my second car last year.

    Rot kun thee sawng seu meua pee thee laeo.

        รถคันที่สองซื้อเมื่อปีที่แล้ว

even/odd - koo/kee - "Even number" is *lek koo* and "odd number" is *lek kee*.

Even-numbered soi's are on the right, odd numbers are on the left.

    Soi lek koo ja yoo dan kwa, lek kee ja yoo dan sai.

        ซอยเลขคู่จะอยู่ด้านขวา เลขคี่จะอยู่ด้านซ้าย

half - "One-half" is *kreung neung*. To describe half of something put *kreung* before the classifier.

We didn't eat all the cake. Half of it is left.

    Rao gin kayk mai mot. Leua yoo kreung neung.

        เรากินเค้กไม่หมด เหลืออยู่ครึ่งหนึ่ง

Today we work half a day.

    Wan-nee tham-ngan kreung wan.

        วันนี้ทำงานครึ่งวัน

two or three/five or ten/ten to twenty - No word is needed between sequential numbers. Put *theung* between non-sequential numbers

We're going with five or six friends.

    Rao ja pai gap pheuan eeg ha hok kon.

        เราจะไปกับเพื่อนอีกห้าหกคน

These dolls are sold for from 60 to 100 baht.

    Took-ga-ta nee kai tua la hok-sip theung roi baht.

        ตุ๊กตานี้ขายตัวละ 60 ถึง 100 บาท

percent - peuh-sen - This is from English. There are three ways to say "seven percent"—
jet peuh-sen, jet nai roi, and *roi la jet.*

A: What percentage of people who come here are foreigners?

Kon thee ma, mee fa-rang gee peuh-sen?

คนที่มามีฝรั่งกี่เปอร์เซนต์

B: Around 50 percent.

Rao-rao ha-sip peuh-sen.

ราวๆ 50 เปอร์เซนต์

Tourism will increase by around ten percent this year.

Pee nee (gan) thawng-thio ja pheuhm keun pra-man roi la sip.

ปีนี้(การ)ท่องเที่ยวจะเพิ่มขึ้นประมาณร้อยละ 10

times - thao - This word also means "equal".

Things in Thailand are about two times cheaper than in France.

Kawng thee meuang Thai thook gwa thee Fa-rang-set pra-man sawng thao.

ของที่เมืองไทยถูกกว่าที่ฝรั่งเศสประมาณสองเท่า

Bangkok is many times bigger than Chiang Mai.

Groong-thayp yai gwa Chiang Mai lai thao.

กรุงเทพฯ ใหญ่กว่าเชียงใหม่หลายเท่า

QUANTITY/PART/POINT/LEVEL/LIMIT

quantity/amount - jam-nuan - This word means "amount", "number", "quantity", and
also "the quantity of/the quantity being".

There's a lot of gold for sale here.

Thee-nee mee thawng kai jam-nuan mak.

ที่นี่มีทองขายจำนวนมาก

In the country there aren't enough teachers for the number of students.

Thee ban-nawk jam-nuan kroo mai phaw gap nak-rian.

ที่บ้านนอกจำนวนครูไม่พอกับนักเรียน

She's the owner of five taxis.

Kao pen jao kawng rot thaek-see jam-nuan ha kun.

เค้าเป็นเจ้าของรถแท็กซี่จำนวนห้าคัน

pa-ree-man - This is another word for "amount" but it's not used with measured quantities.

If there's a lot of rice in the market, it should be cheap.

Tha pa-ree-man kao nai ta-lat mak, kao ja thook.

ถ้าปริมาณข้าวในตลาดมากข้าวจะถูก

ban-joo - This is a verb meaning "to contain", "hold", or "to fill (a container with)". *Kanat ban-joo* is "contents". The word *ban-joo* is written on cartons of merchandise before the stated quantity.

This barrel holds 100 liters.

Thang nee ban-joo (dai) roi lit.

ถังนี้บรรจุ(ได้)ร้อยลิตร

part - suan/phak - The first is also translated as "portion" or "share". The second is used with regions of a country and also with movie sequels.

Some parts of Bangkok are very crowded.

Bang suan kawng Groong-thayp ae-at mak.

บางส่วนของกรุงเทพฯ แออัดมาก

Ann had a part in helping him pass the test.

Ann mee suan chuay hai kao sawp dai.

แอนมีส่วนช่วยให้เค้าสอบได้

You pay your own share, OK?

Koon jai suan kawng koon, na.

คุณจ่ายส่วนของคุณนะ

point - joot - This word is used for physical points, points reached in an undertaking, and points in an argument or discussion. It also means "decimal point" and "period".

This is the highest point the water has ever come up to.

Nee pen joot (thee) soong (thee) soot thee nam keuy keun ma.

นี่เป็นจุด(ที่)สูง(ที่)สุดที่น้ำเคยขึ้นมา

Will we reach the point where we can speak Japanese well?

Rao ja theung joot thee phoot pha-sa Yee-poon geng mai, nia?

เราจะถึงจุดที่พูดภาษาญี่ปุ่นเก่งมั้ยเนี่ย

level - ra-dap/chan - *Chan* is used for grades in school, floors/stories of buildings, and shelves in bookcases.

He's a world class boxer.

Kao pen nak muay ra-dap lok.

เค้าเป็นนักมวยระดับโลก

This grade studies beginning level and that grade studies intermediate level.

Chan nee rian ra-dap ton lae chan nan rian ra-dap glang.

ชั้นนี้เรียนระดับต้นและชั้นนั้นเรียนระดับกลาง

The level of these students is higher than those.

Nak-rian gloom nee yoo ra-dap soong gwa gloom nan.

นักเรียนกลุ่มนี้อยู่ระดับสูงกว่ากลุ่มนั้น

kae - This means "level", "point", "as far as", and "up to".

Last year, the flood water came up to here.

    Meua pee thee laeo, nam thuam keun ma theung kae nee. (or ka-nat nee, ra-dap

    nee, trong nee)

        เมื่อปีที่แล้วน้ำท่วมขึ้นมาถึงแค่นี้

That's enough.

    Kae nee (gaw) phaw laeo.

        แค่นี้(ก็)พอแล้ว

limit - jam-gat - This means "to limit", "to define", and "to be limited".

We have a limited amount of food.

    Rao mee a-han jam-gat.

        เรามีอาหารจำกัด

We have a limited number of these shoes. When they're gone, they're gone.

    Rawng-thao baep nee mee jam-nuan jam-gat. Mot laeo, mot leuy.

        รองเท้าแบบนี้มีจำนวนจำกัด หมดแล้วหมดเลย

You should limit the amount of fat you eat every day.

    Koon kuan (ja) jam-gat jam-nuan kai-mun thee koon gin thook wan.

        คุณควร(จะ)จำกัดจำนวนไขมันที่คุณกินทุกวัน

limit/stipulate - gam-not - This means "to limit", "set/fix", "earmark", or "stipulate". It differs from *jam-gat* in that a person or agency is fixing or stipulating the limit. It's also used for scheduling, limiting, and stipulating times.

He drives faster than the speed limit.

    Kao kap rot reo gwa gam-not./ Kao kap rot reo geuhn gam-not.

        เค้าขับรถเร็วกว่ากำหนด/เค้าขับรถเร็วเกินกำหนด

People of any age can work here. There's no age limit.

    Kon thook wai tham-ngan thee-nee dai. A-yoo mai mee gam-not. (or *Mai mee*

    gam-not a-yoo/Mai jam-gat a-yoo)

        คนทุกวัยทำงานที่นี่ได้ อายุไม่มีกำหนด

I have a set amount of work that I have to do every day.

    Chan mee jam-nuan ngan thee gam-not wai sam-rap chan thook wan. (or *hai*

    instead of *sam-rap*)

        ฉันมีจำนวนงานที่กำหนดไว้(สำหรับ)ฉันทุกวัน

12. COMPARISONS

THE SAME

the same as/like - meuanɈ - *Meuan* is "to be the same", "to be like", or "to resemble".
Variations are *meuan gap, meuan-gan gap,* and *meuan-meuan gap*.

Your shirt is the same as mine.

Seua koon meuanɈ (gap) kawnɈ phomɈ.

เสื้อคุณเหมือน(กับ)ของผม

These shoes are the same as the ones that Noi bought.

Rawng-thao koo nee meuanɈ (koo) thee Noi seu ma.

รองเท้าคู่นี้เหมือน(คู่)ที่น้อยซื้อมา

Bangkok has the same problems as many capital cities.

Groong-thayp mee pan-haɈ meuanɈ meuang luangɈ kawnɈ laiɈ pra-thet.

กรุงเทพมีปัญหาเหมือนเมืองหลวงของหลายประเทศ

You like going to movies the same as I do.

Koon chawp pai doo nangɈ meuanɈ (gap) chan leuy.

คุณชอบไปดูหนังเหมือน(กับ)ฉันเลย

It's nice and cool here like at the beach.

Thee-nee yen dee meuanɈ (gan) gap (thee) chai tha-lay.

ที่นี่เย็นดีเหมือน(กัน)กับ(ที่)ชายทะเล

not the same as/not like - mai meuanɈ (gap) -

Thai restaurants in America aren't the same as those in Thailand.

Ran-a-hanɈ Thai nai A-may-ree-ga mai meuanɈ gap thee nai meuang Thai.

ร้านอาหารไทยในอเมริกาไม่เหมือนกับที่ในเมืองไทย

Lek's not hard-working like his father.

Lek mai ka-yanɈ meuanɈ gap phaw (kawnɈ kao).

เล็กไม่ขยันเหมือนกับพ่อ(ของเค้า)

In general, Jill doesn't do things the way other foreigners do.

Jill tham a-rai mai meuanɈ fa-rang thua pai.

จิลทำอะไรไม่เหมือนฝรั่งทั่วไป

are the same/aren't the same - Put *meuan-gan* or *mai meuan-gan* at the end of the sentence. "Exactly the same" is *meuan-gan leuy* or *meuan-gan thook yang*.

These two people act exactly the same way.

> Sawngj kon nee nee-saij meuanj-gan leuy.
>
> สองคนนี้นิสัยเหมือนกันเลย

Thai and European customs aren't the same at all.

> Pra-phay-nee Thai gap Yoo-rop mai meuanj-gan leuy.
>
> ประเพณีไทยกับยุโรปไม่เหมือนกันเลย

With verbs - Responding with *meuan-gan* after a verb means "sure" (the same meaning as the particle *see*).

A: Are you going to the sports field today?

> Wan-nee pai sa-namj gee-la mai?
>
> วันนี้ไปสนามกีฬามั้ย

B: Sure.

> Pai meuanj-gan./Pai see.
>
> ไปเหมือนกัน/ไปซิ

the same thing/person/place - (classifier) dio-gan - *Dio-gan* refers to "one and the same" person, place, or thing. *Meuan-gan* is used only to describe characteristics.

We live in the same place./We live together.

> Rao yoo thee dio-gan. (or *ban dio-gan*)
>
> เราอยู่ที่เดียวกัน

Phet lives in the same place as me.

> Phet yoo thee dio (gan) gap chan.
>
> เพชรอยู่ที่เดียว(กัน)กับฉัน

She's the same person who came here yesterday.

> Kao pen kon dio (gan) gap kon thee ma meua-wan-nee.
>
> เค้าเป็นคนเดียว(กัน)กับคนที่มาเมื่อวานนี้

A: Is she the same person I met in Bangkok?

> Kon nan pen kon thee phomj jeuh thee Groong-thayp reu plao?
>
> คนนั้นเป็นคนที่ผมเจอที่กรุงเทพฯ รึเปล่า

B: Yes, she's the same person./No, she's not the same person.

> Chai. Kon dio-gan./Mai chai kon dio-gan.
>
> ใช่ คนเดียวกัน/ไม่ใช่คนเดียวกัน

"The same" may be omitted when you're referring to a specific object, as in English.
This isn't the (same) knife you borrowed.

    Nee mai chai meet thee koon yeum pai.

    นี่ไม่ใช่มีดที่คุณยืมไป

same as before/original - deuhm -

Do you live in the same place?

    Yang yoo thee deuhm reu plao?

    ยังอยู่ที่เดิมรึเปล่า

the same kind/style - The words for "kind" or "type" are explained on page 30.

We have the same style shirt.

    Rao mee seua baep dio-gan.

    เรามีเสื้อแบบเดียวกัน

This car is the same model that I have.

    Nee pen rot roon dio gap thee phom mee.

    นี่เป็นรถรุ่นเดียวกับที่ผมมี

He's making the same kind of food as yesterday.

    Kao tham a-han yang dio gap thee tham meua-wan-nee.

    เค้าทำอาหารอย่างเดียวกับที่ทำเมื่อวานนี้

THE SAME—OTHER PHRASES

the same as before - meuan deuhm - Also "as (it was) previously".

This place is as beautiful as before.

    Thee-nee (yang) suay meuan deuhm.

    ที่นี่(ยัง)สวยเหมือนเดิม

The service at this hotel isn't the same as before.

    Rong-raem nee baw-ree-gan mai meuan deuhm.

    โรงแรมนี้บริการไม่เหมือนเดิม

A: How's Ko Chang?

    Gaw Chang pen yang-ngai?

    เกาะช้างเป็นยังไง

B: The same as before.

    Meuan deuhm.

    เหมือนเดิม

meuang (meua) gawn/meuang gao - These phrases have the same meaning but aren't as common.

He's not a teacher like before.

Kao mai dai sawng nang-seu meuang meua-gawn laeo.

เค้าไม่ได้สอนหนังสือเหมือนเมื่อก่อนแล้ว

Everything is changed. It's not the same as before.

A-rai a-rai gaw plian pai. Mai meuang gao laeo.

อะไรๆ ก็เปลี่ยนไป ไม่เหมือนเก่าแล้ว

the same as the last time - meuang krang thee laeo - Also *yang krang thee laeo, meuan krang gawn,* or use *krao* instead of *krang.*

This time I'm not as excited as the last time.

Krang nee phom mai teun-ten meuang krang thee laeo.

ครั้งนี้ผมไม่ตื่นเต้นเหมือนครั้งที่แล้ว

the same as then - meuang tawn-nan/yang tawn-nan -

This time it's not as easy as it was the other time.

Krang nee mun mai ngai meuang tawn-nan laeo, na.

ครั้งนี้มันไม่ง่ายเหมือนตอนนั้นแล้วนะ

as it used to be - meuang keuy -

She still plays music as well as she used to.

Kao yang len don-tree geng meuang keuy.

เค้ายังเล่นดนตรีเก่งเหมือนเคย

the same experience - Use *meuan gap, meuan-meuan gap,* or *klai-klai gap* (which means "similar to").

A: Last night my car was stolen because I forgot to lock it ("lock the door").

Meua-keun-nee rot chan don ka-moy phraw leum lawk pra-too.

เมื่อคืนนี้รถฉันโดนขโมยเพราะลืมล็อคประตู

B: Oh, that's the same thing that happened to me when I was in England.

Oh, un nee meuang gap tawn thee chan yoo Ang-grit leuy.

โอ้ อันนี้เหมือนกับตอนที่ฉันอยู่อังกฤษเลย

not like other people - mai meuang krai/mai meuang kon eun - Also *mai meuan krai eun* which is more formal and used mostly in writing.

Moo doesn't think like other people.

Moo kit mai meuang krai.

หมูคิดไม่เหมือนใคร

not like any other place - maî meuaɲ theê-naĭ/maî meuaɲ theê eun -
They have strange food here that's not like anywhere else.

    Theê-neê mee a-haɲ plaek-plaek maî meuaɲ theê eun.

       ที่นี่มีอาหารแปลกๆ ไม่เหมือนที่อื่น

EXPRESSIONS: keu gan laê/phaw-phaw gan laê - Both are "that's the same/that's no different". *Keu* is Laotian for "the same".

A: Is she taller than me?

    Kao soonɲ gwa phomɲ maî?

       เค้าสูงกว่าผมมั้ย

B: No. You're the same height.

    Maî rawk. Keu gan laê.

       ไม่หรอก คือกันแหละ

SIMILAR

meuaɲ-meuaɲ/klai/klai-klai - These have slightly different meanings. Things that are *meuan-meuan* are more similar than if they're *klai-klai*. *Klai* alone has a stronger meaning than when it's doubled. To put them in order from the most to the least similar, it's *meuan, meuan-meuan, klai*, then *klai-klai*. *Gap* and *gan* are used as in the previous sections.

Her face looks a lot like her mother's.

    Naˇ kao klai maeˇ mak.

       หน้าเค้าคล้ายแม่มาก

These two people are both quiet. ("similarly quiet")

    Sawnɲ kon nee ngiap klai-klai gan.

       สองคนนี้เงียบคล้ายๆ กัน

I love my children the same way my parents love me.

    Chan rak look meuaɲ-meuaɲ gap theê phaw-maeˇ rak chan.

       ฉันรักลูกเหมือนๆ กับที่พ่อแม่รักฉัน

We have things in common.

    Raˇo mee a-raˇi meuaɲ-meuaɲ gan.

       เรามีอะไรเหมือนๆ กัน

These examples have a clause after "similar". Use *klai-klai (wa)*, *klai-klai gap*, or *klai-klai gap wa* and the same with *meuan-meuan*.

Going there is like going to Tokyo.

    Paˇi theê-nan gaw meuaɲ-meuaɲ (gap) (wa) paˇi To-gio, laê.

       ไปที่นั่นก็เหมือนๆ (กับ)(ว่า)ไปโตเกียวแหละ

He acted (rather) as if he loved me.

    Kao tham klai-klai (gap) (wa) kao rak chan.

    เค้าทำคล้ายๆ (กับ)(ว่า)เค้ารักฉัน

klai kiang - This is the same as *klai-klai*. A similar phrase is *glai kiang* for "nearly the same", referring to amounts or distances. See page 278.

They act almost the same.

    Kao nee-sai klai kiang gan.

    เค้านิสัยคล้ายเคียงกัน

It's not the same, but similar.

    (Mun) mai meuang-gan tae klai kiang.

    (มัน)ไม่เหมือนกันแต่คล้ายเคียง

similarity/similarities - kwam klai (kleung) -

Thai and Burmese culture have some similarities.

    Wat-tha-na-tham Thai gap wat-tha-na-tham Pha-ma mee kwam klai (kleung) gan bang.

    วัฒนธรรมไทยกับวัฒนธรรมพม่ามีความคล้าย(คลึง)กันบ้าง

DIFFERENT

There are three words, *tang*, *phit*, and *taek-tang*, which are translated as both "different" and "to differ". For example, "People here are different from the people where I live" is also "People here differ from the people where I live".

1. tang - *Tang* is also in the phrases *tang pra-thet* ("foreign") and *tang-tang* ("various" or "varied"). "From" can be *gap* or *jak*.

People here are different from the people where I live.

    Kon thee-nee tang gap kon thee ban.

    คนที่นี่ต่างกับคนที่บ้าน

Thai and Japanese cultures are very different. ("differ from each other a lot")

    Wat-tha-na-tham Thai gap Yee-poon tang gan mak.

    วัฒนธรรมไทยกับญี่ปุ่นต่างกันมาก

It's different from what he told me.

    Mun tang gap thee kao bawk phom.

    มันต่างกับที่เค้าบอกผม

Ubon isn't very different from Udorn.

    Oo-bon mai tang (pai) jak Oo-dawn thao-rai. (or *tang gap*)

    อุบลไม่ต่าง(ไป)จากอุดรเท่าไหร่

2. phit - This is used in the same way as *tang*. It also means "wrong" or "guilty" and *phit-jai gan* is "to have a disagreement". Don't confuse it with *phit* pronounced high/short which means "poisonous".

Life in the city is different from life in the countryside.

> Chee-wit nai meuang phit gap chee-wit nai chon-na-bot.
>
> ชีวิตในเมืองผิดกับชีวิตในชนบท

Thai food and Western food are very different.

> A-han Thai gap a-han fa-rang nee phit gan yeuh.
>
> อาหารไทยกับอาหารฝรั่งนี้ผิดกันเยอะ

3. taek-tang - This is a formal, written form of "to differ". *Taek* means "to break" or "shatter". For "different from" use *taek-tang gap* or *taek-tang jak*.

Northern Thais are different from Central Thais.

> Kon neua taek-tang gap kon phak glang.
>
> คนเหนือแตกต่างกับคนภาคกลาง

The weather in Thailand is different from England.

> A-gat thee meuang Thai taek-tang jak Ang-grit.
>
> อากาศที่เมืองไทยแตกต่างจากอังกฤษ

These two houses aren't different at all. ("don't have anything that differs")

> Ban sawng lang nee mai mee a-rai taek-tang gan leuy.
>
> บ้านสองหลังนี้ไม่มีอะไรแตกต่างกันเลย

a difference - kwam taek-tang -

There are a lot of differences between the weather here and in Korea.

> A-gat thee-nee gap thee Gao-lee mee kwam taek-tang gan mak.
>
> อากาศที่นี่กับที่เกาหลีมีความแตกต่างกันมาก
>
> Kwam taek-tang kawng a-gat thee Gao-lee gap thee-nee mee mak.
>
> ความแตกต่างของอากาศที่เกาหลีกับที่นี่มีมาก

How are they different? - tang gan yang-ngai? - *Phit* may be used here instead of *tang* but it's less common.

A: How do you think those two people differ?

> Koon kit wa sawng kon nan tang gan yang-ngai?
>
> คุณคิดว่าสองคนนั้นต่างกันยังไง

B: They're different in that Jack is more easygoing than Joe.

> Tang gan trong thee Jack jai-yen gwa Joe.
>
> ต่างกันตรงที่แจ๊คใจเย็นกว่าโจ

What's the difference? - mee a-rai taek-tang gan? - Also with *reu plao* at the end for "Is there any difference?"

A: What's the difference between Northeastern food and Northern food?

> A-hang Ee-sang gap a-hang neuang mee a-rai taek-tang gan (bang)?
>
> อาหารอีสานกับอาหารเหนือมีอะไรแตกต่างกัน(บ้าง)

B: Northern food isn't sour like Northeastern food.

> A-hang neuang mai prio meuang a-hang Ee-sang.
>
> อาหารเหนือไม่เปรี้ยวเหมือนอาหารอีสาน

each is different - There are two patterns:

1. kon la... - *Kon* is "person", but here it can refer to anything—people, places or things. Following are common phrases:

kon la baep	each is different in its own way
kon la seeng	each is a different color
kon la thang	each place is in a different direction
kon la thee	each person or thing is in a different place, each place is a separate place
kon la yang	each is different/of a different kind/done in a different way
kon la kon	they're different people, not the same person

This is the same style, but in a different color.

> Nee baep dio-gan, tae kon la seeng (gan).
>
> นี่แบบเดียวกันแต่คนละสี(กัน)

We don't live in the same place. We live in different places.

> Rao mai dai yoo thee dio-gan. Yoo kon la thee (gan).
>
> เราไม่ได้อยู่ที่เดียวกัน อยู่คนละที่(กัน)

Kanchanaburi and Korat are in different directions.

> Gan-ja-na-boo-ree gap Ko-rat pai kon la thang (gan).
>
> กาญจนบุรีกับโคราชไปคนละทาง(กัน)

A: Is it better to buy clothes at Jatujak or Pratunam?

> Pai seu seua-pha thee Ja-too-jak reung Pra-too-nam dee?
>
> ไปซื้อเสื้อผ้าที่จตุจักรหรือประตูน้ำดี

B: They're both good in different ways.

> Dee kon la yang (gan).
>
> ดีคนละอย่าง(กัน)

A: Is Thai harder than English?

> Pha-sang Thai yak gwa pha-sang Ang-grit mai?
>
> ภาษาไทยยากกว่าภาษาอังกฤษมั้ย

B: They're both difficult in their own way.

    Mun yak gan kon la baep.

    มันยากกันคนละแบบ

2. tang...tang... - "A different..., a different...". Put one of the things that's different after each *tang*.

We'll go to different places./We'll go at different times.

    Tang kon tang pai.

    ต่างคนต่างไป

COMPARATIVE—BIGGER/BETTER

With adjectives/adverbs - (adj/adv) gwa - The comparative is formed by putting *gwa* after the adjective or adverb.

This hotel is better than other hotels.

    Rong-raem nee dee gwa rong-raem eun.

    โรงแรมนี้ดีกว่าโรงแรมอื่น

This shirt is cheaper than the one I bought.

    Seua tua nee thook gwa thee phom seu.

    เสื้อตัวนี้ถูกกว่าที่ผมซื้อ

She's better in school than I am. ("She studies better")

    Theuh rian geng gwa phom.

    เธอเรียนเก่งกว่าผม

Gan is usually included at the end of questions asking for a comparison.

A: America or here - which place is more fun?

    Thee-nee gap thee A-may-ree-ga - thee-naij sa-nook gwa (gan)?

    ที่นี่กับที่อเมริกา ที่ไหนสนุกกว่า(กัน)

B: They're both fun.

    Sa-nook meuan-gan.

    สนุกเหมือนกัน

With verbs ("like more than") - (verb) mak gwa - *Mak gwa*, not *gwa* alone, is put after verbs. *Chawp mak gwa* is "like more", or "prefer".

I want to go to Hong Kong more than Singapore.

    Chan yak pai Hawng Gong mak gwa Sing-ka-po.

    ฉันอยากไปฮ่องกงมากกว่าสิงคโปร์

I like bread more than rice./I prefer bread to rice.

    Phom chawp ka-nom pang mak gwa kao.

    ผมชอบขนมปังมากกว่าข้าว

He (that person) plays more than he works.

   Kon nan len mak gwa tham-ngan.

   คนนั้นเล่นมากกว่าทำงาน

There are more restaurants in Thailand than where I live.

   Meuang Thai mee ran-a-han mak gwa thee ban chan.

   เมืองไทยมีร้านอาหารมากกว่าที่บ้านฉัน

A: Which place do you like better - Hua Hin or Cha-am?

   Hua Hin gap Cha-am - chawp thee-nai mak gwa (gan)?

   หัวหินกับชะอำชอบที่ไหนมากกว่า(กัน)

B: I like Hua Hin more.

   (Chan) chawp Hua Hin mak gwa.

   (ฉัน)ชอบหัวหินมากกว่า

Thee for "than" - *Thee* is "than" when a comparative is followed by a clause.

The beaches here are more beautiful than the ones I saw in Malaysia.

   Hat-sai thee-nee suay gwa thee chan hen thee Ma-lay-sia.

   หาดทรายที่นี่สวยกว่าที่ฉันเห็นที่มาเลเซีย

The village is bigger than when I came here last year.

   Moo-ban yai gwa thee phom ma meua pee thee laeo.

   หมู่บ้านใหญ่กว่าที่ผมมาเมื่อปีที่แล้ว

COMPARATIVE—OTHER PHRASES

(better) than this - (dee) gwa nee - This phrase may also mean "better than this place" or "better than here".

On Phuket the beaches are more beautiful than this.

   Thee Phoo-get chai-hat suay gwa nee.

   ที่ภูเก็ตชายหาดสวยกว่านี้

Yesterday the weather was better than this.

   Meua-wan-nee a-gat dee gwa (wan) nee.

   เมื่อวานนี้อากาศดีกว่า(วัน)นี้

this place is (better) - thee-nee (dee) gwa - There's possible confusion here with English. In Thai, the phrase is "this place is better" (*thee-nee dee gwa*) not "it's better here". *Dee gwa thee-nee* would mean that another place is better than this one. "It's hotter here" is *thee-nee rawn gwa*, not *rawn gwa thee-nee*.

It's hotter here than in Europe./This place is hotter than Europe.

   Thee-nee rawn gwa Yoo-rop.

   ที่นี่ร้อนกว่ายุโรป

Bangkok is hotter than here.

Groong-thayp rawn gwa thee-nee.

กรุงเทพฯ ร้อนกว่าที่นี่

A: What's this place like?

Thee-nee pen yang-ngai?

ที่นี่เป็นยังไง

B: It's better than Bangkok.

(Thee-nee) dee gwa Groong-thayp.

(ที่นี่)ดีกว่ากรุงเทพฯ

A: It's hard to find a job here.

Thee-nee haj ngan tham yak.

ที่นี่หางานทำยาก

B: It's better in Bangkok.

(Thee) Groong-thayp dee gwa, na. (not *dee gwa thee Groong-thayp*)

(ที่)กรุงเทพฯ ดีกว่านะ

much (better) - (dee) gwa mak/(dee) gwa yeuh - Also *dee gwa eeg mak* and *eeg yeuh*.
This place is much cleaner than Bangkok.

Thee-nee sa-at gwa Groong-thayp mak.

ที่นี่สะอาดกว่ากรุงเทพฯ มาก

much more - ying gwa -
He's much happier than other people.

Kao dee-jai ying gwa kon eun.

(เค้า)ดีใจยิ่งกว่าคนอื่น

(better) than before - (dee) gwa gawn/gwa deuhm/gwa gao - Also *gwa tae gawn* and
gwa meua-gawn.

Dam can cook better now than before.

Tawn-nee Dam tham a-han dai geng gwa deuhm.

ตอนนี้ดำทำอาหารได้เก่งกว่าเดิม

Other phrases with *gwa* - These are similar to phrases with *meuan*. Any adjective can
replace *suay*.

suay gwa pok-ga-tee	more beautiful than usual, unusually beautiful
suay gwa krang thee laeo	more beautiful than the last time
suay gwa tawn-nan	more beautiful than then/than that time

EVEN

With adjectives/adverbs - (dee) <u>gwa</u> <u>eeg</u> - *Yang* ("still") can be included when both things are mentioned, as in the third example.

Today it's even hotter than yesterday.

  Wan-nee rawn <u>gwa</u> meua-wan <u>eeg</u>.

  วันนี้ร้อนกว่าเมื่อวานอีก

He can play even better than Lek.

  Kao len dai dee <u>gwa</u> Lek <u>eeg</u>.

  เค้าเล่นได้ดีกว่าเล็กอีก

I run slowly, but he runs even more slowly than I do.

  Phom wing cha laeo, (<u>tae</u>) kao yang cha <u>gwa</u> <u>phom</u> <u>eeg</u>.

  ผมวิ่งช้าแล้ว(แต่)เค้ายังช้ากว่าผมอีก

With verbs - yang...(<u>eeg</u>) duay -

I help him all the time. Sometimes I even give him money.

  Phom chuay kao ta-lawt. Bang krang yang hai ngeuhn kao duay.

  ผมช่วยเค้าตลอด บางครั้งยังให้เงินเค้าด้วย

She always comes on time. Sometimes she even comes early.

  Kao ma trong way-la pen pra-jam. Bang krang kao yang ma chao <u>gwa</u> (<u>eeg</u>) duay.

  เค้ามาตรงเวลาเป็นประจำ บางครั้งเค้ายังมาเช้ากว่า(อีก)ด้วย

With nouns - mae <u>tae</u>/mae gra-thang - The second is more specific.

Jane can cook Thai food. She can even cook Chinese food.

  Jane tham a-han Thai dai. Mae <u>tae</u> a-han Jeen gaw tham dai.

  เจนทำอาหารไทยได้แม่แต่อาหารจีนก็ทำได้

I've never killed an animal, not even a mouse.

  Chan mai keuy ka <u>sat</u> leuy, mae gra-thang <u>noo</u> tua neung.

  ฉันไม่เคยฆ่าสัตว์เลยแม่กระทั่งหนูตัวหนึ่ง

SUPERLATIVE—THE BIGGEST/THE BEST

With adjectives/adverbs - (adj/adv) thee-soot - *Soot* means "at the extreme" or "the end".

Saigon is the biggest city in Vietnam.

    Meuang Sai-ngawn pen meuang thee yai thee-soot nai Wiat Nam.

    เมืองไซ่ง่อนเป็นเมืองที่ใหญ่ที่สุดในเวียดนาม

Singha is the best beer here.

    Bia Sing pen bia (thee) dee thee-soot kawng thee-nee.

    เบียร์สิงห์เป็นเบียร์(ที่)ดีที่สุดของที่นี่

I'm absolutely bored.

    Chan beua thee-soot leuy.

    ฉันเบื่อที่สุดเลย

With verbs - (verb) (mak) thee-soot - *Mak* is optional after verbs.

Accidents are the thing I'm afraid of most. (*glua* is a verb—"I fear")

    Oo-bat-tee-hayt pen sing thee chan glua (mak) thee-soot.

    อุบัติเหตุเป็นสิ่งที่ฉันกลัว(มาก)ที่สุด

A: Which place do you like the most?

    Koon chawp thee-nai (mak) thee-soot?

    คุณชอบที่ไหน(มาก)ที่สุด

B: I like many places.

    Chawp lai thee.

    ชอบหลายที่

extremely - soot yawt/pen thee-soot - *Yawt* means "peak".

The food here is really delicious.

    A-han thee-nee a-roi soot yawt.

    อาหารที่นี่อร่อยสุดยอด

I'm very unhappy.

    Phom sia-jai pen thee-soot.

    ผมเสียใจเป็นที่สุด

EXPRESSION: gwa pheuan - This means "the most", literally "more than its friends".

The flowers in this shop are the most beautiful.

    Dawk-mai thee-nee suay gwa pheuan.

    ดอกไม้ที่นี่สวยกว่าเพื่อน

OTHER PATTERNS—COMPARATIVE & SUPERLATIVE

the most/the least (amounts) - mak thee-soot/ noi thee-soot -

This place has the most tourists in December.

   Thee-nee mee nak thawng-thio mak thee-soot nai deuan Than-wa-kom.

   ที่นี่มีนักท่องเที่ยวมากที่สุดในเดือนธันวาคม

Monday is the day fewest people go shopping.

   Wan Jan ja pen wan thee kon pai seu kawng noi thee-soot.

   วันจันทร์จะเป็นวันที่คนไปซื้อของน้อยที่สุด

at most/at least - yang mak/yang noi -

This shirt should be at most 200 baht.

   Seua tua nee, yang mak, na ja pra-man sawng roi baht.

   เสื้อตัวนี้ อย่างมากน่าจะประมาณสองร้อยบาท

We'll spend at least 100 dollars a day.

   Rao ja chai ngeuhn yang noi roi dawn-la taw wan.

   เราจะใช้เงินอย่างน้อยร้อยดอลลาร์ต่อวัน

At least she won't forget me.

   Yang noi, kao kong mai leum phom.

   อย่างน้อยเค้าคงไม่ลืมผม

bad/worse/worst - yae/leo - Formally, *yae* is used to describe things and *leo* people, but informally they're interchangable. Include *gwa* for "worse" and *thee-soot* for "the worst". Other words that describe people as "bad" are *chua* (falling tone) and *rai* (high tone).

This is the worst hotel.

   Rong-raem nee yae thee-soot.

   โรงแรมนี้แย่ที่สุด

The hotel in Korat was a lot worse than this.

   Rong-raem nai Ko-rat yae gwa nee mak.

   โรงแรมในโคราชแย่กว่านี้มาก

He's the worst person I've ever met.

   Kao pen kon leo thee-soot thee chan jeuh ma.

   เค้าเป็นคนเลวที่สุดที่ฉันเจอมา

the (bigger) the (better) - ying...ying... -

The bigger the better.

   Ying yai ying dee.

   ยิ่งใหญ่ยิ่งดี

The more people there are the more fun it is.

Ying mee kon mak, ying sa-nook.

ยิ่งมีคนมากยิ่งสนุก

can't compare to/can't beat - soo mai dai - This is a common expression in Thai. *Soo* means "fight with", "struggle", or "compete", and *soo mai dai* is "can't beat", "can't match", "can't compete with", or "can't compare with".

London is beautiful, but it can't beat Paris.

Lawn-dawn suay mak, tae soo Pa-reet mai dai.

ลอนดอนสวยมากแต่สู้ปารีสไม่ได้

I can't beat John at speaking Thai.

Chan phoot Thai soo John mai dai.

ฉันพูดไทยสู้จอห์นไม่ได้

can't lose to - mai phae - *Phae* is "lose" or "lose to".

No one beats Thais at pleasing others.

Reuang ao-jai, kon Thai mai phae krai.

เรื่องเอาใจคนไทยไม่แพ้ใคร

He's as tall as (or taller than) his father. ("In height he doesn't lose to his father.")

Kao soong mai phae phaw kao leuy.

เค้าสูงไม่แพ้พ่อเค้าเลย

These two sisters both do things well.

Phee-nawng koo nee geng mai phae gan.

พี่น้องคู่นี้เก่งไม่แพ้กัน

BECOME BIGGER/BETTER

become better/improve - dee keun - Use *dee keun*, not *dee gwa*, when talking about a condition improving or getting better.

Bangkok would be better if there were fewer vehicles.

Groong-thayp ja dee keun tha mee rot noi long.

กรุงเทพฯ จะดีขึ้นถ้ามีรถน้อยลง

New model vehicles are of better quality.

Rot roon mai-mai ja mee koon-na-phap dee keun.

รถรุ่นใหม่ๆ จะมีคุณภาพดีขึ้น

She's a lot better than before.

Kao dee keun gwa deuhm eeg yeuh.

เค้าดีขึ้นกว่าเดิมอีกเยอะ

A: Do you feel better?

    Koon roo-seuk dee keun reu plao?

    คุณรู้สึกดีขึ้นรึเปล่า

B: Yes. I'm a lot better.

    Ka. Dee keun mak laeo.

    ค่ะ ดีขึ้นมากแล้ว

Other adjectives and adverbs - Use *keun* if the change is seen as going up and *long* if the change is going down. *Mak* is put before *keun* when the action isn't really up or down, as with "dry" and "dirty".

With *keun* -

geng keun	become better at doing something
haeng-laeng mak keun	become drier (for places)
kaeng-raeng keun	become stronger
law keun	become more handsome
mak keun/pheuhm keun	become more (an amount—see pages 218-219)
nak keun	become heavier
phaeng keun	become more expensive
phat-tha-na keun	become more developed
reo keun	become faster
ruay keun	become richer
sa-at keun	become cleaner
sok-ga-prok mak keun	become dirtier
suay keun	become more beautiful
uan keun	become fatter
yai keun	become bigger
yao keun	become longer

With *long* -

cha long	become slower
jon long	become poorer
lek long	become smaller
noi long	become less (pages 219-220)
phawm long	become thinner
sun long	become shorter (in length)
thook long	become cheaper
yae long	become worse
yen long	become cooler (as in the late afternoon)

With both -

    gae keun/gae long   both mean "getting older"

Noi runs a lot faster now.
    Tawn-nee Noi wing reo keun yeuh.
    ตอนนี้น้อยวิ่งเร็วขึ้นเยอะ

He drives a lot slower since he had an accident.
    Kao kap rot cha long mak tang-tae kao mee oo-bat-tee-hayt.
    เค้าขับรถช้าลงมากตั้งแต่เค้ามีอุบัติเหตุ

Things are more expensive than before.
    Kawng phaeng keun gwa gawn.
    ของแพงขึ้นกว่าก่อน

People here are richer than before.
    Kon thee-nee ruay keun gwa tae gawn.
    คนที่นี่รวยขึ้นกว่าแต่ก่อน

EQUAL

as (tall) as - thao (gap) -

You're as tall as I am.
    Koon soong thao (gap) phom.
    คุณสูงเท่า(กับ)ผม

Lek's the same age as me.
    Lek a-yoo thao (gap) chan.
    เล็กอายุเท่า(กับ)ฉัน

He can speak Thai as well as Ann.
    Kao phoot pha-sa Thai dai dee thao (gap) Ann.
    เค้าพูดภาษาไทยได้ดีเท่า(กับ)แอน

I can't eat as much as you can.
    Phom gin yeuh-yeuh thao koon mai dai.
    ผมกินเยอะๆ เท่าคุณไม่ได้

are equal - thao-gan -

These two pieces of cloth are the same price.
    Pha sawng chin nee ra-ka thao-gan.
    ผ้าสองชิ้นนี้ราคาเท่ากัน

The flowers here and in Japan are equally beautiful.
    Dawk-mai thee-nee gap thee Yee-poon suay thao-gan. (or *suay meuan-gan*)
    ดอกไม้ที่นี่กับที่ญี่ปุ่นสวยเท่ากัน

These two rooms are equal in size.

    Sawngɟ hawngɟ nee yai thao-gan.

    สองห้องนี้ใหญ่เท่ากัน

Our salaries aren't the same./We don't receive the same salary.

    Rao dai ngeuhn deuan mai thao-gan.

    เราได้เงินเดือนไม่เท่ากัน

We're not the same age.

    Rao a-yoo mai thao-gan./A-yoo rao mai thao-gan.

    เราอายุไม่เท่ากัน/อายุเราไม่เท่ากัน

A: Are they the same age?

    Kao a-yoo thao-gan mai?

    เค้าอายุเท่ากันมั้ย

B: No. Lek is older.

    Mai thao-gan. Lek gae gwa.

    ไม่เท่ากัน เล็กแก่กว่า

approximately equal - thao-thao -

I like basketball as much as football.

    Chan chawp "bat" thao-thao (gap) foot-bawn.

    ฉันชอบบาสเท่าๆ (กับ)ฟุตบอล

Things in these two shops are equally expensive.

    Sawngɟ ran nee kawngɟ phaeng thao-thao gan.

    สองร้านนี้ของแพงเท่าๆ กัน

phaw-phaw gap/gan - This is used when the exact measurement isn't stressed or when the things being compared aren't exactly equal.

Today it's as hot as yesterday.

    Wan-nee rawn phaw-phaw gap meua-wan-nee.

    วันนี้ร้อนพอๆ กับเมื่อวานนี้

They run equally fast.

    Kao wing reo phaw-phaw gan.

    เค้าวิ่งเร็วพอๆ กัน

not as...as - mai...thao (gap) - Also with *meuan* and *yang* if the measurement isn't being stressed. Compare the first three sentences.

Thailand isn't as big as India.

    Meuang Thai mai yai thao (gap) In-dia.

    เมืองไทยไม่ใหญ่เท่า(กับ)อินเดีย

It's not as hot as last year./It's not hot like last year.

  Mun mai rawn meuang pee thee laeo.

   มันไม่ร้อนเหมือนปีที่แล้ว

Germany isn't as much fun as Thailand./Germany isn't fun like Thailand.

  Yeuh-rà-mun mai sà-nook yang (gàp) meuang Thai.

   เยอรมันไม่สนุกอย่าง(กับ)เมืองไทย

I don't have as much money as he does.

  Chan mai mee ngeuhn (mak) thao kao.

   ฉันไม่มีเงิน(มาก)เท่าเค้า

Food is expensive in Bangkok, but it's (still) not as much as in other countries.

  Thee Groong-thayp a-han phaeng, tae yang mai thao (thee) meuang nawk.

   ที่กรุงเทพฯ อาหารแพงแต่ยังไม่เท่า(ที่)เมืองนอก

even/level/equal - sà-meuhŋ/jao - The first is for level surfaces and tied scores. It also means "always/all the time". The second comes from Chinese and is slang for "even" or "equal".

We're tied with Rayong's team./We tied with Rayong's team.

  Rao sà-meuhŋ gàp theem Rà-yawng.

   เราเสมอกับทีมระยอง

equivalent - thiap-thao - For "the equivalent of" or "the same amount or level".

Maw five is equivalent to the eleventh grade.

  Chan maw ha thiap-thao (gàp) grayt sìp-èt.

   ชั้น ม.ห้า เทียบเท่า(กับ)เกรดสิบเอ็ด

equal status - thao-thiam - This means "equal", "on the same level", or "with equal rights".

Men and women are equal.

  Phoo-ying gàp phoo-chai thao-thiam gan.

   ผู้หญิงกับผู้ชายเท่าเทียมกัน

OTHER PHRASES WITH "EQUAL"

as much as/as long as - thao thee -

I've helped her as much as I've had the time to.

  Phom chuay kao mak thao thee mee way-la.

   ผมช่วยเค้ามากเท่าที่มีเวลา

I'll tell you as much as I know.

  Chan ja bawk koon thao thee chan roo.

   ฉันจะบอกคุณเท่าที่ฉันรู้

I've stayed here as long as he has. (or "I'll stay here...")

    Phŏm yoo thee-nee (nan) thaŏ gàp thee kao yoo.

    ผมอยู่ที่นี่(นาน)เท่ากับที่เค้าอยู่

As long as you're helping her she won't go anywhere.

    Thaŏ thee koon yang chuay kao yoo, kao gâw jà mai pai nai.

    เท่าที่คุณยังช่วยเค้าอยู่เค้าก็จะไม่ไปไหน

equal to this/that - thaŏ-nee/thaŏ-nan - Also translated as "equal to this much/that much" and "as much as this/that".

I'm never seen a place as nice as this.

    Chan mai keuy heng thee-nai suay thaŏ-nee leuy.

    ฉันไม่เคยเห็นที่ไหนสวยเท่านี้เลย

I can only pay that much.

    Phŏm jai dai thaŏ-nan lae.

    ผมจ่ายได้เท่านั้นแหละ

as much as it should be - thaŏ thee kuan -

I'm afraid I won't be able to do it as well as I should.

    Phŏm glua wa jà tham dai mai dee thaŏ thee kuan.

    ผมกลัวว่าจะทำได้ไม่ดีเท่าที่ควร

as (well) as I can - thaŏ thee jà tham dai - Substitute other verbs for *tham* as in the second example.

I'll do it as well as I can.

    Phŏm jà tham hai dee thee-soot thaŏ thee jà tham dai.

    ผมจะทำให้ดีที่สุดเท่าที่จะทำได้

I'll help her as much as I can.

    Chan jà chuay theuh thaŏ thee jà chuay dai.

    ฉันจะช่วยเธอเท่าที่จะช่วยได้

as far as I know - thaŏ thee roo/thaŏ thee sap - *Sap* is more polite than *roo*.

As far as I know, he's well.

    Thaŏ thee sap, kao sà-bai dee.

    เท่าที่ทราบเค้าสบายดี

As far as I can remember he told me he was coming next Monday.

    Thaŏ thee jam dai, kao bawk wa kao jà ma wan Jan na.

    เท่าที่จำได้เค้าบอกว่าเค้าจะมาวันจันทร์หน้า

the (best) I've ever seen - thao̓ thee̓ keuy phop - Also *thao thee keuy jeuh, thao thee keuy hen,* and *thao thee keuy doo* (the last if you're actively looking at something, such as a movie).

This place is the most beautiful I've ever seen.

Thee-nee <u>suay</u> thee-<u>soot</u> thao̓ thee̓ keuy phop ma.

ที่นี่สวยที่สุดเท่าที่เคยพบมา

equal to before - thao̓ deuhm - This is for prices and amounts, otherwise use *meuan deuhm.*

The number of teachers is the same as before.

Jam-nuan kroo ya̓ng thao̓ deuhm.

จำนวนครูยังเท่าเดิม

equal to what there used to be - thao̓ thee̓ keuy - Or "equal to what I've experienced before".

There aren't as many people coming here as before.

Mee kon ma thio̓ thee-nee ma̓i mak thao̓ thee̓ keuy ma.

มีคนมาเที่ยวที่นี่ไม่มากเท่าที่เคยมา

Compared to other places I've eaten at, this is the best.

Thao̓ thee̓ keuy gin ma, thee-nee a-<u>roi</u> thee-<u>soot</u>.

เท่าที่เคยกินมาที่นี่อร่อยที่สุด

as much as possible - thao̓ thee̓ pen pai dai̓ -

We should try to spend as little money as possible.

Ra̓o tawng̓ pha̓-ya-yam chai ngeuhn noi thee-<u>soot</u> thao̓ thee̓ pen pai dai̓.

เราต้องพยายามใช้เงินน้อยที่สุดเท่าที่เป็นไปได้

as much as necessary - thao̓ thee̓ jam-pen -

Buy only what's necessary and that will be enough.

Seu̓ <u>kawng</u> ma thao̓ thee̓ jam-pen gaw̓ phaw laeo.

ซื้อของมาเท่าที่จำเป็นก็พอแล้ว

the same amount as - thao̓ jam-nuan/tam jam-nuan -

Please give the same amount to everyone who comes.

Chuay̓ <u>jaek</u> thao̓ jam-nuan kon thee̓ ma duay̓.

ช่วยแจกเท่าจำนวนคนที่มาด้วย

Buy whatever amount of food is needed for the number of guests.

Seu̓ a-<u>han</u> ma tam jam-nuan <u>kaek</u>, na̓.

ซื้ออาหารมาตามจำนวนแขกนะ

THE VERB "COMPARE"

priap thiap - *Priap thiap* can be shortened to *priap* or *thiap* alone except in the first sentence, which is a request.

Please compare Canada and America.

Chuay priap thiap Kae-na-da gap A-may-ree-ga hai fang noi.

ช่วยเปรียบเทียบแคนาดากับอเมริกาให้ฟังหน่อย

When you compare Thais and Westerners, Thais are a lot smaller.

Meua priap thiap kon Thai gap fa-rang, kon Thai tua lek gwa mak.

เมื่อเปรียบเทียบคนไทยกับฝรั่ง คนไทยตัวเล็กกว่ามาก

When you compare Russia and Canada, they have similar weather.

Priap thiap gan laeo, Rut-sia gap Kae-na-da mee a-gat klai-klai gan.

เปรียบเทียบกันแล้ว รัสเซียกับแคนาดามีอากาศใกล้ๆ กัน

Thailand isn't big when you compare it to China.

Meuang Thai mai yai leuy, meua thiap gap meuang Jeen.

เมืองไทยไม่ใหญ่เลย เมื่อเทียบกับเมืองจีน

no one compares to - *Soo* (falling tone) may be used in place of *priap* or *thiap* in both examples.

In talking, no one compares to her.

Reuang phoot nee, mai mee krai thiap kao dai.

เรื่องพูดนี่ไม่มีใครเทียบเค้าได้

No place compares to Krabi.

Mai mee thee-nai priap Gra-bee dai.

ไม่มีที่ไหนเปรียบกระบี่ได้

LIKE THIS/LIKE THAT

yang-ngee/yang-ngan/baep nee/baep nan - These phrases are interchangable for "like this", "like that", "this way", or "that way". *Ngee* (or *nee*) is sometimes translated as "that" in English. In general "this" is more common in Thai while "that" is more common in English. For "this kind/that kind" with things see pages 30-31.

With "do" -

It's not good to do that/to do it that way.

Tham yang-ngan mai dee.

ทำยังงั้นไม่ดี

It would be better to do it this way.

Tham yang-ngee dee gwa.

ทำยังงี้ดีกว่า

Don't do that./Don't do it like that./Don't do it that way.

Ya tham yang-ngan.

อย่าทำยังงั้น

You can't do that./You can't do it that way.

Tham yang-ngan mai dai.

ทำยังงั้นไม่ได้

A: Why are you doing that?/Why did you do it like that/that way?

Tham-mai (theung) tham yang-ngee?

ทำไมถึงทำยังงี้

B: Because the manager told me to.

Phraw phoo jat-gan bawk (hai tham) yang-ngan.

เพราะผู้จัดการบอก(ให้ทำ)ยังงั้น

With other verbs -

We should study like this every day.

Rao kuan ja rian yang-ngee thook wan.

เราควรจะเรียนยังงี้ทุกวัน

Playing football like that isn't any fun.

Len foot-bawn baep nan (mun) mai sa-nook leuy.

เล่นฟุตบอลแบบนั้น(มัน)ไม่สนุกเลย

How could she say that? It's unbelievable.

Kao phoot yang-ngan dai yang-ngai? Mai na-cheua leuy.

เค้าพูดยังงั้นได้ยังไง ไม่น่าเชื่อเลย

Why do you think like that/that way?

Tham-mai koon kit yang-ngan?

ทำไมคุณคิดยังงั้น

I think the same way./I agree.

Chan kit yang-ngee duay.

ฉันคิดยังงี้ด้วย

With adjectives and adverbs - This is translated as "so hot", "hot like this" or "as hot as this".

I can't eat food that's so hot.

Chan gin a-han thee phet yang-ngee mai dai rawk.

ฉันกินอาหารที่เผ็ดยังงี้ไม่ได้หรอก

If she drives so fast, don't go with her anymore.

Tha kao kap rot reo yang-ngan, ya pai gap kao eeg, na.

ถ้าเค้าขับรถเร็วยังงั้นอย่าไปกับเค้าอีกนะ

to be like this - pen yang-ngee/pen baep nee - Also *pen yang-ngan* and *pen baep nan*. These also mean "it's this way/it's that way".

Things are like this because he didn't believe me.

    Mun pen yang-ngee phraw kao mai cheua phom.

    มันเป็นยังงี้เพราะเค้าไม่เชื่อผม

I don't want it to be like that.

    Chan mai chawp thee mun pen yang-ngee.

    ฉันไม่ชอบที่มันเป็นยังงี้

    Chan mai yak hai mun pen yang-ngee rawk.

    ฉันไม่อยากให้มันเป็นยังงี้หรอก

A: You don't want to go?

    Koon mai yak pai reuh?

    คุณไม่อยากไปเหรอ

B: It's not that. I really have a lot of things to do.

    Mai chai yang-ngan. Chan mee thoo-ra jing-jing.

    ไม่ใช่ยังงั้น ฉันมีธุระจริงๆ

if it's like this - tha (pen) yang-ngee - "In that case" is *tha yang-ngan* or *tha ngan*.

If it's going to be like this, I want a divorce.

    Tha pen yang-ngee, chan (gaw) (ja) kaw ya.

    ถ้าเป็นยังงี้ฉัน(ก็)(จะ)ขอหย่า

If it's like that, I'm not going.

    Tha (pen) yang-ngan, phom (gaw) (ja) mai pai.

    ถ้า(เป็น)ยังงั้นผม(ก็)(จะ)ไม่ไป

A: OK. We'll meet in front of the movie theater.

    OK, jeuh gan (thee) na rong-nang, na.

    โอเค เจอกันที่หน้าโรงหนังนะ

B: But I don't know where the movie theater is.

    Tae chan mai roo wa rong-nang yoo thee-nai.

    แต่ฉันไม่รู้ว่าโรงหนังอยู่ที่ไหน

A: In that case I'll pick you up at home.

    Tha ngan phom pai rap thee ban.

    ถ้างั้นผมไปรับที่บ้าน

LIKE/AS

With adjectives/adverbs ("big like") - *Yang, baep,* and *meuan* are interchangable for "like" here. With *meuan* the two things are more exactly the same. *Thao* can also be used if the two things are really equal (page 245).

Bangkok is big like Jakarta. (or "as big as Jakarta")

Groong-thayp yai meuan Ja-ga-ta.

กรุงเทพฯ ใหญ่เหมือนจาร์การ์ต้า

He's tall like his father.

Kao soong meuan phaw.

เค้าสูงเหมือนพ่อ

I want to be tall like John.

Phom yak soong yang John.

ผมอยากสูงอย่างจอห์น

She's beautiful in the way that Thai women are beautiful.

Theuh suay baep phoo-ying Thai.

เธอสวยแบบผู้หญิงไทย

Someone as nice as you must have a lot of friends.

Kon thee nee-sai dee yang koon tawng mee pheuan yeuh nae leuy.

คนที่นิสัยดีอย่างคุณต้องมีเพื่อนเยอะแน่เลย

I'd like to play football like Steve/as well as Steve.

Chan yak len foot-bawn geng meuan Steve.

ฉันอยากเล่นฟุตบอลเก่งเหมือนสตีฟ

Negative - Use *yang, baep,* or *meuan,* and also *thao* if the things being compared are measured. *Gap* is optional with *yang.*

Food in Sweden isn't cheap like in Thailand. (or "isn't as cheap as")

A-han nai Sa-wee-den mai thook yang (gap) nai meuang Thai.

อาหารในสวีเด็นไม่ถูกอย่าง(กับ)ในเมืองไทย

Piak's not a good person like his (older) brother.

Piak mai chai kon dee baep phee-chai.

เปี้ยกไม่ใช่คนดีแบบพี่ชาย

With verbs ("think like") - Use *meuan* for "the same as" and *yang/baep* for "in the same way as". Variations are *meuan wa, meuan gap, meuan gap wa,* and *baep wa.* Compare the first two examples.

She talks like she doesn't want to go.

Theuh phoot meuan mai yak pai.

เธอพูดเหมือนไม่อยากไป

She talks like someone who doesn't have any teeth.

    Theuh phoot baep kon mai mee fun.

      เธอพูดแบบคนไม่มีฟัน

You should think like her.

    Koon kuan kit baep kao.

      คุณควรคิดแบบเค้า

Can you do it like him?/Can you do it the same way as him?

    Koon tham yang kao dai mai?

      คุณทำอย่างเค้าได้มั้ย

She doesn't sing like a Westerner.

    Kao rawng phlayng mai meuang fa-rang.

      เค้าร้องเพลงไม่เหมือนฝรั่ง

He acts as if he never knew me.

    Kao tham meuang gap mai keuy roo-jak chan.

      เค้าทำเหมือนกับไม่เคยรู้จักฉัน

He drives (fast) like he's not afraid to die.

    Kao kap rot reo baep (wa) mai glua tai.

      เค้าขับรถเร็วแบบ(ว่า)ไม่กลัวตาย

A: Do Westerners get married the same way as Thais?

    Kon fa-rang taeng-ngan meuang kon Thai mai?

      คนฝรั่งแต่งงานเหมือนคนไทยมั้ย

B: No. Westerners get married in a church.

    Mai meuang-gan. (Kon) fa-rang taeng-ngan thee bot.

      ไม่เหมือนกัน (คน)ฝรั่งแต่งงานที่โบสถ์

Meuan is the most common with adverbs.

I can't swim as well as Nit.

    Phom wai-nam dai mai geng meuang Nit.

      ผมว่ายน้ำได้ไม่เก่งเหมือนนิด

in the same way as - yang dio gap/baep dio gap -

I'd like to have a beautiful car like this.

    Chan yak dai rot suay-suay yang dio gap kun nee.

      ฉันอยากได้รถสวยๆ อย่างเดียวกับคันนี้

He talks like his brother.

    Kao phoot baep dio gap phee-chai kao. (or *kao phoot meuan*)

      เค้าพูดแบบเดียวกับพี่ชายเค้า

such as/for example - yang/chen - The second is more formal.

I want to visit a country that's developed like Japan.

> Chan yak pai pra-thet thee phat-tha-na laeo yang Yee-poon.

> ฉันอยากไปประเทศที่พัฒนาแล้วอย่างญี่ปุ่น

For example, myself, I don't like to work too hard.

> Yang phom ngee, phom mai chawp tham-ngan nak geuhn pai.

> อย่างผมงี้ ผมไม่ชอบทำงานหนักเกินไป

Two clauses - yang thee/baep thee/meuan thee - These can be expanded to *yang dio-gan gap thee*, etc. *Yang* means "in the way that", *baep* is "like/in the style of", and *meuan* is "the same as". See page 267 for "as" meaning "according to" (*tam thee*).

You didn't help me like you promised.

> Koon mai dai chuay chan yang thee koon sun-ya.

> คุณไม่ได้ช่วยฉันอย่างที่คุณสัญญา

Can you do it the same way that he's doing it?

> Koon tham meuan thee kao tham dai mai?

> คุณทำเหมือนที่เค้าทำได้มั้ย

I want to get a job like I used to have in Kuwait.

> Phom yak dai ngan baep thee (phom) keuy tham nai Koo-wayt.

> ผมอยากได้งานแบบที่(ผม)เคยทำในคูเวต

as I thought - Some common phrases:

yang thee kit	as I thought
yang thee wa	as it's said, as people say
yang thee phoot	as I said
yang thee bawk	as I told you/her/him/them
yang thee wang	as hoped
yang thee tang-jai	as intended

It's not as you think/thought.

> Mai pen yang thee kit rawk.

> ไม่เป็นอย่างที่คิดหรอก

As I told you, I have to go home next month.

> Yang thee chan bawk (wai), chan tawng glap ban deuan na.

> อย่างที่ฉันบอก(ไว้) ฉันต้องกลับบ้านเดือนหน้า

It's like I said, Dam's not sincere with anyone.

> Yang thee keuy phoot (wai), (wa) Dam mai jing-jai gap krai rawk.

> อย่างที่เคยพูด(ไว้)(ว่า)ดำไม่จริงใจกับใครหรอก

NOTES ON "AS/LIKE":

1. and things like that - a-rai yang-ngee/a-rai yang-ngia - These are common expressions in informal Thai. *Yang* can be omitted.

I like to eat vegetables such as *phak boong, phak kana*, and things like that.

Phom chawp gin phak, yang phak boong, phak ka-na, a-rai yang-ngia.

ผมชอบกินผัก อย่างผักบุ้ง ผักคะน้า อะไรยังเงี้ย

Like, guitars and things like that, I don't like playing them at all.

Yang gee-ta a-rai nee, phom mai chawp len leuy.

อย่างกีต้าร์อะไรนี้ ผมไม่ชอบเล่นเลย

It's a cartoon, or something like that.

Pen ga-toon, a-rai ngee.

เป็นการ์ตูนอะไรงี้

2. formal - chen/nai lak-sa-na - The first is the formal equivalent of *yang*. The second is literally "in the charactisteric of" and is used for "as" with nouns.

Doing it that way isn't good.

Tham chen nan mai dee rawk.

ทำเช่นนั้นไม่ดีหรอก

She's tall like her father.

Kao soong chen dio gap phaw.

เค้าสูงเช่นเดียวกับพ่อ

We like each other as friends more than as lovers.

Rao kop gan nai lak-sa-na pheuan mak gwa faen.

เราคบกันในลักษณะเพื่อนมากกว่าแฟน

3. with adverbs - *Yang* and *baep* are put before adverbs of manner and motion to mean "in a....way".

He's sitting there comfortably.

Kao nang baep sa-bai sa-bai.

เค้านั่งแบบสบายๆ

4. like/you know - baep/baep wa/yang - These are included informally to create a pause.

Like, I don't want it at all.

Baep, chan mai ao leuy.

แบบ ฉันไม่เอาเลย

This was a forest before, like, ten years ago there were no houses at all.

Thee-nee pen pa ma gawn, yang, sip pee thee laeo mai mee ban kon yoo leuy.

ที่นี่เป็นป่ามาก่อน อย่างสิบปีที่แล้วไม่มีบ้านคนอยู่เลย

He's sort of a selfish person.

Kao pen kon, baep wa, heŋ gae tua.

เค้าเป็นคนแบบว่าเห็นแก่ตัว

5. using *rao* - *Rao gap* is the formal equivalent of *meuan* where an action is being compared to something else. It's also used with similes as in the second sentence.

She acts like she's the boss.

Theuh tham rao gap (wa) theuh pen huaŋ-na.

เธอทำราวกับ(ว่า)เธอเป็นหัวหน้า

She's as beautiful as an angel.

Theuh suayŋ rao gap nang-fa.

เธอสวยราวกับนางฟ้า

LOOKS/LOOKS LIKE/SEEMS

looks (adjective) - doo (meuaŋ) -

He looks rich.

Kao doo (meuaŋ) ruay, na.

เค้าดู(เหมือน)รวยนะ

This shirt looks too old.

Seua tua nee doo gao geuhn pai laeo.

เสื้อตัวนี้ดูเก่าเกินไปแล้ว

looks like (noun) - doo meuaŋ (gap) -

This place looks like old Thailand.

Thee-nee doo meuaŋ (gap) meuang Thai sa-maiŋ gawn.

ที่นี่ดูเหมือน(กับ)เมืองไทยสมัยก่อน

She looks like a (certain) movie star.

Kao doo meuaŋ (gap) da-ra naŋ kon neung.

เค้าดูเหมือน(กับ)ดาราหนังคนหนึ่ง

looks similar to - doo meuaŋ-meuaŋ (gap)/doo klai-klai (gap) -

Laos looks similar to northern Thailand.

Pra-thet Lao doo meuaŋ-meuaŋ phak neuaŋ kawngŋ Thai.

ประเทศลาวดูเหมือนๆ ภาคเหนือของไทย

Those two people look alike.

Sawngŋ kon nee doo klai-klai gan.

สองคนนี้ดูคล้ายๆ กัน

you look/it looks like/it seems - doo meuanj (gạp/wả) - Other translations are "you look like", "you look as if", "it looks as if", and "it seems that/like/as if/as though". Words are ordered in many ways in Thai.

You look tired./It looks like you're tired./It seems that you're tired.

> Koon doo (meuanj) neuay./Koon doo meuanj gạp neuay.
>
> คุณดู(เหมือน)เหนื่อย/คุณดูเหมือนกับเหนื่อย
>
> Koon doo meuanj (gạp) wả neuay.
>
> คุณดูเหมือน(กับ)ว่าเหนื่อย
>
> Doo koon (meuanj) neuay./Doo koon meuanj gạp neuay.
>
> ดูคุณ(เหมือน)เหนื่อย/ดูคุณเหมือนกับเหนื่อย
>
> Doo koon meuanj (gạp) wả neuay.
>
> ดูคุณเหมือน(กับ)ว่าเหนื่อย
>
> Doo meuanj (gạp) koon neuay./Doo meuanj (gạp) wả koon neuay.
>
> ดูเหมือน(กับ)คุณเหนื่อย/ดูเหมือน(กับ)ว่าคุณเหนื่อย

Your girlfriend looks like she wants to go home.

> Faen (koon) doo meuanj yak glạp ban.
>
> แฟน(คุณ)ดูเหมือนอยากกลับบ้าน

It looks like Yawt's upset.

> Doo meuanj gạp Yawt mai sa-bai-jai.
>
> ดูเหมือนกับยอดไม่สบายใจ

It looks like it's going to rain.

> Doo meuanj wả fonj ja tok.
>
> ดูเหมือนว่าฝนจะตก

It seems that she's not coming.

> Doo kao meuanj ja mai ma.
>
> ดูเค้าเหมือนจะไม่มา

A: The work here looks easy.

> Ngan thee-nee doo meuanj sa-bai.
>
> งานที่นี่ดูเหมือนสบาย

B: No. It looks easy but it's really very hard.

> Plao rawk. Doo meuanj sa-bai, tae jing-jing laeo nạk mak.
>
> เปล่าหรอก ดูเหมือนสบายแต่จริงๆแล้วหนักมาก

IT APPEARS THAT—USING *THA*

The word *tha* means "manner", "pose", or "attitude". Here a situation is being sensed or judged from its appearance.

seems that/might be - tha ja -

It seems that the water is all gone.

Nam tha ja mot laeo.

น้ำท่าจะหมดแล้ว

The rice is almost ready.

Kao tha ja sook laeo.

ข้าวท่าจะสุกแล้ว

the manner/actions/bearing that - tha thang ja - With *thang* the phrase refers more to physical appearance and manner.

You look hungry.

Tha thang koon ja hiuŋ laeo.

ท่าทางคุณจะหิวแล้ว

This ring seems to be fake.

Tha thang waeŋ wong nee ja pen kawngŋ plawm.

ท่าทางแหวนวงนี้จะเป็นของปลอม

She looks Chinese. (Her manner is Chinese.)

Kao tha thang meuaŋ kon Jeen./Kao doo meuaŋ kon Jeen.

เค้าท่าทางเหมือนคนจีน/เค้าดูเหมือนคนจีน

it appears that - mee (thee) tha wa - Other translations are "it seems that" and "there are some indications that".

It seems that it's going to flood.

Mee (thee) tha wa nam ja thuam.

มี(ที)ท่าว่าน้ำจะท่วม

it seems that - doo tha - This is for external events that are looked at.

It seems that Jack's not coming.

Doo tha Jack ja mai ma.

ดูท่าเจ๊คจะไม่มา

It looks like it's going to rain.

Doo tha fonŋ ja tok.

ดูท่าฝนจะตก

I see that/sense that - hen̝ thee/hen̝ tha̅ - Here *hen* is "see", "notice", or "think" and the subject of the sentence is "I". *Wa* is optional after the phrases and *ja* can be included to make the meaning hypothetical.

I guess I won't go there again.

Phǒm̝ hen̝ thee jà ma̅i pài thee̅-nân eeg la̅eo.

ผมเห็นทีจะไม่ไปที่นั่นอีกแล้ว

I don't think I can stand it anymore.

Hen̝ thee jà ma̅i wa̲i̝ la̅eo.

เห็นทีจะไม่ไหวแล้ว

It seems that the situation is getting more confusing.

Hen̝ tha̅ wa̅ reuang̅ jà yoong̝ keun̝.

เห็นท่าว่าเรื่องจะยุ่งขึ้น

Other expressions with *tha* -

kào tha̅	that's great
ma̅i kào tha̅	not so great, that's not very good
tha̅ jà cha̅i	I guess so.
tha̅ dee	looks good (but really isn't)
len̝ tha̅	refers to trying to trick someone by hesitating or not doing what you're supposed to do

13. PREPOSITIONS

Some of the words in this section wouldn't be classified as prepositions in English grammar but are included because they refer to locations. In Thai a single verb is sometimes used where a verb and a preposition are used together in English, for example *keun* is "go up", *long* is "go down" and *kam* is "go across".

ABOUT

There are three words for "about"—*theung, gio-gap,* and *reuang.*

theung - This means "concerning", "regarding", or "of" with verbs like "think", "talk", and "dream".

A: What was he just talking about?

    Meua-gee-nee kao phoot theung a-rai?

    เมื่อกี้นี้เค้าพูดถึงอะไร

B: I couldn't understand it either.

    Chan gaw fang mai roo reuang meuang-gan.

    ฉันก็ฟังไม่รู้เรื่องเหมือนกัน

gio-gap - This is "about" when it means "concerning" or "relating to".

Tell me a little about him.

    Phoot gio-gap kao hai fang noi.

    พูดเกี่ยวกับเค้าให้ฟังหน่อย

A: What do you study?

    Rian gio-gap a-rai?

    เรียนเกี่ยวกับอะไร

B: Hotel Administration.

    Gan baw-ree-hang rong-raem.

    การบริหารโรงแรม

Gio gap (or *gio/gio kawng*) is also the verb "to concern/to involve".

We can do it ourselves. We don't have to get involved with him.

    Rao tham gan ayng gaw dai. Mai tawng pai gio (kawng) gap kao.

    เราทำกันเองก็ได้ ไม่ต้องไปเกี่ยว(ของ)กับเขา

USES OF *REUANG*

Reuang has many meanings, and in some sentences can be interpreted in more than one way. Following are the main uses:

- the preposition "about"
- a noun with the generalized meaning of "story", "subject", "situation", "matter", "problem, and "affair" or the classifier for the same ("this problem" is *panha reuang nee*)
- the classifier for movies; also used to refer to names of movies, plays, and novels
- in the idiom *mee reuang*, meaning "have a fight" (conflict/argument)

As a preposition - As a preposition *reuang* means "about/on the subject of" or "about the situation of".

I'm worried about my children's education.

Phŏm pen huang reuang gan seuk-sa kawng look.

ผมเป็นห่วงเรื่องการศึกษาของลูก

A: What's this book about?

Nang-seu nee reuang a-rai?

หนังสือนี้เรื่องอะไร

B: It's about dinosaurs.

Reuang dai-no-sao.

เรื่องไดโนเสาร์

As a noun - Here *reuang* is a noun meaning "story", "matter", "subject", "situation", "affair", or "problem".

Looking for work is a bother.

Ha ngan pen reuang thee lam-bak.

หางานเป็นเรื่องที่ลำบาก

This matter doesn't concern you.

Reuang nee mai gio (kawng) gap koon (rawk).

เรื่องนี้ไม่เกี่ยว(ของ)กับคุณ(หรอก)

I know that he has deceived foreigners. ("about the story that")

Chan roo reuang thee kao keuy lawk fa-rang.

ฉันรู้เรื่องที่เค้าเคยหลอกฝรั่ง

Gio-gap reuang is "concerning the matter of", "the subject of", etc.

I don't know anything about that situation/matter/problem.

Mai roo gio-gap reuang nan leuy.

ไม่รู้เกี่ยวกับเรื่องนั้นเลย

A: What's this book about?

    Nang-seu̯ (lem) nee gio-gap reuang a-rai?

    หนังสือ(เล่ม)นี้เกี่ยวกับเรื่องอะไร

B: It's for studying Thai.

    Gio-gap gan rian pha-sa̯ Thai.

    เกี่ยวกับการเรียนภาษาไทย

As a classifier - *Reuang* is also the classifier for stories, situations, subjects, and problems. In this sentence it's used with *eun* ("other") and *nan* ("that"), patterns that require classifiers.

We didn't talk about anything but that.

    Rao mai dai kui reuang eun, nawk-jak reuang nan leuy.

    เราไม่ได้คุยเรื่องอื่นนอกจากเรื่องนั้นเลย

Here *reuang* is either "about" or the classifier for the situation/problem.

What are they talking about?

    Kao kui gan reuang a-rai? ("about what" or "what story/situation/matter")

    เค้าคุยกันเรื่องอะไร

Who yelled at you? What was it about?

    Krai da koon? Reuang a-rai?

    ใครด่าคุณ เรื่องอะไร

Noun and preposition - Here *reuang* and *gio-gap* are interchangable for "about". They may also be used together in the phrase *reuang gio-gap* where *reuang* is the noun or classifier for "story", "matter", or "situation" and *gio-gap* is "about".

I like to read books about history. (3 ways to say)

    Chan chawp an nang-seu̯ reuang pra-wat-sat.

    ฉันชอบอ่านหนังสือเรื่องประวัติศาสตร์

    Chan chawp an nang-seu̯ gio-gap pra-wat-sat.

    ฉันชอบอ่านหนังสือเกี่ยวกับประวัติศาสตร์

    Chan chawp an nang-seu̯ reuang gio-gap pra-wat-sat.

    ฉันชอบอ่านหนังสือเรื่องเกี่ยวกับประวัติศาสตร์

A: What's this story about, Joe?

    Nee reuang gio-gap a-rai, Joe?

    นี่เรื่องเกี่ยวกับอะไรโจ

B: It's a story about India.

    Pen reuang gio-gap In-dia.

    เป็นเรื่องเกี่ยวกับอินเดีย

Moo is studying birds.

    Mooj gam-lang seuk-saj reuang/gio-gap nok.

    หมูกำลังศึกษาเรื่อง/เกี่ยวกับนก

It's a problem concerning his health.

    Mun pen pan-haj reuang/gio-gap sook-ka-phap kawngj kao.

    มันเป็นปัญหาเรื่อง/เกี่ยวกับสุขภาพของเขา

With movies - *Reuang* is also used to refer to the names of movies, plays, and novels as in the first question, and as the classifier for movies as in the second.

A: What's the name of the movie?

    Nangj reuang a-rai?

    หนังเรื่องอะไร

B: It's called "Karma Couple".

    Reuang "Koo Gam".

    เรื่องคู่กรรม

A: What's this movie about?

    (Nangj) reuang nee gio-gap a-rai?

    (หนัง)เรื่องนี้เกี่ยวกับอะไร

B: It's (a movie) about Native Americans.

    (Pen nangj) gio-gap In-dia daeng.

    (เป็นหนัง)เกี่ยวกับอินเดียนแดง

ABOVE/OVER/NORTH OF

neuaj -

Chiang Rai is north of Chiang Mai.

    Chiang Rai yoo neuaj Chiang Mai.

    เชียงรายอยู่เหนือเชียงใหม่

We're flying over the Gulf of Thailand.

    Rao gam-lang bin yoo neuaj Ao Thai.

    เรากำลังบินอยู่เหนืออ่าวไทย

ACROSS FROM

trong-kam - This is literally "straight-across". *Kam* is the verb "to go across".

My house is across from the post office.

    Ban phomj yoo trong-kam prai-sa-nee.

    บ้านผมอยู่ตรงข้ามไปรษณีย์

It's across the street./It's on the other side.

    Yoo (trong) kam tha-non pai./Yoo fang trong-kam.

    อยู่(ตรง)ข้ามถนนไป/อยู่ฝั่งตรงข้าม

To say that a place is "across the river" say that it's across from a certain place, or use the verb *kam*.

Vientiane is across from Sri Chiang Mai in Nong Khai province.

    Wiang Jan yoo trong-kam (gap) See Chiang Mai nai jang-wat Nawng Kai.

    เวียงจันทร์อยู่ตรงข้าม(กับ)ศรีเชียงใหม่ในจังหวัดหนองคาย

Across the river is Malaysia.

    Kam mae-nam (pai) gaw pen (pra-thet) Ma-lay-sia.

    ข้ามแม่น้ำ(ไป)ก็เป็น(ประเทศ)มาเลเซีย

straight across from - trong gap -

Ayk's company is just opposite my house.

    Baw-ree-sat kawng Ayk yoo trong gap ban chan leuy.

    บริษัทของเอกอยู่ตรงกับบ้านฉันเลย

AROUND/IN THE AREA OF

thaeo/thaeo-thaeo - *Thaeo* also means "row", and is the classifier for rows of things.

Is there a restaurant around here?

    Mee ran-a-han thaeo nee mai?

    มีร้านอาหารแถวนี้มั้ย

He lives right around here.

    Kao yoo thaeo nee, lae.

    เค้าอยู่แถวนี้แหละ

She's around here somewhere.

    Kao yoo thaeo-thaeo nee.

    เค้าอยู่แถวๆ นี้

Children like to play around my house.

    Dek-dek chawp len yoo thaeo-thaeo ban chan.

    เด็กๆ ชอบเล่นอยู่แถวๆ บ้านฉัน

There are a lot of thieves around here.

    Thaeo nee mee ka-moy yeuh.

    แถวนี้มีขโมยเยอะ

There's no barber shop around here.

    Thaeo nee mai mee ran tat phom (yoo) leuy.

    แถวนี้ไม่มีร้านตัดผม(อยู่)เลย

go around/surrounding - rawp - *Rawp* is also the classifier for circular trips and laps.

There's a garden surrounding the house.

    Mee suan yoo rawp ban.

        มีสวนอยู่รอบบ้าน

The losers have to run around the field five times.

    Kon phae tawng wing rawp sa-nam ha rawp.

        คนแพ้ต้องวิ่งรอบสนามห้ารอบ

AS/ALONG/ACCORDING TO

as/by the - pen -

These things are sold as a set.

    Phuak nee kai pen choot.

        พวกนี้ขายเป็นชุด

We're going as a group.

    Rao ja pai pen gloom.

        เราจะไปเป็นกลุ่ม

I bought it for a gift.

    Chan seu pen kawng-kwan.

        ฉันซื้อเป็นของขวัญ

along/according to - tam - Also "in accordance with".

Go along this street.

    Pai tam tha-non nee, na.

        ไปตามถนนนี้นะ

I work according to my duties.

    Chan gaw tham-ngan tam na-thee kawng chan.

        ฉันก็ทำงานตามหน้าที่ของฉัน

I like to travel in the provinces.

    Phom chawp thio (tam) tang jang-wat.

        ผมชอบเที่ยว(ตาม)ต่างจังหวัด

A: Are there flowers for sale here?

    Mee <u>dawk</u>-mai <u>kaij</u> mai?

    มีดอกไม้ขายมั้ย

B: They're for sale in the market.

    Mee <u>kaij</u> tam <u>ta-lat</u>.

    มีขายตามตลาด

as/according to (conjunction) - tam <u>thee</u> -

According to what Phet told me, he's going to Australia next year.

    Tam thee Phet <u>bawk</u>, kao ja pai Awt-sa-tray-lia pee na.

    ตามที่เพชรบอกเค้าจะไปออสเตรเลียปีหน้า

He doesn't do as I say.

    Kao mai tham tam thee chan <u>bawk</u>.

    เค้าไม่ทำตามที่ฉันบอก

BEFORE (A PLACE)

<u>gawn</u>/<u>gawn</u> <u>theung</u> - *Gawn* means "before", "in advance of", or "ahead of" for both locations and time. *Gawn theung* is literally "before arriving at" or "before reaching".

The gas station is before the intersection.

    Pum <u>yoo</u> <u>gawn</u> (<u>theung</u>) <u>see-yaek</u>.

    ปั๊มอยู่ก่อน(ถึง)สี่แยก

Before (you reach) my house there's a flower shop.

    <u>Gawn</u> <u>theung</u> ban chan mee ran <u>kaij</u> <u>dawk</u>-mai (<u>yoo</u>).

    ก่อนถึงบ้านฉันมีร้านขายดอกไม้(อยู่)

BEHIND

(<u>kang</u>) <u>lang</u>/<u>thaeo</u> <u>lang</u> - *Kang* is optional when "behind" is a preposition but needed for the noun "the back".

The disco is behind the hotel.

    Thek <u>yoo</u> (<u>kang</u>) <u>lang</u> rong-raem.

    เท็คอยู่(ข้าง)หลังโรงแรม

John's house is behind the police station.

    Ban John <u>yoo</u> <u>thaeo</u> <u>lang</u> rong-phak.

    บ้านจอห์นอยู่แถวหลังโรงพัก

There's a parking garage behind the hospital.

    Mee rong <u>jawt</u> rot <u>yoo</u> <u>lang</u> rong-pha-ya-ban.

    มีโรงจอดรถอยู่หลังโรงพยาบาล

the back/the rear - kang lang - Another phrase is *dan lang* which is more formal (*dan* has a falling tone).

In front of the house it's clean, but the back is very messy.

> (Kang) na ban sa-at, tae kang lang rok mak.
>
> (ข้าง)หน้าบ้านสะอาดแต่ข้างหลังรกมาก

BETWEEN

ra-wang -

Your house is between here and the (three-way) intersection, isn't it?

> Ban koon yoo ra-wang thee-nee gap samj-yaek, chai mai?
>
> บ้านคุณอยู่ระหว่างที่นี่กับสามแยกใช่มั้ย

Between me and Noi, everything is just friends.

> Ra-wang phomj gap Noi, thook yang pen kae pheuan.
>
> ระหว่างผมกับน้อยทุกอย่างเป็นแค่เพื่อน

BY

done by a person - doy - This is for "written by", "made by", etc.

This song is sung by Sayan Sunya.

> Phlayng nee rawng doy Saj-yan Sunj-ya.
>
> เพลงนี้ร้องโดยสายันต์ สัญญา

These things were made by prisoners.

> Kawnj phuak nee tham doy nak-thot.
>
> ของพวกนี้ทำโดยนักโทษ

by means of (noun) - duay -

This basket was made by hand.

> Ta-gra nee tham duay meu.
>
> ตะกร้านี้ทำด้วยมือ

by means of (action) - duay/doy - Here a result is achieved by doing an action. *Duay* or *doy* here are prepositions followed by a gerund (see page 13). *Doy* is more formal.

He won the election by buying votes.

> Kao cha-na gan leuak-tang duay gan seu siangj.
>
> เค้าชนะการเลือกตั้งด้วยการซื้อเสียง

They entered the house by breaking down the door.

> Phuak kao kao ban duay gan phang pra-too (kao pai).
>
> พวกเค้าเข้าบ้านด้วยการพังประตู(เข้าไป)

by car/bus/etc - The easiest way to say "I'm going by bus" is literally "I-go-bus"—*chan pai rot-may*. Another way is to include "drive", "ride", or "sit" depending the vehicle and whether you're driving or going as a passenger.

A: How did you go?/How are you going?

Pai rot a-rai?

ไปรถอะไร

B: By motorcycle.

Kee rot (kreuang) pai./Pai rot kreuang.

ขี่รถ(เครื่อง)ไป/ไปรถเครื่อง

A: Should we go by airplane?

Nang kreuang bin pai dee mai?

นั่งเครื่องบินไปดีมั้ย

B: It would be better to go by train.

Nang rot-fai pai dee gwa.

นั่งรถไฟไปดีกว่า

My (younger) sister came by bus.

Nawng-sao nang rot-may ma.

น้องสาวนั่งรถเมล์มา

I'm driving to Lopburi.

Phom ja kap rot pai Lop-boo-ree.

ผมจะขับรถไปลพบุรี

by way of/in the direction of - thang - *Thang* has several uses as a preposition and is also a noun meaning "path", "route", or "way". Here it means "by way of".

I'm going by airplane.

Phom (ja) pai (thang) kreuang-bin.

ผม(จะ)ไป(ทาง)เครื่องบิน

I like to watch the news on TV.

Chan chawp doo kao thang tho-ra-that.

ฉันชอบดูข่าวทางโทรทัศน์

Here it shows the direction you're going.

For Ko Lanta you have to go south.

Gaw Lan-ta tawng pai thang tai.

เกาะลันตาต้องไปทางใต้

It's behind the house.

Yoo thang lang ban.

อยู่ทางหลังบ้าน

It's also used with the home and institutions to show the origin of an action.

The Thai government won't extend Jack's visa.

(Thang) rat-tha-ban Thai mai yawm taw wee-sa kawng Jack.

(ทาง)รัฐบาลไทยไม่ยอมต่อวีซ่าของแจ๊ค

A: Why isn't Nok going to school anymore?

Tham-mai Nok mai rian taw?

ทำไมนกไม่เรียนต่อ

B: Her family won't support her studies.

Thang ban mai sa-nap sa-noon hai rian.

ทางบ้านไม่สนับสนุนให้เรียน

Use *phan thang* for "go by way of" when you're traveling to one place by way of another.

On the way to Hualamphong can you go through Ratprasong?

Pai Huaj-lam-phong phan thang Rat-pra-song dai mai?

ไปหัวลำโพงผ่านทางราชประสงค์ได้มั้ย

in the area of - *Thang* as a preposition also means "about/in the area of/with". It can be combined with *dan* which means "area" or "in the area of".

She doesn't have any problems with her studies.

Kao mai mee pan-haj thang (dan) gan rian.

เค้าไม่มีปัญหาทางด้านการเรียน

I have no knowledge in that area.

Phom mai mee kwam-roo thang nee leuy.

ผมไม่มีความรู้ทางนี้เลย

"by" with dimensions - koon -

A jumbo picture measures four by six.

Roop ka-nat jum-bo keu ka-nat see koon hok.

รูปขนาดจัมโบ้คือขนาดสี่คูณหก

FAR (FROM)

glai (jak) -

A: Is Bang Saen far from here?

Bang Saenj glai jak thee-nee mai?

บางแสนไกลจากที่นี่มั้ย

B: It's not far, around 30 kilometers.

Mai glai mak rawk. Rao samj-sip gee-lo dai.

ไม่ไกลมากหรอก ราวสามสิบกิโลได้

My house is far from town.

Ban chan yoo glai jak tua meuang.

บ้านฉันอยู่ไกลจากตัวเมือง

Kanchanaburi isn't far from here.

Gan-ja-na-boo-ree yoo mai glai jak thee-nee.

กาญจนบุรีอยู่ไม่ไกลจากที่นี่

You've come a long way today.

Wan-nee koon ma glai laeo.

วันนี้คุณมาไกลแล้ว

I don't want to think that far ahead.

Chan mai yak kit glai ka-nat nan.

ฉันไม่อยากคิดไกลขนาดนั้น

to be at a distance - hang - Other meanings are "distant", "separate", and "far apart".

How far is Bangkok from Pattaya?

Groong-thayp hang jak Phat-tha-ya thao-rai? (or *gee gee-lo* instead of *thao-rai*)

กรุงเทพฯ ห่างจากพัทยาเท่าไหร่

Groong-thayp gap Phat-tha-ya yoo hang gan thao-rai?

กรุงเทพฯ กับพัทยาอยู่ห่างกันเท่าไหร่

Bangkok is about 150 kilometers from Pattaya.

Groong-thayp hang jak Phat-tha-ya pra-man roi ha-sip gee-lo.

กรุงเทพฯ ห่างจากพัทยาประมาณร้อยห้าสิบกิโล

Jak Groong-thayp pai Phat-tha-ya pra-man roi ha-sip gee-lo.

จากกรุงเทพฯ ไปพัทยาประมาณร้อยห้าสิบกิโล

In remote villages there are a lot of poor people.

Nai moo-ban thee hang glai awk pai, mee kon jon yoo yeuh.

ในหมู่บ้านที่ห่างไกลออกไปมีคนจนอยู่เยอะ

A: Is there a chicken farm around here?

Thaeoj nee mee fam liang gai mai?

แถวนี้มีฟาร์มเลี้ยงไก่มั้ย

B: Around here there isn't, but if you go further outside of town there are a lot of them.

Thaeoj nee mai mee, tae tha hang awk pai nawk meuang mee yeuh.

แถวนี้ไม่มีแต่ถ้าห่างออกไปนอกเมืองมีเยอะ

FOR

There are three words—*hai, sam-rap*, and *pheua*.

for you - hai/sam-rap - The first is "to give" and the second is more formal. The verb *fak* (meaning "entrust") can be used instead of "for" in sentences like "I bought something for you", as in the first example. See pages 140-141 for more examples with *hai* and page 206 for "enough for".

I bought some fruit for you (to eat).

    Phom seu phong-la-mai ma hai koon gin./Phom seu phong-la-mai ma fak.

    ผมซื้อผลไม้มาให้คุณกิน/ผมซื้อผลไม้มาฝาก

Who is this for?

    Un nee hai krai?/Un nee sam-rap krai?

    อันนี้ให้ใคร/อันนี้สำหรับใคร

This one is for my mother.

    Un nee hai mae./Un nee sam-rap mae.

    อันนี้ให้แม่/อันนี้สำหรับแม่

I made it for her. (also means "I did it for her" with *hai*)

    Chan tham hai kao./Chan tham sam-rap kao.

    ฉันทำให้เค้า/ฉันทำสำหรับเค้า

In this sentence *hai phom tham* means "for me to do".

There's no work for me in that project.

    Nai krong-gan nan mai mee ngan hai phom tham.

    ในโครงการนั้นไม่มีงานให้ผมทำ

designated for - sam-rap -

This computer is for teachers only.

    Kawm-phiu-teuh kreuang nee sam-rap kroo thao-nan.

    คอมพิวเตอร์นี้สำหรับครูเท่านั้น

This is a book for studying Cambodian.

    Nee pen nang-seu sam-rap rian pha-sa Ka-men.

    นี่เป็นหนังสือสำหรับเรียนภาษาเขมร

I bought it for dinner.

    Chan seu ma sam-rap pen a-han yen.

    ฉันซื้อมาสำหรับเป็นอาหารเย็น

We don't have seats for people without tickets.

    Rao mai mee thee-nang sam-rap kon thee mai mee tua.

    เราไม่มีที่นั่งสำหรับคนที่ไม่มีตั๋ว

considering the usual nature of/as for - sǎmɱ-ràp -

For a small town like this, it's an expensive hotel.

    Sǎmɱ-ràp meuang lék-lék yàng-ngee, rong-raem nee phaeng.

    สำหรับเมืองเล็กๆ ยังงี้โรงแรมนี้แพง

It's easy for adults, but not easy for children.

    Mǔn ngaî sǎmɱ-ràp phoô-yài, tae mâi ngaî sǎmɱ-ràp dèk-dèk.

    มันง่ายสำหรับผู้ใหญ่ แต่ไม่ง่ายสำหรับเด็กๆ

To me this place is like home.

    Sǎmɱ-ràp chǎn, thêe-nêe (pèn) meuanɱ bân.

    สำหรับฉัน ที่นี่(เป็น)เหมือนบ้าน

As for Bangkok I'm indifferent.

    Sǎmɱ-ràp Groong-thâyp, chǎn (jà roô-sèuk) cheuy-cheuɱ.

    สำหรับกรุงเทพ ฉันจะรู้สึกเฉยๆ

used for - sǎmɱ-ràp/chái - The first is more formal and the second is the verb "to use". Both are in the complete phrase—*chai sam-rap*.

A: What's this for?/What's this used for?

    Un nee sǎmɱ-ràp thǎm a-rai?/Un nee chái (sǎmɱ-ràp) thǎm a-rai?

    อันนี้สำหรับทำอะไร/อันนี้ใช้(สำหรับ)ทำอะไร

B: It's for teaching.

    Sǎmɱ-ràp sǎwnɱ nák-rian./Chái (sǎmɱ-ràp) sǎwnɱ nák-rian.

    สำหรับสอนนักเรียน/ใช้(สำหรับ)สอนนักเรียน

for the sake of - pheuà - This also means "for the purpose of" as in the last example. The difference between *pheua* and *hai* is shown by the first two sentences. *Pheua* is also on page 100 ("to/in order to"), page 138 ("in order to cause") and pages 164-165 ("so that/in order to").

Everything I do is for her. (for her sake)

    Phǒmɱ thǎm thóok yàng pheuà theuh.

    ผมทำทุกอย่างเพื่อเธอ

I do everything for her. (she doesn't do it)

    Phǒmɱ thǎm hâi theuh thóok yàng.

    ผมทำให้เธอทุกอย่าง

We're working for the future.

    Rao thǎm-ngan pheuà a-na-kót.

    เราทำงานเพื่ออนาคต

I gave him 20 baht for washing my car/to wash my car.

    Chǎn hâi ngeuhn kǎo yêe-sìp baht pheuà láng rót hâi chǎn.

    ฉันให้เงินเค้ายี่สิบบาทเพื่อล้างรถให้ฉัน

"pay for/buy for" with prices - "For" isn't used in Thai.

I bought it for 200 baht. (use *ma* for the object coming to you)

    Phŏmj seu ma sawngj roi baht.

      ผมซื้อมาสองร้อยบาท

Do I have to pay for the room? (*ka* is "the fee for/the charge for")

    Chan tawng jai ka hawng reu plao?

      ฉันต้องจ่ายค่าห้องรึเปล่า

FROM

jak - *Jak* can also be a verb when it refers to going away from a person or place permanantly, as in the second sentence without *awk*.

I leave the house at 4 A.M. (or "I left")

    Chan awk jak ban tawn tee see.

      ฉันออกจากบ้านตอนตีสี่

I'd like to leave this place fast.

    Phŏmj yak (awk) jak thee-nee reo-reo.

      ผมอยาก(ออก)จากที่นี่เร็วๆ

The book fell out of my bag.

    Nang-seuj tok jak gra-paoj (phŏmj).

      หนังสือตกจากกระเป๋าผม

A: Who did you learn your work from?

    Koon rian (roo) ngan (ma) jak krai?

      คุณเรียน(รู้)งาน(มา)จากใคร

B: I trained at a factory.

    Chan rian jak rong-ngan.

      ฉันเรียนจากโรงงาน

A: Where did you buy it?

    Seu ma jak naij?

      ซื้อมาจากไหน

B: I bought it at home.

    Seu ma jak ban.

      ซื้อมาจากบ้าน

from a person - găp/jak - These are interchangable here.

Gaeo went to get some money from a friend.

> Gaeŏ păi aŏ ngeuhn găp pheuan.

> แก้วไปเอาเงินกับเพื่อน

from...to... - jak...(jŏn) theŭng... -

From here to Loei, there were no other vehicles at all.

> Jak theĕ-neĕ theŭng Leuy, măi mee rót leuy.

> จากที่นี่ถึงเลยไม่มีรถเลย

IN/AT

For "in" or "at" a place use *thee, yoo,* or *nai* singly or in various combinations.

With *thee* -

I want to call my boyfriend in Japan.

> Chan yak tho păi hăj faen theĕ Yee-pŏon.

> ฉันอยากโทรไปหาแฟนที่ญี่ปุ่น

Lek went to see him at his house.

> Lek păi hăj (kaŏ) theĕ ban.

> เล็กไปหา(เค้า)ที่บ้าน

In Chonburi there are a lot of shopping centers.

> Theĕ Chon-bŏo-ree mee soonj gan-kā laij haeng.

> ที่ชลบุรีมีศูนย์การค้าหลายแห่ง

How many people live in your house?

> Theĕ ban mee thang-mót gee kŏn?

> ที่บ้านมีทั้งหมดกี่คน

With *yoo/yoo thee* - *Yoo* has the connotation of "staying" at a place. *Yoo thee* can also mean "I have it/it's with me" as in the last example.

Maem's at home.

> Maem yoo (theĕ) ban.

> แหม่มอยู่(ที่)บ้าน

Nok's home is in Chiang Mai.

> Ban Nok yoo (theĕ) Chiang Mai.

> บ้านนกอยู่(ที่)เชียงใหม่

He also has another house in Rayong.

> Kaŏ mee ban yoo Ră-yawng eeg langj neung duay.

> เค้ามีบ้านอยู่ระยองอีกหลังหนึ่งด้วย

The camera is in the room.

> Glawng yoo thee hawng. (or *yoo nai hawng*)
>
> กล้องอยู่ที่ห้อง

I have the book.

> Nang-seu yoo thee chan.
>
> หนังสืออยู่ที่ฉัน

in/inside - (kang) nai - This is the preposition "in/inside" so *kang* is optional before *nai* in all examples.

My (younger) sister is in the house.

> Nawng-sao yoo nai ban.
>
> น้องสาวอยู่ในบ้าน

There's a mouse in the cupboard.

> Mee noo tua neung (yoo) nai too.
>
> มีหนูตัวหนึ่ง(อยู่)ในตู้

A: Why don't you want to go to the disco?

> Tham-mai mai yak pai thek.
>
> ทำไมไม่อยากไปเท็ค

B: It's very noisy in there.

> (Kang) nai nan siang dang mak.
>
> (ข้าง)ในนั้นเสียงดังมาก

Nai can also be used for "in" a city, but *thee* is more common.

My child goes to school in Bangkok.

> Look rian nang-seu (yoo) nai Groong-thayp.
>
> ลูกเรียนหนังสือ(อยู่)ในกรุงเทพฯ

the inside - kang nai/phai nai - This is the noun so *kang* isn't optional. The second phrase is more formal and means "the inner part" or "within", used for both space and time and also for "within" the mind.

A: Is there anyone in the house?

> (Kang) nai ban mee krai yoo mai?
>
> (ข้าง)ในบ้านมีใครอยู่มั้ย

B: No, there's no one inside at all.

> Kang nai mai mee krai yoo leuy.
>
> ข้างในไม่มีใครอยู่เลย

in the area of - dan - This is for areas of study or expertise and also for physical areas.

My (older) brother studies business administration.

> Phee-chai rian dan baw-ree-han thoo-ra-git.
>
> พี่ชายเรียนด้านบริหารธุรกิจ

right at - trong - This means "straight" and may be used for "straight/directly" as in the third sentence.

It's right here.

> Yoo trong nee (leuy).
>
> อยู่ตรงนี้(เลย)

Right here is the mouth of the cave.

> Trong nee pen pak tham.
>
> ตรงนี้เป็นปากถ้ำ

Walk straight ahead, and my house is right next to the gas station.

> Deuhn trong pai, ban chan yoo trong kang pum nam-mun, nan lae.
>
> เดินตรงไป บ้านฉันอยู่ตรงข้างปั้มน้ำมันนั่นแหละ

IN FRONT

(kang) na/trong na/beuang na - The second is "right in front (of)". The third is formal.

My car is parked in front of the house.

> Rot phom jawt (kang) na ban.
>
> รถผมจอด(ข้าง)หน้าบ้าน

I ran into Jane right in front of Robinson's.

> Chan pai jeuh Jane trong na Ro-bin-san phaw dee.
>
> ฉันไปเจอเจนตรงหน้าโรบินสันพอดี

My mother sells noodles in front of the market.

> Mae kai guay-tio (thee) na ta-lat.
>
> แม่ขายก๋วยเตี๋ยว(ที่)หน้าตลาด

(Kang) na is also an adjective meaning "the one in front".

The car in front is going very slowly.

> Rot kun (kang) na kap cha jing-jing.
>
> รถคัน(ข้าง)หน้าขับช้าจริงๆ

the front - kang na - This is a noun so kang isn't optional.

The front of these shops should be repainted.

> Kang na ran phuak nee na ja tha see mai, na.
>
> ข้างหน้าร้านพวกนี้น่าจะทาสีใหม่นะ

in front of others - taw n̄a -

He/she doesn't act nicely in front of other people.

    Kon nan mai mee ma-ra-yat taw n̄a kon eun.

    คนนั้นไม่มีมารยาทต่อหน้าคนอื่น

NEAR

glai (gap)/tit (gap) - These are interchangable. *Glai* and *tit* may also be doubled for "rather near". Some meanings of *tit* are "to stick", "be stuck", "attach", "adjoin", "become attached to", and "be close to".

Maha Sarakam is near Khon Kaen.

    Ma-haj Saj-ra-kam yoo glai-glai (gap) Kawnj Gaen.

    มหาสารคามอยู่ใกล้ๆ (กับ)ขอนแก่น

The post office is near the fire station.

    Prai-sa-nee yoo tit-tit gap sa-thaj-nee dap phleuhng.

    ไปรษณีย์อยู่ติดๆ กับสถานีดับเพลิง

A: Ayuthaya is near Bangkok, isn't it?

    A-yoot-tha-ya yoo glai gap Groong-thayp, chai mai?

    อยุธยาอยู่ใกล้กับกรุงเทพฯ ใช่มั้ย

B: It's not very far. Just a little over 70 kilometers.

    Gaw mai glai mak. Kae jet-sip gwa gee-lo.

    ก็ไม่ไกลมาก แค่เจ็ดสิบกว่ากิโล

close/nearly the same - glai kiang - This is similar to the phrase *klai kiang* which describes characteristics as "similar" (page 234).

The price of these two cars is nearly the same.

    Rot sawnj kun nee, ra-ka glai kiang gan.

    รถสองคันนี้ราคาใกล้เคียงกัน

Provinces that are near Chiang Mai are Chiang Rai, Lamphoon, and Mae Hong Son.

    Jang-wat thee yoo glai kiang gap Chiang Mai gaw mee Chiang Rai, Lam-phoon, lae

    Mae Hawnj Sawnj.

    จังหวัดที่อยู่ใกล้เคียงกับเชียงใหม่ก็มี เชียงราย ลำพูน และแม่ฮ่องสอน

NEXT TO

kang-kang/tit gap - These are interchangable.

There's an amusement park next to the shopping center.

    Mee suanɹ sà-nook (yoo) tit gap soonɹ gan-ka.

    มีสวนสนุก(อยู่)ติดกับศูนย์การค้า

His house is next to Daeng's.

    Ban kao (yoo) kang-kang ban Daeng.

    บ้านเค้า(อยู่)ข้างๆ บ้านแดง

Things in rows - taw pai (nan)/that pai (nan) - These refer to things that are next to each other in rows or lines. They're also used for naming things in order.

This is a hospital. Next to that is a school.

    Nee pen rong-phà-ya-ban. Taw pai nan pen rong-rian.

    นี่เป็นโรงพยาบาล ต่อไปนั่นเป็นโรงเรียน

This is Gai. Next to her is Pet.

    Kon nee Gai. Taw pai nan Pet.

    คนนี้ไก่ ต่อไปนั่นเป็ด

That next picture I drew myself.

    Roop that pai nan chan wat ayng.

    รูปถัดไปนั่นฉันวาดเอง

OF

kawngɹ - This word is used for the possessive and is also the noun "thing/things".

Following are the details of the news.

    Taw pai pen rai-là-iat kawngɹ kao.

    ต่อไปเป็นรายละเอียดของข่าว

The management of this factory is very good. (or "This factory's management")

    Fai baw-ree-hanɹ kawngɹ rong-ngan nee dee mak.

    ฝ่ายบริหารของโรงงานนี้ดีมาก

made of - tham duay/tham jak - These are literally "made with" and "made from". They're interchangable here.

Is this table made completely of teak?

    To nee tham duay mai-sak thang-mot reu plao?

    โต๊ะนี้ทำด้วยไม้สักทั้งหมดรึเปล่า

What's green curry made of?

    Gaeng kioɹ-wanɹ tham duay a-rai?

    แกงเขียวหวานทำด้วยอะไร

ON/ATTACHED TO

<u>tit</u> - In the second example *fa hawng* is "the wall of the room" and *noon* is included for "over there".

There's ice cream on your shirt.

    Mee ai teem <u>tit</u> (bon) seua koon.

    มีไอติมติด(บน)เสื้อคุณ

A: Where's the mirror?

    Gra-<u>jok</u> <u>yoo</u> <u>naj</u>?

    กระจกอยู่ไหน

B: It's on the wall over there.

    <u>Yoo</u> <u>tit</u> faj hawng noon.

    อยู่ติดฝาห้องโน่น

ON/ON TOP OF

(kang) bon - *Kang* is optional before *bon* in all examples.

The pictures are on the table.

    Roop <u>yoo</u> bon to.

    รูปอยู่บนโต๊ะ

You can sleep on the bed.

    Nawn bon tiang, na.

    นอนบนเตียงนะ

There are bungalows on the mountain.

    Mee bung-ga-lo <u>yoo</u> bon kaoj.

    มีบังกะโลอยู่บนเขา

You can sleep on the bus.

    Nawn bon rot gaw dai.

    นอนบนรถก็ได้

Here *(kang) bon* means "up in".

There are birds in the trees.

    Nok <u>yoo</u> bon ton-mai.

    นกอยู่บนต้นไม้

Clouds are floating in the sky.

    Mayk loi <u>yoo</u> bon fa.

    เมฆลอยอยู่บนฟ้า

the top/up there/upstairs - kang bon - This is the noun so *kang* isn't optional. Another phrase for "upstairs" is *chan bon* which refers more to the floors than to the general area (high/short on chan).

Look up there.

> Doo kang bon nan, see.
>
> ดูข้างบนนั้นซิ

A: What's upstairs?

> Kang bon mee a-rai?
>
> ข้างบนมีอะไร

B: There are two bedrooms.

> Mee hawng-nawn sawng hawng.
>
> มีห้องนอนสองห้อง

OUTSIDE

(kang) nawk - This is the preposition.

Joe's house is outside of town.

> Ban Joe yoo nawk meuang.
>
> บ้านโจอยู่นอกเมือง

Outside the house it's cold.

> (Kang) nawk ban mun naoj, na.
>
> (ข้าง)นอกบ้านมันหนาวนะ

the outside - kang nawk/phai nawk - This is the noun. The second phrase is more formal.

There are two people outside.

> Mee kon yoo kang nawk sawng kon.
>
> มีคนอยู่ข้างนอกสองคน

Paint the outside of the building white.

> Teuk nee phai nawk tha duay seej kaoj.
>
> ตึกนี้ภายนอกทาด้วยสีขาว

A: Where did Kaek go?

> Kaek (awk) pai naij?
>
> แขก(ออก)ไปไหน

B: I guess he went outside.

> Awk pai kang nawk mung.
>
> ออกไปข้างนอกมั้ง

OVER

k͞am - This is a verb meaning "cross", "go across", or "step over".

They like to throw trash over the wall.

 P͞hua͞k͞ ka͞o chawp kwa͞ng kȧ-yȧ k͞am ġam-phaeng.

 พวกเค้าชอบขว้างขยะข้ามกำแพง

PAST/BEYOND

leuy - This is used with both places and time.

The factory is past the market.

 Rong-ngan <u>yoo</u> leuy tȧ-lȧt ṗai.

 โรงงานอยู่เลยตลาดไป

A: Where's your house?

 B͞an <u>yoo</u> t͞hee-nȧiɟ?

 บ้านอยู่ที่ไหน

B: It's about two kilometers past the school.

 <u>Yoȯ</u> leuy rong-rian ṗai <u>eeg</u> prȧ-man <u>sawngɟ</u> gėe-lo.

 อยู่เลยโรงเรียนไปอีกประมาณสองกิโล

TO

There are seven words for "to". Two of them are formal.

1. t͞hee - For going "to" places, but often omitted.

I'm going to Roi Et.

 <u>P͞homɟ</u> jȧ ṗai (t͞hee) R͞oi E͟t.

 ผมจะไป(ที่)ร้อยเอ็ด

2. <u>theungɟ</u> - This refers to reaching a place and can be expanded to *jon theung*.

I rode my bike to Lamphoon.

 C͞han <u>kee</u> jȧk-grȧ-yan ṗai (jȯn) t͞heȯungɟ L͞am-phoon.

 ฉันขี่จักรยานไป(จน)ถึงลำพูน

Who are you calling?

 Tho ṗai t͞heȯungɟ krȧi?/Tho ṗai haɟ krȧi?

 โทรไปถึงใคร/โทรไปหาใคร

3. ha͞i̇ - This means "give" and is used for "to" with verbs like "send", "bring", and "take".

Please bring it to me.

 A͟o ma ha͞i̇ c͞han, n͞ȧ.

 เอามาให้ฉันนะ

I'm buying it to send to a friend.

    Chan ja seu song pai hai pheuan.

    ฉันจะซื้อส่งไปให้เพื่อน

4. gap - This is "to" in "good to" (*dee gap*), "do to" (*tham gap*), and "give to" (*hai gap*). Including *gap* with "give" puts emphasis on "to".

He's nice to me.

    Kao dee gap chan.

    เค้าดีกับฉัน

I gave it right to Bob.

    Phom hai gap Bob ayng.

    ผมให้กับบ๊อบเอง

A: What did he do to her?

    Kao tham a-rai (gap) theuh?

    เค้าทำอะไร(กับ)เธอ

B: He lured her into prostitution.

    Kao lawk theuh pai kai tua.

    เค้าหลอกเธอไปขายตัว

5. taw - This means "to" or "toward".

She's really nice to me.

    Kao dee taw phom leua geuhn.

    เค้าดีต่อผมเหลือเกิน

Say it to his face.

    Phoot taw na kao leuy.

    พูดต่อหน้าเค้าเลย

We have to be sincere with each other.

    Rao tawng jing-jai taw gan.

    เราต้องจริงใจต่อกัน

It's dangerous for you. ("toward yourself")

    Mun an-ta-rai taw tua ayng, na.

    มันอันตรายต่อตัวเองนะ

6. gae - This is a formal form of "to", used with "give".

She donated money to the school.

    Kao baw-ree-jak ngeuhn hai (gae) rong-rian.

    เค้าบริจาคเงินให้(แก่)โรงเรียน

She made us happy. ("She gave us happiness.")

Theuh hai kwam-sook (gae) rao.

เธอให้ความสุข(แก่)เรา

7. soo - This is a formal word for "to" or "toward".

Welcome to Thailand.

Yin dee tawn rap soo pra-thet Thai.

ยินดีต้อนรับสู่ประเทศไทย

TOWARD/AT

sai - For "at" or "toward" a place.

Shoot toward the tree.

Ying sai ton-mai leuy.

ยิงใส่ต้นไม้เลย

He was drunk and threw a bottle at my friend.

Kao mao lao laeo kwang kuat sai pheuan.

เค้าเมาแล้วเลยขว้างขวดใส่เพื่อน

thang - This means "route" or "way" and is used for "in the direction of".

Drive in the direction of Ubon.

Kap pai thang Oo-bon.

ขับไปถึงอุบล

UNDER

(yoo) tai/(kang) lang - *Tai* refers to one object being under another. It also means "south", and *tai din* is "underground". *(Kang) lang* is "below", "down below", "under this", "the lower part", or "downstairs".

There's a snake under the rock.

Mee ngoo yoo tai hin.

มีงูอยู่ใต้หิน

Hua Hin is south of Petchburi.

Hua Hin yoo tai Phet-boo-ree.

หัวหินอยู่ใต้เพชรบุรี

Tim's room is below mine.

Hawng (kawng) Tim yoo (kang) lang hawng chan.

ห้อง(ของ)ทิมอยู่(ข้าง)ล้างห้องฉัน

downstairs/the part below - kang lang - This is the noun.

Could you take the fan downstairs?

     Ao phat-lom pai kang lang dai mai?

      เอาพัดลมไปข้างล่างได้มั้ย

Below this is a friend's room.

     Kang lang nee pen hawng kawng pheuan.

      ข้างล่างนี้เป็นห้องของเพื่อน

the bottom - tai/kang lang - These are interchangable.

The bucket is at the bottom of the well.

     Gra-pawng nam yoo kang lang baw.

      กระป๋องน้ำอยู่ข้างล่างบ่อ

EXPRESSION: tai thoong ban - This is "under the house" for Thai elevated houses.

They have a lot of chickens under the house.

     Tai thoong ban kao mee gai yeuh-yae.

      ใต้ถุนบ้านเค้ามีไก่เยอะแยะ

WITH

See also "together" (pages 55-56) and "using *ruam*" (page 58).

gap -

I sent the pictures with Gop.

     Chan fak roop pai gap Gop.

      ฉันฝากรูปไปกับกบ

I saw him with my own eyes.

     Phom heng gap ta.

      ผมเห็นกับตา

duay - Here *duay* means "along with" or "by using". See also "by", page 268.

I don't have anyone to go with.

     Mai mee pheuan pai duay.

      ไม่มีเพื่อนไปด้วย

You should slice these vegetables with a knife.

     Phak nee tawng hun duay meet.

      ผักนี้ต้องหั่นด้วยมีด

I bought it with a credit card.

     Chan seu duay bat kray-dit.

      ฉันซื้อด้วยบัตรเครดิต

I didn't buy it with cash.

    Chan mai dai seu duay ngeuhn sot.

    ฉันไม่ได้ซื้อด้วยเงินสด

I killed the mice with poison.

    Phom ka noo duay ya phit.

    ผมฆ่าหนูด้วยยาพิษ

doy thee - This is for two clauses.

He drove with his wife helping to look at the map.

    Kao kap rot doy thee faen kao chuay doo phaeng-thee.

    เค้าขับรถโดยที่แฟนเค้าช่วยดูแผนที่

WITHOUT

doy mai - *Thee* may be included with two clauses (last sentence).

I went to work without my ID.

    Chan pai tham-ngan doy mai mee bat pra-jam tua.

    ฉันไปทำงานโดยไม่มีบัตรประจำตัว

Jaeo left without telling me.

    Jaeo pai doy mai bawk.

    แจ๋วไปโดยไม่บอก

She went off to work in Bangkok without her parents knowing.

    Kao nee awk jak ban pai tham-ngan Groong-thayp doy (thee) phaw-mae mai roo
    reuang.

    เค้าหนีออกจากบ้านไปทำงานกรุงเทพโดย(ที่)พ่อแม่ไม่รู้เรื่อง

"don't put/not having" - mai sai/mai mee -

He eats it without chili pepper.

    Kao gin mai sai phrik.

    เค้ากินไม่ใส่พริก

We want a house without furniture.

    Rao yak dai ban thee mai mee feuh-nee-jeuh.

    เราอยากได้บ้านที่ไม่มีเฟอร์นิเจอร์

Formal/with nouns - rai - This is more formal and is followed by a noun.

He likes doing things that have no benefit.

    Kao chawp tham a-rai rai pra-yot.

    เค้าชอบทำอะไรไร้ประโยชน์

14. PARTICLES & INTERJECTIONS

PARTICLES

Particles are short words included at the end of sentences that affect the meaning in the same way that stress or inflection does in English. Except for the polite words *ka/krup* listed here first, the use of particles depends on a person's individual speaking style: some people use them a lot and others don't. In general they add informality and playfulness to spoken Thai.

KA/KRUP AND VARIATIONS

krup/ka̅/ka̲/ka̅ - *Krup* for men and *ka* for women are included for politeness. They should be used with people who are older than you are, people in high positions, people you've just met, or anyone in general you want to be polite to. *Krup* and *ka* are also used alone as a polite way to answer "yes". *Krup* always has a high tone/short vowel length. *Ka* can have three pronunciations—high/short when it's at the end of questions, low/short with statements, responses and commands, and falling/short for emphasis on statements, responses, and commands.

A: What's that?

    Nan a-rai, ka̅?   *(ka is high/short with a question)*

    นั่นอะไรคะ

B: Oh, it's a toy.

    Aw! Kawng len dek, ka̲.   (low/short with a response)

    ออ! ของเล่นเด็กคะ

Please do it quickly./Please go a little faster.

    Reo-reo noi, ka̅.   (falling/short for emphasis)

    เร็วๆ หน่อยคะ

ha̅ - This can replace *ka* or *krup* informally.

A: Are you going?

    Pai mai, ha̅?

    ไปมั้ยฮะ

B: Yes.

    Pai, ha̅.

    ไปฮะ

ja/ja - These are more friendly and informal than *ka/krup*. The pronunciation is high/short with questions or when you're offering something to someone (written with the third tone marker—*mai tree*) and falling/short with responses (written with a *mai tho*).

A: Noi, are you going to Hua Hin?

Noi ja pai Huaɟ Hiɲ mai, ja?

น้อยจะไปหัวหินมั้ยจ๊ะ

B: Yes.

Pai, ja.

ไปจ๊ะ

jaɟ - This is flowery language used with your mother, child, or spouse. It shows more tenderness than the previous *ja*. It's written with the fourth tone marker (*mai jattawa*).

What's this, my dear?

Nee a-rai jaɟ, thee-rak?

นี่อะไรจ๋า ที่รัก

LA AND VARIATIONS

la/la ka/la krup - *La* comes from *reu*. It's used with questions and negative responses to invitations, making them sound less serious and abrupt. *La* is low/short when used alone and high/short when *ka* or *krup* are included.

He's not well? What's wrong?

Kao mai sa-bai reuɲ? Pen a-rai, la?

เค้าไม่สบายเหรอ เป็นอะไรล่ะ

Lek didn't come with you? Why not?

Lek mai ma duay reuɲ? Tham-mai, la ka?

เล็กไม่มาด้วยเหรอ ทำไมล่ะคะ

A: Are you going?

Pai mai, la?

ไปมั้ยล่ะ

B: No.

Mai la.

ไม่ล่ะ

la ha - This is an informal, friendly version of *la ka/la krup*.

A: I'm not free today.

Wan-nee phomɟ mai wang.

วันนี้ผมไม่ว่าง

B: So what about tomorrow?

> Laeo phroong-nee, la ha?
>
> แล้วพรุ่งนี้ละฮะ

La may also be included to create a pause after bringing up a topic (first sentence), when a situation has changed (second), to express a strong feeling (third), and to soften a command (fourth).

And what about French, can you speak it?

> Laeo pha-saj Fa-rang-set la, phoot dai mai?
>
> แล้วภาษาฝรั่งเศสละ พูดได้มั้ย

In that case I won't buy it.

> Tha yang-ngan chan mai seu, la.
>
> ถ้ายังงั้นฉันไม่ซื้อละ

It's very cold.

> Naoj mak leuy, la.
>
> หนาวมากเลยละ

Don't forget to feed the bird.

> Ya leum hai a-hanj nok, la.
>
> อย่าลืมให้อาหารนกละ

Laeo is sometimes pronounced *la* (high/short).

I'd better be going now.

> Chan tawng pai gawn la na.
>
> ฉันต้องไปก่อนละนะ

MUNG

mung/la-mung - These are included with statements and responses for "I guess" or "maybe". A formal form is *gra-mang*. See also pages 75-76 and 202.

I guess she's busy.

> Kao (kong ja) mee thoo-ra la-mung.
>
> เค้า(คงจะ)มีธุระละมั้ง

I think he might like it.

> Kit wa kao kong ja chawp mung.
>
> คิดว่าเค้าคงจะชอบมั้ง

I see it's a little too much.

> Henj ja mak pai la-mung.
>
> เห็นจะมากไปละมั้ง

mung - This is included when you're contradicting someone and want to sound confident but not too aggressive. It's similar to *mai chai rawk*. *Mung* is held out longer here.

A: Gaeo has a lot of money.

Gaeo mee ngeuhn yeuh, na.

แก้วมีเงินเยอะนะ

B: No, he doesn't.

Mai chai mung.

ไม่ใช้มั้ง

There (probably) won't be any problem.

Kong mai mee pan-haj mung.

คงไม่มีปัญหามั้ง

mung/mang - This pronunciation of *mung* is a variation of *bang* and means "some", "somewhat", or "sometimes". See also pages 75-76.

A: Do you ever go and get a massage?

Keuy pai ab op nuat mai?

เคยไปอาบอบนวดมั้ย

B: Sometimes.

Gaw keuy mung./Keuy pai mung.

ก็เคยมั้ง/เคยไปมั้ง

NA AND VARIATIONS

na/naw - These are put after statements for "Don't you agree?".

The weather is nice today, isn't it?

Wan-nee a-gat dee, na?

วันนี้อากาศดีนะ

na - This is for requests, friendly warnings, and telling people things directly. It means "mind you" or "OK".

Please drive carefully.

Kap dee-dee, na.

ขับดีๆ นะ

Don't tell anyone.

Ya bawk krai, na.

อย่าบอกใครนะ

Be careful. It's hot.

Ra-wang na, mun rawn.

ระวังนะมันร้อน

Ka and *krup* may be included after *na* for politeness. They're both high/short.

I'm going back.

> Glap gawn, na ka.
>
> กลับก่อนนะคะ

Please close the door.

> Chuay pit pra-too duay, na krup.
>
> ช่วยปิดประตูด้วยนะครับ

Na is also used to add encouragement to an invitation.

Please go (with me).

> Pai, na!
>
> ไปนะ

na - *Na* with a falling tone means "please".

Please smile./Try to smile.

> Yim noi, na.
>
> ยิ้มหน่อยนะ

na/na - *Na* with a low tone is put after the question words "what" and "who" to point out the person or object you're referring to. It's also used to refer back to something, as in the third example. The meaning is stronger when the vowel length is long.

Who?

> Krai, na?
>
> ใครน่ะ

What are you doing?

> Tham a-rai, na.
>
> ทำอะไรน่ะ

Have you found the key?

> Goon-jae, na, jeuh reu yang?
>
> กุญแจน่ะ เจอรึยัง

Na with this pronunciation is also used to create a pause after a subject pronoun and with requests. It sounds less strong than the other pronunciations.

I really didn't want to go, but a friend invited me.

> Chan, na, mai yak pai, tae pheuan chuan.
>
> ฉันน่ะไม่อยากไปแต่เพื่อนชวน

Go with me as a friend. (to accompany me)

> Pai pen pheuan noi, na.
>
> ไปเป็นเพื่อนหน่อยนะ

ah - This comes from *na*. It's used informally at the end of questions.

What do you want to eat?

    Gin a-rai, ah?

        กินอะไรอะ

NEE AND VARIATIONS

nee/niå - These words are the pronoun "this". Here they're put at end of statements and questions to refer back to what is being talked about. See also page 5.

What's this?

    A-rai niå?

        อะไรเนี่ย

Should I go?

    Chan kuan ja pai mai niå?

        ฉันควรจะไปมั้ยเนี่ย

I'm not satisfied with these glasses I bought.

    Chan mai phaw-jai gap waen-ta thee seu ma nee.

        ฉันไม่พอใจกับแว่นตาที่ซื้อมานี่

Nee is also put at the end of answers or explanations to show that it's the only simple answer possible.

I don't know.

    Gaw, phom mai roo nee.

        ก็ผมไม่รู้นี่

There's nothing wrong.

    Gaw mai mee a-rai nee.

        ก็ไม่มีอะไรนี่

She's gone home already.

    Kao glap ban laeo nee.

        เค้ากลับบ้านแล้วนี่

nee - This is an alternative pronunciation with the same meaning.

A: He's your boyfriend?

    Kao pen faen koon reuh?

        เค้าเป็นแฟนคุณเหรอ

B: No.

    Mai chai nee.

        ไม่ใช่นี่

nun̆ lae/nan̆ lae/na̅ lae - These mean "exactly" and put emphasis on the point being made.

A: Whose notebook is this?

Sǎ-mòot nee kawngɟ krài, krup?

สมุดนี่ของใครครับ

B: It's yours.

Gaw̆ kawngɟ kòon, nun̆ lae.

ก็ของคุณนั่นแหละ

na̅e - This is included to show that an amount is considered large.

Oh, you're buying a house for three million baht!

Oh̆, jà seu ban̆ tâng samɟ lan̆, na̅e.

โอ้ จะซื้อบ้านตั้งสามล้านแหนะ

RAWK

rawk/ra̅wk - This is included mostly with the negative and means "not as stated", "not as thought", or "not really". The pronunciation is either low/long or low/short.

A: It's expensive.

Mùn phaeng, na̅.

มันแพงนะ

B: No, not really.

Ma̅i phaeng rawk.

ไม่แพงหรอก

A: Do I have to go?

Phomɟ tawnɡ̆ pài ma̅i?

ผมต้องไปมั้ย

B: No, not really.

Ma̅i, ra̅wk.

ไม่หรอก

If you don't go, I'm not going either.

    Thᾱ theuh mᾱi pᾱi, chᾰn gᾱw mᾱi pᾱi rawk.

    ถ้าเธอไม่ไปฉันก็ไม่ไปหรอก

With the affirmative *rawk* puts emphasis on something someone else doesn't believe.

It's because she likes you that she's helping you.

    Kᾱo chawp koon rawk, kᾱo jeung chuay koon.

    เค้าชอบคุณหรอก เค้าจึงช่วยคุณ

Be careful or it'll break (shatter).

    Ra-wᾱng, dioɟ (mᾰn) gᾱw taek rawk.

    ระวัง เดี๋ยว(มัน)ก็แตกหรอก

THEE

Thee with a mid tone means "time/occasion" and is included with requests to mean "this one time", making them milder by indicating that the person only has to do the action once. This is similar to adding *noi* to requests.

Excuse me.

    Kawɟ-thot thee.

    ขอโทษที

Please mail this letter.

    Chuay song jot-maiɟ hᾱi thee.

    ช่วยส่งจดหมายให้ที

Let him see it just once.

    Kawɟ hᾱi kᾱo doo thee.

    ขอให้เค้าดูที

SA—SAK AND SIA

The examples here include either *sak, sia,* or *sa. Sak* is an indefinite quantifier that minimizes or estimates amounts (explained on page 194). *Sia* means "lose", "be lost", "break", or "waste" and is put after verbs to emphasize that you want an action done completely or quickly. *Sa* is shortened from either *sak* or *sia* depending on its meaning in the sentence.

sak thee/*siaɟ* thee/*sa* thee - These are for actions you want to do or have happen: *sak* to minimize and *sia* to show that the action is done (or wanted done). *Thee* is "once" as in the previous section.

I didn't go. (even once)

    Mᾱi dᾱi pᾱi sak thee.

    ไม่ได้ไปซักที

I waited a long time but she didn't come.

Raw nan laeo, tae kao mai ma sak thee.

รอนานแล้วแต่เค้าไม่มาซักที

I can finally go home. I've been really homesick.

Dai glap ban siaj thee. Kit theung ban mak.

ได้กลับบ้านเสียที คิดถึงบ้านมาก

I still haven't graduated.

Phom mai jop sak thee.

ผมไม่จบซักที

I'd like to go just this once.

Chan yak ja pai sa thee.

ฉันอยากจะไปชะที

siaj/sa/siaj thee/sa thee - These phrases all come from *sia*, not *sak*, and are included with commands for encouragement or to mean "do it quickly". Including *thee* makes the meaning stronger and more polite, as *sa* or *sia* alone can sound abrupt.

Go home.

Glap ban sa.

กลับบ้านชะ

Let's go back. I'm hungry.

Glap sa thee see. Chan hiu laeo.

กลับชะทีซิ ฉันหิวแล้ว

Eat now. The food will get cold.

Gin siaj (thee) see, gap kao ja yen mot laeo.

กินเสีย(ที) กับข้าวจะเย็นหมดแล้ว

sa noi - This is shortened from *sak noi* and is included with statements to minimize the action. It shouldn't be used when requesting something as it would sound too abrupt; use *sak noi* instead (page 213).

Have some water.

Deum nam sa noi, see.

ดื่มน้ำซะหน่อยซิ

I think I'll go and get a haircut.

Phom wa ja pai tat phom sa noi.

ผมว่าจะไปตัดผมซะหน่อย

With amounts - *Sia* or *sa* are included informally when you're referring to part of an amount.

I have ten thousand baht. I'm going to spend five thousand on a TV.

> Mee ngeuhn <u>meun</u> <u>neung</u>. Ja seu thee-wee sa ha phan.
>
> มีเงินหมื่นหนึ่ง จะซื้อทีวีชะห้าพัน

Five of them are women.

> Pen phoo-<u>ying</u> sa ha kon.
>
> เป็นผู้หญิงชะห้าคน

Other phrases - Following are common phrases with *sa* and *sia*:

We haven't seen each other for a long time.

> Mai dai jeuh sa nan. (or *sia nan*)
>
> ไม่ได้เจอชะนาน

He took it already.

> Kao ao pai sa laeo. (or *sia laeo*)
>
> เค้าเอาไปชะแล้ว

You're going out? Wash the clothes first.

> Ja pai thio <u>reuh</u>? Sak pha sa <u>gawn</u>.
>
> จะไปเที่ยวเหรอ ซักผ้าชะกอน

Today he wore a suit! (shows surprise)

> Wan-nee kao <u>sai</u> <u>soot</u> sa duay!
>
> วันนี้เค้าใส่สูทชะด้วย

I've eaten it till I'm sick of it.

> Gin sa <u>beua</u> laeo.
>
> กินชะเบื่อแล้ว

SEE

<u>see</u> - This means "surely" or "really".

A: Shall we go?

> Pai reu <u>plao</u>?
>
> ไปรึเปล่า

B: Sure.

> Pai <u>see</u>.
>
> ไปซิ

see - This is stronger, meaning "of course".

A: Would you like some beer.

> Ao bia mai?
>
> เอาเบียร์มั้ย

B: Sure.

   Ao see.

     เอาซิ

noi see - This is used with requests.

Please let me through./Please let me pass by.

   Kawj thang noi see./Kawj phomj (phan) pai noi see.

     ขอทางหน่อยซิ/ขอผม(ผ่าน)ไปหน่อยซิ

Please bring some water for your mother. (said to child)

   Chuay ao nam hai mae noi see, look.

     ช่วยเอาน้ำให้แม่หน่อยซิลูก

na see - *Na* changes from high/short to mid/short when it's followed by *see*. The meaning here is "it's obvious", "of course", or "what else can it be?"

A: Hey, where has Tom gone?

   Ao, Tom pai naij laeo?

     อ้าว ทอมไปไหนแล้ว

B: He's gone home.

   Kao gaw glap ban pai laeo, na see.

     เค้าก็กลับบ้านไปแล้วนะซิ

THEUH

theuh - This word adds encouragement and also means "let's". In the third sentence *sa* is shortened from *sia*.

Come and eat with us.

   Ma gin gan theuh.

     มากินกันเถอะ

Alright, have it your way.

   Ao theuh./Tam-jai theuh.

     เอาเถอะ/ตามใจเถอะ

Eat it up.

   Koon gin sa theuh.

     คุณกินซะเถอะ

INTERJECTIONS

calling attention - ah̄ - This is said when finishing an action or to call attention to something that's going to happen. It may sound abrupt.

OK. That's enough.

> Ah. Phaw laeo.
>
> อ้า พอแล้ว

well! - ao̅ - For chiding someone or showing surprise or dismay.

Well, why do you say that?

> Ao, tham-mai koon phoot yang-ngan?
>
> อ้าว ทำไมคุณพูดยังงั้น

oh, now I understand - aw̅ -

Oh, it's he who's your brother.

> Aw, kao nee ayng thee pen phee-chai.
>
> ออ เค้านี่เองที่เป็นพี่ชาย

uh - <u>ay</u> - For when you can't remember or can't figure something out—"What was that again?"

Uh - who told me that?

> <u>Ay</u> - krai, na, <u>bawk</u> <u>phom</u>?
>
> เอ ใครนะบอกผม

hey! - ay̅ - For surprise or wonder.

Hey! What are they doing?

> Ay! Kao gam-lang tham a-rai gan <u>yoo</u>, na?
>
> เอ๊ะ เค้ากำลังทำอะไรกันอยู่นะ

angry - ba̅ - When angry or annoyed (not polite).

Huh! You knew that already. Why did you have to ask me?

> Ba. Roo laeo, ma <u>tham</u> tham-mai?
>
> บะ รู้แล้วมาถามทำไม

whiew - heuh̄ - Said when relieved.

Whiew, it's finished.

> Heuh, <u>set</u> laeo.
>
> เฮอ เสร็จแล้ว

hey! - heuy! - Used when angry, when you want someone to stop doing something, or for shouting to someone from a distance (not polite).

Hey! Stop arguing!

Heuy! Leuhk tha-law gan sa thee.

เฮ้ย เลิกทะเลาะกันซะที

my! - mae - Shows surprise or admiration.

My, you've drawn a beautiful picture.

Mae, koon wat phap suay jing-jing.

แหม คุณวาดภาพสวยจริงๆ

wondering - nee -

Hey, are you staying or going?

Nee, theuh ja yoo reu ja pai, ja?

นี่ เธอจะอยู่หรือจะไปจ๊ะ

What's happening? (something surprising)

Geuht a-rai nee?

เกิดอะไรนี่

well, what about that! - oh-ho -

Well, your house is a great place to live.

Oh-ho, ban koon na-yoo jang leuy.

โอโห้ บ้านคุณน่าอยู่จังเลย

ouch! - oy - This is also said to show pain or that you're tired or fed up.

Ouch - it hurts.

Oy - jep!

โอ๊ย เจ็บ

Oh, I'm tired.

Oy - neuay.

โอ๊ย เหนื่อย

oh come on! - tho/tho euy - This is said when you were expecting something other than what actually happened.

Oh come on, please try to understand me. (said to an older person)

Tho euy, phee, kao-jai chan bang, see.

โธ่เอ๊ย พี่เข้าใจฉันบ้างซิ

uncomfortable/surprised - ūi -

Oh, excuse me. I forgot.

> Ūi, kaw-thot, na. Phom leum pai.
>
> อุ๊ย ขอโทษนะ ผมลืมไป

emphasis - wa - This adds emphasis. It isn't polite and is used only with friends or when you're very angry.

What's wrong? Are you sick or what?

> Pen a-rai, wa? Mai sa-bai reu plao?
>
> เป็นอะไรวะ ไม่สบายรึเปล่า

What the ****'s going on?

> Reuang a-rai wa!
>
> เรื่องอะไรวะ

What the ****!!

> A-rai wa!!
>
> อะไรวะ

shocked - wai - This is used mostly by women.

Oh! Help me! A snake!

> Wai! Chuay duay! Ngoo, ngoo!
>
> ว้าย ช่วยด้วย งู งู

angry/calling attention - woy/weuy/wooy - Said loudly to show anger or to draw attention to yourself.

What's going on! Stop it!

> A-rai gan woy! Yoot dai laeo!
>
> อะไรกันโว๊ย หยุดได้แล้ว

don't! - ya -

Don't! It's dangerous.

> Ya! Mun an-ta-rai.
>
> อย่า มันอันตราย

15. TIME PHRASES

GENERAL PATTERNS WITH TIME

Meua with time phrases - *Meua* is optional before any past time word or phrase.

I came here two days ago.

> Chan ma thee-nee (meua) sawng wan thee laeo.

> ฉันมาที่นี่(เมื่อ)สองวันที่แล้ว

Tawn with time phrases - *Tawn* is optional before clock times, times of day, days of the week, months, or any other time word or phrase. *Tawn nai?* is "What time of day?"

She told me that she would go next week.

> Kao bawk wa kao ja pai (tawn) a-thit na.

> เค้าบอกว่าเค้าจะไป(ตอน)อาทิตย์หน้า

in (a certain) month/year - *Nai* is optional before months and years but is used with dates only formally. "On December 15" informally is *sip-ha Than-wa*, or formally *nai wan thee sip-ha deuan Than-wa-kom.*

I'm leaving in December.

> Phom ja glap (nai) deuan Than-wa nee.

> ผมจะกลับ(ใน)เดือนธันวานี้

I bought this car in 2539.

> Chan seu rot kun nee (nai) pee sawng ha sam gao.

> ฉันซื้อรถคันนี้(ใน)ปี 2539

With *gaw* - Time phrases are usually put first in Thai sentences, and *gaw* may be included optionally to link the time phrase and subject with the rest of the sentence.

Before, I was a farmer, but now I sell things.

> Meua-gawn (phom) (gaw) tham na, tae tawn-nee ka-kai.

> เมื่อก่อน(ผม)(ก็)ทำนาแต่ตอนนี้ค้าขาย

On Monday there's a temple fair.

> Wan Jan (gaw) (ja) mee ngan wat.

> วันจันทร์(ก็)(จะ)มีงานวัด

By 10 P.M. I'll have gone already. (or in the past - "I was already gone" without *ja*)

> See thoom (gaw) ja glap laeo.

> สี่ทุ่ม(ก็)จะกลับแล้ว

With *nee* - Two different tones can be put on *nee* when it's after a time word. A high tone means "this" and a falling tone emphasizes that the fact is realized—"for sure".

Moo's coming at 10 A.M.

    Mooj jà ma sìp mong nee.

    หมูจะมา 10 โมงนี้

It's not yet 8 o'clock.

    Yàng maî sawng thoom nee.

    ยังไม่สองทุ่มนี่

Doubling time words - There are two meanings. First, if the time word is doubled after *pen* it emphasizes that the time is long. Secondly it means "day-by-day", "month-by-month", etc.

He travels around the world for months at a time.

    Kao àwk pài thiò tang prà-thet pen deuan-deuan.

    เค้าออกไปเที่ยวต่างประเทศเป็นเดือนๆ

Living here is easy. The days go by and you don't have to go anywhere.

    Yoo thee-nee sà-bai. Wàn-wàn maî tawng pài naij.

    อยู่ที่นี่สบาย วันๆ ไม่ต้องไปไหน

"TO BE" WITH TIME

Pen is used in various patterns with time.

Large amounts - *Pen way-la* is included before phrases with amounts of time to emphasize that the time is long. *Pen* alone can be put before the word "year" or "month"—*pen pee* means "It's been a whole year". (In the previous point the time word is doubled after *pen*.)

I haven't been to Hua Hin for a long time.

    Phòmj maî daî pài Huaj Hinj pèn way-la nan laeo.

    ผมไม่ได้ไปหัวหินเป็นเวลานานแล้ว

I haven't cut my hair for a whole year.

    Chan maî daî tàt phomj pèn pee leuy.

    ฉันไม่ได้ตัดผมเป็นปีเลย

today is - *Pen* is optional here.

Friday's my birthday.

    Wàn Sook (pèn) wàn geuht phomj.

    วันศุกร์(เป็น)วันเกิดผม

This is the day that salaries are given out.

    Wàn-nee (pèn) wàn (thee) ngeuhn deuan awk.

    วันนี้(เป็น)วัน(ที่)เงินเดือนออก

This is the month for Loy Krathong.

    Deuan nee (pen deuan thee) mee ngan Loi Gra-thong.

    เดือนนี้(เป็นเดือนที่)มีงานลอยกระทง

What time was it? -

A: What time was it that you arrived?

    Mun pen way-la thao-rai thee koon ma theung?

    มันเป็นเวลาเท่าไหร่ที่คุณมาถึง

B: It was around 10 P.M.

    Gaw rao-rao see thoom.

    ก็ราวๆ สี่ทุ่ม

With "probably/might/have to" -

A: When will you be finished?

    Koon ja set meua-rai?

    คุณจะเสร็จเมื่อไหร่

B: It will probably be next week.

    Kong ja (pen) a-thit na./Na ja pen a-thit na, na.

    คงจะ(เป็น)อาทิตย์หน้า/น่าจะเป็นอาทิตย์หน้านะ

It could be next month before it arrives.

    At ja pen deuan na gwa mun ja ma theung.

    อาจจะเป็นเดือนหน้ากว่ามันจะมาถึง

But this week I won't be here. It has to be next week.

    Tae a-thit nee mai yoo. Tawng (pen) a-thit na.

    แต่อาทิตย์นี้ไม่อยู่ ต้อง(เป็น)อาทิตย์หน้า

that was - nan gaw (pen) -

I started working here when I was 20. That was five years ago.

    Chan reuhm tham-ngan thee-nee meua tawn a-yoo (dai) yee-sip. Nan gaw (pen)

    meua ha pee thee laeo.

    ฉันเริ่มทำงานที่นี่เมื่อตอนอายุ(ได้) 20 นั่นก็(เป็น)เมื่อห้าปีที่แล้ว

QUANTIFIERS WITH TIME

exactly - trong/phaw dee - The first means "straight" and the second is "just right". *Trong* can also mean "correct" to describe time on a clock, and *phaw dee* is also "at that very moment", under "simultaneously" on page 350.

Right now it's exactly 9 A.M.

    Tawn-nee, sam mong trong leuy./Tawn-nee, sam mong phaw dee.

    ตอนนี้สามโมงตรงเลย/ตอนนี้สามโมงพอดี

right at/exactly at - ayng - This emphasizes "right at" or "just".

A: What day are you going?/When are you going?

    Ja pai wan nai?/Pai meua-rai?

    จะไปวันไหน/ไปเมื่อไหร่

B: Today.

    (Pai) wan-nee ayng.

    (ไป)วันนี้เอง

a little after/a little over - gwa/gwa-gwa - Doubling *gwa* shows that you're estimating the amount.

The program starts at a little after 9 P.M.

    Rai-gan reuhm samj thoom gwa.

    รายการเริ่มสามทุ่มกว่า

I've gone to school here for over two years.

    Phomj rian thee-nee ma sawngj pee gwa laeo.

    ผมเรียนที่นี่มาสองปีกว่าแล้ว

one or two/five or ten - "One or two days" is *wan sawng wan*, also with months and years. For other consecutive numbers use *sawng-sam*, *sam-see*, etc. For non-consecutive numbers put *reu* or *theung* between them.

Before going back to Denmark he plans to go to Maeo's house for a few days.

    Gawn glap Dayn-mak kao wa ja pai thio ban Maeo sak wan sawngj wan.

    ก่อนกลับเดนมาร์คเค้าว่าจะไปเที่ยวบ้านแมวสักวันสองวัน

Please come back in ten or fifteen days.

    Ga-roo-na glap ma eeg nai sip theung sip-ha wan, na ka.

    กรุณากลับมาอีกในสิบถึงสิบห้าวันนะคะ

In five or ten years Thai students will speak English better than now.

    Eeg ha reuj sip pee dek Thai kong phoot pha-saj Ang-grit geng gwa nee.

    อีกห้าหรือสิบปีเด็กไทยคงพูดภาษาอังกฤษเก่งกว่านี้

about/around - pra-man/rao/rao-rao -

I'm going at around 7 A.M.

    Pai pra-man jet mong chao.

    ไปประมาณ 7 โมงเช้า

A: Do you know what time Gai is bringing her friends here?

    Roo mai, Gai ja pha pheuan-pheuan ma thee-nee gee mong?

    รู้มั้ย ไก่จะพาเพื่อนๆ มาที่นี่กี่โมง

B: I don't know, but I think they'll probably come around 5 P.M.

> Mai roo, na, tae kit wa kong ma rao ha mong (yen).
>
> ไม่รู้นะ แต่คิดว่าคงมาราวห้าโมง(เย็น)

maybe/I guess - mung - This is put at the end of sentences.

A: What time is it?

> Gee mong laeo nee?
>
> กี่โมงแล้วนี่

B: It's probably around 1 P.M.

> Bai mong, mung.
>
> บ่ายโมงมั้ง

almost - geuap -

I waited for John for almost two hours.

> Chan koi John geuap sawng chua-mong dai.
>
> ฉันคอยจอห์นเกือบสองชั่วโมงได้

nearly/approaching - glai (theung)/geuap -

It's nearly midnight now.

> Tawn-nee glai (theung) thiang keun laeo.
>
> ตอนนี้ใกล้(ถึง)เที่ยงคืนแล้ว

It's almost eight o'clock.

> Geuap paet mong laeo.
>
> เกือบแปดโมงแล้ว

only/just - kae/thao-nan/ayng - These may be used singly or together, with *kae* before the amount and *thao-nan* or *ayng* after it.

I can only work two or three hours a day.

> Chan tham-ngan dai kae wan la sawng-sam chua-mong.
>
> ฉันทำงานได้แค่วันละสองสามชั่วโมง

We rented the car for only a week.

> Rao chao rot kae a-thit dio thao-nan.
>
> เราเช่ารถแค่อาทิตย์เดียวเท่านั้น

I've been in Thailand for just over a year.

> Phom ma yoo meuang Thai dai kae pee gwa ayng.
>
> ผมมาอยู่เมืองไทยได้แค่ปีกว่าเอง

in only - kae/nai way-la kae/phai nai kae -

They built this house in just a month.

Kao sang ban lang nee set (nai way-la) kae neung deuan.

เค้าสร้างบ้านหลังนี้เสร็จ(ในเวลา)แค่หนึ่งเดือน

only/just/recently - pheung (ja) - There are more examples on page 314.

I've only studied Thai for six months.

Chan pheung (ja) rian pha-sa Thai dai hok deuan.

ฉันเพิ่ง(จะ)เรียนภาษาไทยได้หกเดือน

Gaeo just left.

Gaeo pheung pai dioj-nee ayng.

แก้วเพิ่งไปเดี๋ยวนี้เอง

a whole/the whole - tem/tem-tem - These are interchangable.

I lived in Israel a whole year.

Phom yoo thee It-sa-ra-eol neung pee tem.

ผมอยู่ที่อิสราเอลหนึ่งปีเต็ม

whole/complete - krop - This refers to completing a cycle.

I've lived in Udon for almost a whole year.

Chan yoo Oo-dawn ma geuap krop pee laeo.

ฉันอยู่อุดรมาเกือบครบปีแล้ว

INDEFINITE QUANTIFIERS WITH TIME

Tang and *sak* are explained on page 194. Here they're included with amounts of time.

a long time - tang/tang-nan - The first is put before time words to show that the time is long. The second means "a very long time".

He skipped work for three whole days.

Kao kat ngan tang sam wan.

เค้าขาดงานตั้งสามวัน

I haven't exercised for a long time.

Chan mai dai awk gam-lang gai tang-nan.

ฉันไม่ได้ออกกำลังกายตั้งนาน

a short time/estimating the time - sak - *Sak* shows that the amount of time is being minimized or estimated.

I'd like to stop working for a day, but I have too much to do.

Yak yoot ngan sak wan, tae ngan yeuh mak.

อยากหยุดงานซักวันแต่งานเยอะมาก

It will probably take around three days.

    Kong chai way-la sak samɲ wan.

    คงใช้เวลาซักสามวัน

Please wait. I'll be through in ten minutes.

    Raw dioɲ na. Eeg sak sip na-thee gaw set.

    รอเดี๋ยวนะ อีกซักสิบนาทีก็เสร็จ

A: How many days will the shop be closed?

    Koon ja pit ran sak gee wan?

    คุณจะปิดร้านซักกี่วัน

B: Two or three days.

    Sak sawnɲ-samɲ wan.

    ซักสองสามวัน

TIMES OF DAY

in the morning - tawn chao/way-la chao -

In the morning I like to go jogging.

    Way-la chao phomɲ chawp pai jawk-ging.

    เวลาเช้าผมชอบไปจ็อกกิ้ง

early afternoon - tawn bai/way-la bai/bai-bai - This is between one o'clock and four o'clock in the afternoon.

He'll call early this afternoon.

    Tawn bai nee kao ja tho ma.

    ตอนบ่ายนี้เค้าจะโทรมา

late afternoon - tawn yen/way-la yen/yen-yen - This is approximately from 5 P.M. to 7 P.M.

We'll play golf late tomorrow afternoon.

    Tawn yen phroong-nee rao ja pai len gawp, na.

    ตอนเย็นพรุ่งนี้เราจะไปเล่นกอล์ฟนะ

morning light/daybreak/dawn - sa-wang/roong chao -

It's daylight already.

    Sa-wang laeo.

    สว่างแล้ว

early morning - chao/chao-chao/tae chao/chao troo - *Chao-chao* means "very early" if the first *chao* is held out and stressed, but just "early in the morning" if it's doubled with the same stress on both words. *Tae chao* comes from *tang-tae chao* ("since morning"). The last phrase, *chao troo*, is formal.

I got up early.

Chan teun tae chao.

ฉันตื่นแต่เช้า

The first bus leaves early in the morning.

Rot kun raek awk (tae) chao-chao leuy.

รถคันแรกออก(แต่)เช้าๆ เลย

late morning - saiɲ/saiɲ-saiɲ - *Sai* is also generalized to mean "late" at any time of the day.

It's late. Hurry and get up. (said to your child—*look*)

Saiɲ laeo. Teun reo, look.

สายแล้ว ตื่นเร็วลูก

daytime/at night - (tawn) glang wan/(tawn) glang keun -

Bats sleep in the daytime and search for food at night.

Kang-kao nawn (tawn) glang wan, haɲ gin glang keun.

ค้างคาวนอน(ตอน)กลางวัน หากินกลางคืน

early evening - tawn kam/kam-kam/huaɲ kam/tae huaɲ kam - These mean "evening", "dusk", or "nightfall".

Nit will come again this evening. (*thee* here is "time/occation")

Nit ja ma eeg (thee) tawn kam. (or *eeg krang*)

นิดจะมาอีกทีตอนค่ำ

I've been here since early evening.

Phomɲ ma tae huaɲ kam laeo.

ผมมาแต่หัวค่ำแล้ว

What time of day? - tawn naiɲ? -

A: When shall we go - in the morning or (late) afternoon?

Pai tawn naiɲ dee - tawn chao reuɲ tawn yen?

ไปตอนไหนดี ตอนเช้าหรือตอนเย็น

B: Morning is OK, and so is the afternoon.

Tawn chao gaw dee, reuɲ tawn yen gaw dai meuanɲ-gan.

ตอนเช้าก็ดีหรือตอนเย็นก็ได้เหมือนกัน

dark/late evening - meut -

I have to go home. It's already dark.

> Chan tawng glap ban, la. (Mun) meut laeo.

> ฉันต้องกลับบ้านล่ะ (มัน)มืดแล้ว

late at night - deuk -

I might come back late.

> Chan at glap deuk, na.

> ฉันอาจกลับดึกนะ

I went to sleep late last night.

> Meua-keun-nee phomj nawn deuk.

> เมื่อคืนนี้ผมนอนดึก

this morning/afternoon/etc -

this morning	chao nee
late this morning	saij nee
early this afternoon	bai nee
late this afternoon	yen nee
late today	kam nee
early this evening	huaj kam nee
tonight	keun nee
late tonight	glang deuk

PHRASES WITH DAYS

yesterday morning/etc - *Wan* here has a long vowel length. It means "yesterday", not "day". *Meua* indicates the past.

yesterday	(meua) wan nee
yesterday morning	chao wan nee/meua wan tawn chao
yesterday afternoon (early)	bai wan nee/meua wan tawn bai
yesterday afternoon (late)	yen wan nee/meua wan tawn yen
last night	keun wan (nee)/meua keun nee

I called you yesterday morning but you weren't there.

> Phomj tho theungj koon chao wan nee, tae koon mai yoo.

> ผมโทรถึงคุณเช้าวานนี้แต่คุณไม่อยู่

today, in the past -

this morning	meua chao nee
this afternoon (early)	meua bai nee
this afternoon (late)	meua yen nee
this evening	meua kam nee

tomorrow -

tomorrow morning	phroong-nee chao/chao phroong-nee
tomorrow afternoon (early)	phroong-nee bai/bai phroong-nee
tomorrow afternoon (late)	phroong-nee yen/yen phroong-nee
tomorrow night	phroong-nee tawn glang keun/keun phroong-nee

With days of the week -

Monday morning	chao wan Jan/wan Jan tawn chao
Monday afternoon (early)	bai wan Jan/wan Jan tawn bai
Monday afternoon (late)	yen wan Jan/wan Jan tawn yen
Monday night	keun wan Jan/wan Jan tawn glang keun.

A: Will you be at home on Sunday afternoon?

Bai wan A-thit koon ja yoo ban mai?

บ่ายวันอาทิตย์คุณจะอยู่บ้านมั้ย

B: Not in the early afternoon, but by late afternoon I'll be there.

Tawn bai kong mai yoo, tae ja yoo tawn yen-yen.

ตอนบ่ายคงไม่อยู่ แต่จะอยู่ตอนเย็นๆ

the day after/before -

the day after tomorrow	(wan) ma-reun-nee
the day after that (future)	wan taw pai/wan that pai/wan roong keun
the day before yesterday	meua wan seun

Are you free the day after tomorrow? Shall we go to the floating market?

Ma-reun-nee wang mai? Ja pai ta-lat nam gan mai?

มะรืนนี้ว่างมั้ย จะไปตลาดน้ำกันมั้ย

this coming Monday - wan Jan thee ja theung nee -

A: When's the test?

Ja sawp meua-rai?

จะสอบเมื่อไร

B: It's this coming Saturday.

Ja sawp wan Sao thee ja theung nee.

จะสอบวันเสาร์ที่จะถึงนี้

last Monday/this past Monday - wan Jan thee laeo/thee phan ma - Include *nee* (*thee phan ma nee*) for "this past (time/event)".

This past December I went back to Germany.

    Deuan Than-wa (kom) thee phan ma nee, chan glap pai Yeuh-ra-mun (ma).

    เดือนธันวา(คม)ที่ผ่านมานี่ฉันกลับไปเยอรมัน(มา)

A: You weren't here last Wednesday?

    Wan Phoot thee laeo koon mai yoo reuh?

    วันพุธที่แล้วคุณไม่อยู่เหรอ

B: No. Last Wednesday I went to visit some relatives.

    Mai yoo krup. Wan Phoot thee phan ma chan pai yiam yat.

    ไม่อยู่ครับ วันพุธที่ผ่านมาฉันไปเยี่ยมญาติ

PRESENT TIME PHRASES

now - tawn-nee/dioj-nee - The first is the general word for "now" and the second is "right now".

I don't want to eat yet ("now").

    Chan yang mai yak gin kao tawn-nee.

    ฉันยังไม่อยากกินข้าวตอนนี้

Change your shoes right now. We're going mountain climbing.

    Koon plian rawng-thao dioj-nee leuy, krup. Rao ja pai peen kaoj gan.

    คุณเปลี่ยนรองเท้าเดี่ยวนี้เลยครับ เราจะไปปีนเขากัน

now/at this time - way-la nee/(nai) ka-na nee -

It's raining a lot now.

    Way-la nee fonj tok mak.

    เวลานี้ฝนตกมาก

At this time farmers are harvesting rice.

    Ka-na nee chao na gam-lang gio kao.

    ขณะนี้ชาวนากำลังเกี่ยวข้าว

at this period of time - (nai) chuang nee/ra-ya nee - The second phrase is a little more formal.

Right now this shop is having a sale.

    (Nai) chuang nee ran nee gam-lang lot ra-ka.

    (ใน)ช่วงนี้ร้านนี้กำลังลดราคา

It's not raining now, so the weather is very hot.

    Ra-ya nee fon mai tok, a-gat leuy rawn mak.

    ระยะนี้ฝนไม่ตก อากาศเลยร้อนมาก

nowadays/in these times - sa-mai nee/thook wan nee/yook nee - The last is more formal.

These days Thais like to wear jeans.

    Sa-mai nee kon Thai chawp sai gang-gayng yeen.

    สมัยนี้คนไทยชอบใส่กางเกงยีนส์

These days everything is business.

    Thook wan nee thook yang pen thoo-ra-git pai mot.

    ทุกวันนี้ทุกอย่างเป็นธุรกิจไปหมด

the present - pat-joo-ban - This word is used alone or in the phrases *nai pat-joo-ban* and *(nai) pat-joo-ban nee*, which mean "presently" "currently", "nowadays", or "at the present time". They're synonymous with *dio-nee*, *sa-mai nee* and *ka-na nee*.

At this time the English language is very important.

    (Nai) pat-joo-ban nee, pha-sa Ang-grit sam-kan mak.

    (ใน)ปัจจุบันนี้ภาษาอังกฤษสำคัญมาก

At the present time a lot of Thais are going to work in the Middle East.

    Pat-joo-ban kon Thai pai tham-ngan nai Ta-wan Awk Glang yeuh mak.

    ปัจจุบันคนไทยไปทำงานในตะวันออกกลางเยอะมาก

PAST TIME PHRASES

the past - a-deet - "In the past" is *nai a-deet*.

I used to be a bad person, but that was in the past.

    Phom (keuy) pen kon mai dee ma gawn, tae nan mun pen a-deet pai laeo.

    ผม(เคย)เป็นคนไม่ดีมาก่อนแต่นั่นมันเป็นอดีตไปแล้ว

A: I heard he's been in jail?

    Chan dai-yin wa kao keuy tit kook reuh?

    ฉันได้ยินว่าเค้าเคยติดคุกเหรอ

B: That's something in his past.

Nan pen reuang nai a-deet kawng kao.

นั่นเป็นเรื่องในอดีตของเค้า

two days ago - sawng wan thee laeo - Also *sawng wan ma laeo* and *sawng wan gawn*. *Meua* is optional at the beginning of the phrase (as with any past time phrase).

Two years ago I couldn't speak Thai at all.

(Meua) sawng pee thee laeo, chan phoot pha-sa Thai mai dai leuy.

(เมื่อ)สองปีที่แล้วฉันพูดภาษาไทยไม่ได้เลย

thee laeo/laeo - "She went five days ago" can be expressed with both *ha wan thee laeo* and *ha wan laeo*. The second means that she has gone and been at the place for five days. *Laeo* is used alone with actions that can be seen as continuing over a period of time, while *thee laeo* is for short action verbs such as "buy" and "decide". ("Go" and "come" are used with both.)

She went to Chiang Mai two days ago.

Theuh pai Chiang Mai (meua) sawng wan thee laeo. (she left two days ago)

เธอไปเชียงใหม่(เมื่อ)สองวันที่แล้ว

Theuh pai Chiang Mai (dai) sawng wan laeo. (she's been there for two days)

เธอไปเชียงใหม่(ได้)สองวันแล้ว

"since" with "ago" - In Thai, "since" may be used with actions that happened in the past, literally "I came since two days ago".

I decided five days ago.

Chan tat-sing-jai tang-tae ha wan thee laeo.

ฉันตัดสินใจตั้งแต่ห้าวันที่แล้ว

I came two days ago.

Phom ma tang-tae sawng wan thee laeo.

ผมมาตั้งแต่สองวันที่แล้ว

last month - deuan thee laeo/deuan gawn - Also with weeks and years.

Last month I ran into Ayk on Ko Samet.

(Meua) deuan thee laeo chan jeuh Ayk thee Gaw Sa-met.

(เมื่อ)เดือนที่แล้วฉันเจอเอกที่เกาะเสม็ด

a long time ago - nan (ma) laeo - *Ma* is optional except when the phrase is at the beginning of the sentence, as in the first example. Don't confuse this with *ma nan laeo* which means "for a long time" (page 360).

My parents traveled to Thailand a long time ago.

Nan ma laeo phaw-mae (phom) ma thio meuang Thai.

นานมาแล้วพ่อแม่(ผม)มาเที่ยวเมืองไทย

A: Does Gaeo still get letters from that guy?

    Gaeo yang dai jot-mai jak phoo-chai kon nan yoo reu plao?

    แก้วยังได้จดหมายจากผู้ชายคนนั้นอยู่รึเปล่า

B: He stopped writing a long time ago.

    Kao yoot kiang nan (ma) laeo.

    เค้าหยุดเขียนนาน(มา)แล้ว

many years ago - lai pee ma laeo - Or *thee laeo*. Also for days, etc.

Nok has met her relatives, but it was many years ago.

    Nok keuy jeuh yat (kawng kao), tae lai pee ma laeo.

    นกเคยเจอญาติ(ของเค้า)แต่หลายปีมาแล้ว

not long ago - meua mai nan ma nee -

It wasn't long ago that this was all rice fields.

    Thee-nee keuy pen thoong na meua mai nan ma nee ayng.

    ที่นี่เคยเป็นทุ่งนาเมื่อไม่นานมานี่เอง

not many days ago - mai gee wan thee laeo - Also weeks, months, etc.

He left his things here a few days ago and went traveling.

    Kao thing kawng wai thee-nee meua mai gee wan thee laeo, laeo gaw pai thio.

    เค้าทิ้งของไว้ที่นี่เมื่อไม่กี่วันที่แล้ว แล้วก็ไปเที่ยว

a moment ago - meua-gee (nee) -

A: Your friend was on the boat that just left. Where were you?

    Pheuan koon yoo bon reua thee pheung awk pai meua-gee (nee). Koon pai (yoo)

    nai ma?

    เพื่อนคุณอยู่บนเรือที่เพิ่งออกไปเมื่อกี้(นี้) คุณไป(อยู่)ไหนมา

B: I just went to buy some things.

    Meua-gee-nee phom pai seu kawng.

    เมื่อกี้นี้ผมไปซื้อของ

just/recently/only - pheung (ja) - This means both "only" and "recently". *Ja* is optional.

There's also a formal pronunciation that has the vowel sound *euh*.

I just bought it today.

    Pheung (ja) seu wan-nee ayng.

    เพิ่ง(จะ)ซื้อวันนี้เอง

I'd just turned fifteen when I went to work in a factory.

Chan pheung (ja) a-yoo dai sip-ha pee, tawn chan (pai) tham-ngan rong-ngan.

ฉันเพิ่ง(จะ)อายุได้สิบห้าปีตอนฉัน(ไป)ทำงานโรงงาน

recently - meua reo-reo nee -

Recently there was a Songkran festival here.

Meua reo-reo nee mee ngan Song-gran thee-nee.

เมื่อเร็วๆ นี้มีงานสงกรานต์ที่นี่

on a recent day - wan gawn -

The other day I went looking for jobs with some friends, but we didn't find anything.

Wan gawn phom pai ha ngan gap pheuan-pheuan, tae mai jeuh a-rai.

วันก่อนผมไปหางานกับเพื่อนๆ แต่ไม่เจออะไร

that day - wan nan -

I arrived here on Monday. On that day I didn't have any place to stay at all.

Phom ma theung thee-nee wan Jan. Wan nan mai mee thee-phak leuy.

ผมมาถึงที่นี่วันจันทร์ วันนั้นไม่มีที่พักเลย

recently/lately - tawn lang nee/lang-lang (ma) nee/moo nee -

Lately I've been having a lot of colds.

Tawn lang nee chan pen wat boi.

ตอนหลังนี้ฉันเป็นหวัดบ่อย

I haven't seen her recently./She hasn't come here recently.

Moo nee mai hen kao ma leuy.

หมู่นี้ไม่เห็นเค้ามาเลย

Have you been to Phuket recently?

Lang-lang nee pai Phoo-get ma bang reu plao?

หลังๆ นี้ไปภูเก็ตมาบ้างรึเปล่า

once - krang neung -

Once when I was in Singapore I was fined for littering.

Krang neung tawn thee phom yoo Sing-ka-po phom thook prap phraw thing ka-ya.

ครั้งหนึ่งตอนที่ผมอยู่สิงคโปร์ ผมถูกปรับเพราะทิ้งขยะ

one day/one day it happened that - wan neung/mee yoo wan neung -

One day she decided to start being serious about work.

Wan neung theuh gaw tat-sin-jai tham-ngan yang jing-jang.

วันหนึ่งเธอก็ตัดสินใจทำงานอย่างจริงจัง

He's a strange person. One day he wore a coat when it was very hot.

    Kao pen kon plaek. Mee yoo wan neung, kao sai seua gan naoj ka-na thee a-gat

    rawn mak.

    เค้าเป็นคนแปลก มีอยู่วันหนึ่งเค้าใส่เสื้อกันหนาวขณะที่อากาศร้อนมาก

before/at a time in the past - meua-gawn/tae gawn - Other translations are "in the past", "in former times", and "previously".

The economy is a lot better now than before.

    Tawn-nee sayt-tha-git dee gwa tae gawn yeuh.

    ตอนนี้เศรษฐกิจดีกว่าแต่ก่อนเยอะ

A: Before, there were a lot of canals in Bangkok, weren't there?

    Meua-gawn, mee klawng mak mai nai Groong-thayp, chai mai?

    เมื่อก่อนมีคลองมากมายในกรุงเทพฯ ใช่มั้ย

B: Yes. People in Bangkok used to travel by boat.

    Chai, ka. Meua-gawn, kon Groong-thayp deuhn-thang duay reua.

    ใช่ค่ะ เมื่อก่อนคนกรุงเทพฯ เดินทางด้วยเรือ

before this - (tae) gawn nee -

Before this, there weren't any factories here at all.

    Tae gawn nee thaeoj nee mai mee rong-ngan leuy.

    แต่ก่อนนี้ แถวนี้ไม่มีโรงงานเลย

already (before) - gawn laeo -

I knew before that she was your sister.

    Chan roo (ma) gawn laeo wa kao pen nawng-saoj koon.

    ฉันรู้(มา)ก่อนแล้วว่าเค้าเป็นน้องสาวคุณ

When I got there my friends were already waiting.

    Meua chan pai theung, pheuan gaw nang raw yoo gawn laeo.

    เมื่อฉันไปถึงเพื่อนก็นั่งรออยู่ก่อนแล้ว

have experienced before - keuy...ma gawn -

A: Have you ever done this kind of work?

    Koon keuy tham-ngan baep nee ma gawn mai?

    คุณเคยทำงานแบบนี้มาก่อนมั้ย

B: Never.

    Mai keuy ma gawn leuy, krup.

    ไม่เคยมาก่อนเลยครับ

in past times - să-maǐ gawn - *Samai* is for past periods of time, both historical and from your own past. In the first example the phrase is a modifier.

Some old fashions were very beautiful.

Fae-chuň să-maǐ gawn bang yang gaw suay jing-jing.

แฟชั่นสมัยก่อนบางอย่างก็สวยจริงๆ

A: Can you do farming?

Tham na pen maǐ?

ทำนาเป็นมั้ย

B: I used to do farming when I was a child.

Să-maǐ gawn, tawn pen děk, phǒmɲ keuy tham na.

สมัยก่อนตอนเป็นเด็กผมเคยทำนา

at that time/then - tawn-nán/way-la nán - Also *nai tawn-nan* and *nai way-la nan*. These refer back to something already mentioned.

Pattaya used to be a village. The water was very clean then.

Phat-thá-ya keuy pen moo-bân. (Nai) tawn-nán nam să-at mak.

พัทยาเคยเป็นหมู่บ้าน (ใน)ตอนนั้นน้ำสะอาดมาก

(nai) kà-ná nán - This also refers back to a time already mentioned but as an extra phrase in Thai sentences that isn't included in English.

During World War II I was still very young.

Tawn sǒng-kram lok krang theě sawng, (nai) kà-ná nán chan yang lek mak.

ตอนสงครามโลกครั้งที่สอง (ใน)ขณะนั้นฉันยังเล็กมาก

during that period of time - (nai) chuang nán/ra-ya nán/să-maǐ nán - Another phrase is *yook nan* which is more formal.

Five years ago I was very poor. Sometimes I only had two baht on me.

Meuả hǎ pee theě laeo phǒmɲ jon mak. Chuang nán phǒmɲ keuy mee ngeuhn tit tua kae sawng baht.

เมื่อห้าปีที่แล้วผมจนมาก ช่วงนั้นผมเคยมีเงินติดตัวแค่สองบาท

A: When you were young was it fun? (talking to an older uncle/older man—*loong*)

Să-maǐ loong pen nòom să-nook maǐ?

สมัยลุงเป็นหนุ่มสนุกมั้ย

B: Yes, it was a lot of fun then.

Să-maǐ nán să-nook mak.

สมัยนั้นสนุกมาก

PAST PHRASES WITH *PHAN MA*

Phan is "pass by" and *ma* indicates that the action came from the past.

for the past two months - sawng deuan thee phan ma - This can also mean "two months ago" depending on the context. Include *nee* for "these past two months" *(thee phan may be omitted with nee—sawng deuan ma nee)*.

For the past two days I've been in Chiang Mai./Two days ago I was in Chiang Mai.

> Sawng wan thee phan ma chan yoo Chiang Mai.
>
> สองวันที่ผ่านมาฉันอยู่เชียงใหม่

the time that has passed by - way-la thee phan ma/way-la thee phan pai - *Ma* and *pai* may both refer to the past here, with the passing time seen as either coming or going. With *pai* the phrase can also refer to the future.

The passing time has made her more of an adult.

> Way-la thee phan pai tham hai kao pen phoo-yai keun.
>
> เวลาที่ผ่านไปทำให้เค้าเป็นผู้ใหญ่ขึ้น

Recently I haven't gone traveling at all.

> Way-la thee phan ma, phom mai dai thio leuy.
>
> เวลาที่ผ่านมาผมไม่ได้เที่ยวเลย

the event that happened - (event) thee phan ma/thee phan pai - *Phan* can also be doubled as in the first sentence to show that there were several events. With a single *phan* the first example would mean there was only one party.

The other parties weren't as much fun as this one.

> Ngan liang thee phan-phan ma sa-nook mai thao krang nee.
>
> งานเลี้ยงที่ผ่านๆ มาสนุกไม่เท่าครั้งนี้

That problem is something in the past now. Forget about it.

> Pan-ha nan pen sing thee phan pai laeo. Leum mun, sa.
>
> ปัญหานั้นเป็นสิ่งที่ผ่านไปแล้ว ลืมมันซะ

FUTURE TIME PHRASES

the future - a-na-kot - "In the future" is *nai a-na-kot*.

The future should be better than this.

> A-na-kot na ja dee gwa nee.
>
> อนาคตน่าจะดีกว่านี้

In the future I hope to meet someone nice.

> (Nai) a-na-kot chan wang wa ja jeuh krai thee dee sak kon.
>
> (ใน)อนาคตฉันหวังว่าจะเจอใครที่ดีสักคน

in two days - (nai) eeg sawng wan - Also with hours, weeks, etc. *Eeg sawng wan* can also mean "for two more days" (explained on page 364). Because the meaning of *eeg* could be confused for "again" the phrase should be put at the beginning of the sentence, or *nai* included when it's after the verb. *Kang na*, meaning "in front", may also be included as in the second example.

I'll be back in five days.

Chan ja glap ma nai eeg ha wan./(Nai) eeg ha wan chan ja glap ma.

ฉันจะกลับมาในอีกห้าวัน/(ใน)อีกห้าวันฉันจะกลับมา

In four months I'll be going to India.

Eeg see deuan kang na, phom ja pai In-dia.

อีกสี่เดือนข้างหน้าผมจะไปอินเดีย

A: In how many days will you be leaving?

Eeg gee wan (koon) ja pai?

อีกกี่วันจะไป

B: I'll go in two or three days.

Eeg sawng-sam wan (ja pai).

อีกสองสามวัน(จะไป)

Future with *laeo* ("happen by then") - *Laeo* may be included with the future to show that an action will already have happened by the time stated. The following sentences show the different variations that include *gaw* and *ja*, with "I" omitted. See page 90 for more examples.

I'm going back in two days./In two days I'll have already gone back.

Eeg sawng wan pai laeo./Eeg sawng wan ja pai (laeo).

อีกสองวันไปแล้ว/อีกสองวันจะไป(แล้ว)

Eeg sawng wan laeo gaw ja pai./Eeg sawng wan gaw (ja) pai (laeo).

อีกสองวันแล้วก็จะไป/อีกสองวันก็(จะ)ไป(แล้ว)

next month - deuan na (nee) - Also with weeks and years.

We're getting married next month.

Rao ja taeng-ngan deuan na (nee).

เราจะแต่งงานเดือนหน้านี้

A: How will the weather be next month?

Deuan na a-gat ja pen yang-ngai, ka?

เดือนหน้าอากาศจะเป็นยังไงคะ

B: Next month the weather will be nice and cool.

Deuan na a-gat ja yen sa-bai.

เดือนหน้าอากาศจะเย็นสบาย

in/within the next two days - Also with weeks, months, and years. *Kang na nee* ("in front of") can be included at the end. *Phai nai* emphasizes "within".

in/within two days	nai eeg sawng wan (nee)
	phai nai (eeg) sawng wan (nee)
	nai way-la sawng wan
in the next day or two	nai wan sawng wan nee
in the next two or three days	nai sawng-sam wan nee

I've got to hand in the report in/within four days.

    Chan tawng song rai-ngan nai eeg see wan.

        ฉันต้องส่งรายงานในอีกสี่วัน

He'll come in the next two days.

    Kao ja ma nai sawng wan nee.

        เค้าจะมาในสองวันนี้

I can't finish it in a week.

    Phom tham hai set nai neung a-thit mai dai.

        ผมทำให้เสร็จในหนึ่งอาทิตย์ไม่ได้

I'll contact you in four or five days. ("within these four or five days")

    Chan ja tit-taw koon phai nai (way-la) see ha wan nee.

        ฉันจะติดต่อคุณภายใน(เวลา)สี่ห้าวันนี้

by (tomorrow) - phai nai -

You have to finish reading this book by tomorrow.

    Nang-seu nee tawng an hai jop phai nai phroong-nee.

        หนังสือนี้ต้องอ่านให้จบภายในพรุ่งนี้

in a long time - eeg nan - This also means "for a long/longer time" (page 365).

It'll probably be a long time before I come back again.

    Kong ja eeg nan gwa chan ja glap ma dai.

        คงจะอีกนานกว่าฉันจะกลับมาได้

A: When are you coming back?

    Koon ja ma eeg meua-rai?/Meua-rai koon ja ma eeg?

        คุณจะมาอีกเมื่อไหร่/เมื่อไหร่คุณจะมาอีก

B: It'll be a long time.

    Gaw, eeg nan.

        ก็อีกนาน

in not long/soon - eeg mai nan/eeg noi - See also "for not much longer" (page 365).

It'll be your birthday soon.

Eeg mai nan ja theung wan geuht (koon).

อีกไม่นานจะถึงวันเกิด(คุณ)

She'll be having her baby soon.

Kao ja mee look (nai) eeg mai nan nee.

เค้าจะมีลูก(ใน)อีกไม่นานนี้

I'm moving to Korat soon.

Eeg noi chan ja yai pai Ko-rat.

อีกหน่อยฉันจะย้ายไปโคราช

in not many days/etc - eeg mai gee wan -

In not many months I'll be able to buy a car.

Eeg mai gee deuan (laeo), phom (gaw) ja seu rot dai laeo.

อีกไม่กี่เดือน(แล้ว)ผมก็จะซื้อรถได้แล้ว

soon - reo-reo nee/(nai) mai cha nee/(nai eeg) mai nan nee - *Reo* is "fast", *cha* is "slow".

He'll probably hire an assistant for you soon.

Kao kong ja ha phoo-chuay ma hai koon reo-reo nee.

เค้าคงจะหาผู้ช่วยมาให้คุณเร็วๆ นี้

I'll tell you soon.

Phom ja bawk koon (nai) mai cha nee.

ผมจะบอกคุณ(ใน)ไม่ช้านี้

I'll probably go to work in Cambodia soon.

Chan kong ja pai tham-ngan thee Gum-phoo-cha (nai eeg) mai nan nee.

ฉันคงจะไปทำงานที่กัมพูชา(ในอีก)ไม่นานนี้

in just a moment - eeg paep dio/eeg sak kroo/dio - *Sak kroo* is a little more polite than *paep dio* and refers to a slightly longer period of time. *Dio* with a rising tone means "in a short time" and here is "In a moment I'll..." or "Wait, I'll...".

Wait just a moment, the food will come.

Raw eeg sak kroo, a-han ja ma krup.

รออีกสักครู่ อาหารจะมาครับ

It'll be finished in just a moment.

Eeg paep dio gaw set.

อีกแป๊บเดียวก็เสร็จ

I'll be finished getting dressed in a minute.

Dio chan gaw taeng tua set laeo.

เดี๋ยวฉันก็แต่งตัวเสร็จแล้ว

immediately/right away - thǎn-thee - Other meanings are "promptly", "at once", and "instantly". See also "as soon as" on page 342 for *than-thee thee*.

If this factory closes you should be able to find another job right away.

Thâ rong-ngan nee pit, kong hǎy ngan thâm dâi thǎn-thee.

ถ้าโรงงานนี้ปิดคงหางานทำได้ทันที

immediately/just/simply - leuy -

If I haven't come by 8 P.M. you can just go without me.

Thâ sawng thoom phǒm yang mâi ma, koon pai leuy, nâ.

ถ้าสองทุ่มผมยังไม่มาคุณไปเลยนะ

After you graduate will you get a job right away or keep studying?

Jòp laeo jà thâm-ngan leuy reuy jà rian taw?

จบแล้วจะทำงานเลยหรือจะเรียนต่อ

another day/some other day - wǎn nâ/wǎn lǎng -

I'll come back another day.

Wǎn nâ jà ma mài.

วันหน้าจะมาใหม่

Try doing it again another day.

Wǎn lǎng kôi lawng thâm mài.

วันหลังค่อยลองทำใหม่

in the future/later - phai (phak) nâ/phai lǎng - These have the same meaning as *wan na* and *wan lang* but are higher-level language. Another less common phrase is *nai beuang na* (falling tone on *beuang*).

If you work hard today you'll be happy in the future.

Thâm-ngan nàk wǎn-nee, phai nâ jà dâi sà-bai.

ทำงานหนักวันนี้ภายหน้าจะได้สบาย

next time/later - thee lǎng - Also "at any time after this". *Thee* means "time" or "occasion" and has a mid tone.

In the future don't be late again.

Thee lǎng yà ma sǎy eeg, nâ.

ทีหลังอย่ามาสายอีกนะ

on a day in the future - wǎn kang nâ/wǎn neung - *Sak* may be included to estimate the time—"some day, I don't know when".

One day I might come back here again.

Sàk wǎn neung phǒm àt jà dâi glàp ma thee-nee eeg.

สักวันหนึ่งผมอาจจะได้กลับมาที่นี่อีก

Some time in the future, if you have time, you should take a trip to Switzerland.

    Nai wan kang na, tha mee way-la, koon kuan ja pai thio Sa-wit bang, na.

    ในวันข้างหน้าถ้ามีเวลาคุณควรจะไปเที่ยวสวิสบ้างนะ

One day I'll go and visit you at your house.

    Wan neung chan ja pai yiam koon thee ban.

    วันหนึ่งฉันจะไปเยี่ยมคุณที่บ้าน

at another time/another day - way-la eun/wan eun -

Right now I'm not ready. Can you come another time?

    Tawn-nee chan yang mai phrawm. Koon ma way-la eun dai mai?

    ตอนนี้ฉันยังไม่พร้อม คุณมาเวลาอื่นได้มั้ย

Today I'm not free. I might be free another day.

    Wan-nee mai wang. Wan eun at ja wang.

    วันนี้ไม่ว่าง วันอื่นอาจจะว่าง

At other times traffic isn't as congested as this.

    Way-la eun gan ja-ra-jawn mai ae-at meuang tawn-nee.

    เวลาอื่นการจราจรไม่แออัดเหมือนตอนนี้

the passing time (in the future) - way-la thee phan pai -

With the passing time you might understand more.

    Way-la thee phan pai koon at ja kao-jai mak keun.

    เวลาที่ผ่านไปคุณอาจจะเข้าใจมากขึ้น

this coming event - (event) thee ja theung -

This coming Valentine's Day are you buying something for your boyfriend?

    Wan Wa-len-thai thee ja theung ja seu a-rai hai faen reu plao?

    วันวาเลนไทน์ที่จะถึงจะซื้ออะไรให้แฟนรึเปล่า

WHEN (AS A CONJUNCTION)

In the past - tawn (thee)/meua - These are both used for "when" in the past. *Meua* sounds more formal and general than *tawn*.

I came when he wasn't here.

    Phom ma tawn kao mai yoo.

    ผมมาตอนเค้าไม่อยู่

We met when she was a student.

    Rao phop gan tawn (thee) theuh rian nang-seu.

    เราพบกันตอน(ที่)เธอเรียนหนังสือ

I got married when I was twenty.

Chan taeng-ngan meua (chan) a-yoo yee-sip.

ฉันแต่งงานเมื่อฉันอายุยี่สิบ

When I got there she was sleeping.

Tawn (thee) phom pai theung, kao gam-lang lap yoo.

ตอน(ที่)ผมไปถึงเค้ากำลังหลับอยู่

When he came to see me I wasn't at home. When I came back he was already gone.

Tawn thee kao ma ha phom, phom mai yoo ban. Meua phom glap kao gaw pai laeo.

ตอนที่เค้ามาหาผม ผมไม่อยู่บ้าน เมื่อผมกลับเค้าก็ไปแล้ว

when—in the future - tha/tawn (thee) - In Thai "if" can be used for "when" in the future even if you're sure the action will happen. *Gaw* is included to emphasize the hypothetical and to mean "subsequently".

When I get to England, I'll call you./I'll call you when I get to England.

Tha pai theung Ang-grit laeo, phom (gaw) ja tho ma ha.

ถ้าไปถึงอังกฤษแล้วผม(ก็)จะโทรมาหา

Phom ja tho ma ha tawn (thee) pai theung Ang-grit laeo.

ผมจะโทรมาหาตอน(ที่)ไปถึงอังกฤษแล้ว

When you have children you can't go out much.

Tha mee look, koon gaw ja pai thio mak mai dai.

ถ้ามีลูกคุณก็จะไปเที่ยวมากไม่ได้

Mee look laeo, ja pai thio mak mai dai.

มีลูกแล้วจะไปเที่ยวมากไม่ได้

When you're fixing it, don't get your shirt dirty.

Tawn (thee) sawm, ya hai seua leuh, na.

ตอน(ที่)ซ่อมอย่าให้เสื้อเลอะนะ

meua - *Meua* is also used with the future if you're very sure the action will happen, but it's not as common as *tha*. It may be translated as "after".

I'll go right away, when/after I get my visa.

Chan (gaw) ja pai leuy, meua dai wee-sa laeo.

ฉัน(ก็)จะไปเลยเมื่อได้วีซ่าแล้ว

Here *meua* is used with a generalization—"if" or "when".

If he doesn't love you, just forget him.

Meua kao mai rak koon, gaw leum kao, sa.

เมื่อเค้าไม่รักคุณก็ลืมเค้าซะ

OTHER WORDS FOR "WHEN"

during the period that - chuang (thee) -

When I was a student I had a lot of friends.

    Chuang (thee) phŏmʲ pen nák-rian phŏmʲ mee pheuan yeuh-mák.

    ช่วง(ที่)ผมเป็นนักเรียนผมมีเพื่อนเยอะมาก

When I'm in China I'm going to take a lot of pictures.

    Chuang thee yoo nai meuang Jeen, chan ja thai roop wai yeuh-yeuh.

    ช่วงที่อยู่ในเมืองจีนฉันจะถ่ายรูปไว้เยอะๆ

sà-maiʲ (thee) - This is "when" for past periods of time only. *Thee* may be included if it's followed by a verb or a clause, but phrases like *sa-mai dek* ("when I was a child") don't include it.

When I was a child I had to take care of the water buffalo.

    Sà-maiʲ dèk phŏmʲ tawnɡ liang kwai.

    สมัยเด็กผมต้องเลี้ยงควาย

I used to eat Thai food when I lived in Los Angeles.

    Chan keuy gin a-hanʲ Thai sà-maiʲ (thee chan) yoo L.A.

    ฉันเคยกินอาหารไทยสมัย(ที่ฉัน)อยู่ แอล.เอ.

while - kà-na (thee)/rá-wang (thee) - "While" is used when something occurs while another action is going on. *Tawn* can also be used here for a more general meaning. *Rawang* with this pronunciation also means "during" and "between".

Some kids came and picked the mangoes while I wasn't at home.

    (Mee) phuak dèk-dèk ma gèp mà-muang rà-wang (thee) chan mai yoo ban.

    (มี)พวกเด็กๆ มาเก็บมะม่วงระหว่าง(ที่)ฉันไม่อยู่บ้าน

When you're driving, don't be careless.

    Kà-na kàp rot, ya prà-mat.

    ขณะขับรถอย่าประมาท

during - rá-wang/chuang - These are interchangable, and *nai* can be included before both of them. Include *thee* if it's followed by a clause ("during the time that...").

My father was in Thailand during the Vietnam War.

    Phaw phŏmʲ yoo nai meuang Thai (nai) chuang sŏng-kram Wiat Nam.

    พ่อผมอยู่ในเมืองไทย(ใน)ช่วงสงครามเวียดนาม

He stayed in the car while it was raining.

    Kao yoo nai rot rà-wang thee fonʲ tòk. (or *rawang mee fon tok*)

    เค้าอยู่ในรถระหว่างที่ฝนตก

During the time of my divorce I was very unhappy.

    (Nai) chuang thee ya gan, chan siaʲ-jai mák.

    (ใน)ช่วงที่หย่ากันฉันเสียใจมาก

NOTES ON "WHEN":

1. "When" may be omitted if the meaning is obvious in the sentence.

When I went to Phnom Penh that time, I didn't know anybody.

    Pai Pha-nom Pen tawn-nan mai roo-jak krai leuy.

    ไปพนมเปญตอนนั้นไม่รู้จักใครเลย

When I get home I'm going to hurry and take a bath.

    Theung ban (gaw) ja reep ab-nam.

    ถึงบ้าน(ก็)จะรีบอาบน้ำ

What are you going to do when you go back to Burma?

    Glap Pha-ma laeo ja tham a-rai, ka?

    กลับพม่าแล้วจะทำอะไรค่ะ

2. "When" in English can be expressed as "after" in Thai if you're talking about two events happening consecutively.

When I get to Cambodia I'll find out how to go to Angkor Wat.

    Lang-jak thee pai theung Gum-phoo-cha laeo, phom (gaw) ja haj thang pai thio
    Na-kawn Wat.

    หลังจากที่ไปถึงกัมพูชาแล้วผม(ก็)จะหาทางไปเที่ยวนครวัด

3. "When" in English can be "as soon as" in Thai (*phaw*).

People said that the movie was good, but when I saw it I didn't like it much.

    Krai-krai gaw wa nang reuang nee dee, tae phaw pai doo laeo gaw cheuy-cheuy.

    ใครๆ ก็ว่าหนังเรื่องนี้ดีแต่พอไปดูแล้วก็เฉยๆ

TALKING ABOUT TIME

time - way-la -

My watch is broken. I don't know what time it is.

    Na-lee-ga siaj. Chan mai roo wa way-la thao-rai. (or *wa gee mong laeo*)

    นาฬิกาเสียฉันไม่รู้ว่าเวลาเท่าไหร่

A: Do you have time to do it?

    Mee way-la tham mai?

    มีเวลาทำมั้ย

B: Yes. I have lots of time.

    Mee, yeuh leuy krup./Mee, mak leuy krup.

    มีเยอะเลยครับ/มีมากเลยครับ

A: If you don't have time, please tell me.

    Tha mai mee way-la gaw bawk, na.

    ถ้าไม่มีเวลาก็บอกนะ

give me time to... - kaw̌ɟ way-la -

Give me five more minutes and I'll be through.

Kaw̌ɟ way-la (phǒmɟ) eeg hǎ na-thee gaŵ set.

ขอเวลา(ผม)อีกห้านาทีก็เสร็จ

Let me rest for five minutes.

Kaw̌ɟ way-la (chǎn) phak sak hǎ na-thee, na.

ขอเวลา(ฉัน)พักสักห้านาทีนะ

it's time to - theungɟ way-la/dâi way-la - These are interchangable.

It's time to stop working.

Dâi way-la leuhk ngan laeo.

ได้เวลาเลิกงานแล้ว

It's not time to go back yet.

Yang mâi theungɟ way-la glap leuy.

ยังไม่ถึงเวลากลับเลย

take the time/waste time - Following are some common phrases:

siaɟ way-la	waste time
chai way-la	use time
sa-lǎ way-la	sacrifice time
gin way-la	use time, literally "eat time"

All three examples use *sia* and the third can also use *chai* or *sa-la*.

He doesn't want to take the time to help you.

Kao mâi yak siaɟ way-la chuay koon.

เค้าไม่อยากเสียเวลาช่วยคุณ

Doing it that way will/would waste a lot of time.

Tham baep nan ja siaɟ way-la mak.

ทำแบบนั้นจะเสียเวลามาก

I'll take the time to study this matter.

Chan ja sa-lǎ way-la seuk-saɟ reuang nee.

ฉันจะสละเวลาศึกษาเรื่องนี้

free/free time - wang/way-la wang -

Today I'm free. Tomorrow I'm not free.

Wan-nee wang. Phroong-nee gaŵ mâi wang.

วันนี้ว่าง พรุ่งนี้ก็ไม่ว่าง

If I'm free, I'll come and see you.

    Tha wang gaw ja ma yiam.

        ถ้าว่างก็จะมาเยี่ยม

I have lots of free time.

    Chan mee way-la wang mak.

        ฉันมีเวลาว่างมาก

when I have free time - Use *way-la wang, wan wang* ("a free day") or *wang-wang*.

When I have a free day I'll come.

    Wan wang ja ma.

        วันว่างจะมา

When you're free let's go and see a movie.

    Wang-wang gaw pai doo nang, see.

        ว่างๆ ก็ไปดูหนังซิ

ON TIME/EARLY/LATE

on time - than (way-la)/trong way-la -

She always comes on time.

    Theuh ma than (way-la) sa-<u>meuh</u>.

        เธอมาทัน(เวลา)เสมอ

I got there on time.

    <u>Phom</u> pai <u>theung</u> (thee-<u>nan</u>) trong way-la.

        ผมไปถึง(ที่นั่น)ตรงเวลา

it's past the time - leuy way-la -

It's past time already. Could you hurry a little?

    Leuy way-la laeo. Reo-reo <u>noi</u> dai mai?

        เลยเวลาแล้ว เร็วๆ หน่อยได้มั้ย

It's past bedtime. What are you doing?

    Leuy way-la nawn laeo. Tham a-rai <u>yoo</u>, na?

        เลยเวลานอนแล้ว ทำอะไรอยู่นะ

not on time/late - mai than/<u>sai</u>/cha - These words are used with verbs. "He was late" is "He came late" or "He went late". The word *sai* actually refers to late morning but the meaning may be extended to "late" in general. *Cha* is "slow".

Today Daeng didn't come on time.

    Wan-nee Daeng ma mai than.

        วันนี้แดงมาไม่ทัน

I'll never get there on time.

> Chan kong ja pai mai than nae-nae.

> ฉันคงจะไปไม่ทันแน่ๆ

I arrived there late because the driver didn't pick me up. ("the car didn't pick me up")

> Phom pai cha phraw rot mai dai ma rap phom.

> ผมไปช้าเพราะรถไม่ได้มารับผม

She hurried because it was late.

> Kao reep phraw wa mun sai laeo.

> เค้ารีบเพราะว่ามันสายแล้ว

on time (for) - than - Use *than* before nouns and verbs for "on time for/on time to".

Were you on time for the bus?

> Than rot mai?

> ทันรถมั้ย

I got here right on time for the train.

> Phom ma than rot-fai phaw dee.

> ผมมาทันรถไฟพอดี

He was too late to meet Noi.

> Kao mai than jeuh Noi.

> เค้าไม่ทันเจอน้อย

Mai than before a verb can also mean that you didn't have time to do the action.

I had to hurry here, so I didn't have time to eat.

> Chan reep ma, leuy mai than gin kao.

> ฉันรีบมาเลยไม่ทันกินข้าว

I didn't have time to tell her. She'd already gone.

> Yang mai than bawk kao. Kao gaw pai sa gawn.

> ยังไม่ทันบอกเค้า เค้าก็ไปซะก่อน

Mai than after a verb means that you didn't do the action in time for a deadline, etc.

A: Will you finish it on time?

> Koon ja tham set than (way-la) mai?

> คุณจะทำเสร็จทัน(เวลา)มั้ย

B: I probably won't get it done. There's not enough time.

> Phom kong ja tham set mai than. (Gaw) mun mai koi mee way-la.

> ผมคงจะทำเสร็จไม่ทัน (ก็)มันไม่ค่อยมีเวลา

early/so soon - reo - *Reo* means "fast".

Today I'm quitting work early.

    Wan-nee leuhk ngan reo.

    วันนี้เลิกงานเร็ว

A: Why are you going back so soon?

    Tham-mai reep glap?/Tham-mai glap reo jang?

    ทำไมรีบกลับ/ทำไมกลับเร็วจัง

B: Well, I don't have anything to do.

    Gaw, mai mee a-rai tham laeo nee, ka.

    ก็ไม่มีอะไรทำแล้วนี่ค่ะ

early (in the morning) - chao -

Sometimes she's early, sometimes she's late.

    Kao ma chao bang, saij bang.

    เค้ามาเช้าบ้างสายบ้าง

early/before time - gawn way-la -

Going early for an interview is better than going late.

    Pai theung gawn way-la samj-phat dee gwa pai saij.

    ไปถึงก่อนเวลาสัมภาษณ์ดีกว่าไปสาย

according to the designated time - tam way-la -

If I go to school and don't come home on time she gets worried.

    Way-la phomj pai rong-rian laeo mai glap tam way-la, kao ja pen huang.

    เวลาผมไปโรงเรียนแล้วไม่กลับตามเวลาเค้าจะเป็นห่วง

16. ORDER OF EVENTS

BEFORE

Three words are used for "before"—*gawn, gwa*, and *theung.*

1. *gawn* with phrases ("before Monday") - gawn/gawn theung -
I hurried here, but she arrived before me.

    Phom reep ma laeo, na, tae kao gaw ma gawn phom eeg.

    ผมรีบมาแล้วนะ แต่เค้าก็มาก่อนผมอีก

I'll probably have it done before Saturday.

    Gawn (theung) wan Sao nee chan kong set.

    ก่อน(ถึง)วันเสาร์นี้ฉันคงเสร็จ

***Gawn* with clauses ("before I go")** - gawn/gawn ja/gawn thee ja - The subject of the second clause can be put between *thee* and *ja* (second example).

Before I go home I have to buy some things.

    Gawn glap ban, chan ja pai seu kawng.

    ก่อนกลับบ้านฉันจะไปซื้อของ

I want to call Noi before she goes to work.

    Chan yak tho pai ha Noi gawn thee kao ja pai tham-ngan.

    ฉันอยากโทรไปหาน้อยก่อนที่เค้าจะไปทำงาน

Before I could use this program I had to study it for a long time.

    Gawn thee phom ja chai po-gaem nee dai, phom tawng rian (yoo) lai wan.

    ก่อนที่ผมจะใช้โปรแกรมนี้ได้ผมต้องเรียน(อยู่)หลายวัน

He took some medicine before he went to sleep.

    Kao gin ya gawn nawn.

    เค้ากินยาก่อนนอน

With *thee* alone ("It'll be...") - Here *gawn* is omitted.

It'll probably be a long time before I come back to Thailand.

    Kong eeg nan thee chan ja glap meuang Thai.

    คงอีกนานที่ฉันจะกลับเมืองไทย

It'll be past April before I get to go home.

    Kong ja leuy deuan May-sa pai laeo thee phom ja dai glap ban.

    คงจะเลยเดือนเมษาไปแล้วที่ผมจะได้กลับบ้าน

2. attempting to do something - (jon) *gwa* - This is "before" when an attempt has to be made or something has to be done before something else can happen. Variations are *gwa ja* and *gwa thee ja* (*jon* is usually omitted). Compare the first two sentences. The first has *gwa* and means that the person was trying to get to the bus before it left. The second has *gawn* and doesn't include that meaning. *Jon gwa* also means "until".

Before he was able to get here, the bus had already left.

Gwa kao ja ma theung, rot gaw awk pai laeo.

กว่าเค้าจะมาถึงรถก็ออกไปแล้ว

The bus left before he got here.

Rot awk pai laeo gawn thee kao ja ma theung.

รถออกไปแล้วก่อนที่เค้าจะมาถึง

It'll be a long time before we get to see each again, won't it?

Kong eeg nan (jon) gwa rao ja jeuh gan eeg, na.

คงอีกนาน(จน)กว่าเราจะเจอกันอีกนะ

Before I could get to sleep it was past 1 A.M.

Gwa ja nawn, gaw pra-man tee neung gwa-gwa.

กว่าจะนอนก็ประมาณตีหนึ่งกว่าๆ

3. before it reaches the point that - *theung/gaw* - Here a stated time or action is necessary before the action "reaches" the point of happening. Informally *gaw* may be used alone (in the statements only, not the question). Compare *theung* and *gaw* with "then" (page 335) and *gaw* with "happen by then" (pages 90-91)—*gaw* means "subsequently" in all three patterns. The first sentence compares *theung*, *gwa*, and *gaw*.

It will probably be next year before he comes back.

Kong pee na kao theung ja ma eeg./Kong pen pee na (jon) gwa kao ja ma eeg.

คงปีหน้าเค้าถึงจะมาอีก/คงเป็นปีหน้า(จน)กว่าเค้าจะมาอีก

Kong pee na kao gaw (ja) ma eeg.

คงปีหน้าเค้าก็(จะ)มาอีก

It will be two years before there's another fair.

Eeg sawng pee theung ja mee ngan eeg.

อีกสองปีถึงจะมีงานอีก

A: How many years did you have to work before you had enough money to come here?

Koon tham-ngan gee pee theung mee ngeuhn ma thio?

คุณทำงานกี่ปีถึงมีเงินมาเที่ยว

B: Not many years.

Mai gee pee.

ไม่กี่ปี

yang mai theung wan Sao - This is "before Saturday" when it means "it wasn't yet Saturday" or "it won't yet be Saturday".

She said she'd go back on Sunday, but before Sunday she'd already left.

> Kao wa ja glap wan A-thit, tae yang mai theung wan A-thit kao gaw glap pai laeo.
> เค้าว่าจะกลับวันอาทิตย์แต่ยังไม่ถึงวันอาทิตย์เค้าก็กลับไปแล้ว

BEFORE THIS/BEFORE THAT

before this - gawn nee -

Before, this was a forest.

> Gawn nee, thee-nee pen pa.
> ก่อนนี้ที่นี่เป็นป่า

Were you a student before this?

> Gawn nee, koon rian reu plao?
> ก่อนนี้คุณเรียนรึเปล่า

A: You must be good at skiing.

> Koon na ja len sa-gee geng, na.
> คุณน่าจะเล่นสกีเก่งนะ

B: Before this, yes, but not anymore.

> Gawn nee chai, tae tawn-nee mai chai laeo.
> ก่อนนี้ใช่ แต่ตอนนี้ไม่ใช่แล้ว

before that - gawn nan/gawn na nan -

A: I started working as a driver ten years ago. Before that I sold things in the market.

> Phom reuhm kap rot meua sip pee thee laeo. Gawn (na) nan phom pen phaw-ka.
> ผมเริ่มขับรถเมื่อสิบปีที่แล้ว ก่อน(หน้า)นั้นผมเป็นพ่อค้า

B: And before that what did you do?

> Laeo gawn na nan, la, koon tham a-rai?
> แล้วก่อนหน้านั้นละ คุณทำอะไร

A: Before that I just stayed at home.

> Gawn nan phom gaw yoo ban cheuy-cheuy.
> ก่อนนั้นผมก็อยู่บ้านเฉยๆ

the year before that - pee gawn (na) nan - Also with days, weeks, etc.

I came here in 1990. The year before that I was in Russia.

> Pee neung gao gao soon phom ma thee-nee. Pee gawn (na) nan phom yoo thee
> Rut-sia.
>
> ปี 1990 ผมมาที่นี่ ปีก่อน(หน้า)นั้นผมอยู่ที่รัสเซีย

FIRST, BEFORE SOMETHING ELSE

gawn - *Gawn* means both "before" and "first, before something else".

I'm going to Ko Phi Phi first, then to Phuket, before I go to Malaysia.

> Phom ja pai Gaw Phee-Phee gawn, laeo gaw Phoo-get, gawn ja pai Ma-lay-sia.
>
> ผมจะไปเกาะพีพีก่อนแล้วก็ภูเก็ตก่อนจะไปมาเลเซีย

A: I'm really sleepy. Don't you want to go home?

> Nguang jang leuy. Mai yak (ja) glap ban reuh?
>
> ง่วงจังเลย ไม่อยาก(จะ)กลับบ้านเหรอ

B: You go home first, Lek. I want to go to another place.

> Lek glap ban gawn, na. Chan ja pai thio taw.
>
> เล็กกลับบ้านก่อนนะ ฉันจะไปเที่ยวต่อ

before anything else - gawn eun - Another translation is "first of all".

First of all I'd like to introduce myself. My name is Frank.

> Gawn eun, phom kaw nae-nam tua ayng gawn. Phom cheu Frank, krup.
>
> ก่อนอื่นผมขอแนะนำตัวเองก่อน ผมชื่อแฟรงค์ครับ

in advance - luang na -

Here you have to pay for the hotel room in advance.

> Thee-nee koon tawng jai ka rong-raem luang na.
>
> ที่นี่คุณต้องจ่ายค่าโรงแรมล่วงหน้า

THEN

There are many ways to say "then", which is similar to "after" in Thai.

1. laeo (gaw) - *Gaw* is included to link the first action with the subsequent action. *Ja* may be included with the future. *Laeo (gaw)* also means "and".

I have to go to the embassy, then I'm going to the airport.

> Chan tawng pai sa-thany-thoot, laeo gaw pai sa-nam bin.
>
> ฉันต้องไปสถานทูตแล้วก็ไปสนามบิน

I had a flat tire, then it started raining.

> Yang rot chan baen, laeo fon gaw tok.
>
> ยางรถฉันแบนแล้วฝนก็ตก

I'll read it first, then give it to the manager.

> Phom ja an gawn, laeo phom ja song taw hai phoo jat-gan.
>
> ผมจะอ่านก่อนแล้วผมจะส่งต่อให้ผู้จัดการ

2. laeo (gaw) leuy - This is used mostly with "go" and emphasizes the continuity of the action. It means "then" or "after that".

Yesterday I went out shopping, then I went and got a haircut.

    Meua-wan-nee phom awk pai seu kawng, laeo leuy pai tat phom.

    เมื่อวานนี้ผมออกไปซื้อของแล้วเลยไปตัดผม

3. laeo theung - This emphasizes that the first action is complete before the second is done or "arrived at".

We'll eat, then go to a movie.

    Gin kao set laeo theung ja pai doo nang (thee lang).

    กินข้าวเสร็จแล้วถึงจะไปดูหนัง(ทีหลัง)

I studied Thai, then I watched a video.

    Chan rian pha-sa Thai, laeo theung doo wee-dee-o.

    ฉันเรียนภาษาไทยแล้วถึงดูวีดีโอ

4. koi - This means "gradually" and is included for "then", "later", or "after having waited awhile". *Koi* is used with the future only and replaces *ja*. There are more examples on page 129.

We'll eat, then go to a movie.

    Gin kao set laeo koi pai doo nang.

    กินข้าวเสร็จแล้วค่อยไปดูหนัง

You should get a job first, then think about getting married, son.

    Dai ngan tham laeo theung koi kit reuang taeng-ngan, na look.

    ได้งานทำแล้วถึงค่อยคิดเรื่องแต่งงานนะลูก

5. gaw - *Gaw* is used alone here for "then" or "subsequently". *Laeo* isn't needed or is optional in these sentences because it can be seen from the meaning that the first action happened before the second.

I'll go for three months, then come back.

    Chan (ja) pai sam deuan, gaw ja glap.

    ฉัน(จะ)ไปสามเดือนก็จะกลับ

She worked on it for only two months and finished it.

    Tham kae sawng deuan gaw set.

    ทำแค่สองเดือนก็เสร็จ

When I get home I'm going right to sleep.

    Theung ban gaw ja nawn leuy.

    ถึงบ้านก็จะนอนเลย

He called and the police came soon after that.

    Kao tho pai mai nan, tam-ruat gaw ma.

    เค้าโทรไปไม่นานตำรวจก็มา

6. <u>dioɉ</u> - This is "in just a moment" with the meaning of "then".

Take this medicine and it will go away.

    Gin ya nee laeo, <u>dioɉ</u> gaw haiɉ./Gin laeo jà haiɉ.

        กินยานี้แล้วเดี๋ยวก็หาย/กินแล้วจะหาย

Wait, I'll be right there.

    Raw na, <u>dioɉ</u> phomɉ ma.

        รอนะ เดี๋ยวผมมา

Dio is also put before repeated verbs.

Eat some, then eat some more, then eat some more again.

    Dioɉ gin, <u>dioɉ</u> gin, <u>dioɉ</u> gaw gin eeg.

        เดี๋ยวกิน เดี๋ยวกิน เดี๋ยวก็กินอีก

AFTER

There are four ways to say "after" in Thai.

1. with "stop/finish" - The pattern here is "I'll finish doing something, then I'll...".
Three words meaning "stop" or "finish"—*set, jop,* or *leuhk*—are followed by *laeo* or *gaw*.
Laeo shows that the first action is over before the second begins, while *gaw* means "subsequently". Other words that may be included are *gawn, koi,* and *taw*.

After I take a bath I'm going to work.

    <u>Ab</u>-nam <u>set</u> gaw (jà) pai tham-ngan.

        อาบน้ำเสร็จก็(จะ)ไปทำงาน

    <u>Ab</u>-nam (<u>set</u>) laeo (gaw) (jà) pai tham-ngan.

        อาบน้ำ(เสร็จ)แล้ว(ก็)(จะ)ไปทำงาน

    <u>Ab</u>-nam <u>set</u> gawn laeo (gaw) (jà) pai tham-ngan.

        อาบน้ำเสร็จก่อนแล้ว(ก็)(จะ)ไปทำงาน

    <u>Ab</u>-nam <u>set</u> laeo koi pai tham-ngan.

        อาบน้ำเสร็จแล้วค่อยไปทำงาน

We'll eat, then go to the concert.

    Rao than kao gan set laeo, (gaw) (ja) pai doo kawn-seuht taw, na ka.

    เราทานข้าวกันเสร็จแล้ว(ก็)(จะ)ไปดูคอนเสิร์ตต่อนะคะ

After this program there's one on world boxing.

    Rai-gan nee jop laeo (gaw) ja pen rai-gan muay lok.

    รายการนี้จบแล้ว(ก็)จะเป็นรายการมวยโลก

Tam's gone to work, but after work he's coming back here.

    Tam pai tham-ngan, tae leuhk ngan laeo kao ja glap ma thee-nee.

    ตุ้มไปทำงานแต่เลิกงานแล้วเค้าจะกลับมาที่นี่

Shortened sentences - In these examples the number of words is reduced to a minimum. *Laeo* is needed to show that the first action is over before the second begins.

After I ate it I got diarrhea.

    Gin laeo thawng siaj.

    กินแล้วท้องเสีย

This movie, after you see it you'll want to see it again.

    Nangj reuang nee, doo laeo gaw yak doo eeg.

    หนังเรื่องนี้ดูแล้วก็อยากดูอีก

I thought it was sweet, but when I ate it, it was sour.

    Phomj kit wa wanj, tae gin laeo prio.

    ผมคิดว่าหวานแต่กินแล้วเปรี้ยว

2. lang/lang-jak - This is "after" in Thai but it's less common than the first pattern. These sentences have *lang* followed by a phrase.

We'll go to the airport after four o'clock.

    Rao ja pai sa-namj bin langj see mong.

    เราจะไปสนามบินหลังสี่โมง

After breakfast I like to water the plants.

    Langj a-hanj chao, chan chawp rot nam ton-mai.

    หลังอาหารเช้าฉันชอบรดน้ำต้นไม้

With clauses - *Thee* is optional after *lang* or *lang-jak*.

After I get to Chiang Rai, I'll go to Noi's house to see her.

    (Langj-jak) phomj pai theungj Chiang Rai (laeo), phomj ja pai haj Noi thee ban.

    (หลังจาก)ผมไปถึงเชียงราย(แล้ว)ผมจะไปหาน้อยที่บ้าน

We'll meet again after (stopping) work.

    Jeuh gan langj leuhk ngan, na./(Langj-jak) tham-ngan set laeo koi jeuh gan, na.

    เจอะกันหลังเลิกงานนะ/(หลังจาก)ทำงานเสร็จแล้วค่อยเจอกันนะ

Two weeks after I graduated I got this job.

  (Lang-jak) rian jop dai sawng a-thit chan gaw dai ngan.

  (หลังจาก)เรียนจบได้สองอาทิตย์ฉันก็ได้งาน

3. leuy - This is used for "past" or "after" a time (and also for "past" or "beyond" a place).

Before he gets home it'll probably be after midnight.

  Gwa kao ja glap ban gaw kong leuy thiang keun pai laeo.

  กว่าเค้าจะกลับบ้านก็คงเลยเที่ยงคืนไปแล้ว

A: When should we have another meeting?

  Rao ja pra-choom gan eeg meua-rai dee?

  เราจะประชุมกันอีกเมื่อไหร่ดี

B: It should probably be after Friday. How about Monday?

  Gaw kong leuy wan Sook pai laeo. Wan Jan pen yang-ngai?

  ก็คงเลยวันศุกร์ไปแล้ว วันจันทร์เป็นยังไง

4. phai lang jak thee - This is formal. *Phai lang* alone is a formal way to say "later".

EXPRESSION: pai-pai-ma-ma - This is "after some time passed by" or "after many things had happened". Another meaning is "coming and going".

At first I decided to leave, but after some time I stayed and got married.

  Tawn raek tat-sin-jai wa ja pai, tae pai-pai-ma-ma phom gaw yoo taeng-ngan.

  ตอนแรกตัดสินใจว่าจะไปแต่ ไปๆ มาๆ ผมก็อยู่แต่งงาน

AFTER THIS/FROM NOW ON

Some of these phrases include *pai* to show time going away into the future.

after this - lang-jak nee -

After this, I'm not having anything to do with Maeo again.

  Lang-jak nee, chan ja mai kop (gap) Maeo eeg laeo.

  หลังจากนี้ฉันจะไม่คบ(กับ)แมวอีกแล้ว

next/later on - taw pai - Other meanings are "after this/that", "following this/that", and "in the future".

After we eat, what do you want to do?

  Gin set laeo, taw pai tham a-rai dee?

  กินเสร็จแล้วต่อไปทำอะไรดี

If, after this, you still haven't stopped coming late, you'll have your pay cut.

  Tha taw pai, koon yang mai leuhk ma sai, koon ja don tat ngeuhn deuan.

  ถ้าต่อไปคุณยังไม่เลิกมาสายคุณจะโดนตัดเงินเดือน

two days after this/after two days - lang-jak nee (eeg) sawng wan - Also *sawng wan lang-jak nee.*

After three months you'll get a raise.

    Lang-jak nee (eeg) sam deuan, koon gaw ja dai ngeuhn deuan pheuhm.

    หลังจากนี้(อีก)สามเดือนคุณก็จะได้เงินเดือนเพิ่ม

the day after this - wan taw pai/wan that pai - *Taw pai* means "the following" or "the one after this". *That* is "the next" for things in rows. Also weeks, months, etc.

A: Next week we're going to the North. So, where should we go the week after that?

    A-thit na rao pai thang neua. Laeo a-thit taw pai ja pai nai dee?

    อาทิตย์หน้าเราไปทางเหนือ แล้วว่าอาทิตย์ต่อไปจะไปไหนดี

B: How about Burma?

    Pai Pha-ma dee mai?

    ไปพม่าดีมั้ย

from now on - taw pai (nee)/taw nee pai -

From now on I'm not believing in astrology anymore.

    Taw pai nee chan mai cheua reuang duang eeg laeo.

    ต่อไปนี้ฉันไม่เชื่อเรื่องดวงอีกแล้ว

lang-jak/tang-tae nee (pen ton) pai - Also *jak nee pai, taw jak nee (pai),* and *tae nee taw pai.*

After this I'll never lend money to anyone again. ("let anyone borrow money")

    Taw jak nee pai, chan ja mai hai krai yeum ngeuhn eeg.

    ต่อจากนี้ไปฉันจะไม่ให้ใครยืมเงินอีก

reuay pai - This means "continually from now on".

I'll help you like this from now on.

    Phom ja chuay (leua) koon yang-ngee reuay pai.

    ผมจะช่วย(เหลือ)คุณยังงี้เรื่อยไป

from this year on (future) - lang-jak/tang-tae (time) (pen ton) pai - *Tang-tae* or *lang-jak* are optional when first in the sentence. *Lang-jak* can be shortened to *lang.*

I'll be living here from January on.

    Chan ja ma yoo thee-nee tang-tae deuan Mok-ga-ra pen ton pai.

    ฉันจะมาอยู่ที่นี่ตั้งแต่เดือนมกราเป็นต้นไป

After this year they won't sell it anymore.

    Lang-jak pee nee pai ja mai mee kai eeg laeo.

    หลังจากปีนี้ไปจะไม่มีขายอีกแล้ว

From next month on Ning's living (moving in) with me.

(Tang-tae) deuan na pen ton pai, Ning ja yai ma yoo gap chan.

(ตั้งแต่)เดือนหน้าเป็นต้นไปหนิงจะย้ายมาอยู่กับฉัน

AFTER THAT (PAST/FUTURE)

These phrases can refer to both the past and future.

after that - lang-jak nan/taw jak nan - These can be shortened to *jak nan*.

You have to finish it by next Friday. After that I won't accept it. ("receive it")

Koon tawng hai set wan Sook na, na. Lang-jak nan pai chan mai rap, na.

คุณต้องให้เสร็จวันศุกร์หน้านะ หลังจากนั้นไปฉันไม่รับนะ

I waited, and he came at 9 o'clock (A.M.).

Phom raw, laeo jak nan kao gaw ma tawn sam mong.

ผมรอแล้วจากนั้นเค้าก็มาตอนสามโมง

two days after that/two days later - lang-jak nan (eeg) sawng wan - Also *eeg sawng wan (lang) jak nan* and *eeg sawng wan taw jak nan*.

I'm going to Hong Kong next week. Three days after that I'll go back to Taiwan.

Chan ja pai Hawng Gong a-thit na. Lang-jak nan eeg sam wan chan ja glap
Tai-wan.

ฉันจะไปฮ่องกงอาทิตย์หน้า หลังจากนั้นอีกสามวันฉันจะกลับไต้หวัน

I was very unhappy then, but two days later I met someone new.

Tawn-nan phom siaj-jai mak, tae sawng wan taw jak nan gaw jeuh kon mai.

ตอนนั้นผมเสียใจมากแต่สองวันต่อจากนั้นก็เจอคนใหม่

not long after that - lang-jak nan (eeg) mai nan - Also *lang-jak nan mai gee wan* and *eeg mai gee wan lang-jak nan* (also weeks, months, years).

She came and worked here for a year, then soon after that she quit.

Kao ma tham-ngan thee-nee dai pee neung, lang-jak nan mai nan gaw la awk.

เค้ามาทำงานที่นี่ได้ปีหนึ่ง หลังจากนั้นไม่นานก็ลาออก

a long time after that - lang-jak nan eeg nan - Also *lang-jak nan eeg lai wan* and *eeg lai wan lang-jak nan* (months, years, etc).

I applied for the job, and a long time after that I got it.

Chan sa-mak ngan wai, laeo gaw lang-jak nan eeg nan gwa ja dai.

ฉันสมัครงานไว้แล้วก็หลังจากนั้นอีกนานกว่าจะได้

AFTER THAT/FROM THEN ON (PAST)

These include *ma* to show time coming from the past.

next/later (after that) - taw ma - With the present and future use *taw pai.*

First he called me at home. Later he invited me out.

    Raek-raek kao tho ma thee ban. Taw ma kao chuan chan pai thio.

    แรกๆ เค้าโทรมาที่บ้าน ต่อมาเค้าชวนฉันไปเที่ยว

the day after that - wan taw ma/wan that ma - This is also translated as "the following day" (or with weeks, years, etc).

Last Friday we arrived at the guest house and the following day we went rafting.

    Wan Sook thee laeo rao pai theung get hao, laeo wan taw ma gaw pai lawng

    phae.

    วันศุกร์ที่แล้วเราไปถึงเกสท์เฮาส์ แล้ววันต่อมาก็ไปล่องแพ

two days after that - (eeg) sawng wan taw ma -

At first Lek couldn't play football well, but two years later he was the team captain.

    Tawn raek Lek len foot-bawn mai koi geng, tae sawng pee taw ma kao gaw dai

    pen gap-tun theem.

    ตอนแรกเล็กเล่นฟุตบอลไม่ค่อยเก่งแต่สองปีต่อมาเค้าได้เป็นกัปตันทีม

many days after that - eeg lai wan taw ma -

During Songkran he went to Chiang Mai, and long time after that I saw him in Bangkok.

    Chuang Song-gran kao pai Chiang Mai, eeg lai wan taw ma phom gaw jeuh kao

    thee Groong-thayp.

    ช่วงสงกรานต์เขาไปเชียงใหม่ อีกหลายวันต่อมาผมก็เจอเขาที่กรุงเทพฯ

from that year on/after that year - lang-jak/tang-tae (time) (pen ton) ma - Also *lang* instead of *lang-jak. Pen ton* refers to the beginning of something.

After that month I never called him again.

    Lang-jak deuan nan (pen ton) ma, phom gaw mai keuy tho pai ha kao eeg.

    หลังจากเดือนนั้น(เป็นต้น)มาผมก็ไม่เคยโทรไปหาเค้าอีก

A: How long have you been the manager?

    Koon pen phoo jat-gan ma nan thao-rai laeo?

    คุณเป็นผู้จัดการมานานเท่าไหร่แล้ว

B: It's been since 2540.

    Gaw pen tang-tae pee see-sip pen ton ma.

    ก็เป็นตั้งแต่ปี 40 เป็นต้นมา

AS SOON AS

There are three ways to say "as soon as" in Thai.

1. phaw - *Phaw* can be omitted and *gaw* (meaning "subsequently") used alone if the meaning is understood in context.

As soon as you left, he arrived.

(Phaw) koon pai, kao gaw ma theung.

(พอ)คุณไปเค้าก็มาถึง

As soon as we arrived we had a meeting.

(Phaw) pai theung laeo, rao gaw pra-choom gan. (or *gaw ja* for "we'll have")

(พอ)ไปถึงแล้วเราก็ประชุมกัน

As soon as I see you do it, I'll be able to do it.

Phaw heng, gaw ja tham dai leuy.

พอเห็นก็จะทำได้เลย

With time words - Use *phaw* or *phaw theung* before time words. With *theung* the meaning is "when the time arrived".

Right at noon she started cooking.

Phaw thiang, (theuh) gaw reuhm tham a-hang.

พอเที่ยง(เธอ)ก็เริ่มทำอาหาร

Dam told me that he'd come on Friday, but on Friday he didn't come.

Dam bawk wa kao ja ma wan Sook, tae phaw theung wan Sook kao gaw mai ma.

ดำบอกว่าเค้าจะมาวันศุกร์แต่พอถึงวันศุกร์เค้าก็ไม่มา

2. than-thee thee - *Than-thee* is "immediately", and the second *thee* is "that".

I'll hurry to see Steve as soon as I get to Bangkok.

Chan ja reep pai hay Steve than-thee thee theung Groong-thayp.

ฉันจะรีบไปหาสตีฟทันทีที่ถึงกรุงเทพฯ

A: When can you tell me?

Ja bawk phong (dai) meua-rai?

จะบอกผม(ได้)เมื่อไหร่

B: I'll tell you as soon as I know.

Phong ja bawk koon than-thee thee phong roo.

ผมจะบอกคุณทันทีที่ผมรู้

3. reo thao thee - This is literally "as fast as". *Reo* is "fast" and *thao thee* is "equal to/as much as".

Please tell me as soon as possible.

Chuay bawk chan hai reo thao thee ja reo dai.

ช่วยบอกฉันให้เร็วเท่าที่จะเร็วได้

SINCE

See also "It's been...since" on pages 361-362.

tanḡ-tae - This is used with phrases ("since Friday") and also clauses ("since I came").

Lek has been out of the house since morning.

Lek awk jak ban̄ tanḡ-tae chao.

เล็กออกจากบ้านตั้งแต่เช้า

I've been on Ko Pha-ngan since I came to Thailand.

Phǒmɉ yoo Gāw Pha-ngǎn tanḡ-tae (phǒmɉ) ma yoo meuang Thai.

ผมอยู่เกาะพงันตั้งแต่(ผม)มาอยู่เมืองไทย

She's been smoking since she was a student. ("She started smoking since...")

Theuh reuhm sǒop boo-ree tanḡ-tae sà-maiɉ yang rian yoo.

เธอเริ่มสูบบุหรี่ตั้งแต่สมัยยังเรียนอยู่

Laeo may be included to emphasize that the action began at an earlier time.

A: Hey, why are you still here?

Aw̄. Thǎm-maiɉ yang yoo thee-nee, là?

อ้าว ทำไมยังอยู่ที่นี่ล่ะ

B: I've wanted to leave since yesterday, but my husband's passport isn't ready yet.

Chan yak pai tanḡ-tae meua-wan-nee laeo, tae phat-sà-pawt faen yang maiɉ riap-roi.

ฉันอยากไปตั้งแต่เมื่อวานนี้แล้ว แต่พาสปอร์ตแฟนยังไม่เรียบร้อย

since then - tanḡ-tae nan (ma) -

A: Toom hasn't come home at all?

Toom maiɉ glap ban̄ leuy, reuhɉ?

ตุ้มไม่กลับบ้านเลยเหรอ

B: I saw him last year. Since then I haven't seen him again.

Phǒmɉ jeuh kao meuā pee thee laeo. Tanḡ-tae nan (ma) gaw̄ maiɉ jeuh kao eeg leuy.

ผมเจอเค้าเมื่อปีที่แล้ว ตั้งแต่นั้น(มา)ก็ไม่เจอเค้าอีกเลย

"since" for "on/from/for" - *Tang-tae* is used in Thai where "on", "from", and "for" are used with time in English. It's also used with "ago" in Thai where it isn't used in English. See also page 313 and pages 361-362.

This fair started on June 23. ("since June 23")

Ngan nee reuhm tanḡ-tae yee-sip samɉ Mee-thoo-na.

งานนี้เริ่มตั้งแต่ 23 มิถุนา

I'm going to exercise from now on. ("since today on")

Phǒmɉ jà awk gam-lang tanḡ-tae wan-nee pen ton pai.

ผมจะออกกำลังตั้งแต่วันนี้เป็นต้นไป

Why didn't you tell me from the beginning? ("since the first")

    Tham-mai (koon) mai bawk chan tang-tae raek?

    ทำไม(คุณ)ไม่บอกฉันตั้งแต่แรก

I haven't had a vacation for two years. ("since two years ago")

    Chan mai dai mee wan yoot tang-tae sawng pee thee laeo.

    ฉันไม่ได้มีวันหยุดตั้งแต่สองปีที่แล้ว

from...to... - tang-tae...theung.../jak...theung... - *Jon* is optional before *theung*.

I work from Monday to Saturday.

    Phom tham-ngan tang-tae wan Jan theung wan Sao.

    ผมทำงานตั้งแต่วันจันทร์ถึงวันเสาร์

From 9 P.M. to midnight I'm not free.

    Jak sam thoom theung thiang keun chan ja mai wang.

    จากสามทุ่มถึงเที่ยงคืนฉันจะไม่ว่าง

UNTIL

With phrases ("until Friday") - (jon) theung - *Theung* means "arrive at" or "reach to" and *jon* is "up to" or "as far as". *Jon* is optional in all examples.

I can stay until next week.

    Phom yoo dai (jon) theung a-thit na.

    ผมอยู่ได้จนถึงอาทิตย์หน้า

I probably won't see you until next year.

    Kong mai dai jeuh gan (jon) theung pee na.

    คงไม่ได้เจอกัน(จน)ถึงปีหน้า

A: Until what day are you staying, Jill?

    Jill ja yoo (jon) theung wan nai?

    จิลจะอยู่(จน)ถึงวันไหน

B: I'll probably be here until Thursday.

    Kong yoo theung wan Pha-reu-hat, na.

    คงอยู่ถึงวันพฤหัสนะ

Jon **alone with phrases** - *Jon* can be used alone in these phrases:

until morning	jon chao
until noon	jon thiang
until late afternoon	jon yen
until late	jon deuk

Last night I worked late.

>   Meua-keun-nee phom̯ tham-ngan jon deuk.

>   เมื่อคืนนี้ผมทำงานจนดึก

until after - jon lang̯/jon leuy -

I won't go back until after Friday.

>   Chan ja yang mai glap jon leuy wan Sook pai.

>   ฉันจะยังไม่กลับจนเลยวันศุกร์ไป

after all these days - jon theung̯ thook wan nee - Literally "until all these days".

After all these days I'm still a farmer like before.

>   Jon theung̯ thook wan nee phom̯ gaw yang tham na, meuan̯ deuhm.

>   จนถึงทุกวันนี้ผมก็ยังทำนาเหมือนเดิม

With clauses ("until he comes") - jon (gra-thang̯) - Use *jon* or *jon gra-thang* instead of *(jon) theung* when "until" is followed by a clause. The clause may be reduced to only a verb as in the last example ("drunk" can be interpreted as a verb).

I was sick from the time I left Malaysia until you gave me the medicine.

>   Phom̯ mai sa-bai tang-tae (tawn) awk jak Ma-lay-sia jon koon hai ya phom̯.

>   ผมไม่สบายตั้งแต่(ตอน)ออกจากมาเลเซียจนคุณให้ยาผม

Gai bought clothes until she didn't have any money left at all.

>   Gai seu seua-pha jon (gra-thang̯) mai mee ngeuhn leua̯ leuy.

>   ไก่ซื้อเสื้อผ้าจน(กระทั่ง)ไม่มีเงินเหลือเลย

He drank until he was drunk.

>   Kao gin lao jon mao.

>   เล็กเค้ากินเหล้าจนเมา

"until" with an expectation - jon gwa - *Gwa* may be included when "until" is followed by a future expectation. This is similar to *gwa* for "before". The phrase may also be expanded to *jon gwa ja theung* if it's followed by a time phrase, not by a clause (as in the second example).

I'll wait until she comes.

>   Chan ja raw jon gwa kao ja ma.

>   ฉันจะรอจนกว่าเค้าจะมา

He can't come back again until next year./It'll be next year before he comes back.

>   Kao kong ma mai dai jon gwa ja theung̯ pee na, nun lae.

>   เค้าคงมาไม่ได้จนกว่าจะถึงปีหน้านั่นแหละ

>   Jon (theung̯) pee na, nun lae, thee kao ja ma eeg.

>   จน(ถึง)ปีหน้านั่นแหละที่เค้าจะมาอีก

***Hai* for "until"** - *Hai* ("give") is "until" when it means "and let" or "and cause to be".
Wait until he's better.

    Koi hai kao haiŋ puay gawn./Koi jon kao haiŋ puay gawn.

    คอยให้เค้าหายป่วยก่อน/คอยจนเค้าหายป่วยก่อน

Boil the vegetables until they're done, then take them off.

    Tom phak hai sook, laeo (koi) yok long. (or *Tom phak jon sook*)

    ต้มผักให้สุกแล้ว(ค่อย)ยกลง

Wait until 8 P.M., then we'll go out and eat.

    Koi hai theung sawng thoom gawn, koi awk pai gin kao.

    คอยให้ถึงสองทุ่มก่อนค่อยออกไปกินข้าว

EXPRESSION: jon dai - This is "until finally successful in the end". It's used in the past
only. For the future use *hai dai*, under "expressions with *hai*" on page 141.
Studying here was very difficult, but I managed to graduate.

    Thee-nee rian yak mak, tae phom gaw jop jon dai.

    ที่นี่เรียนยากมากแต่ผมก็จบจนได้

up until now - theung tawn-nee - Also *theung way-la nee*, or use "before this" (*meua
gawn, ma gawn*, or *gawn nee*).
Until now I'd forgotten all that.

    Theung tawn-nee chan leum (mun) mot laeo.

    ถึงตอนนี้ฉันลืม(มัน)หมดแล้ว

Up to now I still don't know where she is.

    Theung way-la nee phom gaw yang mai roo wa theuh yoo thee-nai.

    ถึงเวลานี้ผมก็ยังไม่รู้ว่าเธออยู่ที่ไหน

Up until now I hadn't known he was coming.

    Gawn nee chan mai roo wa kao ja ma./Chan mai roo ma gawn wa kao ja ma.

    ก่อนนี้ฉันไม่รู้ว่าเค้าจะมา/ฉันไม่รู้มาก่อนว่าเค้าจะมา

AT FIRST/LATER/FINALLY

at first - tawn raek/thee raek/raek-raek/mai-mai - *Thee* with a mid tone means "time" or
"occasion". *Krang raek* ("the first time") is also used informally for "at first".
A: When you first came to Thailand could you speak Thai?

    Tawn raek thee ma meuang Thai koon phoot pha-saŋ Thai dai mai, ka?

    ตอนแรกที่มาเมืองไทยคุณพูดภาษาไทยได้มั้ยคะ

B: When I first came? No, not at all.

    Tawn raek thee ma, reuh ka? Phoot mai dai leuy.

    ตอนแรกที่มาเหรอคะ พูดไม่ได้เลย

At first I'll stay with a friend. After that I'll rent an apartment.

Raek-raek chan ja (pai) yoo gap pheuan. Lang-jak nan (gaw) ja chao hawng.

แรกๆ ฉันจะ(ไป)อยู่กับเพื่อน หลังจากนั้น(ก็)จะเช่าห้อง

Since I first came here, she's been nice to me.

Tang-tae ma mai-mai, kao dee gap chan ma ta-lawt.

ตั้งแต่มาใหม่ๆ เค้าดีกับฉันมาตลอด

later (on) - thee lang/tawn lang - Other phrases are *tawn lang-lang* and *phai lang* (the second is formal).

I came first, then Lek came later.

Phom ma gawn, laeo Lek ma thee lang.

ผมมาก่อนแล้วเล็กมาทีหลัง

She did it first and told me later.

Kao tham pai gawn, laeo ma bawk phom tawn lang.

เค้าทำไปก่อนแล้วมาบอกผมตอนหลัง

At first he didn't want to go, but later he changed his mind.

Tawn raek kao mai yak pai, tae tawn lang-lang kao plian-jai.

ตอนแรกเค้าไม่อยากไปแต่ตอนหลังๆ เค้าเปลี่ยนใจ

A: What subjects will I study at first?

Raek-raek nee chan tawng rian a-rai bang? (or "wee-cha nai bang")

แรกๆ นี่ฉันต้องเรียนอะไรบ้าง

B: At first you'll study only English, but later on you'll study other subjects.

Tawn raek-raek theuh ja rian cha-phaw pha-sa Ang-grit, tae tawn lang theuh tawng rian wee-cha eun-eun duay.

ตอนแรกๆ เธอจะเรียนเฉพาะภาษาอังกฤษ แต่ตอนหลังเธอต้องเรียนวิชาอื่นๆด้วย

(nai) way-la taw ma - This is a little more formal.

The first year he couldn't read at all, but later on he could read very well.

Chuang pee raek kao an mai dai, tae (nai) way-la taw ma kao an geng mak.

ช่วงปีแรกเค้าอ่านไม่ได้แต่(ใน)เวลาต่อมาเค้าอ่านเก่งมาก

after a long time - nan-nan pai - This is also translated as "after some time".

At first it felt very hot, but after a long time I got used to it.

Raek-raek gaw rawn mak, tae nan-nan pai phom gaw chin.

แรกๆ ก็ร้อนมากแต่นานๆ ไปผมก็ชิน

finally/lastly - nai thee-soot/tawn thai - Also translated as "in the end" or "at last". *Thai* here means "end" (it's also in *soot-thai*).

I waited three days, then finally got an e-mail.

    Phom raw yoo sam wan, nai thee-soot gaw dai rap e-mail.

    ผมรออยู่สามวัน ในที่สุดก็ได้รับอีเมลล์

We went to a lot of places, then in the end we stayed at Ko Chang for five days.

    Rao thio gan lai thee, laeo tawn thai rao pai phak thee Gaw Chang ha wan.

    เราเที่ยวกันหลายที่แล้วตอนท้ายเราไปพักที่เกาะช้างห้าวัน

FIRST/NEXT/LAST (PERSON/THING)

The words and phrases here are all put after classifiers.

first/the first - raek - *Reuan* is the classifier for clocks and watches.

The first watch I bought only worked for a week.

    Na-lee-ga reuan raek thee phom seu ma chai dai kae a-thit dio.

    นาฬิกาเรือนแรกที่ผมซื้อมาใช้ได้แค่อาทิตย์เดียว

second/etc - thee sawng - Use *thee* to form ordinal numbers.

The second person is named Gaeo.

    Kon thee sawng cheu Gaeo.

    คนที่สองชื่อแก้ว

the next/the following - taw pai/taw-taw pai/that pai - *Taw-taw pai* is for plurals and *that pai* is for things in a series.

You're the next one who has to wash the dishes.

    Koon pen kon taw pai thee ja tawng lang jan.

    คุณเป็นคนต่อไปที่จะต้องล้างจาน

The children I have after this I'll send to nursury school.

    Look kon taw-taw pai ja song pai rian a-noo-ban.

    ลูกคนต่อๆ ไปจะส่งไปเรียนอนุบาล

The next house is my uncle's.

    Ban lang that pai pen kawng loong phom.

    บ้านหลังถัดไปเป็นของลูกผม

coming up next - taw ma -

That house is my uncle's. The one coming up after that is my sister's.

    Ban lang nan (pen) kawng loong. Lang taw ma (pen) kawng phee-sao.

    บ้านหลังนั้น(เป็น)ของลุง หลังต่อมา(เป็น)ของพี่สาว

last (of a sequence)/final/last remaining - soot-thai -

The last place we'll visit is the national museum.

> Thee soot-thai thee rao ja pai thio keu phee-phit-tha-phan sa-thanj haeng chat.
>
> ที่สุดท้ายที่เราจะไปเที่ยวคือพิพิธภัณฑสถานแห่งชาติ

latest/most recent/last - la-soot/soot-thai - *La-soot* is "the most recent" or "the latest" while *soot-thai* is "the last up to now" or "the very last/final". Use *la-soot* to emphasize "latest", as with styles, or if there could be confusion between "latest" and "last/final".

This is the latest model.

> Nee pen roon la-soot.
>
> นี่เป็นรุ่นล่าสุด

On my last trip I went to Singapore.

> Deuhn-thang krang la-soot phomj pai Singj-ka-po.
>
> เดินทางครั้งล่าสุดผมไปสิงค์โปร์

This song is in her latest/last album.

> Phlayng nee yoo nai choot soot-thai kawngj kao.
>
> เพลงนี้อยู่ในชุดสุดท้ายของเค้า

last/previous - thee laeo/gawn - Also "the one before this".

The last car I had broke down a lot.

> Rot kun thee laeo siaj boi.
>
> รถคันที่แล้วเสียบ่อย

My last job was manager of a pizza restaurant.

> Ngan gawn chan pen phoo jat-gan ran peet-sa.
>
> งานก่อนฉันเป็นผู้จัดการร้านพิซซ่า

previous/old/former - gao -

My old car was red.

> Rot kun gao kawngj phomj seej daeng.
>
> รถคันเก่าของผมสีแดง

original/same as before - deuhm -

I'm living with the same friend as before.

> Tawn-nee chan yoo gap pheuan kon deuhm.
>
> ตอนนี้ฉันอยู่กับเพื่อนคนเดิม

SIMULTANEOUSLY/AT THE SAME TIME

at the same time - way-la dio-gan/nai ka-na dio-gan - These are interchangable.

We're going at the same time but in different cars.

    Rao ja pai way-la dio-gan tae rot kon la kun gan.

    เราจะไปเวลาเดียวกันแต่รถคนละคันกัน

I'm so busy. I have to do all the housework and at the same time watch the kid(s).

    Chan yoong mak. Tawng tham ngan-ban thook yang, laeo nai ka-na dio-gan tawng

    doo-lae look duay.

    ฉันยุ่งมาก ต้องทำงานบ้านทุกอย่างแล้วในขณะเดียวกันต้องดูแลลูกด้วย

the same day - wan dio-gan - Also with years, etc.

He and I started working here the same day.

    Phom gap kao reuhm tham-ngan thee-nee wan dio-gan.

    ผมกับเค้าเริ่มทำงานที่นี่วันเดียวกัน

the same time period (historical) - sa-mai dio-gan/yook dio-gan - The second is more formal.

These two Buddha statues were made ("built") in the same era.

    Phra-phoot-tha-roop sawng ong nee sang nai yook dio-gan.

    พระพุทธรูปสององค์นี้สร้างในยุคเดียวกัน

together - phrawm gan/phrawm gap - *Phrawm* is "together" or "at the same time". It can also be doubled to mean "at one and the same time". See also pages 55-56.

The two of them left the bar at the same time.

    Kao sawng kon awk jak ba phrawm gan.

    เค้าสองคนออกจากบาร์พร้อมกัน

He got here at the same time that I did.

    Kao ma theung phrawm (gan) gap chan. (or *way-la dio-gan gap chan*)

    เค้ามาถึงพร้อม(กัน)กับฉัน

Together with this we'll have an elephant show.

    Phrawm gan nee rao ja mee gan sa-daeng kawng chang duay.

    พร้อมกันนี้เราจะมีการแสดงของช้างด้วย

at that very moment - phaw dee (leuy) - This also means "at the same time", "just now", "just then", and "just as". It can have the additional meaning of "unexpectedly".

Just as she arrived, he came.

    (Phaw) theuh ma theung, kao gaw ma phaw dee leuy.

    (พอ)เธอมาถึงเค้าก็มาพอดีเลย

Just as we were finishing, the electricity went out.

    Gam-lang ja set yoo laeo, phaw dee fai dap.

        กำลังจะเสร็จอยู่แล้วพอดีไฟดับ

THE BEGINNING/MIDDLE/END

the beginning - ton -

beginning of the month	ton deuan
beginning of the year	ton pee
from the beginning	tang-tae (tawn) ton

I've been doing it since the beginning of the year.

    Phom tham ma tang-tae ton pee leuy.

        ผมทำมาตั้งแต่ต้นปีเลย

At the beginning of this year I thought I'd go back to America.

    Meua ton pee nee, chan kit wa ja glap pai A-may-ree-ga.

        เมื่อต้นปีนี้ฉันคิดว่าจะกลับไปอเมริกา

I'm going home at the beginning of next month.

    Phom ja glap ban ton deuan na.

        ผมจะกลับบ้านต้นเดือนหน้า

You should have told me from the beginning.

    Koon na ja bawk phom tang-tae (tawn) ton.

        คุณน่าจะบอกผมตั้งแต่(ตอน)ต้น

the middle - glang -

middle of the week	glang sap-da
middle of the month	glang deuan
middle of the year	glang pee

I get a two-month vacation in the middle of the year.

    Chan dai phak rawn sawng deuan glang pee nee.

        ฉันได้พักร้อนสองเดือนกลางปีนี้

I want to go sometime in the middle of the month.

    Phom yak pai rao-rao glang deuan.

        ผมอยากไปราวๆ กลางเดือน

the end - sin̄/plai/thai - The following phrases are common:

end of the year	sin̄ pee/plai pee
end of the month	sin̄ deuan/plai deuan
end of the week	plai sap-da/thai sap-da/sin̄ sap-da
end of the hour	thai chua-mong
weekend (first is formal)	wan soot sap-da/(wan) saoj a-thit

We get paid at the end of the month.

Rao dai rap ngeuhn tawn plai deuan.

เราได้รับเงินตอนปลายเดือน

I'm taking a trip at the end of the month.

Chan ja deuhn-thang sin̄ deuan nee.

ฉันจะเดินทางสิ้นเดือนนี้

For stories, movies, songs -

beginning	tawn raek/tawn reuhm raek/tawn ton/
	tawn raek-raek/tawn ton-ton
middle	glang-glang
end	tawn jop

A: What did you think of that story/movie?

Koon kit yang-ngai (gio-gap) reuang nan?

คุณคิดยังไง(เกี่ยวกับ)เรื่องนั้น

B: The beginning was good, but the middle was a little boring.

Tawn ton-ton gaw dee, tae glang-glang reuang, na-beua pai noi.

ตอนต้นๆ ก็ดีแต่กลางๆ เรื่องน่าเบื่อไปหน่อย

I didn't like the end. The heroine shouldn't have died.

Chan mai chawp tawn jop. Nang ayk mai na tai leuy.

ฉันไม่ชอบตอนจบ นางเอกไม่น่าตายเลย

17. HOW LONG?

Patterns with amounts of time have the same grammatical distinctions in Thai as in English between the past ("I stayed there for two weeks"), the present perfect ("I've stayed here for two weeks"), and the future ("I'll stay there for two weeks").

WORDS FOR "PERIOD OF TIME"

There are five words which vary in meaning and use.

1. chuang - *Chuang* is used for periods of time in the day ("late afternoon" is *chuang yen* or *tawn yen*), periods of the year or season (*chuang na rawn* is "hot season"), periods of life (*chuang wai-roon* is "teenage years"), and periods or cycles in business. It's also used with distances and areas. The basic meanings are "duration", "span", "extent", and "interval". Following are phrases with time:

chuang	the period (of)
chuang (thee)	when, the period that
(nai) chuang	during
(nai) chuang nee	now, at this period of time
chuang nan	then, during that period of time
nai chuang samj pee gawn	for/during the past three years
chuang raek	the first time (referring to a long period of time)
pen chuang-chuang	periodically
sak chuang neung	awhile

The Japanese economy at the beginning of the year was better than it is now.

    Sayt-tha-git Yee-poon nai chuang ton pee (nee) dee gwa tawn-nee.

        เศรษฐกิจญี่ปุ่นในช่วงต้นปี(นี้)ดีกว่าตอนนี้

I want to stay here for a while.

    Phomj yak yoo thee-nee sak chuang neung.

        ผมอยากอยู่ที่นี่ซักช่วงหนึ่ง

2. sa-maij - This is for historical periods. It means "age", "era", or "period".

sa-maij	the period (of)
sa-maij (thee)	when, during the time (that)
sa-maij nee	nowadays, in these times
sa-maij gawn/sa-maij gao	in past times, in former times
sa-maij nan	during that period of time

During the Sukothai period Thai art was very beautiful.

    (Nai) sa-maij Soo-koj-thai sinj-la-pa Thai suay-ngam mak.

       (ใน)สมัยสุโขทัยศิลปะไทยสวยงามมาก

3. ra-ya - This is formal and can refer to both time and distance. It means "duration", "period", "stage of development", or "interval". Common phrases are:

ra-ya nee	now, during this period
ra-ya nan	then, during that period of time
ra-ya yao	long term
ra-ya sun	short term
sak ra-ya neung	awhile

The amount of time it takes to go from here to Singapore is four hours.

    Ra-ya way-la jak nee theung Sinj-ka-po see chua-mong phaw dee.

       ระยะเวลาจากนี่ถึงสิงค์โปร์สี่ชั่วโมงพอดี

In the long term there could be very bad effects.

    Nai ra-ya yao at ja mee phonj siaj mak.

       ในระยะยาวอาจจะมีผลเสียมาก

4. phak - This is a noun that refers to a period of time and also a verb that means "to stay" or "to rest". It's used in the following phrases:

la phak	take days off from work, take a vacation
yoot phak/phak way-la	stop to rest, take a break, take a vacation
phak thiang	lunch break
phak rawn	vacation from work
phak rian	vacation from school
phak neuay	rest break
way-la phak	break time, rest time
phak neung/sak phak	a short time
phak gawn	not so long ago
pen phak-phak	from time to time

A: Have you volunteered here long? ("been a volunteer")

    Ma pen a-saj sa-mak thee-nee nan reu yang?

       มาเป็นอาสาสมัครที่นี่นานรึยัง

B: Just a short time.

    Gaw dai sak phak laeo./Sak phak dai.

       ก็ได้ซักพักแล้ว/ซักพักได้

5. wayn - This is for a period when nothing happens. It's also a verb meaning "to omit" or "skip over".

I have to work every day. I don't have any time off at all.

    Chan tawng tham-ngan thook wan. Mai mee wayn leuy.

    ฉันต้องทำงานทุกวัน ไม่มีเว้นเลย

When you're reading, take a break.

    Way-la an, wayn ra-ya duay.

    เวลาอ่านเว้นระยะด้วย

HOW LONG DID YOU? (PAST)

Basic sentences ("I lived") - *Dai* can be included either before or after amounts of time in the past. Before an amount it means that you "did" or "got" the action for that period of time. After, it means "about" or "around".

We lived together for three years.

    Rao yoo duay-gan sam pee./Rao yoo duay-gan dai sam pee.

    เราอยู่ด้วยกันสามปี/เราอยู่ด้วยกันได้สามปี

    Rao yoo duay-gan sam pee dai. ("around three years")

    เราอยู่ด้วยกันสามปีได้

I went to school for four years and got a B.A.

    Chan rian dai see pee gaw jop prin-ya tree.

    ฉันเรียนได้สี่ปีก็จบปริญญาตรี

I waited for my visa for about two weeks.

    Phom raw wee-sa sawng a-thit dai mung.

    ผมรอวีซ่าสองอาทิตย์ได้มั้ง

My (younger) brother came from England just three days ago. ("these three days")

    Nawng-chai (chan) pheung ma jak Ang-grit dai sam wan nee ayng.

    น้องชาย(ฉัน)เพิ่งมาจากอังกฤษได้สามวันนี้เอง

I worked there for five years and after that I went to Indonesia for two years.

    Phom̌ tham-ngan thee-nan (dai) ha pee, lang-jak nan gaw̌ pai yoo In-do-nee-sia

    sawng pee.

    ผมทำงานที่นั่นได้ห้าปีหลังจากนั้นก็ไปอยู่อินโดนีเซียสองปี

Dai can also be put before verbs with the meaning that you "did", "got", or "got the chance" to do the action. This is explained on page 93.

I went traveling for three days.

    Chan dai pai thio sam̌ wan.

    ฉันได้ไปเที่ยวสามวัน

With *keuy* - The same variations are used with *keuy* to refer to past experiences.

I lived in Saudi Arabia for two years. (had the experience)

    Phom̌ keuy yoo Sa-oo sawng pee./Phom̌ keuy yoo Sa-oo dai sawng pee.

    ผมเคยอยู่ซาอุสองปี/ผมเคยอยู่ซาอุได้สองปี

    Phom̌ keuy yoo Sa-oo sawng pee dai. ("about two years")

    ผมเคยอยู่ซาอุสองปีได้

Negative - With the negative *dai* can be put before both the verb and the amount of time. Before the verb it means "didn't", "didn't get to", or "wasn't able to".

He didn't come to work for five days, so the boss fired him.

    Kao mai dai tham-ngan (dai) ha wan, laeo hua-na gaw̌ leuy lai awk.

    เค้าไม่ได้ทำงาน(ได้)ห้าวันแล้วหัวหน้าก็เลยไล่ออก

(for) a long time - nan/nan-nan - The second is "a very long time".

Yesterday I had to wait for Jack at the airport for a really long time.

    Meua-wan-nee chan tawng raw Jack thee sa-nam̌ bin nan-nan.

    เมื่อวานนี้ฉันต้องรอแจ๊คที่สนามบินน้าน นาน

A: Has your phone been broken long?

    Tho-ra-sap siaj nan reu plao?

    โทรศัพท์เสียนานรึเปล่า

B: Not long. Just a day.

    Yang mai nan, rawk. Kae wan dio.

    ยังไม่นานหรอก แค่วันเดียว

(for) a very long time - tang-nan - *Tang* emphasizes that the amount is large.

John spent a long time looking for shoes.

    John siaj way-la hǎj rawng-thao tang-nan.

    จอห์นเสียเวลาหารองเท้าตั้งนาน

(for) not long - măi nan/dăi măi nan/măi dăi (verb) nan -

I didn't live there long.

> Chăn yoo thee-nân (dăi) măi nan./Chan măi dăi yoo thee-nân nan.
>
> ฉันอยู่ที่นั่น(ได้)ไม่นาน/ฉันไม่ได้อยู่ที่นั่นนาน

A: Have you been responsible for this work long?

> Rap-phit-chawp ngan nee ma nan laeo reuŋ?
>
> รับผิดชอบงานนี้มานานแล้วเหรอ

B: Not long.

> Măi nan mâk rawk./Măi nan thaô-rai (rawk).
>
> ไม่นานมากหรอก/ไม่นานเท่าไร(หรอก)

for many days (for a long time) - laiŋ wăn/laiŋ pee - Also with weeks, months, etc. This is common for "a long time".

Yawt came and stayed with me for many days.

> Yawt ma yiam phŏmŋ laiŋ wăn.
>
> ยอดมาเยี่ยมผมหลายวัน

for not many days (not long) - măi gee wăn - Also with months, years, etc.

He hadn't worked there long when he had a disagreement with his co-workers.

> Kao thăm-ngan thee-nân (dăi) măi gee deuan, kaô gaŵ thiangŋ (gáp) phoô ruam ngan.
>
> เค้าทำงานที่นั่น(ได้)ไม่กี่เดือน เค้าก็เถียง(กับ)ผู้ร่วมงาน

How many days did you/were you...? - (dăi) gee wăn? -

A: How many days were you in Europe?

> Yoo Yoo-rop (dăi) gee wăn?
>
> อยู่ยุโรป(ได้)กี่วัน

B: A little over two weeks.

> Sawngŋ a-thit gwa.
>
> สองอาทิตย์กว่า

Did you...long? - (dăi) nan măi?/(dăi) nan reŭ plao? -

A: Did you live in the Karen village long?

> Koon pai yoo moo-ban Ga-riang (dăi) nan măi?
>
> คุณไปอยู่หมู่บ้านกระเหรี่ยง(ได้)นานมั้ย

B: About three months.

> Samŋ deuan dăi mung.
>
> สามเดือนได้มั้ง

Confirmation questions -

A: You stayed in Phuket for a long time, didn't you?

Koon yoo Phoo-get (dai) nan leuy, chai mai?

คุณอยู่ภูเก็ต(ได้)นานเลยใช่มั้ย

B: Yes. I really liked it there.

Chai. Chan chawp thee-nan jing-jing.

ใช่ ฉันชอบที่นั่นจริงๆ

A: You didn't stay in Australia long, did you?

Koon pai yoo Aws-tray-lia mai nan, chai mai?

คุณไปอยู่ออสเตรเลียไม่นานใช่มั้ย

B: No.

Mai nan rawk.

ไม่นานหรอก

How long did you? - nan thao-rai?/nan kae nai? - These phrases are used to ask about exact amounts of time and aren't as common as the previous questions.

A: How long did you teach there?

Koon sawn thee-nan (dai) nan thao-rai?

คุณสอนที่นั่น(ได้)นานเท่าไหร่

B: About five years.

Geuap ha pee.

เกือบห้าปี

How long ago? - Questions with "how long ago" in English are usually formed with "when" in Thai.

A: When did you come here? (instead of "How long ago did you come here?")

Koon ma thee-nee meua-rai?

คุณมาที่นี่เมื่อไหร่

B: I came five days ago.

Phom ma meua ha wan thee laeo.

ผมมาเมื่อห้าวันที่แล้ว

HOW LONG HAVE YOU? (PRESENT PERFECT)

Basic sentences ("I've lived") - The present perfect expresses actions that began in the past and which are still continuing. *Ma* or *dai* (or both) can be included before the amount of time, and *laeo* or *ma laeo* are put at the end for "already". Following are variations:

He's lived here for two years (already)./He's been living here for two years.

> Kao yoo thee-nee sawng pee (ma) laeo.
>
> เค้าอยู่ที่นี่สองปี(มา)แล้ว

> Kao yoo thee-nee ma sawng pee laeo.
>
> เค้าอยู่ที่นี่มาสองปีแล้ว

> Kao yoo thee-nee dai sawng pee (ma) laeo.
>
> เค้าอยู่ที่นี่ได้สองปี(มา)แล้ว

> Kao yoo thee-nee ma dai sawng pee laeo.
>
> เค้าอยู่ที่นี่มาได้สองปีแล้ว

I've been taking this medicine for two days.

> Chan gin ya nee dai sawng wan laeo.
>
> ฉันกินยานี้ได้สองวันแล้ว

She's lived in Thailand for over ten years.

> Kao ma yoo meuang Thai dai sip pee gwa laeo.
>
> เค้ามาอยู่เมืองไทยได้สิบปีกว่าแล้ว

Dai can also be put before the verb. It stresses that the action has been happening over a period of time, and that it is still going on.

It's been flooding for about five days.

> Nam dai thuam ma ha wan laeo mung.
>
> น้ำได้ท่วมมาห้าวันแล้วมั้ง

Laeo or *ma laeo* can also be put before the amount of time (instead of at the end) to emphasize "already".

I've been here for three years already.

> Phom yoo ma laeo sam pee.
>
> ผมอยู่มาแล้วสามปี

Negative - Use the same variations. *Dai* is common before the verb in the negative.

He hasn't paid taxes for three years.

> Kao mai (dai) sia pha-see sam pee (ma) laeo.
>
> เค้าไม่(ได้)เสียภาษีสามปี(มา)แล้ว

> Kao mai (dai) sia pha-see ma sam pee laeo.
>
> เค้าไม่(ได้)เสียภาษีมาสามปีแล้ว

Kao mai (dai) siaj pha-seej dai samj pee (ma) laeo.

เค้าไม่(ได้)เสียภาษีได้สามปี(มา)แล้ว

Kao mai (dai) siaj pha-seej ma dai samj pee laeo.

เค้าไม่(ได้)เสียภาษีมาได้สามปีแล้ว

Yang can be included to mean "haven't yet". It isn't translated in English.

I haven't seen her for two weeks.

Phomj yang mai dai jeuh kao (ma) sawngj a-thit laeo.

ผมยังไม่ได้เจอเค้า(มา)สองอาทิตย์แล้ว

I've...for a long time - *Ma, laeo,* and *dai* can be included with "for a long time". *Ma* shows that the action has happened up to the present, *laeo* emphasizes "already", and *dai* emphasizes that you "got" the time.

I've been waiting for a long time.

Chan koi ma nan./Chan koi (ma) nan laeo./Chan koi (ma) nan-nan.

ฉันคอยมานาน/ฉันคอย(มา)นานแล้ว/ฉันคอย(มา)น้าน นาน

Chan koi dai nan laeo./Chan koi (ma) tang-nan.

ฉันคอยได้นานแล้ว/ฉันคอย(มา)ตั้งนาน

She's been a singer here for a long time.

Theuh pen nak-rawng thee-nee dai nan laeo.

เธอเป็นนักร้องที่นี่ได้นานแล้ว

They've been selling this kind of medicine for a long time.

Ya cha-nit nee mee kaij (ma) tang-nan laeo.

ยาชนิดนี้มีขาย(มา)ตั้งนานแล้ว

A: You haven't gone traveling for a long time, have you?

Koon mai (keuy) dai pai thioj (ma) nan laeo, chai mai?

คุณไม่(เคย)ได้ไปเที่ยว(มา)นานแล้วใช่มั้ย

B: No, I haven't.

Chai.

ใช่

Meaning "can" - *Dai* means "can" if *laeo* isn't included. Compare these sentences.

I've lived with him for a long time.

Phomj yoo gap kao dai nan laeo.

ผมอยู่กับเค้าได้นานแล้ว

I can live with him a long time.

Phomj yoo gap kao dai nan.

ผมอยู่กับเค้าได้นาน

for not long - (dai) mai nan - You can also make the verb negative as in the second example.

I've just started training for boxing.

    Phom pheung hat toi muay dai mai nan.

    ผมเพิ่งหัดต่อยมวยได้ไม่นาน

We haven't known each other long.

    Rao roo-jak gan (dai) mai nan thao-rai./Rao yang mai roo-jak gan nan thao-rai.

    เรารู้จักกัน(ได้)ไม่นานเท่าไหร่/เรายังไม่รู้จักกันนานเท่าไหร่

for many years/etc - (ma) lai pee laeo/dai lai pee laeo - Also weeks, days, months.

Joe has played music for many years.

    Joe len don-tree dai lai pee laeo.

    โจเล่นดนตรีได้หลายปีแล้ว

for not many days/etc - mai gee wan (nee) -

A: How long have you had this restaurant? ("opened this restaurant")

    Peuht ran-a-han nee ma nan thao-rai laeo?

    เปิดร้านอาหารนี้มานานเท่าไหร่แล้ว

B: We just opened it a few months ago.

    Pheung peuht dai mai gee deuan ayng.

    เพิ่งเปิดได้ไม่กี่เดือนเอง

It's been...since - thee/tang-tae/tang-tae thee - *Thee* is used here for a generalized "that/since". *Tang-tae* is also explained on page 313 and pages 343-344.

It's been many months since he left home.

    Pen way-la lai deuan thee kao awk jak ban.

    เป็นเวลาหลายเดือนที่เค้าออกจากบ้าน

    Pen way-la lai deuan tang-tae (thee) kao awk jak ban.

    เป็นเวลาหลายเดือนตั้งแต่(ที่)เค้าออกจากบ้าน

    Kao awk jak ban pen way-la lai deuan laeo.

    เค้าออกจากบ้านเป็นเวลาหลายเดือนแล้ว

    Kao awk jak ban tang-tae lai deuan thee laeo.

    เค้าออกจากบ้านตั้งแต่หลายเดือนที่แล้ว

It's been seven years since they opened that company.

    (Dai) jet pee laeo thee kao (dai) peuht baw-ree-sat nan.

    (ได้)เจ็ดปีแล้วที่เค้า(ได้)เปิดบริษัทนั้น

    Kao (dai) peuht baw-ree-sat nan jet pee ma laeo.

    เค้า(ได้)เปิดบริษัทนั้นเจ็ดปีมาแล้ว

It's been a long time since I talked to her.

> Nan ma laeo (tang-tae) thee phom dai kui gap theuh.

> นานมาแล้ว(ตั้งแต่)ที่ผมได้คุยกับเธอ

It's been seven years since I've gone to the dentist. ("that I haven't gone")

> Pen way-la sawng pee thee mai dai pai ha maw fun.

> เป็นเวลาสองปีที่ไม่ได้ไปหาหมอฟัน

> Phom mai dai pai ha maw fun tang-tae sawng pee thee laeo.

> ผมไม่ได้ไปหาหมอฟันตั้งแต่สองปีที่แล้ว

He's been sick for many days. ("It's been many days that he's been sick.")

> (Dai) lai wan laeo thee kao mai sa-bai.

> (ได้)หลายวันแล้วที่เขาไม่สบาย

Have you...long?/Has it been long? -

A: Have you studied Thai long?

> Rian pha-sa Thai (ma) nan (laeo) reu yang, ka?

> เรียนภาษาไทย(มา)นาน(แล้ว)รึยังคะ

B: Not long. Only two months.

> Yang mai nan rawk. Kae sawng deuan ayng.

> ยังไม่นานหรอก แค่สองเดือนเอง

A: Has it been long since you graduated?

> Koon rian jop (dai) (ma) nan reu yang, krup?

> คุณเรียนจบ(ได้)(มา)นานรึยังครับ

B: About three years.

> Sam pee laeo mung.

> สามปีแล้วมั้ง

A: Have you been raising cattle long?

> Nan reu yang thee koon liang wua?

> นานรึยังที่คุณเลี้ยงควาย

B: It hasn't been two years (yet).

> Yang mai dai sawng pee leuy.

> ยังไม่ได้สองปีเลย

Confirmation questions -

A: You've been in Thailand a long time?

> Ma meuang Thai nan (laeo) reuh? (or *chai mai?*)

> มาเมืองไทยนาน(แล้ว)เหรอ

B: Yes. I've been here a long time.

    Chai, krup. Phom yoo ma nan laeo.

    ใช่ครับ ผมอยู่มานานแล้ว

How many years have you? - (ma) (dai) gee pee laeo? - Also with days, etc.

A: How many years have you been in Thailand?

    Yoo meuang Thai (ma) (dai) gee pee laeo?

    อยู่เมืองไทย(มา)(ได้)กี่ปีแล้ว

B: I've been here for five years.

    Yoo ma (dai) ha pee./(Dai) ha pee laeo./Yoo ma ha pee dai (mung).

    อยู่มา(ได้)ห้าปี/(ได้)ห้าปีแล้ว/อยู่มาห้าปีได้(มั้ง)

How long have you? - (ma) nan thao-rai laeo? - This is for exact amounts of time. The other question types are more common in general conversation.

A: How long have you been selling things here?

    Kai kawng thee-nee (ma) nan thao-rai laeo?

    ขายของที่นี่(มา)นานเท่าไหร่แล้ว

B: For eight months.

    Paet deuan dai.

    แปดเดือนได้

A: How long has it been since we last met?

    Nan thao-rai laeo, tang-tae rao jeuh gan krang gawn?

    นานเท่าไหร่แล้วตั้งแต่เราเจอกันครั้งก่อน

B: It's been four years, hasn't it?

    See pee ma laeo, chai mai?

    สี่ปีมาแล้วใช่มั้ย

for so long - Ask with *lai wan* ("many days") etc.

A: Where have you been for so long?

    Pai nai ma lai wan (laeo)?

    ไปไหนมาหลายวัน(แล้ว)

B: I took a trip to Yunnan.

    Pai thio Yoo-nan ma.

    ไปเที่ยวยูนานมา

HOW LONG WILL YOU? (FUTURE)

for two days - sawng wan - No word is included for "for".

A: How many days will you stay here?

    (Ja) yoo gee wan?

    (จะ)อยู่กี่วัน

B: Probably three or four days.

    Kong sam-see wan.

    คงสามสี่วัน

for two more days - eeg sawng wan - This also means "in two days" (page 319).

A: How many more days will you be here?

    Koon ja yoo eeg gee wan?

    คุณจะอยู่อีกกี่วัน

B: I can stay for five more days.

    Chan yoo dai eeg ha wan.

    ฉันอยู่ได้อีกห้าวัน

I'll keep working here for one more month.

    Chan ja tham-ngan thee-nee taw pai eeg sak neung deuan.

    ฉันจะทำงานที่นี่ต่อไปอีกซักหนึ่งเดือน

We probably won't see each other for two years.

    Rao kong ja mai dai jeuh gan (pen way-la) (eeg) sawng pee.

    เราคงจะไม่ได้เจอกัน(เป็นเวลา)(อีก)สองปี

How much longer? - eeg nan thao-rai -

A: How much longer will he let you use the motorcycle?

    Kao ja hai koon chai rot-kreuang eeg nan thao-rai?

    เค้าจะให้คุณใช้รถเครื่องอีกนานเท่าไหร่

B: One more week.

    Eeg neung a-thit.

    อีกหนึ่งอาทิตย์

Will you...long? -

A: Will you stay in France long?

    Koon ja yoo Fa-rang-set nan mai?

    คุณจะอยู่ฝรั่งเศสนานมั้ย

B: I'll be there quite a long time.

    At ja nan noi.

    อาจจะนานหน่อย

longer/for a longer time - eeg nan - This is also "in a long time" (page 320).

I can stay here a lot longer.

    Phom ja yoo thee-nee dai eeg nan.

    ผมจะอยู่ที่นี่ได้อีกนาน

Will your friend be staying with you much longer?

    Pheuan ja yoo gap koon eeg nan mai?

    เพื่อนจะอยู่กับคุณอีกนานมั้ย

I probably won't come to Thailand for a long time.

    Phom kong mai dai ma Meuang Thai eeg nan, na.

    ผมคงไม่ได้มาเมืองไทยอีกนานนะ

for not much longer - eeg mai nan/eeg noi - The same phrases are used for "in not long/soon" (page 321). The second is common with requests.

I'll be here just a little longer.

    Phom ja yoo thee-nee eeg mai nan.

    ผมจะอยู่ที่นี่อีกไม่นาน

Wait a little longer and I'll be finished.

    Raw eeg noi, ja set laeo.

    รออีกหน่อยจะเสร็จแล้ว

ALWAYS/CONTINUOUSLY

"Always" is used in two ways in English with different patterns in Thai. First, it refers to actions that are going on continually, as in "She always works" (explained here). Secondly it's for actions that happen whenever possible, as in "She always reads at night" (page 378).

always/all the time/constantly - sa-meuh -

The weather is always good here.

    Thee-nee a-gat dee sa-meuh.

    ที่นี่อากาศดีเสมอ

Phet always practices dancing.

    Phet feuk ten-ram yoo sa-meuh.

    เพชรฝึกเต้นรำอยู่เสมอ

continually/all the time - reuay-reuay -

If I had the money I'd just like to travel all the time.

    Tha mee ngeuhn chan gaw yak thio pai reuay-reuay.

    ถ้ามีเงินฉันก็อยากเที่ยวไปเรื่อยๆ

the whole time - tå-<u>lawt</u> - This refers to something happening continuously during a period of time. *Ta-lawt* means "through", "throughout", or "the whole period".

Last week I was on Phuket the whole time.

    A-thit thee laeo <u>phom</u> <u>yoo</u> Phoo-<u>get</u> tå-<u>lawt</u>.

      อาทิตย์ที่แล้วผมอยู่ภูเก็ตตลอด

There are mangoes the whole month of April.

    Nai deuan May-<u>sa</u> jå mee må-muang tå-<u>lawt</u>/så-<u>meuh</u>.

      ในเดือนเมษาจะมีมะม่วงตลอด/เสมอ

all the time - tå-<u>lawt</u> way-la -

I always see her reading./I see that she likes to read all the time.

    Chan <u>hen</u> theuh chawp <u>an</u> nang-<u>seu</u> tå-<u>lawt</u> way-la.

      ฉันเห็นเธอชอบอ่านหนังสือตลอดเวลา

from now on/permanently - leuy -

I want to live here permanantly.

    <u>Phom</u> yak <u>yoo</u> thee-nee leuy.

      ผมอยากอยู่ที่นี่เลย

ALWAYS—PHRASES WITH *MA* AND *PAI*

have always - tå-<u>lawt</u> ma/ma tå-<u>lawt</u>/reuay ma/så-<u>meuh</u> ma - These include *ma* to show the action coming from the past. The last is used with facts more than actions.

Farmers are poor, and it's always been that way.

    Chao na yak-jon. (Mun) pen yang-ngee ma tå-<u>lawt</u>.

      ชาวนายากจน (มัน)เป็นยังงี้มาตลอด

He's always been good to me.

    Kao dee <u>taw</u> chan så-<u>meuh</u> ma.

      เค้าดีต่อฉันเสมอมา

always/from now on/forever - tå-<u>lawt</u> pai/så-<u>meuh</u> pai - These include *pai* to show the action going away into the future.

We can stay together forever.

    Rao <u>yoo</u> duay-gan dai tå-<u>lawt</u> pai.

      เราอยู่ด้วยกันได้ตลอดไป

ALL/THE WHOLE (PHRASES)

all day/all night - thang wan/ta-lawt wan/thang keun -

Today it was cold all day.

    Wan-nee nao ta-lawt wan leuy.

    วันนี้หนาวตลอดวันเลย

A: Why do you look so tired?

    Tham-mai doo koon neuay mak?

    ทำไมดูคุณเหนื่อยมาก

B: Last night I watched videos all night.

    Meua-keun phom doo wee-dee-o thang keun.

    เมื่อคืนผมดูวิดีโอทั้งคืน

all year - ta-lawt pee -

There are tangerines and bananas for sale all year.

    Mee som gap gluay kai ta-lawt pee.

    มีส้มกับกล้วยขายตลอดปี

my whole life - ta-lawt chee-wit -

He's worked hard his whole life, so now he lives well.

    Kao tham-ngan nak ma ta-lawt chee-wit, kao leuy mee chee-wit thee dee nai

    wan-nee.

    เค้าทำงานหนักมาตลอดชีวิตเค้าเลยมีชีวิตที่ดีในวันนี้

the whole three weeks - ta-lawt sam a-thit - Include *nee* or *nan* for "these/those".

I looked for Maem the whole three weeks I was in Singapore.

    Phom tam ha Maem ta-lawt sam a-thit thee yoo Sing-ka-po.

    ผมตามหาแหม่มตลอดสามอาทิตย์ที่อยู่สิงค์โปร์

For the next two weeks I'm going to travel all over Thailand.

    Ta-lawt sawng a-thit nee, chan ja thio hai thua meuang Thai leuy.

    ตลอดสองอาทิตย์นี้ฉันจะเที่ยวให้ทั่วเมืองไทยเลย

For that whole two months I didn't eat any Western food at all.

    Ta-lawt sawng deuan nan, phom mai dai gin a-han fa-rang.

    ตลอดสองเดือนนั้นผมไม่ได้กินอาหารฝรั่ง

that whole time - ta-lawt way-la nan -

That whole time I never spoke to her at all.

    Ta-lawt way-la nan chan mai dai phoot gap theuh leuy.

    ตลอดเวลานั้นฉันไม่ได้พูดกับเธอเลย

SPENDING TIME/TAKING TIME

The phrase is *chai way-la*, literally "use-time", or use a verb with *nan* as in the last question and answer.

I spent two whole hours driving to the party.

Chan chai way-la tang sawng chua-mong kap rot pai ngan liang.

ฉันใช้เวลาตั้งสองชั่วโมงขับรถไปงานเลี้ยง

It won't take long to do this work.

Ngan nee chai way-la tham mai nan.

งานนี้ใช้เวลาทำไม่นาน

How many days does it take to make a suit?

Tat soot (chai way-la) gee wan?

ตัดสูท(ใช้เวลา)กี่วัน

A: How long does it take to get to Wat Phra Kaeo?

Pai Wat Phra Gaeo chai way-la thao-rai?

ไปวัดพระแก้วใช้เวลาเท่าไหร่

B: It (probably) takes about an hour.

(Kong) chai way-la pra-man neung chua-mong.

(คง)ใช้เวลาประมาณหนึ่งชั่วโมง

A long time./It takes a long time.

Nan./Chai way-la nan.

นาน/ใช้เวลานาน

Not long.

Mai nan./Gaw mai nan thao-rai./Chai way-la mai nan.

ไม่นาน/ก็ไม่นานเท่าไหร่/ใช้เวลาไม่นาน

A: Why did it take so long?

Tham-mai chai way-la nan?

ทำไมใช้เวลานาน

B: My car broke down.

Gaw, rot mun siaj nee.

ก็รถมันเสียนี่

A: To learn barbering, do you have to study long?

Rian tat phom, tawng rian nan reu plao?

เรียนตัดผมต้องเรียนนานรึเปล่า

B: No, not long.

Mai tawng rian nan gaw dai.

ไม่ต้องเรียนนานก็ได้

AMOUNTS OF TIME—OTHER PHRASES

awhile - sak kroo/sak kroo neung/sak kroo dio - Also *sak phak, sak phak neung, sak chuang neung,* and *sak ra-ya neung.*

He went into the room for a moment, then came out.

Kao kao pai nai hawng sak kroo neung, gaw awk ma.

เค้าเข้าไปในห้องซักครู่หนึ่งก็ออกมา

a short time - paep dio - This refers to a shorter period of time than *sak kroo.* See page 321 for these phrases with *eeg* meaning "in just a moment".

Wait just a moment.

Raw paep dio, na./Raw sak kroo, na ka.

รอแป๊บเดียวนะ/รอซักครู่นะคะ

I'll have it finished in just a minute.

Tham paep dio, gaw set.

ทำแป๊บเดียวก็เสร็จ

I just waited a short time and you came.

Chan raw paep dio, koon gaw ma laeo.

ฉันรอแป๊บเดียว คุณก็มาแล้ว

up to - theung -

It might take up to three days.

At ja chai way-la theung sam wan.

อาจจะใช้เวลาถึงสามวัน

not up to (past time) - mai theung/mai dai - These phrases are literally "not arrive at" and "not get". Include *yang* for "hasn't yet reached".

I hadn't known her for a week and she asked to borrow my car.

Chan roo-jak theuh mai theung neung a-thit, theuh gaw ma kaw yeum rot chan.

ฉันรู้จักเธอไม่ถึงหนึ่งอาทิตย์ เธอก็มาขอยืมรถฉัน

I haven't even been married for two months.

Phom taeng-ngan yang mai dai sawng deuan leuy.

ผมแต่งงานยังไม่ได้สองเดือนเลย

not up to (future) - (eeg) mai theung - Use only *mai theung,* not *mai dai,* for "it won't reach (a certain time)" in the future.

A: Are you coming back soon?

Ja glap reo reuh?

จะกลับเร็วเหรอ

B: It won't be an hour and I'll be back.

Eeg mai theung chua-mong (gaw) ja glap, la.

อีกไม่ถึงชั่วโมง(ก็)จะกลับล่ะ

Kong mai theung chua-mong gaw glap, la.

คงไม่ถึงชั่วโมงก็กลับล่ะ

longer than - nan gwa - *Mak gwa* can also be used in the first sentence because the amount of time is stated.

We've known each other for more than ten years.

Rao roo-jak gan ma (dai) nan gwa sip pee laeo. (or *mak gwa sip pee laeo*)

เรารู้จักกันมา(ได้)นานกว่าสิบปีแล้ว

A: Have you been here longer than Jane?

Koon yoo thee-nee (ma) nan gwa Jane reu plao?

คุณอยู่ที่นี่(มา)นานกว่าเจนรึเปล่า

B: No, Jane's been here longer than I have.

Plao. Jane yoo ma (dai) nan gwa phom.

เปล่า เจนอยู่มา(ได้)นานกว่าผม

for so long - nan ka-nat nee/nan ka-nat nan -

A: Why was Moo gone so long?

Tham-mai Moo theung pai nan ka-nat nan, la?

ทำไมหมูถึงไปนานขนาดนั้นล่ะ

B: He had a lot of business to do.

Gaw, kao tawng tham thoo-ra lai yang nee.

ก็เค้าต้องทำธุระหลายอย่างนี่

time left - leua - *Leua* means "left" or "leftover".

You don't have to rush. There's still a lot of time.

Mai tawng reep, na. Mee way-la leua (yoo) yeuh.

ไม่ต้องรีบนะ มีเวลาเหลือ(อยู่)เยอะ

A: How much time is left.

Leua way-la thao-rai?

เหลือเวลาเท่าไหร่

B: There are five minutes left.

Leua (yoo) eeg ha na-thee.

เหลือ(อยู่)อีกห้านาที

18. FREQUENCY

OFTEN

often/not often - boi/mai boi -

I call my parents often.

    Chan tho pai haɟ phaw-mae boi.

      ฉันโทรไปหาพ่อแม่บ่อย

But I don't write them often.

    Tae chan kianɟ jot-maiɟ pai haɟ kao mai boi.

      แต่ฉันเขียนจดหมายไปหาเค้าไม่บ่อย

Things get stolen here a lot. (including *ja* makes it hypothetical)

    Thee-nee kawnɟ (ja) haiɟ boi.

      ที่นี่ของ(จะ)หายบ่อย

Lek watches TV a lot.

    Lek (ja) doo thee-wee boi.

      เล็ก(จะ)ดูทีวีบ่อย

happen often - Use *mee/geuht keun* for "happen".

A lot of motorcycles crash on this curve.

    Kong nee (keuy) mee rot kwam boi. (*kwam* is "overturn")

      โค้งนี้(เคย)มีรถคว่ำบ่อย

Around here there are a lot of murders.

    Thaeoɟ nee (keuy) mee kat-ta-gam geuht keun boi.

      แถวนี้(เคย)มีฆาตกรรมเกิดขึ้นบ่อย

Repeated - boi-boi/boi-boi - If both words are low/short the meaning is "rather often". If the first is high/long and the second low/short it means "very often".

The students cheat on tests pretty often.

    Nak-rian chawp lawk kaw-sawp boi-boi.

      นักเรียนชอบลอกข้อสอบบ่อยๆ

She goes to that shop really often.

    Kao pai ran nan boi-boi.

      เค้าไปร้านนั้นบ่อยๆ

not very often - maῖ koῖ <u>boi</u> - There are three variations. *Ja* is optional in all examples.

1. Put the whole phrase after the verb. *Ja* may be included before *boi* and *thao-rai* can be included at the end.

I don't go to Maboonkrong very often.

    Phom̒ paῖ Ma-boon-krawng maῖ koῖ (jà) <u>boi</u>.

    ผมไปมาบุญครองไม่ค่อย(จะ)บ่อย

I play tennis, but not often.

    Phom̒ leñ̒ thèn-nῐt, <u>tae</u> maῖ koῖ <u>boi</u> thao-rai.

    ผมเล่นเทนนิสแต่ไม่ค่อยบ่อยเท่าไหร่

2. Put the verb between *mai koi* and *boi*. *Ja* is optional before the verb.

I don't wear make-up very often. ("make up my face" - a verb)

    Chan̒ maῖ koῖ (jà) taeng-na̒ <u>boi</u> thao-rai.

    ฉันไม่ค่อย(จะ)แต่งหน้าบ่อยเท่าไหร่

3. Put only *mai koi* before the verb without *boi*. This means "not often" or "not much", referring to the quantity of the action.

I don't go very often anymore.

    Phom̒ maῖ koῖ paῖ laeo.

    ผมไม่ค่อยไปแล้ว

I don't eat Western food much.

    Phom̒ maῖ koῖ (jà) daῖ gin a-<u>hang</u> fa-<u>rang</u>.

    ผมไม่ค่อย(จะ)ได้กินอาหารฝรั่ง

TIMES/OCCASIONS

Classifiers for "time/occasion" - krang/<u>hong</u>/thee - These are interchangable but *krang* is the most common. *Thee* is often used for short, sharp actions such as hitting or kissing.

once - krang dio/krang <u>neung</u>/<u>neung</u> krang - Also with *hon* and *thee*.

You use it once and throw it away?

    Koon chai krang dio laeo (gaw̒) thing paῖ leuy <u>reuh</u>?

    คุณใช้ครั้งเดียวแล้ว(ก็)ทิ้งไปเลยเหรอ

A: Have you ever gone to Mexico?

    Koon keuy paῖ Mek-see-go maῖ?

    คุณเคยไปเม็กซิโกมั้ย

B: I've been there once.

    Keuy paῖ (<u>yoo</u>) <u>hong</u> <u>neung</u>.

    เคยไป(อยู่)หนหนึ่ง

sak krang - This means "only once" or "once at an unspecified time". *Sak* minimizes or estimates.

Please help me (just once).

> Chuay phom̒ sak krang theuh, krup.

> ช่วยผมซักครั้งเถอะครับ

I'd like to go and see him some time next year.

> Chan̒ yak ja̒ pai yiam kao sak krang̒ (nai chuang) pee na̒.

> ฉันอยากจะไปเยี่ยมเค้าซักครั้ง(ในช่วง)ปีหน้า

twice/three times - Put the number before *krang*, *thee*, or *hon*.

A: You've been to Phuket before, haven't you?

> Keuy pai Phoo-ge̒t ma laeo, chai̒ mai?

> เคยไปภูเก็ตมาแล้วใช่มั้ย

B: Yes. I've been there three times.

> Chai̒. Pai ma sam̒ krang laeo.

> ใช่ ไปมาสามครั้งแล้ว

I've only been to Thonburi three times.

> Chan̒ pai thio̒ Thon-boo-ree ma kae̒ sam̒ hon̒ thao̒-nan.

> ฉันไปเที่ยวธนบุรีมาแค่สามหนเท่านั้น

She kissed me twice.

> Theuh hawm̒ phom̒ sawng̒ thee.

> เธอหอมผมสองที

Krang is also a classifier referring to events, as in this example.

He hasn't come to the past four meetings.

> Pra̒-choom see̒ krang thee̒ phan ma, kao mai̒ dai̒ kao̒ ruam (pra̒-choom).

> ประชุมสี่ครั้งที่ผ่านมาเค้าไม่ได้เข้าร่วม(ประชุม)

many times - lai̒ krang/boi̒ krang/lai̒ thee/lai̒ hon̒ -

I've tried fixing it many times, but I can't.

> Chan̒ pha̒-ya-yam (ja̒) sawm̒ yoo lai̒ krang, tae gaw̒, sawm̒ mai̒ dai̒.

> ฉันพยายาม(จะ)ซ่อมอยู่หลายครั้งแต่ก็ซ่อมไม่ได้

A: I've been to Bali many times, but I'm still not tired of it.

> Ba-lee̒ nee̒, phom̒ pai ma lai̒ krang̒ laeo, tae yang̒ mai̒ beua.

> บาหลีนี่ ผมไปมาหลายครั้งแล้วแต่ยังไม่เบื่อ

B: I've never even been there once.

> Chan̒ mai̒ keuy pai leuy sak krang.

> ฉันไม่เคยไปเลยซักครั้ง

Other classifiers - thio/rawp/meu - These are for specialized actions—*thio* for trips, *rawp* for circular actions or cycles, and *meu* for meals. *Thio* is used only when the trip is repeated on the same day or within a certain period of time.

I've been to the market twice today already.

    Wan-nee chan pai ta-lat ma laeo sawng thio.

    วันนี้ฉันไปตลาดมาแล้วสองเที่ยว

I've seen this movie three times (already).

    Nang reuang nee phom doo ma sam rawp laeo.

    หนังเรื่องนี้ผมดูมาสามรอบแล้ว

There's enough food to eat twice/for two meals.

    Mee a-han phaw gin dai sawng meu.

    มีอาหารพอกินได้สองมื้อ

How many times? - gee krang? - Also *dai gee krang, ma gee krang,* and *gee krang laeo* (asking about the past) or with *thee* or *hon* in place of *krang.*

A: How many times have you been to Doi Suthep?

    Koon keuy pai Doi Soo-thayp (ma) gee krang laeo?

    คุณเคยไปดอยสุเทพ(มา)กี่ครั้งแล้ว

B: Only once.

    Kae krang dio.

    แค่ครั้งเดียว

FREQUENCY WITH DAYS/WEEKS/ETC

once/twice a week - Use either *la* or *taw.* There are three ways to say "once" and two ways to say other numbers.

once a month	deuan la krang/krang la deuan
	krang (neung) taw deuan
twice a week	a-thit la sawng krang/sawng krang taw a-thit
three times a day	wan la sam krang/sam krang taw wan

In this factory we get a vacation twice a year.

    Rong-ngan nee rao dai phak rawn pee la sawng krang.

    โรงงานนี้เราได้พักร้อนปีละสองครั้ง

Farmers around here plant rice twice a year.

    Chao na thaeo nee plook kao sawng krang taw pee.

    ชาวนาแถวนี้ปลูกข้าวสองครั้งต่อปี

every day/week/etc -

every month (hour/	thook deuan
day/week/year)	thook-thook deuan ("each and every")
	krang neung thook-thook deuan
every night/evening	thook keun
every Monday	thook wan Jan
every weekend	thook sao a-thit
every other day	wan-wayn-wan
every morning	thook chao
every afternoon (early)	thook bai
every afternoon (late)	thook yen

There's a Loi Krathong festival here every year.

Thook pee thee-nee (ja) mee ngan Loi Gra-thong.

ทุกปีที่นี่(จะ)มีงานลอยกระทง

I don't like to stay at home on weekends. ("every weekend")

Phom mai chawp yoo ban thook sao a-thit.

ผมไม่ชอบอยู่บ้านทุกเสาร์อาทิตย์

A: Do you do it every day?/Do they do it every day?

Tham thook wan mai?

ทำทุกวันมั้ย

B: No, not every day.

Mai thook wan.

ไม่ทุกวัน

every three days/etc - There are two common ways to say this.

every three days	thook sam wan/sam wan krang (neung)
every six hours	thook hok chua-mong/hok chua-mong krang (neung)
every two weeks	thook sawng a-thit/sawng a-thit krang (neung)
every three months	thook sam deuan/sam deuan krang (neung)

And also two longer phrases:

every three months	thook sam deuan taw krang
	krang neung (nai) thook-thook sam deuan

In this department we have to write reports every two weeks.

Nai pha-naek nee rao tawng kian rai-ngan sawng a-thit krang (neung).

ในแผนกนี้เราต้องเขียนรายงานสองอาทิตย์ครั้ง(หนึ่ง)

People come to inspect the factory every three months.

    Mee kon ma <u>truat</u> rong-ngan <u>thook</u> <u>samj</u> deuan.

        มีคนมาตรวจโรงงานทุกสามเดือน

Every three or four days the electricity goes off.

    Fai <u>dap</u> thook-thook <u>samj</u> (<u>reuj</u>) <u>see</u> wan leuy.

        ไฟดับทุกๆ สาม(หรือ)สี่วันเลย

daily/annually - pra-jam wan/pra-jam pee -

His daily work is delivering newspapers.

    Ngan pra-jam wan (<u>kawngj</u>) <u>kao</u> keu songj nang-<u>seuj</u> phim.

        งานประจำวัน(ของ)เค้าคือส่งหนังสือพิมพ์

rai - This is "each/every" with time. It's also the classifier for cases and incidents.

rai wan	daily
rai deuan	monthly
rai <u>pak</u>	twice a month (for magazines, etc)
rai tua	one person at a time, individually

"Thai Rath" is a daily newspaper.

    "Thai <u>Rat</u>" pen nang-<u>seuj</u> phim rai wan.

        ไทยรัฐ เป็นหนังสือพิมพ์รายวัน

I'll ask them individually.

    Chan ja <u>thamj</u> <u>phuak</u> <u>kao</u> pen rai tua.

        ฉันจะถามพวกเค้าเป็นรายตัว

QUESTIONS—HOW OFTEN?

"How often?" in Thai is *boi kae nai?*, but questions are more commonly phrased as "Do you...often?", "Do you....every day?", or "How many times a day do you...?" (or with weeks/months/years).

Do you...often? -

A: Do you go to movies often?

    Pai doo nangj <u>boi</u> mai?

        ไปดูหนังบ่อยมั้ย

B: Yes./No./Not very often.

    <u>Boi</u>./<u>Mai</u> <u>boi</u>./<u>Mai</u> <u>koi</u> <u>boi</u>.

        บ่อย/ไม่บ่อย/ไม่ค่อยบ่อย

    I don't go very often. (or other verb from the question to replace *pai*)

    <u>Mai</u> <u>koi</u> (<u>dai</u>) pai.

        ไม่ค่อย(ได้)ไป

Do you...every day? -

A: Do you eat rice every day?

Koon gin kao thook wan mai?

คุณกินข้าวทุกวันมั้ย

B: No, not every day. I eat potatoes and bread too.

Mai (dai gin kao) thook wan. Gin mun fa-rang gap ka-nom pang duay.

ไม่(ได้กินข้าว)ทุกวัน กินมันฝรั่งกับขนมปังด้วย

How many times a week? - a-thit la gee krang? - Also with days, months, etc.

A: How many times a week do you play sports?

Koon len gee-la a-thit la gee krang?

คุณเล่นกีฬาอาทิตย์ละกี่ครั้ง

B: Two or three times. It depends on if I have the opportunity.

Sawng-sam krang. Mai nae, laeo tae o-gat.

สองสามครั้ง ไม่แน่แล้วแต่โอกาส

Taking medicine - The question in Thai is "How do I take this medicine?".

A: How (often) do I take this medicine?

Ya nee gin yang-ngai, ka?

ยานี้กินยังไงคะ

B: Take it every six hours, three times a day.

Gin ya nee thook hok chua-mong, wan la sam krang.

กินยานี้ทุกหกชั่วโมง วันละสามครั้ง

Transportation - Generalize the question—"What time do buses leave?".

A: What time do buses leave?

Mee rot awk gee mong bang?

มีรถออกกี่โมงบ้าง

B: There's a bus leaving every two hours, five times a day.

Mee rot awk thook sawng chua-mong, wan la ha thio.

มีรถออกทุกสองชั่วโมง วันละห้าเที่ยว

Salary - The question in Thai is "How do they pay you?".

A: How (often) do they pay you?

Kao ja jai yang-ngai?

เค้าจะจ่ายยังไง

B: (I get my salary) twice a month./I get paid every two weeks.

(Dai ngeuhn deuan) deuan la sawng krang./Dai thook sawng a-thit.

(ได้เงินเดือน)เดือนละสองครั้ง/ได้ทุกสองอาทิตย์

MORE TIMES

"One more time" is *eeg krang neung* or just *eeg krang* informally (also with *thee* or *hon*). Other numbers are put before *krang, thee,* or *hon.*

I want to go and climb Phu Kradeung again.

   Phǒmȷ yak pai peen Phoo Gra-deung eeg thee.

   ผมอยากไปปีนภูกระดึงอีกที

A: How many more times do I have to come, doctor?

   Tawng ma eeg gee krang, ka mawȷ?

   ต้องมาอีกกี่ครั้งคะหมอ

B: One more time should be enough.

   Eeg honȷ dio gaw phaw.

   อีกหนเดียวก็พอ

eeg sak krang - Including *sak* minimizes or estimates the amount. In the first sentence the phrase means "only one more time" or "this time is the time".

Play that song one more time.

   Len phlayng nan eeg sak krang, see.

   เล่นเพลงนั้นอีกซักครั้งซิ

Even if I read it ten more times I won't understand it.

   (Thěungȷ/mae wǎ) phǒmȷ ja an eeg sak sip krang, gaw mai kaô-jai rawk.

   (ถึง/แม้ว่า)ผมจะอ่านอีกซักสิบครั้งก็ไม่เข้าใจหรอก

ALWAYS/WHENEVER

"Always" can refer to two things—actions done continuously (explained on page 365) and actions done whenever (every time/any time) they're possible (explained here).

always - sǎ-meuhȷ - *Sameuh* can be doubled.

If I have time, I always work in the garden.

   Thǎ mee way-la, phǒmȷ ja thǎm suanȷ sǎ-meuhȷ.

   ถ้ามีเวลาผมจะทำสวนเสมอ

I always see her in the market.

   Chǎn jeuh theuh thee ta-lat sǎ-meuhȷ sǎ-meuhȷ.

   ฉันเจอเธอที่ตลาดเสมอๆ

every time - thook krang/thook-thook krang/thook thee/tae la krang - The first is most common. *Tae la krang* is "each time" and *thook-thook krang* is "each and every time".

Every time I go to the market I see her.

   Thook-thook krang thee chan pai ta-lat ja jeuh theuh (sǎ-meuhȷ).

   ทุกๆ ครั้งที่ฉันไปตลาดจะเจอเธอ(เสมอ)

Every time I ask, he answers like that.

    Phŏmj thamj, kao gâw tawp yàng-ngán thóok thee.

    ผมถาม เค้าก็ตอบยังงั้นทุกที

It floods here every time it rains.

    Thêe-nêe nám (jà) thuam thóok kráng thee fŏnj tòk.

    ที่นี่น้ำ(จะ)ท่วมทุกครั้งที่ฝนตก

Every time I see him, he's driving a new car.

    Jeuh kao tàe lá kráng, gâw kàp rót kun mài.

    เจอเค้าแต่ละครั้งก็ขับรถคันใหม่

A: How long do you stay each time you go home?

    Glàp ban tàe lá kráng nan thâo-rài?

    กลับบ้านแต่ละครั้งนานเท่าไหร่

B: I go home for one month a year.

    Chăn glàp pai pee lá deuan.

    ฉันกลับไปปีละเดือน

at any time - thóok way-la -

You can call me at any time.

    Koon tho ma hăj chăn dâi thóok way-la leuy, na.

    คุณโทรมาหาฉันได้ทุกเวลาเลยนะ

when/whenever - way-la (thêe) - Compare the first example which has *way-la* meaning "whenever" with the second which has *tawn* meaning "when" (referring to a single occurrance). *Thee* is optional in all examples.

When you go to Chiang Mai, where do you stay?   (refers to every time you go)

    Way-la pai Chiang Măi, koon châwp phák thêe-năij?

    เวลาไปเชียงใหม่คุณชอบพักที่ไหน

When you go to Chiang Mai, where are you going to stay?   (refers to this time)

    Tawn pai Chiang Măi, koon jà (pai) phák thêe-năij?

    ตอนไปเชียงใหม่คุณจะ(ไป)พักที่ไหน

When(ever) it rains the weather is good.

    Way-la fŏnj tòk a-gàt (gâw) dee.

    เวลาฝนตกอากาศ(ก็)ดี

When you use the tape recorder you should't touch this button.

    Way-la chái thâyp kreuang nee, yà gòt poom nee, na.

    เวลาใช้เทปเครื่องนี้อย่ากดปุ่มนี้นะ

whenever—repeated verbs with *gaw* - Here *gaw* is put between a repeated verb.

When it's time to work I work. When it's time to play I play.

Way-la tham-ngan gaw tham-ngan. Way-la len gaw len.

เวลาทำงานก็ทำงาน เวลาเล่นก็เล่น

I have trouble sleeping. (Whenever I try to sleep I can't.)

Way-la nawn gaw nawn mai lap.

เวลานอนก็นอนไม่หลับ

When it rains, it rains for a long time.

Tha fon tok gaw tok nan.

ถ้าฝนตกก็ตกนาน

whenever/any time - Here the question word is "whenever". See also page 180.

Any time you come I'll be free.

Meua-rai (gaw dai) thee koon ma, phom gaw wang.

เมื่อไหร่(ก็ได้)ที่คุณมาผมก็ว่าง

(Theung) ma meua-rai phom gaw wang.   ("even if you come at any time")

(ถึง)มาเมื่อไหร่ผมก็ว่าง

(Mai wa) ma meua-rai phom gaw wang.   ("whether you come at any time")

(ไม่ว่า)มาเมื่อไหร่ผมก็ว่าง

Meua-rai gaw wang.   (I'm free any time.)

เมื่อไหร่ก็ว่าง

always/regularly - pra-jam/pen pra-jam - *Pen* is optional when the meaning is "often" as in the first example, but needed when it means "every time" or "regularly" as in the second. Other translations are "usually", "constantly", "habitually", or "whenever possible". *Pra-jam* is also an adjective meaning "regular" or "usual".

I always lose my glasses.

Phom chawp tham waen-ta hai (pen) pra-jam.

ผมชอบทำแว่นตาหาย(เป็น)ประจำ

A: Where do you usually go swimming?

Pok-ga-tee koon pai wai-nam thee-nai?

ปกติคุณไปว่ายน้ำที่ไหน

B: I don't have any swimming pool I go to regularly.

Mai mee sa wai-nam thee chan pai pen pra-jam.

ไม่มีสระว่ายน้ำที่ฉันไปเป็นประจำ

Sa wai-nam thee pai pen pra-jam gaw mai mee.

สระว่ายน้ำที่ไปเป็นประจำก็ไม่มี

"like to" for "always" - In Thai, saying that you like to do something can mean that you always do it.

This dog always steals my shoes.

Maj tua nee chawp ka-moy rawng-thao phomj.

หมาตัวนี้ชอบขโมยรองเท้าผม

SOMETIMES

bang thee/bang krang/bang honj - The first phrase also means "maybe". *Pen* should be included before the phrase when it's in the middle or at the end of the sentence. *Gaw* is commonly included with "sometimes" to reinforce the hypothetical meaning.

Sometimes I go out to see plays.

Bang krang (chan) gaw pai doo la-kawn.

บางครั้ง(ฉัน)ก็ไปดูละคร

(Chan) pai doo la-kawn pen bang krang.

(ฉัน)ไปดูละครเป็นบางครั้ง

Sometimes he makes people upset.

Bang-thee kao gaw tham hai kon mai phaw-jai.

บางทีเค้าก็ทำให้คนไม่พอใจ

A: Do you like to watch TV a lot?

Chawp doo thee-wee boi mai?

ชอบดูทีวีบอยมั้ย

B: Sometimes.

(Pen) bang thee./Gaw pen bang krang.

(เป็น)บางที/ก็เป็นบางครั้ง

sometimes it happens that - mee bang thee thee - Or *bang krang*.

Sometimes the ATM is closed and I can't get any money.

Mee bang thee thee too ATM pit, laeo phomj beuhk ngeuhn mai dai.

มีบางทีที่ตู้เอทีเอ็มปิดแล้วผมเบิกเงินไม่ได้

A: Has it ever happened that you lend money to someone and they don't return it?

Keuy mee mai, thee (koon) hai kon yeum ngeuhn laeo kao mai (chai) keun?

เคยมีมั้ย ที่(คุณ)ให้คนยืมเงินแล้วเค้าไม่(ใช่)คืน

B: Yes, it happens sometimes.

Gaw, mee bang krang.

ก็มีบางครั้ง

some days - (pen) bang wan - This is common for "sometimes".

Sometimes I go and deposit the money, sometimes another person goes.

  Bang wan chan gaw pai fak ngeuhn, bang wan gaw hai kon eun pai.

  บางวันฉันก็ไปฝากเงิน บางวันก็ให้คนอื่นไป

A: Do you cook for yourself?

  Koon tham a-han than ayng reu plao? (or *gin* instead of *than*)

  คุณทำอาหารทานเองรึเปล่า

B: Sometimes.

  (Pen) bang wan.

  (เป็น)บางวัน

With *gaw*—sometimes it is/sometimes it isn't - Here *gaw* is included in the second sentence to mean "also". *Gaw* may also be put in the first sentence, and the two sentences may be reduced to one as in parentheses.

Some days I eat it. Some days I don't.

  Bang wan (gaw) gin. Bang wan gaw mai gin. (shortened to *Bang wan gaw gin.*)

  บางวัน(ก็)กิน บางวันก็ไม่กิน

Sometimes the children are good, but sometimes they're bad.

  Bang krang dek-dek gaw dee, tae bang thee gaw deu.

  บางครั้งเด็กๆ ก็ดีแต่บางทีก็ดื้อ

***Bang* for "sometimes"** - This is explained on page 202.

My parents go out sometimes, but mostly they stay at home.

  Phaw-mae ja awk pai kang nawk bang, tae suan mak gaw yoo ban.

  พ่อแม่จะออกไปข้างนอกบ้างแต่ส่วนมากก็อยู่บ้าน

periodically/once in a while/rarely - There are many phrases:

  pen chuang-chuang/pen krao-krao/pen bang krang/pen thee/

  nan-nan thee/nan-nan (verb) thee/nan-nan (verb) (sak) krang

People visit this place sometimes.

  Kon ma thio thee-nee pen bang krang.

  คนมาเที่ยวที่นี่เป็นบางครั้ง

I drink foreign liquor once in a while.

  Phom gin lao nawk nan-nan thee.

  ผมกินเหล้านอกนานๆ ที

  Nan-nan thee phom ja gin lao nawk (sak krang).

  นานๆ ที่ผมจะกินเหล้านอก(ซักครั้ง)

I take the bus once in awhile.

> Nan-nan phom̌ ja keun̠ rot-may sak krang.
>
> นานๆ ผมจะขึ้นรถเมล์ซักครั้ง

If you just eat it once in a while you won't get tired of it. (*theung* is "so/therefore")

> Nan-nan gin thee, theung̠ ja mai beua.
>
> นานๆ กินทีถึงจะไม่เบื่อ

USUALLY

There are four ways to say "usually".

1. ordinarily/regularly/habitually - tham-ma-da/tam tham-ma-da - The second is a little more formal. *Thammada* is also an adjective meaning "regular".

I'm usually an easygoing person.

> Tham-ma-da chan̠ pen kon a-rai gaw dai. (or "pen kon ngai-ngai")
>
> ธรรมดาฉันเป็นคนอะไรก็ได้

There are usually more tourists here.

> Tham-ma-da thee-nee keuy mee nak thawng-thio ma yeuh gwa nee.
>
> ธรรมดาที่นี่เคยมีนักท่องเที่ยวมาเยอะกว่านี้

Meaning "it's usual" - pen tham-ma-da -

It's usual that a man would like a good woman like you.

> Mun pen tham-ma-da thee phoo-chai ja chawp phoo-ying̠ dee yang koon.
>
> มันเป็นธรรมดาที่ผู้ชายจะชอบผู้หญิงดีอย่างคุณ

2. usually/as usual - pok-ga-tee/doy pok-ga-tee - This is more formal than *thammada*. It means "normally", "routinely", "usually", or "regularly" and is also "normal" as in medical tests. *Pok-ga-tee* alone is used only at the beginning of sentences.

I usually don't come this way.

> Pok-ga-tee mai keuy ma thang nee (leuy).
>
> ปกติไม่เคยมาทางนี้(เลย)

I usually go to bed at nine.

> Chan nawn sam̠ thoom̠ doy pok-ga-tee.
>
> ฉันนอนสามทุ่มโดยปกติ

tam pok-ga-tee - This means "ordinarily", "normally", "as usual", or "usually".

She's back at work today as usual.

> Wan-nee kao glap ma tham-ngan tam pok-ga-tee.
>
> วันนี้เค้ากลับมาทำงานตามปกติ

Noom's someone who doesn't talk much.

    Tam pòk-gà-tee Noom pen kon phôot nói.

        ตามปกติหนุ่มเป็นคนพูดน้อย

as it usually is - meuang pòk-gà-tee - This is also translated as "the same as usual" or "as usual".

Today there's no water as usual. (*mai lai* is "not flowing")

    Wan-nee nam mâi lǎi, meuang pòk-gà-tee.

        วันนี้น้ำไม่ไหลเหมือนปกติ

out of the ordinary - phìt pòk-gà-tee - This is also translated as "unusual", "abnormal", or "irregular".

Today is unusual. You didn't order fried rice.

    Wan-nee phìt pòk-gà-tee, ná. Koon mâi dâi sàng kâo-phàt.

        วันนี้ผิดปกตินะ คุณไม่ได้สั่งข้าวผัด

Lately Maeo's been very lazy, which is unusual.

    Moo nee Maeo kêe-giat mâk, phìt pòk-gà-tee.

        หมู่นี้แมวขี้เกียจมากผิดปกติ

A: Is anything wrong? (meaning "out of the ordinary")

    Mee à-rai phìt pòk-gà-tee mái?

        มีอะไรผิดปกติมั้ย

B: Everything's normal.

    Thôok yang pen pòk-gà-tee dee.

        ทุกอย่างเป็นปกติดี

3. usually/likely to - mák jà - This is put before the verb. *Ja* can be omitted but is usually included. Other meanings are "inclined to" and "frequently".

I usually get a letter from her around New Year's.

    Chán mák jà dâi jòt-mǎi jàk theuh nai chuang pee mài.

        ฉันมักจะได้จดหมายจากเธอในช่วงปีใหม่

In this season it usually rains heavily.

    Nâ nee fǒng mák (jà) tòk nàk.

        หน้านี้ฝนมัก(จะ)ตกหนัก

4. mostly - suan mâk/suan yài - These phrases mean "usually" in the sense of "mostly" or "most of the time" (not "as usual/habitually") and can also modify nouns in phrases like "most Thais" (*kon Thai suan mak*). The first two sentences compare the meanings of *suan mak* and *thammada*.

I usually don't drink beer. I like to drink wine.

   (means "mostly I don't" or "I'm not likely to")

     Suan mak phom̩ mai gin bia. Phom̩ chawp gin lao wai.

     ส่วนมากผมไม่กินเบียร์ ผมชอบกินเหล้าไวน์

Usually I don't drink beer, but today I'll drink some.

   (you don't drink it habitually but today you'll make an exception)

     Tham-ma-da phom̩ mai gin bia, tae wan-nee phom̩ ja gin.

     ธรรมดาผมไม่กินเบียร์แต่วันนี้ผมจะกิน

Phet usually goes out on Sundays. ("every Sunday")

     Suan mak Phet pai thio̧ thook wan A-thit.

     ส่วนมากเพชรไปเที่ยวทุกวันอาทิตย์

THE FIRST TIME/THIS TIME/NEXT TIME/LAST TIME

Krang, thee, hon, and *krao* are all used for "time/occasion" here. *Krang* is the most common and *krao* is more formal.

the first/second time -

The first time I went to Phuket there were no hotels at all. (2 ways to say)

     Krang raek thee (phom̩) pai Phoo-get, mai mee rong-raem leuy.

     ครั้งแรกที่(ผม)ไปภูเก็ตไม่มีโรงแรมเลย

     Phom̩ pai Phoo-get krang raek mai mee rong-raem leuy.

     ผมไปภูเก็ตครั้งแรกไม่มีโรงแรมเลย

The second time I went, there were a lot of hotels.

     Krang thee sawng̩ thee phom̩ pai thee-nan, mee rong-raem keun lai̧ haeng.

     ครั้งที่สองที่ผมไปที่นั่นมีโรงแรมขึ้นหลายแห่ง

     Phom̩ pai thee-nan krang thee sawng̩ mee rong-raem keun lai̧ haeng.

     ผมไปที่นั่นครั้งที่สองมีโรงแรมขึ้นหลายแห่ง

this is the first time that... - The phrase may begin with either *krang nee* (high tone on *nee*) or *nee* alone (with a falling tone).

A: This the first time you've been here, isn't it?

     Nee pen krang raek thee koon ma thee-nee, chai mai? (or "Krang nee pen...")

     นี่เป็นครั้งแรกที่คุณมาที่นี่ใช้มั้ย

B: No, this is the third time.

     Plao. Nee pen krang thee sam̩ laeo, krup.

     เปล่า นี่เป็นครั้งที่สามแล้วครับ

A: When was the first time?

     Ma krang raek meua-rai, ka?

     มาครั้งแรกเมื่อไหร่คะ

B: It was about five years ago.

    Gaw̆ meuả hả pee theê laeo.

    ก็เมื่อห้าปีที่แล้ว

at first - chuang raek̆/rá-yá raek̆ - These refer to longer periods of time.

When I first came to Thailand, I liked to eat fried bananas a lot.

    Chuang raek̆ theê <u>yoo</u> meuang Thai, chăn chawp gin gluaŷ thawt̆ mak̆.

    ช่วงแรกที่อยู่เมืองไทยฉันชอบกินกล้วยทอดมาก

this time - krang nee/krao nee/<u>hoŋ</u> nee/thee nee -

A: Are you going to the Northeast this time?

    Krang nee, jả pải Ee-<u>saŋ</u> mai?

    ครั้งนี้จะไปอีสานมั้ย

B: Not this time. I don't have time.

    Krang nee koŋ mai. <u>Phoŋ</u> mai mee way-la.

    ครั้งนี้คงไม่ ผมไม่มีเวลา

this time (for events) - (event) krang nee/krao nee - Here *krang* and *krao* are the classifiers for incidents and events ("this fire", "this flood", etc). Use *nan* instead of *nee* for past events.

On this trip to Indonesia I'm just going to Sumatra.

    Pai In-do-nee-sia krang nee, <u>phoŋ</u> jả pai kaê <u>Gaw̆</u> Soo-mat̆-tra thaồ-nan.

    ไปอินโดนีเซียครั้งนี้ผมจะไปแค่เกาะสุมาตราเท่านั้น

I didn't stay for the end of that meeting.

    Prả-choôm krao nan, chăn mai daî <u>yoo</u> jon joๆ̀p.

    ประชุมคราวนั้นฉันไม่ได้อยู่จนจบ

the next time - There are many phrases that include either *na* or *taw pai* for "next". *Krao* is the most common, while *o-gat* is more formal.

    krao nả/thee nả/krang nả/o-gat nả/

    krao <u>taw</u> pải/thee <u>taw</u> pải/krang <u>taw</u> pải/<u>hoŋ</u> taw pải

The next time I go on a trip I'm not taking so many things.

    Pải thiồ krao nả, chăn jả mai ao <u>kawŋ</u> pải yeuh.

    ไปเที่ยวคราวหน้าฉันจะไม่เอาของไปเยอะ

The next time you go to Laos, please buy me some silver. ("if you go")

    Krao <u>taw</u> pải thả koon pải Lao, chuaŷ seû kreuang ngeuhn haî duaŷ, nả.

    คราวต่อไปถ้าคุณไปลาวช่วยซื้อเครื่องเงินให้ด้วยนะ

Next time we'll go somewhere else.

O-gat nā (rao jà) pai thee eun, nā.

โอกาสหน้า(เรา)จะไปที่อื่นนะ

A: What should I tell him if he calls again?

Phǒm jà bawk kao yàng-ngai thâ kao tho ma eeg?

ผมจะบอกเค้ายังไงถ้าเค้าโทรมาอีก

B: The next time, if he calls again, tell him I'm not here.

Thee nā, thâ kao tho ma, bawk wâ chan mai yoo, nā.

ที่หน้าถ้าเค้าโทรมาบอกว่าฉันไม่อยู่นะ

the last/final time - krang sòot-thai/krao sòot-thai - The first is more common.

This is the last time I'll come here.

Krang nee pen krang sòot-thai thee phǒm jà ma thee-nee. (or "Nee pen...")

ครั้งนี้เป็นครั้งสุดท้ายที่ผมจะมาที่นี่

the last/previous/most recent time - There are many phrases. Because *krang sòot-thai* also means "the final time (ever)" use a different phrase if there could be confusion.

krang thee laeo/krao thee laeo/hon thee laeo/

krang sòot-thai/krang gawn

The last time, he came alone. This time he brought a friend.

Krang thee laeo kao ma kon dio. Krang nee kao pha pheuan ma duay kon neung.

ครั้งที่แล้วเค้ามาคนเดียว ครั้งนี้เค้าพาเพื่อนมาด้วยคนหนึ่ง

The last time I came here I didn't see you.

Krang sòot-thai thee ma thee-nee chan mai dai jeuh koon.

ครั้งสุดท้ายที่มาที่นี่ฉันไม่ได้เจอคุณ

The last time there was a fire, many shops burned down.

Fai mai krao thee laeo, mai pai lai ran.

ไฟไหม้คราวที่แล้วไหม้ไปหลายล้าน

A: When was the last time you went to Sukothai?

Pai Soo-kon-thai krang sòot-thai meua-rai?

ไปสุโขทัยครั้งสุดท้ายเมื่อไหร่

B: The last time I went was during Loi Krathong.

Phǒm pai krang thee laeo tawn Loi Gra-thong.

ผมไปครั้งที่แล้วตอนลอยกระทง

THE FIRST DAY/THE LAST DAY

Also with days, weeks, months, and years.

the first day	wan raek
the second day	wan thee sawng
the last day	wan soot-thai

The first day he worked here he came late.

Wan raek thee kao ma tham-ngan thee-nee, kao ma saij.

วันแรกที่เค้ามาทำงานที่นี่เค้ามาสาย

The second day he didn't come at all.

Wan thee sawng kao gaw mai ma leuy.

วันที่สองเค้าก็ไม่มาเลย

A: This is the last day you'll be here, isn't it?

Wan-nee pen wan soot-thai thee koon ja yoo thee-nee, chai mai?

วันนี้เป็นวันสุดท้ายที่คุณจะอยู่ที่นี่ใช่มั้ย

B: No. Friday is the last day.

Plao. Wan Sook pen wan soot-thai.

เปล่า วันศุกร์เป็นวันสุดท้าย

CLASSIFIERS

Classifiers are used in phrases that refer to people and things, including numbers, "each", "another", "this/that", "which", "every", "some", and "many". The concept is similar to English in phrases like "two bottles of Coke", "this pair of socks", or "many sheets of paper" but in Thai it's extended to all objects ("two dogs" is "dog—two bodies" and "this car" is "car—this vehicle").

BASED ON CHARACTERISTICS

The following classifiers are used with items based on their shape or other distinguishing characteristics.

animals	tua	ตัว
circular motions	rawp	รอบ
classes/levels	chan	ชั้น
clothing (shirts/pants)	tua	ตัว
flat objects	phaen	แผน
furniture	tua	ตัว
items/objects (in general)	un	อัน
kinds of things	yang/baep	อย่าง/แบบ
kinds of things (formal)	cha-nit/pra-phayt	ชนิด/ประเภท
line-like objects	sen	เส้น
lump-shaped objects	gawn	ก้อน
machines/mechanical things	kreuang	เครื่อง
orders/servings of food or drinks	thee	ที่
pairs of things	koo	คู่
one of a pair (means "side")	kang	ข้าง
pieces of things	chin	ชิ้น
piles/stacks of things	gawng	กอง
places/locations	haeng/thee	แห่ง/ที่
rolls of things	muan	มวน
round things	look	ลูก
rows of things	thaeo	แถว
sets of things	choot	ชุด
small objects (ticket/pillow)	bai	ใบ
very small objects (candy/pills)	met	เม็ด
times/occasions/instances	krang/thee/hon	ครั้ง/ที่/หน
vehicles	kun	คัน

SPECIFIC CLASSIFIERS

Following are classifiers for common objects. Some are from the previous list. Sample phrases are given in various patterns that use classifiers.

airplanes	lum	ลำ
this airplane	kreuang-bin lum nee	เครื่องบินลำนี้
amulets	ong	องค์
that amulet	phra ong nan	พระองค์นั้น
bags of things	thoong	ถุง
How many bags of rice?	Kao gee thoong?	ข้าวกี่ถุง
bamboo (pieces of)	thawn	ท่อน
Which piece of bamboo?	Mai-phai thawn nai?	ไม้ไผ่ท่อนไหน
bananas (bunch)	wee	หวี
two bunches of bananas	gluay sawng wee	กล้วยสองหวี
bananas (single)	bai	ใบ
one more banana	gluay eeg neung bai	กล้วยอีกหนึ่งใบ
(a large bunch of bananas, as on a tree, is called a "kreua")		
batteries	gawn	ก้อน
every battery	than thook gawn	ถ่านทุกก้อน
belts	sen	เส้น
many belts	kem-kut lai sen	เข็มขัดหลายเส้น
blankets	pheun	ผืน
a different blanket	pha-hom pheun eun	ผ้าห่มผืนอื่น
boards (wooden)	phaen	แผ่น
some boards	gra-dan bang phaen	กระดานบางแผ่น
boats	lum	ลำ
this boat	reua lum nee	เรือลำนี้
books	lem	เล่ม
that book	nang-seu lem nan	หนังสือเล่มนั้น
bottles of things	kuat	ขวด
Which bottle of Pepsi?	Pep-see kuat nai?	เป๊ปซี่ขวดไหน
bottles (empty)	bai	ใบ
three empty bottles	kuat sam bai	ขวดสามใบ
bowls (small)	thuay	ถ้วย
How many bowls of food?	Gap kao gee thuay?	กับข้าวกี่ถ้วย
bowls (large)	cham	ชาม
one more bowl of noodles	guay-tio eeg neung cham	ก๋วยเตี๋ยวอีกหนึ่งชาม
bowls (empty)	bai	ใบ
every bowl	thuay thook bai	ถ้วยทุกใบ

boxes of things	glawng	กล่อง
many boxes of durian	thoo-rian lai glawng	ทุเรียนหลายกล่อง
bread (slices of)	phaen	แผ่น
two slices of bread	ka-nom pang sawng phaen	ขนมปังสองแผ่น
bread (loaves of)	thaeo	แถว
a different loaf of bread	ka-nom pang thaeo eun	ขนมปังแถวอื่น
(for a loaf of bread in a plastic bag use "thoong")		
brooms	dam/un	ด้าม/อัน
some brooms	mai-gwat bang dam	ไม้กวาดบางด้าม
buildings	lang	หลัง
this building	teuk lang nee	ตึกหลังนี้
cakes	gawn	ก้อน
that cake	ka-nom kayk gawn nan	ขนมเค้กก้อนนั้น
cans of things	gra-pawng	กระป๋อง
How many cans of beer?	bia gee gra-pawng?	เบียร์กี่กระป๋อง
candy (hard candy)	met	เม็ด
three pieces of "Halls"	"Hawn" sam met	ฮอลล์สามเม็ด
carts (buffalo carts)	lem	เล่ม
Which cart?	Gwian lem nai?	เกวียนเล่มไหน
cases	rai	ราย
(refers to patients and cases of diseases or incidents)		
this patient	kon kai rai nee	คนไข้รายนี้
two cases of malaria	ma-la-ria sawng rai	มาลาเรียสองราย
many accidents	oo-bat-tee-hayt lai rai	อุบัติเหตุหลายราย
chairs	tua	ตัว
one more chair	gao-ee eeg neung tua	เก้าอี้อีกหนึ่งตัว
chopsticks	koo	คู่
many pairs of chopsticks	ta-giap lai koo	ตะเกียบหลายคู่
cigarettes (pack)	sawng	ซอง
every pack of cigarettes	boo-ree thook sawng	บุหรี่ทุกซอง
cigarettes (single)	muan/tua	มวน/ตัว
two cigarettes	boo-ree sawng muan	บุหรี่สองมวน
classes (in school)	hawng	ห้อง
a different class	nak-rian hawng eun	นักเรียนห้องอื่น
clocks/watches	reuan	เรือน
some watches/clocks	na-lee-ga bang reuan	นาฬิกาบางเรือน
coconuts (bunch)	tha-lai	ทะลาย
this bunch of coconuts	ma-phrao tha-lai nee	มะพร้าวทะลายนี้

coconuts (single)	look	ลูก
that coconut	ma-phrao look nan	มะพร้าวลูกนั้น
cups of things	thuay	ถ้วย
How many cups of coffee?	Ga-fae gee thuay?	กาแฟกี่ถ้วย
cups (empty)	bai	ใบ
these two cups	thuay sawng bai nee	ถ้วยสองใบนี้
disks	phaen	แผ่น
Which CD?	CD phaen nai?	ซีดีแผ่นไหน
documents	cha-bap	ฉบับ
many documents	ayk-ga-san lai cha-bap	เอกสารหลายฉบับ
doors	ban	บาน
every door	pra-too thook ban	ประตูทุกบาน
earrings (pair)	koo	คู่
one more pair of earrings	toom-hoo eeg neung koo	ตุ้มหูอีกหนึ่งคู่
earrings (one)	kang	ข้าง
one earring	toom-hoo kang neung	ตุ้มหูข้างหนึ่ง
eggs	fawng/bai	ฟอง/ใบ
every egg	kai thook fawng	ไข่ทุกฟอง
elephants	cheuak	เชือก
many elephants	chang lai cheuak	ช้างหลายเชือก
engines	kreuang	เครื่อง
some engines	kreuang-yon bang kreuang	เครื่องยนต์บางเครื่อง
events	krang	ครั้ง
this election	gan leuak tang krang nee	การเลือกตั้งครั้งนี้
eyeglasses	un	อัน
these glasses	waen-ta un nee	แว่นตาอันนี้
fans	tua	ตัว
that fan	phat-lom tua nan	พัดลมตัวนั้น
flowers (bunch)	chaw	ช่อ
Which bunch of flowers?	Dawk-mai chaw nai?	ดอกไม้ช่อไหน
flowers (single)	dawk	ดอก
How many roses?	Dawk goo-lap gee dawk?	ดอกกุหลาบกี่ดอก
fork s	kun	คัน
three forks	sawm sam kun	ซ่อมสามคัน
fruit (large)	bai	ใบ
one more apple	aep-pun eeg neung bai	แอปเปิ้ลอีกหนึ่งใบ
fruit (any kind)	look	ลูก
many tangerines	som lai look	ส้มหลายลูก

(the formal classifier for fruit is "phon")

furniture	tua	ตัว
every table	to thook tua	โต๊ะทุกตัว
gemstones	met	เม็ด
a different diamond	phet met eun	เพชรเม็ดอื่น
ghosts/giants/hermits	ton	ตน
some ghosts	phee bang ton	ผีบางตน
glasses of drinks	gaeo	แก้ว
this glass of water	nam gaeo nee	น้ำแก้วนี้
glasses (empty)	bai	ใบ
that glass	gaeo bai nan	แก้วใบนั้น
governments	ka-na/choot	คณะ/ชุด
How many governments?	Rat-tha-ban gee ka-na?	รัฐบาลกี่คณะ
groups of people	gloom/moo	กลุ่ม/หมู่
Which group of people?	Kon gloom nai?	คนกลุ่มไหน
guns	gra-bawk	กระบอก
three guns	peun sam gra-bawk	ปืนสามกระบอก
hair (strands of)	sen	เส้น
many strands of hair	phom lai sen	ผมหลายเส้น
hats	bai	ใบ
one more hat	muak eeg neung bai	หมวกอีกหนึ่งใบ
herds/flocks	foong	ฝูง
every herd of buffalo	kwai thook foong	ควายทุกฝูง
hotels	haeng/thee	แห่ง/ที่
a different hotel	rong-raem haeng eun	โรงแรมแห่งอื่น
houses	lang	หลัง
some houses	ban bang lang	บ้านบางหลัง
ice cubes	gawn	ก้อน
many ice cubes	nam-kaeng lai gawn	น้ำแข็งหลายก้อน
installments	nguat	งวด
this loan installment	phawn nguat nee	ผ่อนงวดนี้
irons	tua	ตัว
that iron	tao-reet tua nan	เตารีดตัวนั้น
keys	dawk	ดอก
How many keys?	Goon-jae gee dawk?	กุญแจกี่ดอก
kings	ong	องค์
every king	ga-sat thook ong	กษัตริย์ทุกองค์
(more respectful is "phra-ong"		
knives	lem	เล่ม
two knives	meet sawng lem	มีดสองเล่ม

land (pieces of)	pheun/plaeng	ผืน/แปลง
one more piece of land	thee-din eeg neung pheun	ที่ดินอีกหนึ่งผืน
(the first is for larger pieces of land)		
leaves	bai	ใบ
many leaves	bai-mai lai bai	ใบไม้หลายใบ
legs	kang ("side")	ข้าง
Which leg?	Ka kang nai?	ขาข้างไหน
letters	cha-bap	ฉบับ
a different letter	jot-mai cha-bap eun	จดหมายฉบับอื่น
light bulbs	duang	ดวง
some light bulbs	lawt-fai bang duang	หลอดไฟบางดวง
magazines	cha-bap	ฉบับ
this magazine	nit-ta-ya-san cha-bap nee	นิตยสารฉบับนี้
matches (box)	glak/glawng	กลัก/กล่อง
that box of matches	mai-keet fai glak nan	ไม้ขีดไฟกลักนั้น
matches (single)	gan	ก้าน
this match	mai-keet fai gan nee	ไม้ขีดไฟก้านนี้
mats	pheun	ผืน
Which mat?	Seua pheun nai?	เสื่อผืนไหน
meals	meu	มื้อ
two meals	a-han sawng meu	อาหารสองมื้อ
mirrors	ban	บาน
one more mirror	gra-jok eeg neung ban	กระจกอีกหนึ่งบาน
monks	roop/ong	รูป/องค์
every monk	phra thook roop	พระทุกรูป
(the second is for high-level or highly respected monks)		
mosquito nets	lang	หลัง
many mosquito nets	moong lai lang	มุงหลายหลัง
mountains	look	ลูก
a different mountain	phoo-kao look eun	ภูเขาลูกอื่น
movies	reuang	เรื่อง
some movies	nang bang reuang	หนังบางเรื่อง
necklaces	sen	เส้น
this necklace	soi-kaw sen nee	สร้อยคอเส้นนี้
newspapers	cha-bap	ฉบับ
How many newspapers?	Nang-seu phim gee cha-bap?	หนังสือพิมพ์กี่ฉบับ
noodles	sen	เส้น
those noodles	guay-tio sen nan	ก๋วยเตี๋ยวเส้นนั้น

packages (wrapped)	haw	ห่อ
Which package of noodles?	Guayj-tioj haw naij?	ก๋วยเตี๋ยวห่อไหน
packs of medicine	phaengj	แผง
three packs of medicine	ya samj phaengj	ยาสามแผง
packets of things	sawng	ซอง
every pack of cigarettes	boo-ree thook sawng	บุหรี่ทุกซอง
parcels	haw	ห่อ
a different parcel	phat-sa-doo haw eun	พัสดุห่ออื่น
paintings/drawings	roop	รูป
some paintings	roop-wat bang roop	รูปวาดบางรูป
paper (pieces of)	phaen/bai	แผ่น/ใบ
one more piece of paper	gra-dat eeg neung phaen	กระดาษอีกหนึ่งแผ่น
pencils	dam	ด้าม
this pencil	din-sawj dam nee	ดินสอด้ามนี้
pens	dam	ด้าม
that pen	pak-ga dam nan	ดินสอด้ามนั้น
people (men/women/etc)	kon	คน
How many women?	Phoo-yingj gee kon?	ผู้หญิงกี่คน
people (respected)	than	ทาน
Which lady?	Soo-phap sa-tree than naij?	สุภาพสตรีท่านไหน
pictures	bai	ใบ
two pictures	roop sawngj bai	รูปสองใบ
(a formal classifier for pictures is "ban")		
pillows	bai	ใบ
one more pillow	mawnj eeg neung bai	หมอนอีกหนึ่งใบ
pills/capsules	met	เม็ด
every pill	ya thook met	ยาทุกเม็ด
plates (of food)	jan	จาน
many plates of fried rice	kao-phat laij jan	ข้าวผัดหลายจาน
plates (empty)	bai	ใบ
a different plate	jan bai eun	จานใบอื่น
potatoes (whole)	huaj	หัว
some potatoes	mun fa-rang bang huaj	มันฝรั่งบางหัว
problems	reuang/yang	เรื่อง/อย่าง
this problem	pan-haj reuang nee	ปัญหาเรื่องนี้
refrigerators	langj/kreuang	หลัง/เครื่อง
that refrigerator	too-yen kreuang nan	ตู้เย็นเครื่องนั้น
razor blades	bai	ใบ
How many razor blades?	meet gon nuat gee bai?	มีดโกนหนวดกี่ใบ

rings	wong	วง
Which ring?	Waen wong nai?	แหวนวงไหน
rivers	sai	สาย
every river	mae-nam thook sai	แม่น้ำทุกสาย
rooms	hawng	ห้อง
many bedrooms	hawng-nawn lai hawng	ห้องนอนหลายห้อง
roads/streets	sen/sai	เส้น/สาย
a different road	tha-non sai eun	ถนนสายอื่น
(*sen* refers to the physical road, *sai* to the direction)		
sandwiches	thee/choot/koo	ที่/ชุด/คู่
one more sandwich	saen-wit eeg neung koo	แซนวิชอีกหนึ่งคู่
sarongs	pheun	ผืน
some sarongs	sa-rong bang pheun	โสร่งบางผืน
schools	rong	โรง
this school	rong-rian rong nee	โรงเรียนโรงนี้
sheets (bedsheets)	pheun	ผืน
that bedsheet	pha-poo-thee-nawn pheun nan	ผ้าปูที่นอนผืนนั้น
soap (bars of)	gawn	ก้อน
How many bars of soap?	Sa-boo gee gawn?	สบู่กี่ก้อน
soldiers/officials	nai	นาย
two soldiers	tha-han sawng nai	ทหารสองนาย
spoons	kun	คัน
Which spoon?	Chawn kun nai?	ช้อนคันไหน
stamps	duang	ดวง
one more stamp	sa-taem eeg neung duang	แสตมป์อีกหนึ่งดวง
stars/planets	duang	ดวง
every star	dao thook duang	ดาวทุกดวง
statues (Buddha)	ong	องค์
many Buddha statues	Phra-phoot-tha-roop lai ong	พระพุทธรูปหลายองค์
statues (general)	chin	ชิ้น
a different statue	roop-pun chin eun	รูปปั้นชิ้นอื่น
(also by what the statue depicts, for example an animal may be "tua")		
stones	gawn	ก้อน
some stones	hin bang gawn	หินบางก้อน
sticks (food on sticks)	mai	ไม้
three sticks of meatballs	look-chin sam mai	ลูกชิ้นสามไม้
sugar cubes	gawn	ก้อน
How many sugar cubes?	Nam-tan gee gawn?	น้ำตาลกี่ก้อน

suitcases	bai	ใบ
this suitcase	gra-paoj bai nee	กระเป๋าใบนี้
tables	tua	ตัว
that table	to tua nan	โต๊ะตัวนั้น
tapes, cassette	muan/ta-lap	ม้วน/ตลับ
Which tape?	Thayp muan naij?	เทปม้วนไหน
tape recorders	kreuang	เครื่อง
some tape recorders	thayp bang kreuang	เทปบางเครื่อง
teeth	see	ซี่
every tooth	fun thook see	ฟันทุกซี่
televisions	kreuang	เครื่อง
a different TV	tho-ra-that kreuang eun	โทรทัศน์เครื่องอื่น
temple buildings	lang	หลัง
many temple buildings	bot laij lang	โบสถ์หลายหลัง
tickets	bai	ใบ
three tickets	tuaj samj bai	ตั๋วสามใบ
toilet paper (rolls)	muan	ม้วน
two rolls of toilet paper	thit-choo sawngj muan	ทิชชูสองม้วน
tools (one)	un/tua	อัน/ตัว
that hammer	kawn tua nan	ฆ้อนตัวนั้น
tools (set)	choot	ชุด
these tools	kreuang-meu choot nee	เครื่องมือชุดนี้
towels	pheunj/tua	ผืน/ตัว
How many towels?	Pha-chet-tua gee pheunj?	ผ้าเช็ดตัวกี่ผืน
trains/processions	ka-buan	ขบวน
Which train?	Rot-fai ka-buan naij?	รถไฟขบวนไหน
trees/plants	ton	ต้น
one more tree	ton-mai eeg neung ton	ต้นไม้อีกหนึ่งต้น
tubes of things	lawt	หลอด
some tubes of toothpaste	ya-seej-fun bang lawt	ยาสีฟันบางหลอด
umbrellas	kun	คัน
a different umbrella	rom kun eun	ร่มคันอื่น
windows	ban	บาน
this window	na-tang ban nee	หน้าต่างบานนี้

-SPECIAL RULES-
THE NOUN & CLASSIFIER ARE THE SAME

In some cases the name of the object and the classifier are the same word. Following is a list of these words with some special rules they follow. There are also regular classifiers for some of the words and these follow the normal rules. They're listed after the first word (the noun/classifier) as with "cause", "meaning", and "picture".

boxes	glawng	กล่อง
this box	(glawng) glawng nee	(กล่อง)กล่องนี้
chapters/lessons	bot	บท
one more lesson	(bot) eeg neung bot	(บท)อีกหนึ่งบท
causes	saj-hayt/pra-gan/kaw/yang	สาเหตุ/ประการ/ข้อ/อย่าง
this cause	saj-hayt nee	สาเหตุนี้
(other three classifiers)	saj-hayt pra-gan nee	สาเหตุประการนี้
cities	meuang	เมือง
colors	seej	สี
corpses	sop	ศพ
districts	am-pheuh	อำเภอ
issues/points (discussion)	pra-den	ประเด็น
meanings	kwam-maij/yang	ความหมาย/อย่าง
methods/ways	wi-thee	วิธี
pages (one side)	na	หน้า
pages (both sides)	phaen	แผ่น
person/people	kon	คน
pictures	roop/bai	รูป/ใบ
this picture	roop nee/roop bai nee	รูปนี้/รูปใบนี้
points (location/discussion)	joot	จุด
points (on a list)	kaw/rai-gan	ข้อ/รายการ
provinces	jang-wat	จังหวัด
reasons	hayt-phonj/kaw/yang/ pra-gan	เหตุผล/ข้อ/อย่าง/ ประการ
this reason	hayt-phonj nee	เหตุผลนี้
(other three classifiers)	hayt-phonj kaw nee	เหตุผลข้อนี้
rooms	hawng	แห่ง
shops	ran/haeng	ร้าน/แห่ง
Which shop?	ran naij?/ran haeng naij?	ร้านไหน/ร้านแห่งไหน
this shop	ran nee/ran haeng nee	ร้านนี้/ร้านแห่งนี้
songs	phlayng	เพลง
stories/situations/matters	reuang	เรื่อง
styles	baep	แบบ
sub-districts	tam-bon	ตำบล

subjects	wee-cha	วิชา
temples	wat/haeng	วัด/แห่ง
a different temple	wat eun/wat haeng eun	วัดอื่น/วัดแห่งอื่น
train cars	bo-gee	โบกี้
trips/visits	thio	เที่ยว
ways (directions)	thang/sen/sai	ทาง/เส้น/สาย
every way	thook thang	ทุกทาง
(other two classifiers)	thang thook sai	ทางทุกสาย
words	kam	คำ

this/that - Formally the noun and classifier are both said, so the word is repeated. However the noun is generally omitted informally (here it's in parentheses) and said only once.

I used to stay in this room.

> Chan keuy yoo (hawng) hawng nee.
>
> ฉันเคยอยู่(ห้อง)ห้องนี้
>
> (Hawng) hawng nee chan keuy yoo.
>
> (ห้อง)ห้องนี้ฉันเคยอยู่

That picture, you didn't bring it?

> Roop nan, mai dai ao ma duay reuh? (or *roop bai nan*)
>
> รูปนั้น ไม่ได้เอามาด้วยเหรอ

In this example two words, *kam* and *kwam-mai*, follow the special rules.

This word has many meanings.

> (Kam) kam nee mee lai kwam-mai.
>
> (คำ)คำนี้มีหลายความหมาย
>
> (Kam) kam nee mee kwam-mai lai yang.
>
> (คำ)คำนี้มีความหมายหลายอย่าง

With numbers/many/some - The noun is omitted informally.

The house has five rooms.

> Ban nee mee (hawng) ha hawng.
>
> บ้านนี้มี(ห้อง)ห้าห้อง

She sang many songs.

> Kao rawng (phlayng) lai phlayng.
>
> เค้าร้อง(เพลง)หลายเพลง

I gave him some of the pictures.

    Phom̷ ao (roop) bang roop hai kao.

    ผมเอา(รูป)บางรูปให้เค้า

this is the - There are two patterns. The noun can be repeated in the first but is generally omitted informally.

That's the song I like.

    Nan pen (phlayng) phlayng thee chan chawp.

    นั่นเป็น(เพลง)เพลงที่ฉันชอบ

    Phlayng nan pen phlayng thee chan chawp.

    เพลงนั้นเป็นเพลงที่ฉันชอบ

which/another/every - The noun usually isn't repeated in these patterns.

A: Which room is good?

    Hawng̷ nai̷ dee?

    ห้องไหนดี

B: This room is good.

    Hawng̷ nee dee.

    ห้องนี้ดี

He's sitting in another (train) car.

    Kao nang̷ yoo eeg bo-gee neung.

    เค้านั่งอยู่อีกโบกี้หนึ่ง

He's interested in every subject.

    Kao son̷g-jai thook wee-cha.

    เค้าสนใจทุกวิชา

All of the rooms are full.

    Thook hawng̷ tem mot.

    ทุกห้องเต็มหมด

    Tem mot thook hawng̷.

    เต็มหมดทุกห้อง

Every province of Thailand is hot.

    Meuang Thai thook jang-wat rawn.

    เมืองไทยทุกจังหวัดร้อน

    Meuang Thai rawn thook jang-wat.

    เมืองไทยร้อนทุกจังหวัด

INDEX - THAI

For some Thai words the base meanings are given although there may not be a references for every meaning.

many days after that, 341

many more, 32

more, additional (quantities), 32-33,
    214-215

more, with requests, 213

more people, another person, 51-52

more times, 378

nobody else, 53

not anymore, never again, 110-111

not up to (a future time), 369-370

one more, two more, 32

people in addition to yourself, 45

some more, 215

still, 106-107

two days after that, 341

with "and", 147

within the next two days, 320

eeg kon neung - the other person, 52

eeg laeo - again, 108

    not anymore, never again, 110-111

eeg mai nan - for not much longer, 365

    in not long, soon, 321

eeg mak - a lot more, 32

eeg nan - longer (time)

    a long time after that, 340

    for a long time, 365

    in a long time, 320

eeg noi - a little more, 215

    for not much longer, 365

    in not long, soon, 321

eeg tang hak - also, 148

eeg yang - more things, other things, 37

eun - other, others, another (not this one)

    another one (not this one), 33

    another person (not this one), 52-53

    at another time, another day, 323

    before anything else, 334

    more than anyone, 50

    nobody else, 53

    something else, 38, 40

gae - to (in "give to", formal), 283

gam-lang - strength, force, power, energy

    continuous actions, present tense, 87

    past continuous, 92

    just about to happen, 89

gam-not - to limit, set, fix, earmark,
    stipulate, be limited, stipulated, to
    schedule

    meaning "limit", 228

gan - each other, with each other

    actions in a group, 56-57

    it's believed, 57

    questions about group actions, 67

    together, 55-56

    with "at the same time", 350

    with comparative, 237-238

    with "different", 234-237

    with "equal", 245-247

    with "let's", 102

    with "the same", 229-231

gan ayng - do within a group, 57

gan theuh - let's, 102

gan - prefix used to form gerunds, 12-15

    prefix meaning "affairs of/matters of", 15

gan pen - being, 15

gan thee - that, the fact that, the story that,
    85-86

gan thee ja...dai - in order to, 166

gao - old (for objects)

    better than before, 239

    previous, former, 349

    the same as before, 232

gap - and, with; and, 147

    both...and..., 199

    from (a person), 275

    linking two subjects, 6

    to (good to/do to), 283

    with, 285

    with "enough for", 206

    with "near", 278

    with "so...that", 223

    with "to the extent that", 224

    with "together", 56, 350

    with "up to an amount", 221

INDEX - ENGLISH